£2·50

27/1

NIGHT RAIDERS

Night Raiders

*Burglary and the Making of Modern Urban
Life in London, 1860–1968*

ELOISE MOSS

OXFORD

UNIVERSITY PRESS

OXFORD
UNIVERSITY PRESS

Great Clarendon Street, Oxford, OX2 6DP,
United Kingdom

Oxford University Press is a department of the University of Oxford.
It furthers the University's objective of excellence in research, scholarship,
and education by publishing worldwide. Oxford is a registered trade mark of
Oxford University Press in the UK and in certain other countries

Published in the United States of America by Oxford University Press
198 Madison Avenue, New York, NY 10016, United States of America

British Library Cataloguing in Publication Data
Data available

Library of Congress Control Number: 2018966639

ISBN 978–0–19–884038–1

Printed and bound by
CPI Group (UK) Ltd, Croydon, CR0 4YY

Acknowledgements

It is an absolute joy to finally get to thank everyone who has made this book possible. It began life as my doctoral thesis, entitled Cracking Cribs: Representations of Burglary and Burglars in London, 1860–1939, completed at the University of Oxford in 2013. I could never have undertaken a D.Phil, or the Masters in Modern British History at the University of Manchester that preceded it, without the financial support of the Arts and Humanities Research Council, which funded both degrees. Fourth-year funding to complete the doctorate was acquired from a Bryce Research Studentship and Vice Chancellor's Award from the University of Oxford, as well as a grant from the Andrew Smith Foundation. My 2013–14 post as Past and Present Fellow at the Institute of Historical Research in London gave me the necessary finances and professional stability to extend the chronological scope of the book to 1968 through conducting additional research. In 2017, sabbatical leave from teaching at the University of Manchester finally allowed me to finish it. My thanks to all of these institutions for their support. Oxford University Press, and the fabulous team of editors, Christina Wipf-Perry and Cathryn Steele, as well as eagle-eyed copy-editor Timothy Beck and project manager Markcus Sandanraj, have ultimately seen this book into existence and offered invaluable editorial guidance. I am so grateful to them for their assistance, as well as the anonymous reviewers who commented on the book in draft version, whose suggestions and references vastly enriched its content.

Good research is only ever accomplished through the helpful tips and assistance of the many archivists and librarians historians meet during a project. The staff at the institutions whose collections are referenced in this book do wonderful work preserving our national history and play a significant role in shaping the direction of the research. I would like to pay particular tribute to those at the London Metropolitan Archives, who spent five years trolleying over thousands of court registers for me to trawl for records of burglary. Zoe Richards at Madame Tussauds' archive went above and beyond to dig out an image of the waxwork of burglar Charles Peace for me at the last minute. I am similarly indebted to John Porter at the Prudential Group Archives, Howard Doble at the London Metropolitan Archives, and Paul Johnson at the National Archives, all of whom had dedicated additional time and resources to help supply me with the images I needed. The rare film dealers at Vicpine Videos deserve credit for some truly impressive detective work hunting down various versions of the Raffles films for me. To all those who have helped me research this book over the years, and to everyone who gave feedback on my work at conferences I attended in Britain and internationally, your generous insights are tremendously appreciated.

I scarcely know how to begin to thank my doctoral supervisor, Matt Houlbrook, whose constant intellectual support—which continues more than five years post-viva!—epitomizes that well-worn saying that a PhD supervisor's work is never done. Since day one, Matt's encouragement, kindness, intellectual guidance, and painstaking attention to detail, as well as his sense of humour, have been amazing and crucially made this project and my career development far more fun than I had ever thought it could be: *thank you*. I owe you a beer, as always. At Oxford, Matthew Grimley and Jane Hamlett offered constructive and critical guidance during my transfer from probationer to D.Phil interview. The lovely friends I made there have continued to inspire me through their work and navigation of academic and non-academic challenges over the last few years. For being so great, here's to Eve Colpus, Ceci Flinn Goldie, Charlotte Greenhalgh, Erika Hanna, Sim Koole, Kate McNaboe, Sarah Newman, Will Pooley, Aparna Rao, and Hannah Sikstrom-Walker. Selina Todd and Louise Jackson were my viva examiners, and genuinely made that afternoon one of the highlights of my academic career through their incisive, creative questions and supportive approach. It is thanks to them that this book now ends in 1968. They have also played no small part in making sure my career continues, providing references and offering ideas on new projects ever since. Additionally, my sincere gratitude goes to Selina for giving me a year's Stipendiary Lectureship in History at St. Hilda's College post-viva, where I honed my teaching skills and understanding of post-war culture on her excellent 'Britain from the Bomb to the Beatles' course. I will always be glad to have had the privilege of working at St. Hilda's.

I would like to say a special thank you to Julie-Marie Strange, who over the last ten years has been variously my course tutor, pen-pal, colleague, boss(!), and throughout it all, very much adored friend. Having chivvied me successfully to get this book finished and swapped me innumerable copies of excellent crime novels in the meantime to keep me going, I hope she enjoys the end product, and knows how deeply I have appreciated her support. I also hope she gets a very well-earned rest after finishing her tenure as a fantastic Head of Division! Max Jones, Frank Mort, and Hannah Barker have also known me since those early MA History days and I am now incredibly chuffed to be a lecturer alongside them at Manchester, where I attempt to channel my experience of their wonderful teaching in my own practice every day. In different ways Julie-Marie, Max, Frank, and Hannah shaped the interests and methodological approaches that inform this book, as well as acting as mentors and friends, offering encouragement and advice along the way. Hannah must be singled out for giving me a job—twice!—first as her research assistant and some years later, in a permanent post at the University of Manchester, which I still can't quite believe. I have some (though not many) regrets about the bit where I burst into tears and gabbled about how much I love Manchester 'like a reality show winner' when she offered me that last, much cherished, permanent job. Thank you! (I still love Manchester.)

In a department of circa forty colleagues, it is extraordinarily good luck to discover that everyone is absolutely lovely, hilariously funny, and unfailingly kind. My warmest thanks to everyone with whom I work in the history department at Manchester, for cheering me on with this book and for making me weirdly look forward to departmental meetings and those never-that-far-away away days. I can think of nowhere else I can make analogies to Star Wars or harp on excitedly about the latest Jurassic Park film so frequently without backlash. Among my colleagues, Sasha Handley and Penny Summerfield both proofread drafts of this book, helping hone it into what I hope is an engaging style. Anything lacking is entirely due to my own failure to apprehend their excellent feedback. Frances Houghton and Laure Humbert have shared a great deal of helpful advice about the publication process, as well as constant reassurance, friendship, and gossip on matters professional and personal. They also share my love of tea and cake, which is pretty vital to any working relationship—thanks ladies! Linda Briggs, James Connolly, Eleanor Davey, Clara Dawson, David Jiménez Torres, Frank Eissa Barroso, Jonathan Mair, Sarah Roddy, and Anna Strowe formed my early support and survival group during the first year here, bonding over some incredibly surreal training sessions, dinners, pub quizzes, and cinema trips. Like any endeavour, a book is as much the product of rest as hard work, so my thanks to them all for keeping things in perspective (and my thanks to Charles Insley on this score as well). Charlotte Wildman and Ruth Lamont have become a dream team of research partners and firm friends, whose input throughout this project, and on many topics besides, has been invaluable. My undergraduate students, past and present, on my level 3 course 'Defining the Deviant: Crime and British Society, 1888–2000' continually reinvigorate my modes of thinking and writing about histories of crime, inspiring me to do better.

My non-work friends are all the more amazing for sticking with me through the rollercoaster years of writing this book. Lucy VanEssen-Fishman and Nisha Singh were both, at different times, my flatmates in Oxford, which should merit some sort of award for living with me while I wrestled with the D.Phil. Thank you both for your patience and humour, for seeing me through some major ups and downs, and for letting me have Jurassic Park on in the background while I wrote (since I have now mentioned it twice, I would like to thank Steven Spielberg for making that film, as I can't seem to write without it). Christine Grandy landed in Oxford when there was only one more year to go and instantly reenergized life and work through her common sense, kindness, and encouragement, reading everything and even conducting a mock viva with me. In addition to being a truly awesome friend, Christine co-organized a Crime and Deviance Conference at the University of Lincoln with me in 2015, drawing together a network of scholars whose works appear throughout this book.

Some friends go back further than any of us want to remember. Gina Fay Reynolds, Emma Middleditch, and Rachel Watts have been friends at least as long as I have been a budding historian, and I appreciate their encouragement. Relatives have also offered kind support; my thanks to Anthony and Carol Cox, Winifred and Chris Hickson, Anne and Helmut Schülke, Alan Moss and Su, and Keith and Daria Moss. Much more recently, my lovely fellow-students at the Glossop Spanish class—Jo, Judith and Judith, Gill, Liz, David, and Isabella—our teacher Gemma, and my neighbours Anna, Diane, and Andy, have kept me sane while I put the finishing touches to the book, and I am very grateful for the welcome and friendship they given me during the last, rather momentous year.

Finally, to my family. Katrina Davies and Sophie Hughes are always there with love, laughter, and a sense of adventure. They are the only people who could have persuaded me to visit Dollywood. They have as much of a stake in this book as I do, having listened to me going on about history for well over a decade now, and even offering their thoughts on parts of my work over our (many, many) years of friendship. I really don't know what I would do without you two! But I do know that cocktails are on the horizon when this book is in print. I think the world of you both. Thanks also to my brother, Sandy (by far the cooler one of the two of us), for cheering me on! Finally, to my parents, Kath and Steve Moss, who are the best mum and dad in the world. None of this would have happened without you. This book is small repayment for a lifetime of love, support (financial, emotional, big-spider-rescuing, cup-of-tea-making, cooking-guidance-providing, and trips-outdoors-to-improve-head-space-giving), and all the zillion other things you have given me. I dedicate this book to my parents, with all my love.

Contents

List of Figures   xi

List of Abbreviations   xv

Introduction   1

1. The 'King of All Burglars'   21

2. A. J. Raffles: Gentleman Thief   43

3. Marvellous Mrs Raffles? The Implausible Woman Burglar   66

4. The Cat Burglar as London's Rooftop Threat   89

5. Burglary Insurance and the Culture of Fear   110

6. Designing the Burglar-Proof Home   132

7. Defying the Burglar in Post-War London   158

8. Spy-Burglars and Secrets in the Cold War Capital   185

Epilogue: 'We Are All Burglars'   206

Appendix   215

Bibliography   221

Index   247

List of Figures

I.1. 'Beat the Burglar', Burglary insurance advert issued by Prudential Assurance
Co. Ltd, 1946. Reproduced by kind permission of the Prudential Archives.   7

I.2. 'Wall Boring Burglars', *Daily Mail* (10 April 1930), p. 11. Reproduced by
kind permission of Solo Syndication on behalf of the Daily Mail, Associated
Newspapers Limited.   10

1.1. Plate from Unknown Author, *Charles Peace; or, The Adventures of a Notorious
Burglar. Founded on Fact and Profusely Illustrated* (London: G. Purkess, 1880),
p. 63. British Library, Mic. C10176. Reproduced by kind permission
© The British Library Board.   31

1.2. 'Phrenological Head of Charles Peace, the Burglar', *Illustrated Police News*
(22 Feb. 1879), p. 1. Reproduced by kind permission © The British
Library Board.   34

1.3. Waxwork of Charles Peace on display at Madame Tussaud's (*c.*1900).
Image reproduced by kind permission of Madame Tussaud's Archives.   39

1.4. *Daily Mirror* (19 July 1935), p. 1. Reproduced by kind permission of
Reach Publishing Services Ltd.   41

2.1. 'Raffles, The Amateur Cracksman, at the Comedy', *Sketch* (30 May 1906),
p. 4. Victoria and Albert Museum Theatre and Performance Collections
[VAM] (cutting in file Comedy: Raffles 12 May 1906). Reproduced by
kind permission, @ Victoria and Albert Museum, London.   54

2.2. 'Wyndham's 1915', programme (23 Dec. 1914). VAM. Reproduced
by kind permission, @ Victoria and Albert Museum, London.   57

2.3. Display Advertising, *Evening Standard* (10 Sept. 1930), p. 4.
Reproduced by kind permission © The British Library Board.   60

3.1. *Illustrated Police News* (2 Apr. 1898), p. 1. Reproduced by kind
permission © The British Library Board.   76

3.2. Scene from 'The Last of Mrs. Cheyney' (St. James's Theatre, 1925),
photograph featured in the *Play Pictorial* (Oct. 1925), p. 91.
Reproduced by kind permission © The British Library Board.   82

3.3. 'Estelle Graham (pseud.), 'Confessions of a Girl Cat Burglar',
Glasgow Weekly News (11 Mar. 1933), p. 13. Used by kind permission
of D. C. Thomson & Co Ltd.   86

4.1. 'Burglary Risks', *The Times* (28 Apr. 1926), p. 15.   90

4.2. '"Cat" Burglar's £7,000 Booty', *Daily Mail* (7 Feb. 1925), p. 7.
Reproduced by kind permission of Solo Syndication on behalf of
the Daily Mail, Associated Newspapers Limited.   100

4.3. 'The Way of the Cat Burglar', *Daily Express* (24 Feb. 1937), p. 1.
Reproduced by kind permission of Express Newspapers Syndication.   101

4.4. *Daily Express* (17 Dec. 1924), p. 8. Reproduced by kind permission
of Express Newspapers Syndication. 103

4.5. TNA, MEPO 2/5229, Crime Map of 'X' Division (Kilburn)
(31 Mar. 1937), p. 218. 107

5.1. 'Revolvers and daggers', CII, 9.94 Box 158, Law Accident Insurance
Society, *Burglars and Burgling* (1899), p. 19. Reproduced by kind permission
of the Chartered Insurance Institute Archives. 111

5.2. 'A thief climbing a portico', CII, 9.94 Box 158, Law Accident Insurance
Society, *Burglars and Burgling* (1899). Reproduced by kind permission
of the Chartered Insurance Institute Archives. 112

5.3. '10 Burglaries in One District in 12 Hours', *Scotsman*, (15 Dec. 1920),
p. 7. As published in *The Scotsman* on 15 Dec. 1920 and reproduced
with their kind permission. 122

5.4. 1924 British Empire Exhibition artefact. On the left, before pulling tag;
on the right, after pulling tag. Reproduced by kind permission of
Prudential Group Archives. 125

6.1. LMA, CLC/B/002, Box 264, *Illustrated Price List of Chubb & Son's
Patent Locks and Safes* (Oct. 1882), p. 31. Reproduced by kind permission
of London Metropolitan Archives (City of London). 134

6.2. LMA, CLC/B/002/10/01/008, Jewel safe featured in exhibition booklet
*Chubb's Patent Locks and Safes, International Exhibition, 1862.
Class XXXI. No. 6017* (1862), p. 3. Reproduced by kind permission
of London Metropolitan Archives (City of London). 138

6.3. LMA, CLC/B/002/10/01/008, Door Lock featured in exhibition booklet
*Chubb's Patent Locks and Safes, International Exhibition, 1862. Class
XXXI. No. 6017* (1862), p. 2. Reproduced by kind permission of London
Metropolitan Archives (City of London). 139

6.4. LMA, CLC/B, file 1999/007, 'Milner's Jewellery Safe Cabinets', in
*Milner's Hold-Fast and Fire Resisting Safes, Chests, Strong Rooms,
Strong Room Doors, Powder Magazines, &c. (c.1880)*, p. 24. Reproduced by
kind permission of London Metropolitan Archives (City of London). 140

6.5. LMA, CLC/B/002, Box 264, *Illustrated Price List of Chubb & Son's Patent
Locks and Safes* (Oct. 1882), p. 31. Reproduced by kind permission of
London Metropolitan Archives (City of London). 142

6.6. TNA, MEPO 3/2026, Front Cover of Rely a-Bell pamphlet, in
Burglar Alarms Connected to Police Stations: Policy, 1934–1947 (1936). 149

7.1. TNA, MEPO 2/8052, 'Whitehall 1212: Exhibition at Selfridges,
taken for Exhibitions Division' (May 1950). 167

7.2. TNA, INF 2/124, Home Office, 'Don't Invite Crime' (1965). 172

7.3. TNA, INF 2/124, Home Office, 'Watch Out! There's a
Thief About!' (c.1967). 173

7.4. TNA, CRIM 1/5013, 'Crime Scene Photograph 11', *Rex v. John
William Smith* (1968). 180

7.5. TNA, CRIM 1/5013, 'Crime Scene Photograph 12',
Rex v. John William Smith (1968). 181

8.1. 'The Krogers' Bungalow in Ruislip', in John Bulloch and Henry Miller,
Spy Ring: The True Story of the Naval Secrets Case (London: Secker and
Warburg, 1961), p. 65. Reproduced by kind permission of the
Press Association. 199

List of Abbreviations

BBC	BBC Written Archives Centre
BL	British Library
BTA	British Telecom Archive
CII	Chartered Institute of Insurance Archives
CU	Cambridge University Archives
HCPP	House of Commons Parliamentary Papers
HRC	Harry Ransom Humanities Research Center, University of Texas at Austin
LMA	London Metropolitan Archives
MO	Mass Observation Archive
MODA	Museum of Domestic Design and Architecture Archives
MTA	Madame Tussaud's Archives
NAS	National Archives of Scotland
ODNB	Oxford Dictionary of National Biography
OBP	Old Bailey Papers
OU	Open University Police Archives
PGA	Prudential Group Archives
RMA	Royal Mail Archives
SLA	Sheffield Local Archives
TNA	The National Archives, Public Records Office, United Kingdom
BT	Board of Trade
CAB	Cabinet Papers
CRIM	Criminal Trials Series
FO	Foreign Office
HO	Home Office
INF	Office of Information
J	Justice Department
MEPO	Metropolitan Police
PCOM	Prison Commission
UBA	University of Birmingham Archives
VAM	Victoria and Albert Museum Archives

Introduction

Opening her front door in the comfortable middle-class suburb of Wembley, north-west London late one balmy evening in June 1939, Mrs Kathleen Herd suffered a nasty shock. Tired and laden down with shopping bags, she suddenly realized that *someone else* was in the house with her. It is not difficult to imagine how she felt. A creeping awareness of the sounds of a stranger in her home—the creak of an upstairs floorboard or the jarring crash of an overturned chair—would have triggered an unwelcome rush of adrenalin, signalling immediate physical danger. Mr Herd was unfortunately away at the time. What should she do? Returning outdoors to cry for help held the possibility of being overheard by the burglar, who might move to silence her before her screams caught others' attention. Or, she could look for the nearest telephone box to use the new '999' emergency number, introduced in London as a faster way to call the police in 1937, just two years previously. But then all the while she was doing that, the burglar would be stealing even more of her possessions, or might run away before the police could get there. Kathleen chose a third option. Bravely—some might say foolishly—she walked further into her home.

She was lucky. As the *Daily Mirror* would later report, her entry had 'scared away' the thief, who apparently decided against a confrontation and disappeared, presumably out of a back window or door.[1] Yet Mrs Herd's relief can only have been matched by despair as she began to register that prized personal possessions had disappeared: a bloodstone ring and one very unusual brooch.[2] The loss of the brooch hit particularly hard. Her grief at the theft may even have eclipsed the retreating prospect of violence. For the brooch, though of little financial value, recorded one of the most profound episodes of the Herds' personal history, a story that intersected with one of the nation's darkest hours. Serving with outstanding bravery in the British Army's Royal Field Artillery during the First World War, John Herd, Kathleen's husband, was struck in the leg by a bullet in France. He was temporarily discharged in 1917.[3] Many would (justifiably) have used such an

---

[1] 'SOS to a Burglar with a Kind Heart', *Daily Mirror* (16 June 1939), p. 19.

[2] Bloodstone is a form of jasper, a semi-precious stone. My thanks to Sasha Handley for identifying the material.

[3] The Medal Roll for John Herd records him being awarded the Victory Medal, the 1914–15 Star (Herd appears to have gotten this in 1915), and an additional medal marked in handwriting with an X and the word 'Gordons', which seems likely to refer to the Military Cross for service with the Gordon Highlanders in 1917. TNA, WO/372/9, 'John Herd, Royal Field Artillery: Medal Record' (1915–1919).

injury to request a permanent discharge, an escape from the bloody massacres, mustard gas, disease, and freezing muddiness of trench warfare. John, by contrast, mounted the extracted bullet from his leg on a brooch that he gave to his mother in commemoration of his survival, and returned to the war. The brooch became a talisman. 'He has formed a great sentimental attachment to it', Kathleen would later tell the press. Demobbed in 1919, having managed to survive one of the deadliest conflicts of the twentieth century, John's future seemed bleak. Given the well-documented mental and physical trauma of ex-soldiers returning from the Western Front and the impact this had on their ability to obtain employment and sustain romantic relationships, it was unlikely the 1920s would have loomed as a particularly 'roaring' decade for him.[4] Against all odds, however, John managed both, eventually meeting and marrying his wife 'just a few years' prior to the burglary.[5] And, as a fitting blessing on the couple, at their wedding John's mother gave the brooch to her daughter-in-law. It was this brooch, this priceless fragment of Herd's personal and family history, that was now in the burglar's possession.

Night Raiders is the first history of burglars and burglary in modern Britain. Tapping into rich, untold stories of private heroism and everyday struggle, it charts the confrontation between criminal and householder inside their homes during the period 1860 until 1968. During these decades, burglary acted as a focal point for articulating national values about citizenship, family, and lifestyle, and the 'perils and pleasures' of modern urban living.[6] Accordingly, this book goes on the trail of burglars as they pick up their blow-torches and diamond cutters before heading out into the darkness. *Night Raiders* examines the 'treasures' they stole, the places they stole them from, and the reasons they gave for attempting—in the parlance of the times—to 'crack' another 'crib' (house). It situates the shifting versions and reported experiences of burglary amongst the motives of the state, popular, and commercial sectors, as each sought to evolve a closer relationship and consensus of interests with citizens through the crime. Stoking emotions of fear or pleasure at burglary (the latter, crafted around lurid films depicting suave, handsome burglars seducing lonely female householders and escaping from justice), these sectors mobilized popular feeling on the issue to sell products and services, situating burglary within broader histories of capitalism and liberal democracy. This is also a history of the city, and how burglary energized new ways of knowing, securing, and moving around it.

Burglary haunted city-dwellers' lives for centuries. Extra financial rewards were offered for the capture of burglars from the late-1690s, fuelling the efforts of mercenary 'thief-takers' to pursue them to the hangman's noose.[7] The sinister nature of

---

[4] Michael Roper, *The Secret Battle: Emotional Survival in the Great War* (Manchester: Manchester University Press, 2009), pp. 276–313; Joanna Bourke, *Dismembering the Male: Men's Bodies, Britain, and the Great War* (Chicago: University of Chicago Press, 1996).

[5] 'SOS to a Burglar with a Kind Heart', *Daily Mirror* (16 June 1939), p. 19.

[6] I have taken inspiration here from the title of Matt Houlbrook's seminal *Queer London: Perils and Pleasures in the Sexual Metropolis, 1918–1957* (Chicago: University of Chicago Press, 2005).

[7] Tim Hitchcock and Robert Shoemaker, *London Lives: Poverty, Crime, and the Making of a Modern City, 1690–1800* (Cambridge: Cambridge University Press, 2015), pp. 61–2.

the crime was defined in English common law during the early 1700s, which distinguished burglary as occurring only during the night-time (unlike its daytime counterpart, housebreaking) and requiring some form of 'breaking in'. Amanda Vickery, historian of the eighteenth-century London home, outlines how the crime was seen as the ultimate affront to the tenet that 'An Englishman's Home is his Castle', citing an influential manual for magistrates of the era that insisted '"And so tender is the law in respect of the immunity of a man's house, that it will never suffer it to be violated with impunity."'[8] Accordingly, the penalty for burglary (even if nothing was stolen) was to be fatal, a sentence that remained in law until 1861, although at the Old Bailey trials no one was hanged for it after 1830.[9] One only has to glance through works by influential judges and lawyers published in the eighteenth and nineteenth century, including treatises by Sir William Blackstone, Sir John Jervis, and Herbert Broom, to find that they devoted independent chapters to theft, housebreaking, and burglary due to the gravity of the latter offence.[10] These were understood as very different crimes, despite the tendency of historians to refer to them in the same breath.[11] Admittedly, in certain

---

[8] Amanda Vickery, *Behind Closed Doors: At Home in Georgian England* (London and New Haven: Yale University Press, 2009), p. 31; Vickery, 'An Englishman's Home is his Castle? Thresholds, Boundaries, and Privacies in the Eighteenth-Century London House', *Past and Present* 199 (2008), pp. 154–5.

[9] Simon Devereaux, 'The Bloodiest Code: Counting Executions and Pardons at the Old Bailey, 1730–1837', *Law, Crime, and History* 6:1 (2016), p. 32.

[10] V. A. C. Gatrell, 'The Decline of Theft and Violence in Victorian and Edwardian England', in V. A. C. Gatrell, Bruce Lenman, and Geoffrey Parker (eds.), *Crime and the Law: The Social History of Crime in Western Europe Since 1500* (London: Europa Publications, 1980), p. 319. The deaths of Blackstone in 1780 and Jervis in 1856 did not prevent their works becoming the most widely used by jurists and legal scholars throughout the nineteenth and early twentieth centuries, whilst Broom's work ran into three editions between 1876 and 1883. Wilfrid Prest, 'Blackstone, Sir William (1723–1780), legal writer and judge', *Oxford Dictionary of National Biography*, http://www.oxforddnb.com/view/10.1093/ref:odnb/9780198614128.001.0001/odnb-9780198614128-e-2536 (accessed 26 June 2018) ; Getzler, Joshua S., 'Jervis, Sir John (1802–1856), judge', *Oxford Dictionary of National Biography*, http://www.oxforddnb.com/view/10.1093/ref:odnb/9780198614128.001.0001/odnb-9780198614128-e-14795 (accessed 26 June 2018) ; Lobban, Michael, 'Broom, Herbert (1815–1882), legal writer', *Oxford Dictionary of National Biography*, http://www.oxforddnb.com/view/10.1093/ref:odnb/9780198614128.001.0001/odnb-9780198614128-e-3569 (accessed 26 June 2018). Sir William Blackstone, *Commentaries on the Laws of England: Adapted to the Present State of the Law by Robert Malcolm Kerr, L.L.D* (3rd edn, London: John Murray, 1862), pp. 252–9 ; Sir John Jervis, *Archibold's Pleading and Evidence in Criminal Cases* (20th edn, London: Sweet and Maxwell, 1886), pp. 453–9, 558–75 ; Herbert Broom, *The Philosophy of Common Law* (3rd edn, London: W. Maxwell and Son, 1883), pp. 227–31. Wilfrid Prest, 'Blackstone, Sir William (1723–80)', *Oxford Dictionary of National Biography*, http://www.oxforddnb.com/view/10.1093/ref:odnb/9780198614128.001.0001/odnb-9780198614128-e-2536 (accessed 26 June 2018) ; Joshua S. Getzler, 'Jervis, Sir John (1802–1856)', *Oxford Dictionary of National Biography*, http://www.oxforddnb.com/view/10.1093/ref:odnb/9780198614128.001.0001/odnb-9780198614128-e-14795 (accessed 26 June 2018) ; Michael Lobban, 'Broom, Herbert (1815–1882)', *Oxford Dictionary of National Biography*, http://www.oxforddnb.com/view/10.1093/ref:odnb/9780198614128.001.0001/odnb-9780198614128-e-3569 (accessed 26 June 2018).

[11] To date, historians have taken their cue from the publication *Judicial Statistics*, issued annually by the Home Office to record the levels of crime in England and Wales. Following its pre-1893 practice of collapsing burglary and housebreaking into one crime, they have tended not to dig deeper. Although this certainly demonstrates a point at which officials seemingly collapsed the differences between burglary and housebreaking, it is a relatively minor instance of correlating the two as part of a recording practice that the historian V. A. C. Gatrell has admitted was 'hazy' in the Victorian period.

published statistical records, from which scholars have taken their cue, burglary continued to be collapsed into a broader category of 'theft with violence' prior to 1893. Yet during the years 1860 until 1968, the rules of the 'game' (as it was described by one former burglar) were made more rigid.[12] According to the Larceny Acts of 1861 and 1916, burglary could only be tried as such if it took place during the 'night-time' hours of nine p.m. and six a.m., and from a specifically residential building—a place where people were likely to be at home when the burglar came to call.[13] This was a legal definition shared across the Atlantic until the 1960s, fostering a lively exchange of criminological opinion, news stories, theatre plays, and films about burglary between Britain and America.[14] Burglary needs a fresh appraisal.

Fixed in time and space, burglars were 'Night Raiders': an evocative phrase coined in 1897 by one American criminologist to describe a man (it was generally thought to be perpetrated by men) who would clamber through your windows dressed in black wearing a mask, silently steal your jewels, and then melt away again into the shadowy nocturnal world outside.[15] 'Professionals' of this breed were supposedly the most skilled and intelligent of thieves. In 1894 Sir Charles Edward Troup, chair of the Home Office Committee on the Identification of 'Habitual' Criminals, admitted to parliament that 'A professional burglar, for instance, may, before he is arrested, commit 20 crimes', a pretty damning comment on who then appeared to be winning the 'game' between police and burglars.[16] For the 'experts', athleticism was also involved, since climbing through windows, up stackpipes, and occasionally on rooftops, was no mean feat. This was a crime that would test the resourcefulness, organization, and physical endurance of police as they chased their prey across the cityscape; small wonder, then, that burglary was viewed as a test of national character as well.

The story of the burglary at the Herds' fit easily into this mould. Kathleen's love for her husband, and her bravery in entering her home that night in 1939 despite the danger, was a kind of 'domestic heroism' that complemented John Herd's

---

Gatrell, 'The Decline of Theft and Violence in Victorian and Edwardian England', pp. 318–19; Clive Emsley, *Crime and Society in England, 1750–1900* (London: Routledge, 1987), pp. 23–4, 62, 131–3; Clive Emsley, *Crime and Society in Twentieth-Century England* (Harlow: Longman, 2011), pp. 22, 137–8; William Meier, *Property Crime in London, 1850–Present* (Basingstoke: Palgrave MacMillan, 2011), pp. 13–40.

[12] George Smithson, *Raffles in Real Life* (London: Hutchinson and Co., 1930), p. 25.

[13] Regarding the use of the term burglary in published criminal statistics and in the several thousand police reports I analysed to collate statistics from the London magistrates' courts, the authors of these reports were extremely careful to differentiate burglary from other forms of larceny/theft, particularly the daytime crime of 'housebreaking', taking care to specify the hour at which a crime was committed, in all the records I have seen. Although it could be suggested that a theft from a house might possibly have been recorded as taking place a few minutes before 6 a.m. or after 9 p.m. to sway a jury to deliver a harsher sentence, there is simply no way of proving this, and I have been most struck in my research by the precise attention to the legal definition of those recording this crime.

[14] Wilbur R. Miller, *The Social History of Crime and Punishment in America* (London: Sage, 2012), p. 182; see Chapter 2.

[15] Benjamin P. Eldridge, *Our Rival, the Rascal: A Faithful Portrayal of the Conflict between the Criminals of this Age and the Defenders of our Society* (Boston: Pemberton Publishing Co., 1897), p. 102.

[16] HCPP, Cmd. 8072, C. E. Troup, *Judicial Statistics, England and Wales, 1894* (London, 1896), p. 31; P. W. J. Bartrip, 'Troup, Sir Charles Edward (1857–1941)', *Oxford Dictionary of National Biography*, http://www.oxforddnb.com/view/article/60141 (accessed 21 Dec. 2016).

impressive war record.[17] He himself was a beacon of masculine patriotism that the burglar's actions could not dim. Burglary was a useful analogy to war, with its comparable motifs of invasion, violence, destruction, and loss. Press reports presented the Herds as paragons of stoicism, physical sacrifice, hard work, and heterosexual romance, qualities being energized anew in national culture in the build-up to yet another global conflict. The Second World War witnessed hugely popular films such as *Goodbye Mr Chips* (1939) and *Mrs Miniver* (1942) that fleshed out comparable scenarios of 'ordinary' people resisting invasion for cinema audiences to reflect upon. Mrs Miniver, for example, single-handedly tackled a stranded Nazi pilot in her home when her husband was away fighting. Contributing to circulating ideals of a shared 'British bulldog' spirit, these were narratives designed to inspire triumph over malign German nationalism, with clear parallels to Kathleen Herd's actions in the face of her burglar.[18]

Burglary was also sexualized. Time and again reports emerged of burglars 'penetrating' into the most intimate, private spaces of the home.[19] But this was no mere analogy. By specifying that burglary happened at night, the law implicitly recognized that burglary presented the threat of violence and rape, not just the loss of material goods. British judges were empowered to deliver a sentence of life imprisonment for burglars, in contrast to the more lenient sentences dealt out to 'housebreakers', who stole in daytime. Considering the danger Kathleen Herd had faced, this distinction made sense. The report of the burglary at the Herds' held a subtext of sexual violence all too familiar to regular readers of crime news in the *Daily Mirror*. Fickle good fortune saved Kathleen from being at home all through that evening, instead of crossing paths with the thief momentarily as she walked in. Had she been at home, she could have encountered the burglar in the far more isolated and vulnerable context of her living room, or worse, in the bedroom. The horror of waking up disoriented and alone at the sound of an alien footstep on the landing may well have haunted the thoughts of the *Daily Mirror*'s readers, giving them a few sleepless nights over the security of the locks attached to their own bedroom windows.

These legal conditions were not the only elements that made burglary intrinsic to the national conversation. In a powerful sense, burglary destabilized a funda-mental relationship between citizenship and property-owning forged in the nineteenth century. The 1832 Reform Act made the right to vote contingent on the ability to rent a house or lodgings worth ten pounds or more. Enfranchising large numbers of the middle classes at the expense of working-class citizens, a property qualification endured in varying forms until the terms of the vote were extended to include all men over the age of 21 (and women over 30) in 1918. Yet there were never any guarantees where citizenship was concerned. Wealth

---

[17] 'A woman's love' gained new powers in the novels of Mills and Boon during the 1920s, healing not only the emotional wounds of ex-soldiers (handily ensuring their safe re-integration into civilian life) but also knitting together a new generation of family units, restoring the stability of society. Jay Dixon, *The Romance Fiction of Mills and Boon, 1909–1990s* (London: UCL Press, 1999), p. 100.

[18] *Goodbye Mr Chips* (United Kingdom: Metro Goldwyn Mayer, dir. Sam Wood, 1939). The film won Donat an Oscar for Best Actor.

[19] See Chapter 6.

and status were generally precarious in Victorian and Edwardian Britain. For the lower-middle class especially, meagre wages earned as clerks and secretaries combined with a gruelling cocktail of long hours, high rents, and large family sizes. Targeted advertising piled on the pressure, suggesting buying costly domestic furnishings as a means to visibly 'get ahead' and cultivate networks among important colleagues.[20] Yes, this may have been a good way to encourage the boss to come around for dinner, but these furnishings, including ornaments, could also be delightfully tempting to the roving eyes of a burglar. Burglary insurance—the obvious safeguard, introduced into insurers' policy portfolios during the 1880s—was expensive, and riddled with clauses about what constituted a 'breaking in' that made pay-outs increasingly difficult to claim.[21] Fear of burglary was understandable, when it could easily mark the difference between upwards or downwards social mobility for a family poised on the knife-edge between classes.

The post-1918 increase in affordable housing and removal of the property qualification from the franchise (for men) did not mean that attitudes towards burglary relaxed in later decades. Quite the opposite. Successive economic depressions in 1921 and 1929, and an uncertain job market following each World War meant that (according to both press and insurance advertisers) society would be 'assailed' by hordes of unemployed or recently demobbed young men, looking to turn criminal. Skilled either in the factory or the Armed Services, it was thought they would likely commit burglary as an interim source of income until the economy 'rebalanced' in their favour—frequently achieved through the government ejecting women from the jobs they had acquired as 'reinforcements' during wartime. Hysteria crept into the tone of the *Daily Mail* in 1945, when it headlined a '60% increase in burglaries' as the war's end drew near and burglars supposedly joined forces with Black Market profiteers to sell stolen goods before tighter policing was imposed.[22] These fears were unfounded. Post-war crime 'waves' form what the historian Clive Emsley has called 'relatively small blips' in the overall statistics of crime for the twentieth century, with the volume of media warnings of imminent violence far outweighing the real number.[23] Statistical likelihoods *discouraging* fears about burglary rarely made headlines, however, in a culture where it uniquely emblematized an attack on the sanctity of the home. Juxtaposed alongside stories of rising rates of divorce and juvenile delinquency, fears over sexual promiscuity, and reactions against immigration, these factors collectively seemed perfectly designed to undermine the fragile post-war recovery.[24]

---

[20] A. James Hammerton, 'Pooterism or Partnership? Marriage and Masculine Identity in the Lower Middle Class, 1870–1920', *Journal of British Studies* 38:3 (1999), pp. 291–321; A. James Hammerton, 'The Perils of Mrs Pooter: Satire, Modernity and Motherhood in the Lower Middle Class in England, 1870–1920', *Women's History Review* 8:2 (1999), pp. 261–76.

[21] See Chapter 5.

[22] 'Black Market Spies "Spot" for the Burglars', *Daily Mail* (3 Jan. 1945), p. 3.

[23] Clive Emsley, *Soldier, Sailor, Beggarman, Thief: Crime and the British Armed Services Since 1914* (Oxford: Oxford University Press, 2013), pp. 160–73.

[24] See Frank Mort, *Capital Affairs: London and the Making of the Permissive Society* (London and New Haven: Yale University Press, 2010).

BEAT THE BURGLAR

ISSUED BY THE PRUDENTIAL ASSURANCE CO. LTD.

Fig. I.1. 'Beat the Burglar', Burglary insurance advert issued by Prudential Assurance Co. Ltd, 1946. Reproduced by kind permission of the Prudential Archives.

Men were needed. Popular discourse of the era proposed defending the home against predatory thieves through an active reassertion of 'masculine' authority, reinstating the man of the house in the Victorian 'breadwinner' model: a patriarch who would buy the relevant insurance, affix the appropriate locks, bolts, and bars, and if all else failed, fight the burglar off with his fists. Saturating contemporary media, this ideal conveniently chimed with a broader conservative backlash against the social changes wrought by war. Interwar women were enjoying political emancipation and greater opportunities for employment; they were even marrying later (gasp).[25] But would their new-found independence be enough to save them when the burglar came to call? Advertisements such as Fig. I.1, from the Prudential Assurance Co. in 1946, ensured that the question remained contentious. Its sinister depiction of a ghoulish-looking man reaching to open a door handle through a smashed glass pane was enough to send shivers down the spine of any homeowner. In lurid yellow, the headline 'Beat the Burglar' cleverly positioned insurance as the hidden trump card that would offer financial protection, ensuring the criminal was unable to reduce a family to poverty, whatever the scale of the crime. Yet 'Beat' could also gesture at the possibility of a physical fight in defence of family and possessions, the idea of which few women would have been expected to entertain.

[25] Selina Todd, *Young Women, Work, and Family Life in England, 1918–1950* (Oxford: Oxford University Press, 2005).

The ways in which burglary has been experienced and imagined over time thus offer an important set of insights into the changing nature and ideology of domestic lives and relationships during the nineteenth and twentieth century. To explore the cultural significance of the crime, *Night Raiders* seeks to arrive at the moments where ideas circulating about burglary transformed into what philosopher and sociologist Michel de Certeau famously termed the 'practices of everyday life'.[26] Those practices include securing one's home with the latest anti-burglar technologies, consequently designing and living within the space in subtly different ways, and buying insurance or instructing police officers to keep a careful an eye on rooftops and windowsills for signs of trouble. Moving between the extraordinary and the everyday in understanding the place of crime in society, this book takes inspiration from a body of scholarship that does not classify itself as contributing to histories of crime per se, but uses crime as a lens to explore broader themes and ideas in history.[27] Within this remit, I explore the relationship between burglary and ideas about 'appropriate' ways of acting around and organizing city and home, and the material composition of both. Here, I am influenced by scholars who have been interested in discovering how new ways of knowing and navigating the cityscape grew from changing modes of regulation and surveillance of crime historically.[28] *Night Raiders* charts an important era of transition when the public sense of security shifted away from a reliance on relatives, neighbours, and police, to reside in the promises of insurance companies and a new raft of commercial security technologies. Locks and safes, burglar alarms and brand new emergency telephone numbers were all deployed in the battle of wits between homeowner and thief. How did this alter the relationship between citizen and state? As people fashioned new expectations about security that they could now simply buy, police tried to work with security companies to ensure their products led to more arrests than false alarms and hassle. In a maelstrom of sometimes competing, sometimes complementary interests, the issue of which sector controlled the regulation, identification, and capture of burglars grew muddier. Fears about burglary could lucratively be manufactured through clever press and advertising, if a company so desired (say, when their profit margins were looking a bit fragile). Correspondingly, regardless of whether or not the volume of burglaries had increased, politicians and police officials could only reap benefits publicly from collaborating in upholding the system of insurance and security industry claims, joining them in the 'fight against crime'.

---

[26] Michel de Certeau, *The Practice of Everyday Life* (Berkeley: University of California Press, 1984).
[27] Judith Walkowitz, *City of Dreadful Delight: Narratives of Sexual Danger in Late-Victorian London* (Chicago: University of Chicago Press, 1992); Martin Wiener, *Reconstructing the Criminal: Culture, Law and Policy in England, 1830–1914* (Cambridge: Cambridge University Press, 1990); Martin Wiener, *Men of Blood: Violence, Manliness, and Criminal Justice in Victorian England* (Cambridge: Cambridge University Press, 2004); Ginger Frost, *Promises Broken: Courtship, Class, and Gender in Victorian England* (Virginia: University Press of Virginia, 1995); Shani D'Cruze, *Crimes of Outrage: Sex, Violence, and Victorian Working Women* (London: UCL Press, 1998); Matt Houlbrook, *Prince of Tricksters: The Incredible True Story of Netley Lucas, Gentleman Crook*, (Chicago: University of Chicago Press, 2016).
[28] Walkowitz, *City*; Lynda Nead, *Victorian Babylon: People, Streets, and Images in Nineteenth-Century London* (London and New Haven: Yale University Press, 2000); Houlbrook, *Queer London*.

Their relationship had clear implications for the class and wealth of those the state protected. Trouble frequently began when those who could afford insurance and security devices gained more immediate police attention than those who could not, especially given the volume of false alarm calls. In 1968, a Home Office 'Working Party on False Burglar Alarm Calls' was set up because, as Chief Superintendent of Police F. W. Hudson reflected in the minutes: 'Of the alarm calls to which police respond, 97% were false…as more alarms were installed, to a point at which their number would be beyond police resources, the whole system would break down and the alarm would be virtually useless.'[29] While police were busy chasing alarms to ensure that security customers' clientele remained 'satisfied', real villains were on the loose. Class mattered more and more for victims in a system where regulation of crime was orchestrated in large part by the commercial imperatives of security companies, rather than exclusively by police.

In reality, whether operating as 'cat' burglars slinking athletically along rooftop terraces, or forming a much larger body of clumsily masked men and women clambering hastily through windows into bedrooms, burglars in nineteenth- and twentieth-century London were often desperate, mostly poor.[30] Accordingly, the most common form of 'treasure' the majority ventured to steal amounted to less than five pounds in worth; usually, just a little food or a few coins purloined from a nearby cupboard (Table 1).[31] This was a nonetheless devastating loss in the lives of a working-class family facing the daily struggle of hand-to-mouth survival. The impact burglary had on these families was, in fact, hardly registered outside the courts. Newspapers (particularly the tabloids but also, by the later decades of our period, highbrow publications like *The Times*) progressively spurned reporting on the everyday cases in the local magistrates' courts, instead showering notoriety and renown upon exceptional cases of burglars who targeted the rich and made off with untold sums of money or jewellery worth millions. Admittedly, this sometimes hinged more upon the technique than the loot. In 1930, the theft of £60 from a two-ton safe improbably reached and forced open through a series of drilled-out

---

[29] TNA, HO 287/1676: *Home Office Working Party on False Burglar Alarms Calls* (20 Sept. 1968), p. 3.

[30] Of the 1,436 male defendants for burglary tried at the Old Bailey (CCC) or recorded in the proceedings at the Metropolitan Magistrates Courts and City of London Justice Rooms sampled at five-yearly intervals between 1860 and 1939, the most frequently listed occupations were: building and construction (including casual labourers), 434; road, railway, and dock labourers, 138; warehouse workers, porters, painters and decorators, 118; shop workers and merchants, 95; unemployed and menial labourers (including rag-sorters, street traders, sewer workers, and chimney sweeps), 90; servicemen in the armed forces and mariners, 85; butchers/bakers/fishmongers, 83; dress- and boot-makers, milliners, 53; clerks and insurance-brokers, 50; commercial staff (including hotel employees and waiters), 46; gas-workers and electricians, 41. Certain professions were more pronounced in the statistics for burglary during 1920–39, presumably due to economic depressions of 1921 and 1929. These included workers in road, rail, and on the docks, warehouse workers, merchants, clerks and insurance brokers, and commercial staff. Statistics for women burglars were dominated by unemployment, with 87 unemployed out of 190 women tried in the sample, and just 10 working as servants (the occupation commonly assumed to lead to burglary). For a more detailed breakdown of statistics, see Eloise Moss, 'Cracking Cribs: Representations of Burglars and Burglary in London, 1860–1939', Unpublished D.Phil Thesis, University of Oxford, 2013.

[31] See Appendix.

WALL-BORING BURGLARS

WORK BY LIGHTED PAPER.

ROOF TILES REMOVED

BURGLARS, who, it is believed, worked for two or three hours by the dim light of burning paper, cut through an eighteen-inch wall 200 years old early yes-

A diagram showing the hole in the wall and the course taken by the thieves.

terday morning. to carry out a robbery at the premises of J. H. Worrall, Son, and Co., silversmiths, Aldersgate street. E.C.

Fig. I.2. 'Wall Boring Burglars', *Daily Mail* (10 April 1930), p. 11. Reproduced by kind permission of Solo Syndication on behalf of the Daily Mail, Associated Newspapers Limited.

walls sent journalists into a spin: 'WALL BORING BURGLARS' screamed one headline excitedly (Fig. I.2).[32]

Burglars have haunted the thoughts of those with property to lose (or simply those with a healthy fear of violent crime) for centuries.[33] However, this book does not chart an uncomplicated history of fearful or defensive attitudes towards crime and criminal. Indeed, had Mr and Mrs Herd taken a trip to the cinema in 1940, just over a year after their case made the headlines, they might have been surprised and not a little disgruntled to watch a film that earned millions from celebrating burglary as an opportunity for daring young men to enjoy adventure, romance, and the spoils of incalculable wealth. *Raffles* (1940) starred handsome leading English actor David Niven, and was directed and produced by legendary Hollywood film-makers Sam Wood and Samuel Goldwyn. The latest of nine film adaptations of the stories first written by E. W. Hornung in 1899, *Raffles* brought to the screen the exploits of a bored, suave, wealthy young man who had turned to burgling the mansions of the aristocracy for fun. The film's sole concession to the controversy its message might generate was the burglar appearing to hand himself in to Detective Mackenzie at the end. Yet even the 'resolution' offered by this scene was ambiguous.

---

[32] 'Wall Boring Burglars', *Daily Mail* (10 Apr. 1930), p. 11.
[33] Gillian Spraggs, *Outlaws and Highwaymen: The Cult of the Robber in England from the Middle Ages to the Nineteenth Century* (London: Pimlico, 2001).

As the two men disappeared into the London fog, Raffles' beautiful and wealthy fiancée Gwendolyn (played by Olivia de Havilland, of *Gone with the Wind* fame) pledged to wait for him. Raffles' fate, one suspected, would not be very tragic. Besides this, in all previous versions Raffles gleefully escaped. The new ending prompted Dilys Powell, the *Sunday Times*' famous film critic, to caution audiences likely to be disappointed by the 1940 film that 'if you don't like the ending blame the Hays office [the American board of film censors], not me.'[34]

In these popular narratives of the burglar-as-hero, created to entertain and cultivate pleasure rather than fear, the timing of the crime was vital. Night-time held the potential for criminally imbued erotic fantasy. As historian Joachim Schlör has elegantly explained, 'Fear and fascination meet us as we approach the nocturnal city and accompany us along our way. We enter a world that is both familiar and strange, a landscape full of light and rich with shadows, the receptacle of our desires and our hidden, unspeakable fears.'[35] The prospect of an attractive young man dressed in black finding their way into one's bedroom at night was not all that upsetting for some, especially in stories where the violence was removed. In 'By Night', a short story by romance novelist Robert Hichens published in *Nash's Pall Mall Magazine* in 1930, a 'cat' burglar attempting to steal jewellery from a Mayfair mansion in London's West End accidentally wakes up his victim, a beautiful young heiress. Noticing him standing at the foot of her bed, the heiress does not worry about fear of attack but instead muses that he is 'a young man, handsome, very lean and strong, but not tall, wearing odd, closely-fitting black clothes'. The burglar returned the compliment, noting 'She was very pretty, and she looked very pretty in the big bed, for she was young, fresh in her smooth whiteness, long limbed. And her big eyes, fearless in their interested gaze, looked exotic.'[36]

Whilst it might be tempting to regard this story as a slightly tepid form of early 'burglar porn', the fact that *Nash's Pall Mall Magazine* was a mainstream publication suggests that a tacit acknowledgement of the erotics of burglary was widely accepted. *Night Raiders* looks at the moments these versions, constituting a 'pleasure culture of crime' around burglary, emerged into popular culture. At times, they circulated alongside reports of real burglaries, the narratives of violence and loss sitting uncomfortably alongside exciting and entertaining versions of the crime that appeared frivolous and insensitive by contrast. It would not do to dismiss them as such. The triumph of the burglar over ostentatiously wealthy victims, typical in 'pleasurable' narratives at the time, offered vicarious justice for working- and middle-class readers and cinemagoers during periods of economic depression. While stark inequalities of class and opportunities for employment continued to endure, the ability of the lowly burglar to capture the heart of a beautiful heiress was a kind of social mobility, wherein 'daring' and initiative were valued over formal education or 'manners'. The expectation that burglars would target spaces such as the bedroom

---

[34] Dilys Powell, 'Raffles (Regal)', *Sunday Times* (24 Mar. 1940), p. 3.

[35] Joachim Schlör, *Nights in the Big City: Paris, Berlin, London, 1840–1930* (London: Reaktion, 1998), p. 9.

[36] Robert Hichens, 'By Night', *Nash's Pall Mall Magazine* (June 1930), pp. 46–92.

or boudoir, used to erotic effect by authors such as Hichens, was also a source of inspiration for lock and safe manufacturers, whose designs for 'boudoir safes' channelled the spatial dynamics of burglary into adverts and product designs. As usual, burglary could be invested with an aspect of 'fear or fantasy' depending on the commercial imperatives of those drawing upon it. While burglary as a source of fear was used fairly consistently to promote products and services across the period, burglary-as-fantasy emerged when economic conditions made people receptive to witnessing the triumph of the burglar, indicating important moments of fracture and dissonance in the relationship between citizen, state, and market.

Writing a history of crime presents particular challenges. Most of the subjects of this book would prefer not to be found. They meet the historian's gaze reproachfully, forced to divulge snippets of their lives during their confinement in prison, and encountering us now through the dusty, crumbling pages of court ledgers and long-forgotten police and press reports. Sometimes we catch a more alarming glimpse of them forcing their way into homes in the plots of old films and works of fiction, or somewhat more predictably, in insurance catalogues. Occasionally, the burglars manage to slip away altogether unseen, uncaptured, and unreported. Here, they gleefully join the ranks of those populating the so-called 'dark' figure of unrecorded crimes. Fundamentally, our ability to be absolutely certain about the scale and nature of burglary (or indeed, any crime) is always compromised by these factors. Yet this need not be viewed as 'limitations' to our knowledge. In Matt Houlbrook's spectacular account of the many 'lives' and aliases of interwar confidence trickster Netley Lucas, the historian argues that we may never be able to get at the biographical 'truth' of people purposefully avoiding, or trying to hoodwink, the institutions and interactions designed to register their existence. What we can discover, though, is 'the terrain on which those lives took shape'; this encompasses the social, cultural, political, economic, and technological features of the past that made possible certain forms of criminal behaviour, their regulation, and people's responses to them.[37]

CAPITAL CRIMES

Historians of modern Britain are often, quite rightly, accused of investing too much significance in London by clumsily assuming the capital city works as a 'barometer' for all trends prevalent in national life. Privileging the metropolis in the scholarship this way undoubtedly causes problems. It should be fairly obvious that conditions in London cannot be simply transposed onto those of other urban or regional centres in the past. Particularly in regard to crime, within London itself the sheer diversity of the city's various boroughs and districts, and the forms of criminal activity, policing and regulation within them, require sensitive dissection. On the occasions I deem it appropriate to draw connections between ideas or practices relating to burglary that had currency both in London and at a national

[37] Houlbrook, *Prince of Tricksters*.

level, I identify who was making these comparisons *at the time* and why. Here, I follow Frank Mort's work on sexuality and sexual cultures in the post-war capital. *Night Raiders* builds on his endeavour to understand how specific features of the city at specific historical moments—its population, socio-political and socio-cultural dynamics, geography, architecture, and the role of its institutions in national and world affairs—lent it a 'centrality' in discussions of certain forms of crime and their containment.[38] From this starting point, it is my hope that future historians might subsequently take inspiration from this book and test the 'reach' of my conclusions in other temporal and geographical contexts.

So…why London?

London was the largest urban centre in Britain during the period 1860–1968. In 1861, the 'Administrative County of London' and Middlesex (city and suburbs) had a population of 2,991,314, comprising an area of 254,552 acres. By 1961 the population had nearly doubled to 5,435,027. It had in fact been higher than this (in 1931 it reached 6,035,731) but in the first two decades after the war housing in the city became more expensive, and many young families moved further out into new 'commuter' suburbs. Nonetheless, the numbers continued to grow, and when 'London and Middlesex' merged into 'Greater London' in 1971 the census suddenly recorded two million more 'Londoners'—7,452,346—covering an area of 390,279 acres.[39]

The city's incredibly rapid expansion, due in part to foreign migration as well as increasing life expectancies among the resident population, gave the city its unique socio-geographic composition. London from the mid-nineteenth century, as the historian Judith Walkowitz observes, was 'a multi-ethnic, polyglot settlement of many European diasporas.'[40] Anonymity was a cloak that many could easily adopt, whether for criminal purposes or otherwise, in this 'city of strangers'—a portrait of London life drawn by sociologists throughout the twentieth century.[41] Resident city-dwellers' relationships were, of course, far more complex than this imagining allows. Streetlife in the late Victorian metropolis was, according to the historian Peter K. Andersson, often fraught with intimacies and tensions between different classes, ages, gendered and ethnic groups. 'It was difficult to remain anonymous within the confines of the neighbourhood', Andersson writes, particularly in the cramped conditions of working-class lodgings in the mews (although the term

---

[38] Mort, *Capital Affairs*.

[39] Office of National Statistics, 'Two Hundred Years of the Census: London and Middlesex', (London, 2001), https://data.london.gov.uk/dataset/office-national-statistics-ons-population-estimates-borough (accessed 24 Dec. 2016); HCPP, Cmd.2605, *Report of the Committee on Housing in Greater London* (Mar. 1965), pp. 60–1.

[40] Judith Walkowitz, *Nights Out: Life in Cosmopolitan London* (London and New Haven: Yale University Press, 2012), pp. 5–6.

[41] Peter K. Andersson, *Streetlife in Late Victorian London: The Constable and the Crowd* (Basingstoke: Palgrave MacMillan, 2013), p. 4. This idea is also echoed by historian Stefan Petrow, who describes London as a focus for anxieties as 'the centre of crime and vice, not for its own area alone but for the whole country', at the end of the nineteenth century because 'London attracted a rapidly increasing, largely anonymous, migratory population, a significant proportion being casual labourers, the very poor, and foreign exiles, political and criminal.' Stefan Petrow, *Policing Morals: The Metropolitan Police and the Home Office, 1870–1914* (Oxford: Oxford University Press, 1994), p. 13.

'neighbourhood', as he suggests, registers as far too inclusive a label to adequately describe how one set of Victorian neighbours might consider themselves enemies or, less dramatically, prefer to ignore each other, while another group of residents in the same locale would assert the bonds of friendship quite happily in public).[42] Yet the need for *some* form of privacy, frequently beginning at the closed door of a lodgings, was emphasized by working-class citizens interviewed throughout this era, and in a city the size of London with its rapid turnover of inhabitants, it was quite possible to suddenly find oneself living just a room apart from an accused burglar, as trial transcripts of the period reveal.[43] Accordingly, in 1902 London's famous social surveyor Charles Booth, usually a man with his finger on the pulse of the city, stated that burglary was 'perhaps the most characteristic London crime', a statement that makes sense in light of the conditions of urban life there.[44]

London was also home to the Metropolitan Police. Although this factor might be thought discouraging to the would-be criminal, the reputation of the Force for moral integrity, efficiency, and ability to capture criminals had taken rather a beating by the late 1880s. In 1888, their failure to capture notorious serial killer Jack the Ripper after the horrific murders of five prostitutes in the impoverished East End area of Whitechapel, four of whom were butchered *in the street*, would cast a shadow over the police's reputation well into the twentieth century.[45] The much-vaunted Criminal Investigation Department, founded in 1878 with its legion of detectives, was also well-known for its use of 'violating privacy, spying, and resorting to artifice or entrapment' to capture villains, the success of which was undermined by the network of criminal informants on which they relied, whose 'semi-criminal' activities detectives were willing to overlook and sometimes protect.[46] Although Scotland Yard detectives' reputations had somewhat recovered by the interwar period, with their high-profile captures of 'celebrity' murderers such as Patrick Mahon and Edith Thompson (the latter now regarded as innocent), as well as the armed robbers involved in the Hyde Park Hotel robbery of 1937, their achievements were offset by public and political condemnation over their use of brutal, 'third degree' interrogation tactics on suspects, leading to a parliamentary inquiry in 1928.[47] The shifting fortunes of police produced a kind of mythology surrounding

[42] Ibid., pp. 64–9.   [43] Ibid., p. 65.

[44] Charles Booth, *Life and Labour of the People in London, Vol. IX: Notes on Social Influences and Conclusions* (London: Williams and Norgate, 1902), pp. 138–9.

[45] Robert F. Haggard, 'Jack the Ripper as the Threat of Outcast London', in Alexandra Warwick and Martin Willis (eds.), *Jack the Ripper: Media, Culture, History* (Manchester: Manchester University Press, 2007), pp. 197–214.

[46] Petrow, *Policing Morals*, pp. 45, 75.

[47] Ian Burney and Neil Pemberton, *Murder and the Making of the English CSI* (Baltimore: Johns Hopkins University Press, 2016), pp. 63–79; Lucy Bland, 'The Trials and Tribulations of Edith Thompson: The Capital Crime of Sexual Incitement in 1920s England', *Journal of British Studies* 47:3 (2008), pp. 624–48; Matt Houlbrook, '"A Pin to See the Peepshow": Culture, Fiction and Selfhood in Edith Thompson's Letters, 1921–1922', *Past and Present* 207:1 (2010), pp. 215–49; Angus McLaren, *Playboys and Mayfair Men: Crime, Class, Masculinity, and Fascism in 1930s London* (Baltimore: Johns Hopkins University Press, 2017); Eloise Moss, 'The Scrapbooking Detective: Frederick Porter Wensley and the Limits of "Celebrity" and "Authority" in Interwar Britain', *Social History* 40:1 (2015), pp. 58–81; John Carter Wood, '"The Third Degree": Press Reporting, Crime Fiction and Police Powers in 1920s Britain', *Twentieth Century British History* 21:4 (2010), pp. 464–85.

the pitfalls and opportunities burglars could expect in London. Their uncertain likelihood of capture would be matched by the greater wealth they might steal from all those households available to target. The city presented an irresistible challenge for burglars aspiring to achieve renown.

Symbolically, threats to the metropolis were frequently conflated with threats to Britain as a whole. Capital city and financial centre of nation and empire (until the transition to the Commonwealth), London should have offered a secure home for all Britain's worldly riches. The lack of success in this regard and continued presence of crime and vice in the metropolis were repeatedly associated with broader 'condition of England' questions from the 1830s, as historian Stefan Petrow explores. During the 1870s, these debates re-emerged as part of a sense of national 'crisis' linked to the ascendancy of foreign competitors for industry and global political clout, as well as concerns over secularization and the spread of poverty.[48] The broad social chasm between London's East End (long aligned with criminality because of the area's poverty, lack of infrastructure, and overcrowding) and the more exclusive resorts of its wealthy West End populace offered a clear-cut backdrop to burglars' apparently effortless ability to cross between those 'territories' and blur their social boundaries. Not only were poorer, working-class burglars thought likely to infiltrate the West End to loot the richer properties, but those burglars who attained 'professionalism' at the crime might even be able to mimic their upper-class prey to the extent that they could live and work alongside them. Again, under these conditions it was no surprise that the media lavished attention on those burglaries that took place in these prosperous West End mansions, elevating London's burglars to national and international attention.

Older east/west configurations of London's economic and criminal topography ceased to have the same prominence in the press after the Second World War. This was no doubt accentuated by the altered physical and social landscape following the destruction wrought by the Blitz and accelerated migration into the capital.[49] Crime reporting now turned on a type of 'exposé journalism' that favoured a tone of gritty social realism over the melodramatic forms that had prevailed before the war. Yet these changes did not mean that the relationship between London and burglary became diluted. The crime simply took on new proportions in a city that attracted a thriving post-war celebrity 'scene', where burglars could stalk the homes and hotel rooms of rich, beautiful, international 'stars' of stage, screen, and music. Police continued their attempts to frustrate their criminal nemeses, innovating new methods for knowing and controlling the ever-evolving cityscape such as patrolling with 'panda' cars and installing CCTV (Closed Circuit Television) cameras, though these had mixed success.[50] In a metropolis recovering once again from the staggering physical, social, political, economic, and cultural changes wrought

---

[48] Petrow, *Policing Morals*, pp. 12–13. [49] Frank Mort, *Capital Affairs*, pp. 46–7.

[50] Chris A. Williams, 'Police Surveillance and the Emergence of CCTV in the 1960s', *Crime Prevention and Community Safety*, 5 (2003), reprinted in Williams (ed.), *Police and Policing in the Twentieth Century* (Aldershot: Ashgate Publishing, 2011), pp. 27–37; Sarah Manwaring-White, *The Policing Revolution: Police Technology, Democracy and Liberty in Britain* (Brighton: Harvester, 1983), pp. 17–51.

by war, burglary remained the underlying challenge, acting as a barometer for the state in which the city would re-emerge.

INTERVIEW WITH THE BURGLAR

> In this prison I also made the acquaintance of a professional 'cracksman', or burglar. He was a man of fair education, good appearance, and considerable natural ability; much above the average of his professional brethren. He had been living luxuriously in London, on the fruits of his professional industry and skill. Till now he had escaped all punishment, with the exception of a few months' imprisonment, for a "mistake" committed at the outset of his professional career.
>
> Merchant (pseud.), *Six Years in the Prisons of England*,
> ed. Frank Henderson (London, 1869), 29

We do not know whether this encounter really took place between the 'cracksman' and the author, an anonymous 'Merchant' supposedly sent to prison after a trading venture went sour and bankruptcy, debts, and ruin inevitably followed. Frank Henderson, the book's editor, was in the business of churning out 'convict biographies' that were gaining popularity in late Victorian Britain as part of an emerging campaign against the inhuman deprivation of food and other indignities experienced in prisons.[51] *Six Years in the Prisons of England* contributed to a genre that was taken seriously by prominent prison reformers of the period. It was significant, therefore, that its narrative included an introduction to the 'professional burglar' with a precise set of characteristics: skill, hard work, good looks, intelligence, and the ability to ape one's social 'superiors'. The evasive London burglar enjoyed both an attractive persona and lifestyle, and as such, stood in danger of corrupting other less dangerous prison inmates.[52] In a section entitled 'Indiscriminate Association of Prisoners', the author warned that prisoners who 'had no inclination to repeat the offence, or to pursue a career of crime', were being mixed in with 'the professional thief and housebreaker, the burglar, and the garrotter' to their moral detriment.[53]

This cracksman was a distinctive threat. Listed systematically among other discrete criminal 'types' such as the housebreaker and the garrotter, the burglar was a staging-post between the severity of their crimes. Housebreaking was intrusive, and connoted material loss, but would not take place at night and thus held less threat of violence or rape. Garrotting meant throttling or strangling a victim with a rope or other implement, which was rare in cases of burglary. It had taken time

---

[51] Helen Johnston, *Crime in England 1815–1880: Experiencing the Criminal Justice System* (London: Routledge, 2015), pp. 114–16.

[52] Although the corruption of younger prisoners by more seasoned 'professionals' was a concern from the beginning of incarceration, the reference here is significant for being raised in the context of claims highlighting the example of the danger posed specifically by an incarcerated London burglar in this respect.

[53] Merchant (pseud.), *Six Years in the Prisons of England*, ed. Frank Henderson (London: Richard Bentley, 1869), p. 120.

for this order to develop. During the eighteenth and early nineteenth century, burglary had no temporal specificities in law. In popular culture, as the historian Gillian Spraggs notes, the crime was neither admirable nor regarded as particularly skilled, considered to dwell with other 'low' forms of thieving due to the 'sneakiness' of creeping into someone's house and attempting to escape silently. By contrast, the eighteenth century was the era of the highway robber, a rare and exceptional criminal whose 'bravery' in meeting their victims face to face on the road found immortality in ballads to legends such as Dick Turpin.[54] Indeed, until the 1860s the most famous fictional burglar of the day—Bill Sikes, in Dickens' *Oliver Twist*— was also a murderer and accomplice of Fagin, who groomed boys for pickpocketing as well.[55] The 1860s therefore witnessed a wholesale change in attitudes towards burglars and burglary, which swiftly consolidated into the dominant fear- and pleasure-giving narratives.

Many of the key developments in the history of burglary chronicled in this book take place before the Second World War. As a result, the first two sections concentrate on the period prior to 1939, while the final section moves the story forward, setting it entirely within the post-war period. Section One, 'Burglars', charts the birth of the 'professional' London burglar as a masculine, daring, and diabolically clever criminal type. The story starts with Charles Peace (d. 1879), a notorious burglar and murderer originally from Sheffield, who in 1878 committed twenty-six burglaries in London's Blackheath district single-handed. Peace's inventive disguises, hand-made tools, and extensive and prolific 'career' garnered him unprecedented notoriety and press publicity once finally captured, securing him a notoriety which endured into the late 1930s. Peace was exceptional. His life and criminal exploits were an anomaly among a much larger number of opportunistic thieves, whose burglaries were few and their rewards meagre. Why, then, did Peace become the archetype of burglars, to whom police and public were encouraged to look when deciding how to regulate the city and secure their homes? Chapter 1 discovers how a real-life villain was turned into a legendary criminal, in a process that had profound implications for all subsequent versions of burglary whether legal, criminological, or circulating through popular culture.

Chapter 2 looks at the reverse of this process. Arthur J. Raffles, fictional cracksman and star England cricketer, burst onto the literary scene in 1898. Created by Ernest William Hornung, brother-in-law of *Sherlock Holmes*' author Sir Arthur Conan Doyle, Raffles was Holmes' antithesis: the fun-loving master thief. The ultimate embodiment of the 'pleasure culture' surrounding the burglar, Raffles' physical attractiveness and athleticism blurred the lines between moral virtue and romantic allure. As the original novels were continually remade in theatre and film and their characters reincarnated in those media, newspapers began to label real burglars 'Raffles'. Espying an opportunity, ex-criminals appropriated this sympathetic title for themselves, using the idea of 'real-life Raffles' to fashion glamorous celebrity personae through lucrative autobiographical writings. The character became an

---

[54] Spraggs, *Outlaws and Highwaymen*, pp. 242–5.
[55] Charles Dickens, *Oliver Twist* (1837–9; reprinted London: Penguin, 1994).

international phenomenon, beloved by audiences across Europe and America who flocked to see his exploits at the cinema and continually identified the burglar as an English 'hero', akin to Robin Hood. Yet Raffles was no philanthropist. Keeping the jewels for himself and glorifying in escaping capture by police, Raffles was a figure of danger for many contemporaries, who identified the longevity of his success as a harbinger of popular unrest caused by economic depression that might seduce generations of young people into a life of crime. This chapter examines how, where criminality was concerned, distinguishing between fact and fiction presented unnecessary (and unheeded) complications to commercial success.

Women burglars were supposedly rare. When they were caught in the act, these women were greeted with shock and ridicule, their triumphs and failures as thieves both dismissed as 'amateurish' in comparison with those of male burglars. In the final chapter of this section, I begin to examine the relationship between gender, crime, and the home. Burglary had always been perpetrated by both sexes, albeit in greater numbers by men—at least, of those burglars who were caught. Yet for a woman to raid someone's home during a period when the ideology of women's roles was still intimately entwined with domesticity and family life was seen as a 'betrayal' of their 'nature'. These 'forays' into burglary by women consequently met with denial; as 'freaks' among their sex they were usually portrayed as spinsters or somehow 'wronged' romantically. Burglary was the ultimate symbol of their want of love and the stability of a family. This chapter traces how popular denial of the female burglar responded to fears about women's greater political and social agency following the rise of the suffragette movement, as well as later symbols of female independence such as the Edwardian 'new' woman and the interwar 'flapper'.

Section Two, 'Burglaries', deals with crime and control in the city. Terrifying images of burglars carrying knives and guns, scrambling through windows, and standing silent and masked in the dark beside householders' beds characterized the marketing strategy of the burglary insurance sector, which sprung into existence during the 1880s. Chapter 4 shows how, by exacerbating homeowners' fears of the presence of the burglar within the home, and the prevalence of burglary nationally, insurers merged individual and national concerns about the crime in a calculated bid to attract custom. I analyse fear-mongering insurance adverts, with their promise to act as a bastion of security against financial loss, alongside instances when victims of burglary attempted to make a claim. Caveats dealing with the need to prove that burglars had indeed 'broken' in were contingent on homeowners fitting sophisticated, branded locks and latches at points of vulnerability on windows and doors. Just as this made securing financial compensation more challenging, it also instilled the idea of burglars' expertise and professionalism should they conquer these defences. As the self-styled commercial 'protection' against burglary, burglary insurance became an ordinary household investment. Its prosperity therefore enables us to identify those ideas about crime and criminal that held currency in the minds of consumers. Crucially, this chapter highlights the intersection of media, state, and market discourse about crime in weaving a specific version of burglary into the very fabric of everyday life, uniting three domains that historians of crime have traditionally treated separately.

'Cat' burglars slip silently into focus in the next chapter. First described in 1907, the reputation of these extraordinarily athletic thieves and citizens of the rooftops achieved phenomenal status during the interwar period. Disregarding the regulated concourse of the street to reach their victims via window, wall, and roof, cat burglars forever altered received wisdom on how London as an environment could be manipulated and experienced, and how it needed to be policed. The fact that all this took place at night as well gave added lustre to these thieves' well-publicized exploits. An entirely new sub-category of crime thus emerged as space, time, and identity became intertwined.[56] Concurrently, the material residue of burglars' rooftop escapades—broken tiles and drainpipes, soil-marks on walls, etc.—encouraged new modes of policing and regulation based on the developing practice of forensic science. This chapter considers the geographical signifiers associated with burglars' activities across the 'public' spaces of the city. It argues that accounts of burglars' unusual mobility when travelling to victims' houses evoked fears surrounding the erosion of London's social boundaries, through suburbanization bringing working, middle, and upper classes into closer proximity than ever before, and via disruptive new modes of travel such as the car and Underground railway. In so doing, it shows that contemporary understandings of how London as an environment could be manipulated and experienced were fundamentally revised in relation to burglary.

When officials, press, and public heaped scorn upon the idea of the woman burglar, they did so in part because of the links between burglary and rape (another crime often assumed to always be perpetrated by men against women).[57] The final chapter of this section takes up the story that began in Chapter 3, this time examining the relationship between crime, gender, and the home via a closer look at the security devices that began populating middle-class houses from the mid-nineteenth century. Designed to be both secure and difficult to discover among other furnishings, locks and safes were increasingly decorated with particular rooms in mind, especially the boudoir and the bedroom. I suggest that this reflected the heightened publicity accorded burglaries of women's jewellery, possessions which held their own gendered, emotional significance as tokens of love and familial bonds. Invisible barriers to crime began to reshape domestic space in this era, whether locks and safe doors hidden beneath gloriously elaborate carvings and intricate metalwork or burglar alarms with sensors fitted snugly between carpets, walls, and window-ledges, trailing soft tentacles around the home's perimeter. While existing scholarship on the history of domestic space so far has treated decoration and security separately, this chapter considers how the design and placement of anti-burglar devices crafted an interplay between boundaries and furnishings that maintained the facade of carefree residential harmony.[58]

---

[56] On the relation between these categories see Henri Lefebvre, *The Production of Space*, trans. Donald Nicholson-Smith (Oxford: Oxford University Press, 1992); David Harvey, *The Condition of Postmodernity: An Inquiry into the Origins of Cultural Change* (Oxford: Oxford University Press, 1989).

[57] Joanna Bourke, *Rape: A History from 1860 to the Present* (London: Virago, 2007).

[58] Deborah Cohen, *Household Gods: The British and their Possessions* (London and New Haven: Yale University Press, 2006); Vickery, *Behind Closed Doors*; Jane Hamlett, *Material Relations: Domestic Interiors and Middle-Class Families in England, 1850–1910* (Manchester: Manchester University Press, 2010).

Night Raiders closes after the Second World War. In the last section, I explore how pre-war versions of burglary wrestled to endure within the new world being wrought. Physically and conceptually, London after the war was a radically altered space. Craters were left where prominent buildings once stood. Thousands of homes had been razed to the ground, either bombed directly or having caught fire from adjacent buildings. Among the city's population the 'norms' of social behaviour had been forcibly disregarded for years, along with the everyday rhythms of peacetime life and, subsequently, all economic and political certainties. There was also a whiff of espionage. In the concluding chapter, I consider how, during the 1950s, burglars were implicated in Cold War-led fears of spying through thefts at the London residences of foreign diplomats and officials, including those of Russia and Poland. Burglary was never far from the scene of national and international controversy, even as its profile diminished beneath an onslaught of murder, vice, and sex scandals with which the capital became synonymous in the postwar decades.[59] Ultimately, although the Theft Act of 1968 eventually diluted the distinctions between burglary and other forms of theft, burglary continued to occupy a fundamental place at the heart of national life. Casting its dark shadow, it served to throw broader issues into the light.

[59] Mort, *Capital Affairs*.

1

The 'King of All Burglars'

Two o'clock in the morning, Thursday, 10 October 1878. Patrolling the avenue leading from St. John's Park to Blackheath, a wealthy suburb of south-east London recently plagued by burglaries, Police Constable Edward Robinson noticed a light flickering in the drawing room of a nearby house. After watching carefully for a few minutes, Robinson went in search of his colleagues. Returning with Constable William Girling and Sergeant Charles Brown, they noticed that the light was now moving around several other rooms of the house. It was unlikely to be a member of the family. Had the occupants been restless or hungry they would have likely stayed in one room so as not to disturb the rest of the household, perhaps summoning a servant to bring them a snack. Suspicions raised, the three officers agreed to surround the building. Robinson and Girling climbed over the wall into the back garden, while Brown circled round to the front door and rang the doorbell. As the sound of that ring broke the quiet of the moonlit night, the light in the house was abruptly extinguished and a man dropped from the drawing room window onto the lawn. He began to run.

Robinson gave chase. Just as he was gaining ground towards the bottom of the garden his quarry turned and pointed a revolver at Robinson's head. 'Keep back, keep off, or by God I will shoot you', threatened the burglar. 'You had better not', retorted Robinson, with remarkable cool. The burglar fired three shots and ran again—the bullets whistled past Robinson's head. Robinson made to pounce as a fourth shot was fired, again missing him by inches. Policeman and burglar tumbled to the ground. As they did so, a fifth, slightly muffled shot, rang out from between the wrestling pair, and Robinson uttered a cry: the burglar had fired a shot into the policeman's right arm above the elbow. But the officer did not give up. With the burglar swearing loudly in frustration, they continued to struggle until Sergeant Brown arrived. As Brown reported (with, one suspects, a rather dry sense of humour), the fight concluded when he successfully 'subdued' the thief with the aid of his truncheon. Giving evidence at London's Central Criminal Court, the Old Bailey, five weeks later, the Sergeant testified that the burglar was found in possession of a silver pocket-flask, banker's cheque-book, and letter-case, all belonging to homeowner Mr James Alexander Burness. The prisoner called himself 'John Ward'.[1]

For residents of the neighbouring districts of Blackheath and Greenwich in south-east London, the capture of 'Ward' signalled the end of a year-long plague of twenty-six burglaries that 'had excited much interest and even alarm' throughout

[1] OBP, 18 Nov. 1878 (t18781118–51).

London by their 'regularity', according to *The Times*.[2] Initial press reports of this arrest, however, had not yet made the connection between the dozens of burglaries that had taken place and the lone burglar that had been caught, and as a result, were remarkably concise. Recounting the circumstances of the burglar's capture as a sequence of facts, the story was secreted amongst pages of court reports detailing numerous other similar crimes, offering little indication that the burglary or its perpetrator would attract any unusual public interest. Soon, this would change. On 8 November 1878, acting on a tip from a woman with whom the burglar had been living in London, the police arrested Hannah Peace (wife of Charles) at their Sheffield home. In the process, they discovered stolen goods still missing from Blackheath residences. It was not long before an officer from the Sheffield police force was dispatched to the capital to identify 'Ward', whose description corresponded with that of Charles Peace, a career burglar wanted in Sheffield for the murder of Arthur Dyson in November 1876.[3] Peace's capture, and Robinson's bravery in holding on to him despite his injury, would become the stuff of legend over the next five decades.

Hanged on 25 February 1879, Peace gained a kind of immortality as his life story was retold in countless press articles, criminological texts, novels, theatre plays, and films enduring into the 1930s. In 1894 he was given the notable accolade of being christened the 'King of all Burglars' by the *Strand Magazine*, a publication recently made famous as the home of Sir Arthur Conan Doyle's Sherlock Holmes stories (the first, *A Study in Scarlet*, was published there in 1891).[4] By moulding the new breed of 'professional' burglar in Peace's image, the media anointed the dead crook with a status similar to Holmes, whose talents as a detective—albeit fictional—were to become forevermore the benchmark for the efforts of real police (however unfairly).[5] Their ability to put the burglar on a similar pedestal in the annals of crime was due in part to the posthumous malleability of Peace's character, skills, and exploits, which magnified with each retelling of his story. Sir Edward Abbott Parry, a county court judge in Manchester who one might have expected to offer a rather more sober view of the thief, instead compared Peace to both Caesar and Napoleon in his work *The Drama of the Law* (1924). As Parry wrote, 'His [Peace's] methods of evading the police in these reconnaissances have all the simplicity of true greatness...Nature had gifted him with extraordinary strength and agility.'[6]

Was it a coincidence that the master criminal, in the form of Peace, took shape in the public imagination just as relations between police and public entered a

---

[2] Details on the extent of Peace's burglaries can be found in TNA, PCOM 8 108, Statement of Convict E1138 John Ward (14 Dec. 1878); 'The Burglaries on Blackheath', The Times (8 Nov. 1878), p. 8.

[3] 'The Burglaries on Blackheath', The Times (8 Nov. 1878), p. 8; 'Strange Discovery of a Murderer', The Standard (8 Nov. 1878), p. 5.

[4] Unknown Author, 'Crimes and Criminals', Strand Magazine (Jan. 1894), p. 284.

[5] Michael Saler, ' "Clap if You Believe in Sherlock Holmes": Mass Culture and the Re-enchantment of Modernity, c.1890–c.1940', Historical Journal 46:3 (2003), pp. 599–622.

[6] Sir Edward Abbott Parry, The Drama of the Law (London: T. Fisher Unwin, 1924), pp. 224–30.

period of tension? 1878, the year of Peace's arrest, saw the establishment of the Criminal Investigation Department (CID) at Scotland Yard, the home of the Metropolitan Police. Under command of the Home Secretary, Sir Richard Cross, and directed by Sir Charles Edward Howard Vincent, who had studied the tactics of renowned Paris detective squad the Sûreté when attending the Sorbonne, the CID was set up to replace the disgraced 'Detective Branch', whose senior officers had been convicted of taking bribes from a known con artist in the 1877 'Turf Fraud Scandal'.[7] Whilst the formation of the CID was meant to signal a new professionalism within the Force, during the early 1880s a number of bombs were successfully set off in London by the Fenian Irish nationalists, compromising the credibility of police intelligence again. More embarrassingly, in 1884 the Fenians managed to trigger a bomb planted directly beneath the CID's own offices at Scotland Yard, despite the agency receiving a warning in advance. Even before Jack the Ripper's escape from justice in 1888, the Force's authority to act in the public defence was severely strained.[8]

The emergence of a figure like Peace in this context, his popularity (a term I am using deliberately in place of 'notoriety' due to the romanticizing of criminal and crimes), and the glamour and skills entwined with his spiralling legend raises fascinating questions about how the burglar was used to channel wavering public sentiment towards police.[9] In one sense, Peace's ascent to stardom drew energy from the state's perceived failures at controlling crime, or addressing the economic and social conditions that cultivated it, especially surrounding poverty. Over time, Peace became a tried-and-tested vehicle for renewing debate about police efficiency, his reincarnations in fiction, theatre, and film fuelled by their commercial success as entertainment across various genres of media. In an interesting twist, police also seem to have perceived that they were more vulnerable when facing criminals during these decades, since officers responded with an emphatic 'yes' to a Home Office questionnaire asking if Metropolitan Police wanted to carry guns in 1883. As the historian Clive Emsley notes, their desire to be armed caught both the Home Office and Vincent by surprise, since Vincent was aware of only ten instances between October 1878 and September 1883 when guns had been fired at officers—two were killed, six were wounded and two more had bullets go through their clothing.[10]

Yet something more complicated was also going on. The burglar's intelligence, 'daring', and the longevity of his 'burglarious' activity were qualities celebrated equally in works by noted jurors and police officers. Within the hallowed walls of

---

[7] Haia Shpayer Makov, *The Ascent of the Detective: Police Sleuths in Victorian and Edwardian England* (Oxford: Oxford University Press, 2011), p. 123.

[8] Haia Shpayer Makov, *Ascent*, 210; William J. Fishman, 'Crime and Punishment', in Alexandra Warwick and Martin Willis (eds.), *Jack the Ripper: Media, Culture, History* (Manchester: Manchester University Press, 2007), pp. 231–2.

[9] On the use of celebrity in this fashion and its blurred encounter with 'notoriety' as a concept, see Fred Inglis' discussion of Baudelaire in his *A Short History of Celebrity* (Princeton: Princeton University Press, 2010), p. 95.

[10] My thanks to one of the anonymous reviewers at OUP for drawing my attention to this reference. Clive Emsley '"The Thump of Wood on a Swede Turnip": Police Violence in Nineteenth-Century England', *Criminal Justice History* 6 (1985), pp. 125–49.

Scotland Yard's 'Black Museum', Peace's tools were put on display for posterity to both public and trainee officers. Criminal celebrity, in Peace's case, was as much a product of official institutions as it was the entertainment marketplace. Legal institutions have always been cultural institutions, influenced as much by prevailing popular attitudes towards crime as the rule of law. This is a maxim that the historian Martin Wiener has schooled rigorously, proven time and again in analyses of the legal treatment of rapists and murderers, even holding sway within the divorce courts.[11] Normally, though, where sympathy for the criminal has affected sentencing the main protagonists have gradually drifted out of public consciousness, with the crime itself viewed as a 'one-off' motivated by passion or triggered by years of emotional abuse. Veneration of crime and criminal was more rare; rarer still was the kind of mutual, enduring glorification Peace received from all quarters, ultimately framing burglary as a 'master craft'. While officials might then hail their triumphs over the burglar as incredible feats of policing, it became much less certain who held the power to actually define how a criminal looked and behaved, or dictate the 'hierarchy' of serious crimes and their social and political resonance.

*   *   *

> The burglars in our day are not in general such desperate men as those in former times. They are better known to the police than formerly, and are kept under more strict surveillance. Many of the cracksmen have been repeatedly subjected to prison discipline, and have their spirits in a great measure subdued.[12]
>
> John Binney, writing of London's burglars for social surveyor
Henry Mayhew's volume London Labour and the London Poor (1861)

Burglary was a dying art. In 1861, journalist-turned-social-surveyor John Binney's pessimistic account of the fortunes of London's burglars made for comforting reading for the average householder, predicting a future in which the 'experts' at this crime would finally become extinct under the weight of decades of aggressive penal justice. This must have been a relief, since they were apparently quite difficult to spot. As Binny claimed, 'cracksmen' had:

> in their appearance little or no trace of their criminal character. They have the look of sharp business men.... These crack burglars generally live in the streets adjoining the New Kent Road and Newington Causeway, and groups of them are to be seen occasionally at the taverns beside the Elephant and Castle, where they regale themselves luxuriously on the choicest wines, and are lavish of their gold.[13]

---

[11] Wiener, Reconstructing the Criminal, pp. 248–9; D'Cruze, Crimes of Outrage; Ginger Frost, '"She is but a Woman": Kitty Byron and the English Edwardian Criminal Justice System', Gender & History 16:3 (2004), pp. 538–60; Shani D'Cruze, Sandra Walklate, and Samantha Pegg, Murder: Social and Historical Approaches to Understanding Murder and Murderers (London: Routledge, 2006); Frost, Promises Broken; Anna Clark, Scandal: The Sexual Politics of the British Constitution (Princeton: Princeton University Press, 2004).

[12] John Binny, 'Thieves and Swindlers' (1861), in Henry Mayhew and Others, The London Underworld in the Victorian Period: Authentic First-Person Accounts by Beggars, Thieves and Prostitutes (1861: Reprinted New York: David and Charles, 2005), p. 227.

[13] Binny, 'Thieves', pp. 209, 215.

Gentlemanly in appearance and habits, and positioning themselves in key locations within the London borough of Southwark, these 'experts' lived and socialized just a short walk over the bridge across the river Thames from the city's financial district and the salubrious resorts of the West End. Clearly attuned to 'blending in' in ways that enabled them to move (and to thieve) easily among their upper-class surrounds, burglars of this ilk certainly seemed to possess the intelligence and social acumen to flourish from their crimes. Yet this specimen of criminality was apparently disappearing, increasingly failing to outwit police and now exceeded in numbers by the less-threatening 'low' burglar to be found in London's East End districts. If *London Labour and the London Poor* was to be believed, this meant that burglary was most commonly perpetrated by young, inexperienced, and poverty-stricken men whose crimes were opportunistic and ill thought-through, causing them to swiftly be captured and brought to justice. Commensurately, in lacking the skills of safe-crackers these 'amateurs' would likely steal goods of less value, causing less financial damage to their victims.[14]

Was Binny raising false hopes? Statistical indices of burglary bore out his judgement that the frequency of the crime should cause less concern than that of others (particularly housebreaking and shopbreaking, which proliferated in the tens of thousands), although there was hardly a dramatic decline in its rate. The number of recorded burglaries remained at a relatively constant level in England and Wales, from 1,445 cases in 1893, when the statistics for burglary began to be recorded separately from those of housebreaking, to 1,515 cases in 1938, after which the advent of the Second World War temporarily interrupted data gathering. London witnessed a rather better record, as burglaries decreased from 516 in 1893 to 277 in 1938, but there had been spikes. As recently as 1932 (when the country was still suffering the effects of the Great Depression) 650 burglaries were recorded in the city. These figures hardly amounted to an insurmountable crime 'wave' though.[15] From the numbers alone, it looked like police were winning.

Binny was also right in thinking that the majority of these thieves were desperate rather than 'experts'. As court reports indicate, the occupations of defendants for this crime fell mainly into the category of low-paid manual labourers, whether on building sites, in warehouses, or in the transportation industry. 'White-collar' workers, such as clerks and insurance brokers, and commercial staff such as waiters joined their ranks during the interwar years, when recurrent economic depressions in 1921 and 1929 similarly rendered these jobs less financially secure.[16] The courts were not unsympathetic. Alfred Whittaker, tried for burglary at the Old Bailey in April 1903, had attempted to steal a clock and umbrella from a house at Grosvenor Crescent in the West End. Despite the high-profile West End address, which was usually guaranteed to attract newspaper columnists itching to write up such crimes as an attack on the excessive privilege of the rich (rather than an act borne

---

[14] Ibid.   [15] See Charts 1 and 2, Appendix.
[16] See fn 27, Introduction; Nicholas Crafts, 'Long-Run Growth', in Roderick Floud and Paul Johnson (eds.), The Cambridge Economic History of Modern Britain Vol. II: Economic Maturity, 1860–1939 (Cambridge: Cambridge University Press, 2004), pp. 1–24.

of necessity), Whittaker produced a persuasive written defence. In it, he pleaded 'that he was suffering severely from depression, through being out of employment, and was suddenly seized by temptation, and committed this burglary'. Even though he had two previous convictions, Whittaker's excuse seemed to resonate with the judge, who sentenced him to just two months' hard labour for the crime.[17]

Where did Charles Peace fit into this picture? In the days immediately following his capture as 'John Ward', he seemed destined to achieve little distinction from other burglars. Only his excessive use of violence, as well as some confusion, in the first instance, about his ethnicity made him moderately newsworthy. As *The Standard* reported succinctly on 11 October 1878:

> A half-caste was charged at Greenwich Police Court, yesterday, with committing a burglary at Gifford House, St. John's Park, Blackheath. The police noticed a light flitting about the house during the night, and having given an alarm, the Prisoner came out of the dining-room window. Being confronted with a Constable he fired five shots from a revolver at him, wounding him seriously in the arm, but after much trouble he was secured.[18]

The tone of this description, leading with the supposed mixed race of 'Ward' before enumerating his crimes, was consistent with a period in which stigma against citizens of non-white ethnicities was at a height due to the white supremacist ideology underpinning the British empire. Conditioned by the discourse of 'savagery' that attended non-Western races in Victorian England, thereby legitimizing colonial rule as a 'civilizing' force, this dichotomy was also applied to distinguish criminals and the poor from the rest of society.[19] Consequently, the imaginary boundaries between these social groups became blurred. In their place, a triumvirate of 'problems of class, ethnicity, and criminality became dominant' within contemporary thinking about the likely causes and perpetrators of crime. This was entrenched in part by the discrimination that prevented many immigrants to Britain from obtaining work, thereby condemning them to poverty and occasionally, desperate acts of theft.[20]

Wilkie Collins' novel *The Moonstone* (1868) nourished these assumptions. Often considered the 'first modern detective novel', its premise was the burglary of a cursed Indian diamond known as 'The Moonstone' from the boudoir of English heiress Rachel Verinder in her country mansion. Initially, suspicion fell on a group of travelling Indian men—'three Hindoo conspirators'—for whom the diamond was a stolen sacred artefact, and who had managed to enter the mansion by posing as jugglers and offering Verinder and her guests 'a very bad and clumsy' performance.[21] Traced back to their base in London by the implacable Detective Sergeant Cuff, it

---

[17] OBP, 27 Apr. 1903 (t19030427–412).
[18] 'News', The Standard (11 Oct. 1878), p. 4. Similar or identical reports were also published as follows: 'Police', The Times (11 Oct. 1878), p. 9; 'A Desperate Burglar', Lloyd's Weekly Newspaper (13 Oct. 1878), p. 4; 'A Police Constable Shot by a Burglar', Illustrated Police News (19 Oct. 1878), p. 2.
[19] Preeti Nijhar, 'Imperial Violence: The "Ethnic" as a Component of the "Criminal" Class in Victorian England', Liverpool Law Review 27 (Dec. 2006), p. 349.
[20] Ibid., p. 345.
[21] Wilkie Collins, The Moonstone (1868: reprinted London: Penguin, 1994).

was discovered that the group had been beaten to committing the crime by another member of the household; nevertheless, they functioned as a believable 'red herring', successfully playing with readers' prejudices to sustain the narrative. Even their apparent incompetence chimed with the prevailing infantilization of the racial 'other'.[22] Similarly, by depicting 'Ward' as 'half-caste', the press enjoined readers to view him as a petty bandit, a mediocre villain whose single (known) act of burglary and violence stemmed from an 'impure' heredity and an innate cultural aversion to the forces of 'civilization'.[23]

On 8 November 1878, the police interview with Hannah Peace meant that Ward's existing press persona expired. With it disappeared press references to his ethnicity (*The Times* now claimed he had a 'power of facial contortion in which he appeared to have equalled some of the greatest actors', in order to explain away their assertion he was 'half-caste').[24] Neither was he to remain categorized among a lower 'class' of burglars. Instead, the unveiling of 'John Ward' as Charles Peace marked a decisive shift in the discursive tone and composition of press reports. Now featured in the 'News' sections of *The Times*, *Standard*, and *Lloyd's Weekly Newspaper*, the burglar accumulated even more column inches in the 'Legal' sections of *The Graphic* and *Reynolds's Newspaper* (the 1870s and 1880s witnessed an unprecedented expansion of titles within the press, aiding the swift circulation of news around the country in a new epoch of mass literacy).[25] Journalists collectively heralded Peace and his exploits in a way that recalled 'the romantic language of heroic masculinity' afforded the heroes of Victorian and Edwardian boys' adventure novels.[26] According to *Reynolds's Newspaper*, Peace was

> …a notorious desperado…The manner in which [Peace] has eluded the vigilance of the police is most surprising, especially when it is remembered that he is well known to the police in several large towns. He is an accomplished burglar, but has twice previously fallen into the hands of the police and been sentenced to penal servitude. Throughout his career he has never had an accomplice.[27]

Aged 47 when captured, having committed numerous burglaries for which his intermittent spells in prison seemed never to have dampened his enthusiasm, Peace's outlandish existence was understandably portrayed as nearer fiction than fact. This was confirmed the following week, when revelations about his double life (and third alias) as 'Mr. Thompson', a respectable trader in musical instruments in

[22] Anne McClintock, Imperial Leather: Race, Gender, and Sexuality in the Colonial Contest (London: Routledge, 1995).

[23] John Tosh, Manliness and Masculinities in Nineteenth-Century Britain (London: Routledge, 2005), pp. 192–5.

[24] 'Charles Peace', The Times (5 Feb. 1879), p. 9.

[25] Jonathan Rose, The Intellectual Life of the British Working Classes (London and New Haven: Yale University Press, 2001), pp. 367–79.

[26] Ibid.; 'The Bannercross Murder', The Times (12 Nov. 1878), p. 7; 'Arrest of a Supposed Murderer', Lloyd's Weekly Newspaper (10 Nov. 1878), p. 3; 'Legal', Graphic (9 Nov. 1878), p. 475; 'Arrest of a Supposed Murderer', Reynolds's Newspaper (10 Nov. 1878), p. 6; Martin Francis, 'The Domestication of the Male? Recent Research on Nineteenth- and Twentieth-Century British Masculinity', Historical Journal, 45 (Sept. 2002), p. 640.

[27] 'Arrest of a Supposed Murderer', Reynolds's Newspaper (10 Nov. 1878), p. 6.

Peckham, south-east London, served to underline the burglar's literary potential. As *The Standard* excitedly explained, '... [Peace] was not only a daring burglar, but a man of scientific as well as musical tastes... When he resided at Peckham he lived in affluence on the proceeds of his burglaries, kept a pony and trap, a sumptuous table, and was always most punctilious in his money payments.'[28] Some newspapers offered illustrations, first showing Peace entertaining the public on stage with his violin, then burgling a house in a menacing black mask brandishing a long iron jemmy (a crowbar used to open windows).[29] Newspaper reports emphasizing the duality of Peace's life poked fun at those who had unwittingly welcomed the burglar into their community at face-value. Morality was no longer synonymous with material prosperity in an era when gross and fundamental inequalities were regarded as a matter of fortune rather than merit, a lesson writ large in the popular consciousness by the works of Mayhew, Charles Dickens, and others.[30] Peace, like his disciple Jack the Ripper, could have been *anyone*.

This process of celebrity-making only strengthened as events unfolded. Sentenced to life imprisonment on burglary and assault charges at the Old Bailey on 18 November 1878, Peace was transferred to Leeds' Armley Gaol to face murder allegations for the death of Arthur Dyson. On the train journey to Sheffield, he attempted to escape by jumping out of a window while the train was still moving. The manoeuvre was thwarted; a particularly tenacious warder clung to the criminal's foot before dropping him on the train tracks. It did, however, provide even more fodder for journalists, for whom the jump through the window was 'quick as lightning' and conducted 'with the agility of a cat'.[31] Building on earlier claims about the burglar's elusiveness, and the defiance towards police he had demonstrated during events at Blackheath, the press now explicitly adopted the language of adventure. Florid language was not enough to ensure that papers would sell, though, as writers were pressured to squeeze every last ounce of lucrative detail from the story and its protagonists. Reinstated under lock and key at H.M.P. Leeds, Peace was found guilty of murder and sentenced to be hanged on 25 February 1879. While he sat waiting for the hangman, and fresh developments seemed temporarily suspended, the proprietor of the *Sheffield Daily Telegraph* was forced to write to the Governor of Leeds' Armley Gaol to complain that rival journalists had reduced themselves to bribing Peace's family for his letters, looking for snippets of news.[32]

In the few short months from Peace's arrest at Blackheath in October 1878 to his imminent execution in February 1879, newspapers did their utmost to construct

---

[28] 'The Sheffield Murderer', Standard (12 Nov. 1878), p. 6.

[29] Illustrated Police News (30 Nov. 1878), p. 1.

[30] Seth Koven, Slumming: Sexual and Social Politics in Victorian London (Princeton: Princeton University Press, 2006).

[31] TNA, PCOM 8/108, Letter no. 9335.15 (5 Feb. 1879); Press descriptions of Peace's escape attempt: 'The Banner Cross Murder', Leeds Mercury (23 Jan. 1879), p. 8; 'London, Thursday, Jan. 23', Daily News (23 Jan. 1879), p. 4; 'Attempted Escape of Peace', Freeman's Journal and Daily Commercial Advertiser (23 Jan. 1879), p.8; 'The Bannercross Murder: Attempted Escape of Peace', Bristol Mercury and Daily Post (23 Jan. 1879), p. 2; 'The Banner Cross Murder', Liverpool Mercury (23 Jan. 1879), 7; 'Escape and Recapture of the Convict Peace', Hull Packet and East Riding Times (24 Jan. 1879), p.8; 'Escape and Recapture of the Prisoner Peace', Ipswich Journal (25 Jan. 1879), p.10.

[32] TNA, PCOM 8/108, Letter addressed to A. C. Keene Esq, Governor of Armley Jail (2 Feb. 1879).

a form of celebrity around Peace that was part-truth, part-legend. Only the burglar himself appeared devoid of agency in fashioning his public persona, prevented by his gaolers from giving interviews and having no say in what was written about him. Peace's 'absence' was a marker of how unfamiliar a territory the national press remained to criminals in the early decades of its expansion, despite their providing the most staple form of news. In letters to Sue Bailey, the woman with whom he had been living at Peckham, sent by Peace in his gaol cell at Leeds on 7 February 1879, the burglar wrote that

> I have my kind Governors permission for you to come & see me now at once to come up to the Prison and bring this letter with you…it is my wish that you will obey me in this one thing for you have obeyed me in meney [sic] things, but do obey me in this one and do not let this letter fall into the hands of the press.[33]

Perhaps Peace's mistrust of the newspapers was ironic, since they were offering him a form of immortality. But his unwanted fame also mirrored his loss of control, since renown was anathema to someone whose life had been cloaked in anonymity, enabling him to slip freely between aliases and commit burglaries with relative impunity. Celebrity formed part of the noose tightening around Peace's neck, diminishing opportunities for future escape, and forcing him to bear witness to his own obituary being written while he waited for the hangman. Soon, posthumous accounts of Peace's life and career would take over, carrying the burglar's memory into an uncharted territory where the 'ownership' and meaning of his legacy was still undecided.

'PEACE-WORSHIP'

Found guilty of murder at Leeds Assizes and executed on 25 February 1879 after what *Lloyd's Weekly Newspaper* called 'an indecently hasty and slipshod trial', Peace's peculiar attraction for readers of the press began to cause consternation among contemporary observers.[34] In an article in periodical *The City Jackdaw* entitled 'Criminal Worship', one author fretted,

> For some weeks past the whole of our reading population have been absolutely besotten with Peace-worship…Young and old rush impetuously to bow at the shrine of criminal worship, fascinated by the infamous notoriety which throws a sickly halo around his head; the morbid taste of the whole nation becomes so surfeited, and public morality so vitiated, that every nook and corner of the man's past life is assiduously searched for the purpose of finding out whether he is…connected with the place or person who wishes to mount a pedestal in one of the niches of the temple of fame, hanging to the villain's coat-tails.[35]

[33] SLA, M.D. 5021, Letter from Charles Peace addressed to 'My poor Sue' (7 Feb. 1879), postmarked H.C.M.P. [Her Majesty's Convict Prison].
[34] TNA, PCOM 8 108, Minute Paper No. 60434 (25 Feb. 1879); 'The Life and Adventures of Charles Peace', Lloyd's Weekly Newspaper (9 Feb. 1879), p. 1.
[35] 'Criminal Worship', City Jackdaw (21 Feb. 1879), p. 117.

'Peace-worship', had become a new form of criminal threat. Luring the reading public into idolizing a convicted burglar and murderer, the ability to say 'I knew him!' now apparently held some cachet. Recognizing the widespread 'taste' for articles about Peace, the author had to concede that the burglar was, by this point, far along the path of repackaging from criminal to commercial product, indicating that some deeper dissatisfaction with state and society lay at the heart of this craze. Stories of violent crime were, however, widely embraced as a source of fascination and entertainment in Victorian press and popular culture, even as actual violence was increasingly regulated and suppressed.[36] As historian Rosalind Crone observes of the popularity of characters such as Sweeney Todd (1846), the fictional 'demon barber of Fleet Street' whose murdered clientele were chopped up into meat and sold as pies, the textual 'celebration' of gross violence provided 'an alternative and more suitable way [for readers] to experience and even participate in violence'. Substituting for the 'thrill' of committing a crime, narratives such as those about Charles Peace were repeated and recycled as a useful 'safety valve' for conversations and imaginings about breaking restrictive social codes, often involving wreaking destruction on the lives of the propertied.[37] Commentators could only have hoped that 'Peace-worship' would be a passing trend.

It wasn't. Burglary, more than other types of theft, was a vehicle by which class divisions and antagonisms could acquire clear lines of demarcation. Taking place, in fictional accounts, overwhelmingly within the homes of the wealthy and proper-tied, burglaries' spatial backdrop offered a window onto a level of domestic comfort few working- and middle-class readers could ever hope to achieve. By contrast, the skill demanded of the burglar in negotiating such spaces in silence in the dark and overcoming security devices including locks, bolts, alarms, and safes acted as an analogy for the enterprise and expertise of these classes, upon whose industry the wealthy relied.[38] Accordingly, between 1878 and 1880, Peace's life and crimes became the subject of a serialized 'penny dreadful'. A lowbrow magazine-style publication rich with graphic illustrations and issued in weekly instalments, its remit was to sustain 'emotional and imaginative stimulation' by keeping readers hooked as long as possible.[39] *Charles Peace; or, The Adventures of a Notorious Burglar* (Fig. 1.1) featured Peace in the role of a somewhat 'misguided' hero for its audience of young working-class men and boys.[40] Far from despicable, his burglaries funded life as a 'celebrated young man from the country' in London, among 'Women . . . possessed

[36] Rosalind Crone, Violent Victorians: Popular Entertainment in Nineteenth-Century London (Manchester: Manchester University Press, 2012), pp. 8–9.

[37] Ibid., p. 246.

[38] Maxine Berg and Pat Hudson, 'Rehabilitating the Industrial Revolution', Economic History Review 45:1 (1992), pp. 24–50.

[39] Lise Shapiro Sanders, Consuming Fantasies: Labor, Leisure, and the London Shopgirl, 1880–1920 (Ohio: Ohio Univrsity Press, 2006), p. 130.

[40] John Springhall, '"Pernicious Reading"? The Penny Dreadful as Scapegoat for Late-Victorian Juvenile Crime', Victorian Periodicals Review 27 (1994), pp. 326–49; Gavin Sutter, 'Penny Dreadfuls and Perverse Domains: Victorian and Modern Moral Panics', in Judith Rowbotham and Kim Stevenson (eds.), Behaving Badly: Social Panic and Moral Outrage—Victorian and Modern Parallels (Aldershot: Ashgate Publishing, 2003), pp. 163–7.

Fig. 1.1. Plate from Unknown Author, *Charles Peace; or, The Adventures of a Notorious Burglar. Founded on Fact and Profusely Illustrated* (London: G. Purkess, 1880), p. 63. British Library, Mic. C10176. Reproduced by kind permission © The British Library Board.

of a rare order of beauty; languid swells, sporting and betting men' in a 'city devoted to nothing but pleasure'.[41]

Peace was portrayed as a romantic hero, whose encounters with beautiful and treacherous women played no small part in forcing his slide into lawlessness. Truth no longer mattered, except tenuously; as the preface to *The Adventures of a Notorious Burglar* admitted, 'Probably many of the stories which are told of his exploits have only an element of truth, but the substratum on which they rest is doubtless constituted of actual facts.'[42] What mattered was a good story, and in many respects Peace's exploits held just the right ingredients to ensure its success, although just to be safe the narrative plotted an inevitable journey towards the hangman. Often the source of fears about the 'corruption of the young' through their lurid tales of 'London low-life', penny dreadfuls usually restored balance by executing their villains at the end.[43] Reaching this end was not without its drama. Dissecting the burglar's (imagined) body-language, the author described Peace's 'firm tread' up the steps of the scaffold, and then had him give a long speech of repentance and forgiveness 'in a clear, firm voice, the tones of which must have been heard outside the prison walls'.[44] Villain or no, the burglar was to initiate readers into Victorian

---

[41] Unknown Author, Charles Peace; or, The Adventures of a Notorious Burglar. Founded on Fact and Profusely Illustrated (London: G. Purkess, 1880), p. 136.

[42] Ibid., p. 2.   [43] Springhall, ' "Pernicious Reading" ', p. 337.   [44] Ibid., p. 785.

ideals of 'masculine' physical strength, stoicism, and the desire to uphold Christian values even as he met a grisly death.[45]

Readers didn't need to confront their hero's demise quickly, however, being given two years' worth of instalments to enjoy the combination of unearned wealth, romantic dalliance, and defiance of society's laws that propelled Peace on his journey. A major part of this enjoyment were the allusions to sex. The Victorians were once thought 'prudish' about the subject; yet there was nothing prudish about the illustration in Fig. 1.1, showing Peace leering over a beautiful, wealthy young woman lying 'asleep' in bed. Still wearing her pearl necklace, and reclining expansively in a nightgown festooned with lace through which her breasts were tantalizingly visible, the lady's 'victimhood' was more than a little questionable according to contemporary notions of 'appropriate' women's behaviour.[46] Apparently delighted to find herself in the presence of a burglar brandishing a gun (she was drawn smiling), this flamboyantly dressed, ostentatiously wealthy, sexually provocative woman had more in common with contemporary portrayals of high-class prostitutes than the middle-class 'angel in the home', an innocent, maidenly victim.[47] Here, the penny dreadful instituted an idea that one of the 'perks' of being an 'expert' burglar were the sexual opportunities, profiting from a tension between romance and rape that bespoke little (if any) identification with the experiences of real survivors of the crime.

Little sympathy was likely to be evinced by working-class readers for the wealthy victims of crime during the 1880s, when the legalization of trade unions refocused popular attention on the continued exclusion of millions of working men from basic rights afforded by the franchise.[48] Working people were tired; autobiographies written by those who were children of working-class families in this period recall their parents occupied in an endless cycle of toil and 'making ends meet'. Fathers employed in mines and steel factories performed 'killing work' that sapped their physical strength and stretched thin time with family, while mothers did their best at obtaining the casual, low-paid jobs available to them in cotton factories and cared for children.[49] Trade union activism to try to improve things offered a little hope in a life of struggle—famous strikes, such as the matchgirls' strike at the Bryant and May factory in 1888, had resulted in victory, with a settlement offered to workers

---

[45] Tosh, Manliness and Masculinities.

[46] Amanda Vickery, 'Golden Age to Separate Spheres: A Review of the Categories and Chronology of English Women's History', Historical Journal 36:2 (1993), pp. 383–414.

[47] For contemporary descriptions of prostitutes, see Lucy Bland, Banishing the Beast: Feminism, Sex and Morality (London: I.B. Taurus, 2001), pp. 95–6; for Victorian perceptions of the appropriate demeanours of female victims, see Frost, Promises Broken, pp. 28–30; D'Cruze, Crimes of Outrage, pp. 137–41.

[48] Pat Thane, 'The Working Class and State "Welfare" in Britain, 1880–1914', Historical Journal 27:4 (1984), pp. 877–900.

[49] Julie-Marie Strange, Fatherhood and the British Working Class, 1865–1914 (Cambridge: Cambridge University Press, 2015), pp. 28–33; Sonya Rose, Limited Livelihoods: Gender and Class in Nineteenth-Century England (Berkeley: University of California Press, 1992); Catriona Parratt's study of the hours laboured by working-class women at these sites in the late Victorian and Edwardian periods suggests that despite the introduction of the Factory Acts, women continued to be forced to work much later hours in the evening than men because of their comparative lack of unionization. Catriona Parrott, 'Little Means or Time: Working-Class Women and Leisure in Late-Victorian and Edwardian England', International Journal of the History of Sport, 15 (1998), pp. 22–53.

and national publicity on their dangerous working conditions. Just a few years later, however, a similar strike at the Bell's match factory during 1893–4 failed miserably, leading to acrimonious relations between employers and employees and workers being branded with a reputation for violence by the press.[50] From 1887, the findings of Charles Booth's famous survey of poverty in London revealed that the very poorest in society lived just streets away from the aristocracy, reinforcing the impression that the latter cared little for the fate of the former.[51] Why should the concerns of the poor, therefore, be directed towards the wealthy victims of burglary, when battles remained to be fought over working pay and conditions that impoverished thousands of working-class families? In their world, not having to share a bedroom was a luxury frequently unknown.[52] Small wonder, then, that exaggerated stories of Charles Peace's crimes remained commercial. They even began to acquire a certain aura of 'truth', for it was in this context that definitions of burglary entered an era of slippage.

Controlling how crime was perceived and identified was a battle waged in concert with a crisis of faith in public institutions and officials during the late Victorian period. While police were engulfed in bribery scandals and trying to guard against Fenian bomb plots, members of parliament and the aristocracy were accused of being criminals themselves. Denizens of their ranks fell foul of the laws against homosexuality in several high-profile cases of arrest between 1870 and 1889, while damaging references were made to titled men's involvement in a London child prostitution ring exposed by the *Pall Mall Gazette* in 1885.[53] Company fraud was also rife. During the 1870s successful prosecutions were levelled against successive company 'directors' for swindling shareholders out of tens of thousands of pounds, operating sham enterprises with authentic-sounding names such as the Co-Operative Credit Bank, Ruby Consolidated Mining Company, and Albion Life Assurance Society.[54] Even those espousing the saintliest of motives turned out to be suspect. 'Dr' Thomas Barnardo, founder of the famous children's homes, was taken to court in 1877 after photographs he used in fundraising fallaciously posed children doing menial work they had never endured, having torn their clothing to suggest greater neglect by their parents than they had actually experienced. Barnardo was acquitted, but suffered damage to his reputation.[55]

Hypocrisy and criminality flourished in multiple guises at the top, leaving space for the media and other interested bodies to become arbiters of information about criminal 'types' that would have to be taken seriously to secure public trust. The

---

[50] Seth Koven, The Matchgirl and the Heiress (Princeton: Princeton University Press, 2014), pp. 85–103.

[51] Charles Booth, Life and Labour of the People in London (London: Williams and Norgate, 1887–1902).

[52] Tom Crook, 'Norms, Forms and Beds: Spatializing Sleep in Victorian Britain', Body and Society 14:4 (2008), pp. 19–21.

[53] Matt Cook, London and the Culture of Homosexuality, 1885–1914 (Cambridge: Cambridge University Press, 2003), pp. 15–18, 50–1; Walkowitz, City of Dreadful Delight, pp. 81–120.

[54] James Taylor, Boardroom Scandal: The Criminalization of Company Fraud in Nineteenth-Century Britain (Oxford: Oxford University Press, 2013), pp. 164–72.

[55] Koven, Slumming, pp. 113–15.

potential for Peace's mythologized status as a 'paragon' of burglars to gain purchase in official accounts of crime first reared its head in 1879, with a diagram featured in the *Illustrated Police News* entitled 'Phrenological Head of Charles Peace, the Burglar' (Fig. 1.2). Phrenology was a 'science' popular among budding criminologists— lawyers, journalists, social surveyors, and scientists—seeking to discover new explanations for the causes of criminality. With criminology still in its infancy,

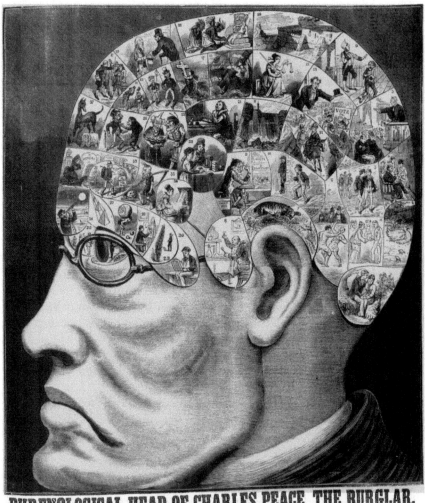

Fig. 1.2. 'Phrenological Head of Charles Peace, the Burglar', *Illustrated Police News* (22 Feb. 1879), p. 1. Reproduced by kind permission © The British Library Board.

phrenology's emphasis on the influence of external factors on the brain's development chimed with its practitioners' growing belief that environment, rather than heredity, determined whether or not people fell into a life of crime.[56]

As the diagram showed, the various emotional characteristics governing Peace's behaviour corresponded to what was thought were the location of the various organs of the brain. Significantly, whilst five of the areas of the brain identified were labelled with explicitly negative characteristics, including 'combativeness', 'destructiveness', and 'acquisitiveness', the rest (comprising thirty-four emotions ranging from 'Amativeness—love between the sexes', through 'Conscientiousness—fair dealing, sense of justice') were either normative or fundamentally 'good' qualities. Minimal difference in the size of these brain regions suggested that 'benevolence—kindness, compassion, charity', or 'constructiveness—mechanical ingenuity' held just as much sway over Peace's mind.[57] Here was a complex criminal personality, one whose existence could be endlessly mined for stories about the 'contest' between police and policed.

The *Illustrated Police News* was a mass-market publication that generally favoured gory tales of violence, particularly when featuring a beautiful and shapely woman, to enervate the pens of its team of illustrators. Like penny dreadfuls, it occupied the hinterland between sensational fiction and the revelation of real events, as despite its title, no formal relationship to police existed. Its article on Peace, however, found its target. Reinforcing the notion that the burglar merited further examination and a place within scientific textbooks on crime, Peace's tools and disguises found their way into Scotland Yard's 'Black' Museum (where they remain today).[58] Instituted in 1875, the museum was a series of rooms devoted to exhibiting relics from 'notable' crimes collected by investigating police officers, with the dual purpose of training young constables in criminals' methods.[59] As such, the logics of the space pitted the professionalism of police against the intelligence and skill of particular 'expert' criminals in a way that obscured their everyday dealings with a less-skilled majority, elevating the 'aristocrat' of burglars—Peace—to exemplar. This could then be rebranded as conventional wisdom. In 1885, the *Strand Magazine*'s report on the exhibition of burglars' tools at the museum declared that the 'professional' and 'most artistic kind of burglar' formed 'the class of men who are the greatest trouble to the police'.[60]

Displayed in the gallery alongside death masks of executed criminals, revolvers, knives, bombs, and bludgeons, and later, letters and bloodied clothes from the Jack the Ripper murders, the Peace artefacts might reasonably have been expected to encourage a sentiment of disgust. Yet appreciation of the ingenuity of his self-made

[56] Roger Cooter, *The Cultural Meaning of Popular Science: Phrenology and the Organisation of Consent in Nineteenth-Century Britain* (Cambridge: Cambridge University Press, 1984), pp. 75–9; Wiener, *Reconstructing*, p. 165.

[57] 'Phrenological Head of Charles Peace, the Burglar', Illustrated Police News (22 Feb. 1879), p. 1.

[58] My thanks to curator Alan McCormick for allowing me to visit in 2012.

[59] Gordon Honeycombe, *More Murders of the Black Museum 1835–1985* (London: Arrow, 1993), p. vii; Bill Waddell, *The Black Museum, New Scotland Yard* (London: Harrap, 1993), p. 5.

[60] 'Crimes and Criminals', Strand Magazine (Jan. 1894), pp. 273–84.

tools and the effectiveness of his disguises provoked admiration. Robert James Power-Berrey, a crime journalist who wrote a book based on his visit to the museum in 1899, asserted that Peace was 'clever... undoubtedly', his modified lantern (the size of a matchbox so as to be portable and not throw too much light) being 'an artful contrivance'.[61] Arthur Griffiths, who served as Inspector of Prisons from 1878–99, included a photograph of Peace's tools within the museum in his 1902 book *Mysteries of Police and Crime*, appending a long list of Peace's false arm, picklocks, vice, and gimlet beside a description of Peace's 'celebrated' and 'daring' escape attempt on the train to Leeds.[62] It seemed to correspond with what Berry had earlier described as some policemen's 'sneaking regard for burglars'.[63] The visiting journalist from *Chambers's Journal* had already alluded to this attitude in 1885, suggesting that Sergeant Bradshaw, the then-curator of the museum, handled Peace's tools 'tenderly, as if he loved them'.[64]

A new phase in the creation of criminal celebrity marked the decades immediately following Peace's death, led by the media but joined by members of the police and the legal sector. The latter had little choice, if they were to maintain their authority. Taking a cue from their museum, police officers and legal experts who wrote published memoirs and autobiographies during the period 1880 to 1930 assiduously paid homage to Charles Peace in these works.[65] Charles Mercier, doctor and Fellow of the Royal College of Surgeons who worked extensively in prisons, wrote in 1913 of the burglar's 'courage and enterprise' as part of an extended 'analysis' of the 'mental and bodily aptitudes' that distinguished burglars from other 'classes' of thief.[66] Jerome Caminada, the famous detective, similarly referred in his autobiography of 1895 to the 'resolute purpose and cool daring' Peace shared with other professional burglars.[67] Politicians got involved as well. Member of Parliament for Sheffield,

---

[61] Robert J. Power-Berrey, Bye-ways of Crime with Some Stories from the Black Museum (London: Greening and Co., 1899), pp. 8–10.

[62] Arthur Griffiths, Mysteries of Police and Crime (London: Cassell and Co., 1902), p. 37.

[63] Power-Berry, Bye-Ways, pp. 43–4.

[64] 'The Black Museum', Chambers's Journal of Popular Literature, Science and Arts (25 Apr. 1885), p. 264.

[65] Montagu Stephen Williams, Leaves of a Life: Being the Reminiscences of Montagu Williams Q.C. (London: MacMillan and Co., 1880), pp. 122–33; Charles Meymott Tidy, Legal Medicine (London: Smith, Elder and Co., 1882), p. 174; James Bent, Criminal Life: Reminiscences of Forty-Two Years as a Police Officer (London: J. Heywood, 1891), p. 243; Jerome Caminada, Twenty-Five Years of Detective Life (Manchester: John Heywood, 1895), p. 192; Griffiths, Mysteries of Police and Crime, pp. 45–52; Richard Storry Deans, Notable Trials: Romances of the Law Courts (London: Cassell and Co., 1906), pp. 170–88; Norman Wise Sibley, Criminal Appeal and Evidence (London: T. Fisher Unwin, 1908), p. 180; Richard Frith Quinton, Crime and Criminals, 1876–1910 (London: Longmans and Co., 1910), p. 91; John William Horsley, How Criminals are Made and Prevented: A Retrospect of Forty Years (London: T. Fisher Unwin, 1913), p. 39; Frederick Lamb, Forty Years in the Old Bailey: With a Summary of the Leading Cases and Points of Law and Practice (London: Stevens and Son, 1913), pp. 228–9; Charles Arthur Mercier, Crime and Criminals: Being the Jurisprudence of Crime, Medical, Biological, and Psychological (London: University of London Press, 1918), p. 245; Ernest Bowen-Rowlands, Seventy-Two Years at the Bar: A Memoir (London: MacMillan and Co., 1924), pp. 177–8; Charles Kingston, A Gallery of Rogues (London: S. Paul and Co., 1924), p. 55; Parry, The Drama of the Law, pp. 225–40; Basil Thomson, The Criminal (London: Hodder and Stoughton, 1925), p. 218.

[66] Mercier, Crime and Criminals, p. 245.

[67] Caminada, Twenty-Five Years of Detective Life, p. 192.

Richard Storry Deans, eulogized in 1906 about Peace's 'audacious robberies; his daring escapes; his wonderful disguises; his reckless jump from the express train'.[68] Given that he was born in Sheffield it may be that Deans anticipated Peace would offer some 'graveyard tourism' for his constituency, but the tone of the work was hardly befitting a public representative charged with promoting law and order.

These books were meant to sell. For their authors, who had seen (exaggerated) narratives of crime become dominant within the media and entertainment industry, the realization that their occupations gave them a unique selling point may have posed a quandary. They must walk a tightrope between retaining their professional authority as 'public men', while being seen to profit from the same literary market-place that lined the pockets of journalists and ex-crooks, who also had a unique perspective from which to market their life stories and increasingly used writing as a post-carceral outlet for a new identity and source of income.[69] Some tried to distance themselves from this murky landscape. John William Horsley, who was chaplain at Clerkenwell prison from 1876 to 1886, wrote in disparaging terms of the media's portrayal of Peace in his 1913 work *How Criminals are Made and Prevented*:

> Owing to the unnecessary prominence given to every detail of his career by fevered pressmen in search of copy, many had their thoughts turned to burglary as a substitute for work, and to imitate him by carrying a revolver became a fashion among thieves, whereby several murders came about.[70]

Horsley offered no evidence to support his claim, and readers would have been forgiven for finding his condemnation of 'pressmen' somewhat disingenuous when his own description of Peace praised 'the astute and inventive burglar'.[71] Over time, therefore, the elision between Peace and the 'typical' burglar gradually grew stronger through officials' complicity in endorsing the idea, sustaining extraordinariness as the stated norm for burglary.

LIFE AFTER DEATH

Peace's story continued to resonate with audiences at the start of the twentieth century, affording him a starring role in a brand new genre of entertainment surfacing in Edwardian Britain: film. At first, it was unclear what role film would occupy in the cultural landscape. Viewed mainly by working-class audiences on makeshift screens erected in music halls and theatres, early films straddled the domains of news-provider and entertainment commodity, akin to the satirical 'variety turns' of performers like Marie Lloyd that mocked upper-class disengagement from real life and the sexual double-standard.[72] Initially showing scenes of London life filmed impromptu on the streets, filmmakers began to experiment

[68] Storry Deans, Notable Trials, p. 170.   [69] Houlbrook, Prince of Tricksters.
[70] Horsley, How Criminals are Made and Prevented, p. 39.   [71] Ibid.
[72] Lynda Nead, The Haunted Gallery: Painting, Photography, Film c.1900 (London and New Haven: Yale University Press, 2007), pp. 122–4; Peter Bailey, 'Conspiracies of Meaning: Music-Hall and the Knowingness of Popular Culture', Past & Present 144 (1994), pp. 138–70.

with communicating the imaginary, as well as recreating famous crimes.[73] In 1905 one of the earliest films ever made in Britain, *The Life and Times of Charles Peace*, gave the burglar flesh again.[74]

Knitted together as a sequence of episodes of between thirty and forty seconds' duration, the film unashamedly revelled in the 'triumph of the underdog'. A comedic montage depicted bumbling policemen falling off roofs in pursuit of Peace; failing to recognize the burglar making a getaway dressed as a parson; and nearly losing him again when in their custody, during an electrifying re-enactment of Peace's jump from the train on the way to face his murder trial. In this last sequence, the visualization of the speed and movement of the train was achieved through juxtaposing a stationary shot of the train's windows against a real-time shot of the blurry, rolling countryside flying past without, impressing viewers with the sheer power and velocity of modern transport. Peace's dive from the rhythmic juggernaut of slick machinery into the abyss of a chaotic moving landscape (managed with the use of a dummy) affirmed his intrepidness, and symbolized his resistance to the strictures of the ordinary, regulated world. Film provided the technological apparatus to marry these qualities with the burglar in a manner that viewers would imbibe as part of a wondrous new sensory experience.

Filmed by pioneering Welsh director William Haggar and acted by members of his family, *The Life and Times of Charles Peace* gained immediate popularity in their native Wales, where it was screened as part of Haggar's travelling cinematograph, often at fairgrounds. Such was its status as a 'hit' that it was bought by film industry giant the Gaumont Picture Corporation, which distributed it around the United Kingdom. Whether concerns were raised about the film's blatant anti-authoritarian sentiments, a hallmark of Haggar's style, is unclear; the power of film was not yet realized, and the British Board of Film Censors was not founded until 1912. One of Haggar's children, Lily, remembered it as 'a classic of its time', while his son Walter recalled the enthusiasm of locals in Pembrokeshire (where scenes were filmed) for the project, one woman loaning the family her house for the burglary, and a local railway guard letting them 'borrow' his train for the escape.[75] Peace was brought to life in a truly democratic medium, and while twenty-six years had passed since his death—and many others had committed burglaries that made headlines— the popularity of his legend seemed unwavering.

Economic growth was painfully slow in Edwardian Britain. Unemployment continued to threaten the most vulnerable, heralding a small swell in the number of recorded burglaries nationally (peaking at 1,885 in 1910) and in the capital (555 in 1907).[76] Yet this was also the era of Liberal reform, when old age pensions,

---

[73] Ibid., p. 164.

[74] The Life and Times of Charles Peace (United Kingdom: dir. William Haggar, 1905). Available to view at the British Film Institute.

[75] Peter Yorke, William Haggar (1851–1925): Fairground Filmmaker (Bedlinog: Accent Press, 2007); Luke McKernan, 'Haggar (Arthur) William (1851–1925)', Oxford Dictionary of National Biography, http://www.oxforddnb.com/view/article/42131 (accessed 14 Jan. 2017); David Berry, 'Haggar, William (1851–1925)', Reference Guide to British and Irish Film Directors, BFI Screenonline http://www.screenonline.org.uk/people/id/449862/ (accessed 15 Jan. 2017).

[76] Charts 1 and 2, Appendix; Crafts, 'Long-Run Growth', pp. 1–24.

insurance for workers against sickness or injury, and the creation of labour exchanges and the dole for the unemployed tended to ameliorate some of the worst causes of poverty. The forms in which Peace's celebrity took shape articulated these moments of change, and the uncertainties they caused, particularly in the nature of his appearance in effigy at Madame Tussaud's wax museum in London (Fig. 1.3).

Public demand for a model of Peace was being anticipated while he sat awaiting the hangman in Leeds. As the minutes of a meeting in Leed's Armley Gaol record, the Secretary of State and High Sheriff of Yorkshire had both had to refuse independent requests to take casts of Peace's head.[77] Tussaud's created an effigy anyway, its catalogue of 1900 describing how Peace was displayed in the Chamber of Horrors 'in the character of "Mr. Thompson"', his respectable alias in Peckham. There was an interesting schism between Peace's respectable guise and the description afforded him in the catalogue, which labelled him a 'miscreant', asserting 'He was "bad-mad", or "mad-bad", and from other points of view the earth was well rid of him.'[78] As a *Daily Express* journalist queried when visiting in 1907, 'Mr Charles Peace, burglar

Fig. 1.3. Waxwork of Charles Peace on display at Madame Tussaud's (*c.*1900). Image reproduced by kind permission of Madame Tussaud's Archives.

[77] TNA, PCOM 8 108, Minute Paper No. 60434.67 (25 Feb. 1879).
[78] George Augustus Sala, Madame Tussaud's Exhibition Guide (London, 1900).

and murderer, is holding a little Court of his own. He is surrounded by a number of people looking at him rather sheepishly. The catalogue has it "that the earth was well rid of him". And yet here he is, immortalised in wax, surrounded every day by a wondering crowd.'[79]

The comment was significant. As in the earlier press reports on 'Peace-worship', the 'wonder' identified here inferred that viewers' fascination with the burglar was symptomatic of a moral vacuum at the heart of British society, despite the changed nature of the cultural context. Describing the 'sheepish' interest of the 'wondering' crowd, the journalist pinpointed the moral ambiguity of Peace's smartly dressed effigy, wrought in wax in a highly sanitized representation to attract a paying crowd whose enjoyment was not disturbed by having to confront similar effigies of the burglar's victims (alive or dead). As Pamela Pilbeam has noted, in the late nineteenth century Tussaud's itself occupied a somewhat ambiguous role in the cultural land-scape. On the one hand a venue frequented by a middle-class audience seeking to enjoy 'the snobbery of mingling with the [waxwork] mighty', Tussaud's also claimed to teach fact, offering 'an intimately corporeal biographical history' of its featured subjects.[80] The Chamber of Horrors, with its grisly name and reputation for indu-cing fear, was a space designed to reflect both journalistic and legal representations of criminals in all their forms, offering a 'history' of crime that was peculiarly attuned to public opinion.[81]

Peace's gentlemanly exterior at Tussaud's was as much about his purported 'mastery of disguise' as it was about social mobility—or fakery. As the embodiment of the 'expert burglar' audiences would have expected any representation of him to allude to the skills and abilities that had become so intrinsic to how burglary was now understood. At the same time, it bespoke a society experiencing the stirrings of far-reaching change, as workers acquired new rights and guarantees from the state so that the burglar, whose life was spent chasing a better lifestyle, emerged as another (illegal) arm of this popular 'movement'. The First World War brought a check on this thinking. Between 1918 and 1925, Tussaud's drastically changed its display of Peace, suggesting an obvious correlation with the government's stated concern in the wake of the war that popular culture impart suitably 'grave' messages of 'shared, stable values'.[82] Duly cautioned, Tussaud's transformed an entire room to resemble the cold brickwork architecture of a prison dungeon, and posed a fresh waxwork of Peace before it clad in drab prison clothes, sat humbly awaiting his fate at the feet of the hangman. The display focused viewers' thoughts squarely on his untimely end, although the existing figurine of Peace as Thompson was also placed alongside the scene to soften the impact.[83]

---

[79] 'Chamber of Horrors', Daily Express (29 Nov. 1907), p. 4.
[80] Pamela Pilbeam, Madame Tussaud and the History of Waxworks (London: Hambledon and London, 2003), pp. 223, 226.
[81] Ibid., pp. 225–7.
[82] See comparable emphasis in contemporary theatre productions highlighted by Gordon Williams, British Theatre in the Great War: A Revaluation (London: Bloomsbury, 2003), pp. 215–57; see also discussion of 'conservative modernism' of interwar fiction in Alison Light, Forever England: Femininity, Literature and Conservatism between the Wars (London: Routledge, 1991).
[83] Madame Tussaud's Exhibition Catalogue (London: Madame Tussaud's, 1925), pp. 43, 48.

In 1925, though, a massive fire ripped through the building. Madame Tussaud's collection was partially ruined, costing them one million pounds in repairs (today it would equate to ten times the amount). The fire provoked renewed assessment of exactly what popular sentiment was invested in the waxwork of the 'celebrated' Peace. As a journalist for the *Manchester Guardian* reported during the height of the fire, the watching crowd 'inquired after the safety of Charlie Peace' with obvious 'concern'.[84] Returned in 1928 to his old position of prominence in the Chamber of Horrors (a full forty-nine years after his execution), Peace's description in the exhibition catalogue was imbued with a new levity that appeared to finally concede defeat to romanticized versions of his life and crimes. In 1930, the updated catalogue genially recorded that the waxwork Peace stood 'in one of his numerous clever disguises', and 'would probably be considered a bit of a "cat burglar" to-day'.[85]

The latter half of the interwar years revised the memory of Peace to reclaim his earlier status as a figure of popular unrest, again notably coinciding with a period of economic depression initiated by the Wall Street Crash of 1929. Ignoring the

SHOCK for Colonel Sir Percy Laurie, the Assistant Commissioner of Police, at the Crime Club luncheon at Grosvenor House, W., yesterday, when he discovers who is Lady Towns-hend's other neighbour: the late Charles Peace (1832-79), the burglar-murderer who lived as a rich, respectable citizen. He has come from Madame Tussaud's.

Fig. 1.4. *Daily Mirror* (19 July 1935), p. 1. Reproduced by kind permission of Reach Publishing Services Ltd.

[84] 'Madame Tussaud's On Fire', Manchester Guardian (19 Mar. 1925), p. 9.
[85] The New Madame Tussaud's Exhibition: Official Guide and Catalogue (London: Madame Tussaud's, 1930), p. 64.

wrinkles that visibly inscribed the signs of middle-age on Peace's waxwork, the catalogue author's claim that Peace would now be identified as a 'cat burglar' demonstrated his resilience as an archetype. 'Cat' burglars were the latest media phenomenon, a supposedly young, unusually athletic, and frequently attractive breed of burglars that had seeped into popular and official usage during the early 1920s.[86] Peace's legacy therefore continued to inform, and be reconstructed by, changing stereotypes of burglary that favoured exceptionalism, acting as a symbolic bridge between older and more recent understandings of the nature of the crime. It continued to highlight the instability of the authority claimed by public officials and institutions concerned with regulating and defining crime, especially as the media and entertainment industry clawed from them ever more power and influence over public opinion. In 1935, Peace's waxwork was surreptitiously beside Colonel Sir Percy Laurie, Assistant Commissioner of Police, and Lady Townshend at a lunch at London's 'Crime Club' (to their apparent bemusement) (Fig. 1.4). In the caption to the photo published by the *Daily Mirror*, the journalist explained how Townshend's 'neighbour' at dinner 'lived as a rich respectable citizen', a eulogy that would have gladly been claimed by any of his fellow celebrities at the table.

* * *

The treatment of Charles Peace shows how a real criminal's life story could be rendered malleable over time in order to shape new ways of identifying and classifying particular types of crime and criminal. This is significant because it illustrates that the actual experiences and corporeality of a criminal was no barrier to his [or her] reinvention to suit changing cultural attitudes towards crime, which, when appropriated and guided by the media, had the capacity to become orthodox in official accounts. In part, the very extraordinariness of Peace's 'story' lent itself uniquely to generalizations about others' crimes. The sheer volume and variety of burglaries effected by Peace, as well as his pioneering methods, meant that other burglars would likely have some facet of their histories in common with him (however tenuous). Additionally, this aspect of Peace's fame ensured that versions of his life remained commercial, and made him first choice as a subject to inhabit new literary genres and forms of media that upheld the burglar's status on the pedestal of criminality, while enhancing his characteristics through emerging technologies. Audiences for Peace's endeavours were secured within an academic context where criminology's disciplinary boundaries remained porous to the interventions of journalists, and in a historical context where wealth and status were often precarious and temporary. Such realities meant that the 'fiction' of burglary seemed just as likely (or attractive) as the fact, a theme I develop in Chapter 2.

---

[86] See Chapter 4.

2

A. J. Raffles
Gentleman Thief

> Raffles was a burglar. I had helped him to commit one burglary, therefore
> I was a burglar too...My blood froze. My heart sickened. My brain whirled.
> How I had liked this villain! How I had admired him! How my liking and
> admiration must turn to loathing and disgust! I waited for the change. I longed
> to feel it in my heart. But—I longed and I waited in vain!
>
> > Thoughts of Bunny Manders, on realizing he had acted as accomplice to
> > Arthur Raffles during a burglary, in 'The Ides of March' (1898),
> > by Ernest William Hornung

To all the world, Arthur J. Raffles appeared an elegant man of leisure. Famed as
a cricketer for Middlesex, he became 'legend' among a team renowned as the
'Gentlemen of England'.[1] By night, he was an expert burglar. Raffles was the
fictional creation of Ernest William Hornung (1866–1921), real-life brother-
in-law of Sir Arthur Conan Doyle, author of Sherlock Holmes. Poking fun at their
relationship, Raffles emerged during the late Victorian period as Holmes' debonair,
sexier criminal alternative. First appearing on the literary scene in *Cassell's Magazine*
in 1898, he conducted his burglaries with the aid of his very own 'Watson': dim-
witted cohort Bunny Manders, in whose narrative voice the stories were written.[2]
Throughout twenty-six short stories and one novel published between 1898 and
1909, as well as successive films until the late 1930s, the young burglars skilfully
plundered the wealthy commercial and residential resorts of London. Stealing
from the jewellers of Bond Street, and the Mayfair mansions of the Lords and
Ladies with whom they dined, their adventures saw them continually elude capture by the police.[3] Yet 'loathing and disgust' barely featured, as readers were
guided to see, through Bunny's eyes, how committing a burglary could provide the

---

[1] Malcolm Tozer, 'A Sacred Trinity—Cricket, School, Empire: E. W. Hornung and his Young Guard',
in J. A. Mangan (ed.), *The Cultural Bond: Sport, Empire, Society* (London: Cass, 1992), pp. 14–15.

[2] E. W. Hornung, 'In the Chains of Crime', *Cassell's Magazine* (June 1898), pp. 3–12.

[3] After their initial appearance in *Cassell's Magazine*, the short stories were published collectively
in volumes *The Amateur Cracksman* (1899), *The Black Mask* (1901), and *A Thief in the Night*
(1905). E. W. Hornung, *The Complete Short Stories of Raffles* (1899–1905: reprinted London: Penguin,
1987); E. W. Hornung, *Mr Justice Raffles* (1909: reprinted Fairfield: Createspace Independent
Publishing Platform, 2007).

thrills of a legitimate sport (with material benefits). Just as Raffles 'seduced' Bunny to act as his accomplice, readers seemed similarly incapable of resisting the burglar, whose wit, cleverness, and physical beauty were used to charm his way into the imaginations of millions of willing audiences.

Concerns were raised. As a reviewer for middlebrow periodical *Academy* despaired of the stories in 1899, 'all one's notions of right and wrong are turned topsy-turvey'.[4] Conan Doyle himself echoed this sentiment more strongly, commenting that 'You must not make the criminal a hero' when he reflected on his rival's success in 1924.[5] Both voiced a genuine fear that young readers would inevitably try to copy the attractive villain, perhaps recognizing that the slippages between fiction and fact in Victorian sensational press reports, with their 'entertaining' ideas of violent crime, might have laid the groundwork for Raffles to function as an irresistible call to arms for the most impressionable audiences.[6] 'Topsy-turvey' seemed a fitting description for audiences' eager embrace of the 'gentleman' burglar. Suggesting the existence of a broader spectrum of attitudes towards crime and criminal than they had previously suspected, for reviewers, Raffles' popularity defied easy or comfortable understanding.[7] It is curious, then, that scholars have belittled Raffles' significance. Casting him as 'an ironic anti-hero' or the stuff of 'lightweight adventure fantasy', scholarly judgements have effectively dismissed the burglar as little more than passing satire, a poor relation to the almighty Sherlock Holmes.[8]

Raffles was no joke; he was an icon. Adopting the mantle left by Charles Peace, Hornung's fictional burglar energized the culture of pleasure towards burglary in this era. Raffles' romanticized burglaries were crimes that audiences were encouraged to revel in and enjoy. Eliciting unambiguous delight in the triumph of the burglar over society and the law, the stories flourished under a demanding entertainment market for further Raffles-centred fiction, plays, and films. Public enthusiasm was hardly surprising. Raffles' lifestyle as a wealthy bachelor in London, acquired through illegitimate means, offered a vicarious opportunity to shed the constraints of everyday life. Renouncing codes of class conduct, property rights, law, and citizenship, he embodied the fantasies of upper-middle-class male readers when conceived in the original novels.[9] Progressively, as the burglar was disseminated

---

[4] 'Fiction', *Academy* (22 Apr. 1899), p. 458.

[5] Arthur Conan Doyle, *Memories and Adventures* (New York: Hodder and Stoughton, 1924), p. 288.

[6] Crone, *Violent Victorians*, pp. 218–19.

[7] See Laura Doan's discussion of 'topsey-turveydom' in the context of interwar analyses of 'gender inversion', and the feelings with which the term was associated: Laura Doan 'Topsy-Turvydom: Gender Inversion, Sapphism, and the Great War', *GLQ: A Journal of Lesbian and Gay Studies* 12:4 (2006), pp. 517–42.

[8] Marty Roth, *Foul and Fair Play: Reading Genre in Classic Detective Fiction* (London: University of Georgia Press, 1995), p. 52; Stephen Knight, *Crime Fiction 1800–2000: Detection, Death, Diversity* (Basingstoke: Palgrave MacMillan, 2004), p. 70.

[9] Here I offer a different perspective from Richard Ireland's argument in relation to Raffles, which suggests that the idea of a 'gentleman burglar' was a particularly striking departure from Victorian criminological notions of a 'criminal class' overwhelmingly composed of the poorest members of society. Ireland suggests that Raffles' status in this regard may not have been the intention of Hornung, but nonetheless functioned in that way; my own reading of Raffles' significance lies in the character's ultimately cross-class aspirational criminality, his assumed 'gentlemanliness' deriving from Hornung's

more widely through the media of theatre and film, he became a criminal 'hero' for viewers of all classes and genders. Introducing a glamorous female accomplice into the mix to appease the appetites of theatregoers, women viewers could now equally identify with the delights of burglary, albeit purely as romantic interests. Sexual allure gave Raffles a potent lustre, his physical attractiveness and athleticism, as well as the beauty of his lovers and associates, piquing audiences' interest and apparently easing any moral qualms they might otherwise have had.

Certainly, the sheer pervasiveness and recurrence of the fictional burglar in British and international popular culture before the Second World War deserves closer scrutiny. Of the books, *The Amateur Cracksman* and subsequent second and third collected volumes of the short stories entitled *The Black Mask* (1901) and *A Thief in the Night* (1905) were commercial triumphs, re-printed in multiple editions and translated in various languages including French and German.[10] Raffles was portrayed on the stage on both sides of the Atlantic, theatre productions enjoying runs in Philadelphia, New York, and Washington in 1903, in Hamburg in 1907, at London's Comedy Theatre in 1906 and Wyndham's Theatre in 1914, and in theatres in Edinburgh and Glasgow in 1909, 1912, 1915, 1917, 1921, and 1937.[11] No less than nine films about the burglar were made in Britain, France, and America between 1907 and 1939, situating Raffles as Holmes' counterpart in enduring cultural currency by resonating with successive generations, and nationalities, of audiences.[12] Raffles' successful transition across genres and ascendancy as an internationally renowned British cultural icon indicates a thriving intellectual

own experiences of public school and social milieu. See Richard Ireland, 'Criminology, Class, and Cricket: Raffles and Real Life', *Legal Studies* 33:1 (2013), pp. 66–84.

[10] See British editions of *The Amateur Cracksman* (London: Grant Richards, 1901); (London: Eveleigh Nash, 1911); (London: John Murray, 1926); (London: Readers Library Publishing Company Ltd, 1930), and (London: Jonathan Cape Ltd, 1936); *A Thief in the Night* (London: Nelson Library, 1914), and (London: George G. Harrap & Co. Ltd, 1926); French and German language editions: E.W. Hornung, *Ein Einbrecher aus Passion* (Stuttgart: Verlag von. J. Engelhorn, 1903), E.W. Hornung, *Le Masque Noir: Aventures de Raffles, Cambrioleur Amateur* (Paris: La renaissance du livre, 1907).

[11] 'At the Theatres', *Washington Times* (11 Oct. 1903), p. 2; 'Raffles and Redwood', *New York Times* (28 Oct. 1903), p. 7; UBA, MS 127, box 5, E. W. Hornung Papers, Letter from E. W. Hornung to Shane R. Chichester (1 Jan. 1907). This letter indicates that translations of the play were being prepared for France, Italy, and Sweden, but the materialization of these plans is unknown. 'Drama', *Athenaeum* (19 May 1906), p. 619; 'Raffles', *Play Pictorial*, 25 (1914), p. 88; 'Entertainments', *Scotsman* (4 May 1909), p. 5; 'Entertainments', *Scotsman* (15 Oct. 1912), p. 4; 'Glasgow "On Trial" At King's', *Scotsman* (5 Oct. 1915), p. 3; 'Glasgow', *Scotsman* (27 Nov. 1917), p. 3; 'Theatre Royal', *Scotsman* (1 June 1921), p. 1; 'Entertainments', *Scotsman* (20 July 1937), p. 8; 'Glasgow Theatres', *Scotsman* (27 July 1937), p. 14.

[12] *Raffles* (United States of America: Vitagraph Company of America, director unknown, 1907); *Raffles, The Amateur Burglar* (France: Gaumont Production Company, director unknown, 1910); *Raffles, The Gentleman Thief* (United Kingdom: New Agency Film Company, director unknown, 1911); *Raffles, The Amateur Cracksman* (United States of America: L. Lawrence Weber Photodrama Corporation, Hyclass Producing Company, dir. George Irving, 1917); *Mr Justice Raffles* (United Kingdom: Hepworth Picture Plays, dirs. Gerald Ames and Gaston Quiribet, 1921); *Raffles* (United States of America: Universal Jewel Production Company, dir. King Baggot, 1925); *Raffles* (United States of America: Samuel Goldwyn Incorporated, dirs. Harry d'Abbadie D'Arrast and George Fitzmaurice, 1930); *The Return of Raffles* (United Kingdom: W.P. Film Company, dir. Mansfield Markham, 1932); *Raffles* (United States of America: Samuel Goldwyn Incorporation, dir. Sam Wood, 1939); Saler, ' "Clap if You Believe in Sherlock Holmes" ', pp. 599–622.

interchange in popular understandings of crime transatlantically, with repercussions for how burglary was regulated and punished on a much grander scale.

For all these reasons, it is surprising that while Raffles languishes understudied, other fictional tales of crime and deviancy have been debated and analysed over and again for decades.[13] Notably, historians and literary scholars have concentrated their efforts on novels upholding the themes of justice and the law, especially by authors such as Edgar Allen Poe, Conan Doyle, or Margery Allingham. These allow us to pinpoint the moments at which, historically, popular culture has become the mechanism for reasserting social order, as when the war profiteer became a dominant villain in crime fiction produced after 1918.[14] Legal scholar Richard Ireland's study of Raffles' significance, which places the novels alongside late nineteenth-century criminological texts, similarly suggests that Raffles' gentlemanly persona functioned to 'shock' Victorian and Edwardian readers into confronting the possibility of the respectable upper classes committing crime. Raffles' novelty thereby drew attention to pervasive 'expectations' that most burglars were working-class and desperate, in Ireland's view.[15] Collectively, these ideas leave little space for stories that celebrated criminal enterprise as a pathway to social mobility (joyfully allowing Raffles and Bunny to escape capture and punishment at the end), standing us in danger of obscuring the full range of meanings attached to crime and criminals in a changing cultural landscape.[16]

Raffles not only instituted a more sympathetic stereotype of burglars, but also intensified perceptions of their expertise. Part of the blame lay with journalists, who established 'Raffles' as a byword for a sanitized, romantic idea of criminal endeavour beyond the realm of fiction by headlining reports of actual burglaries with descriptions like 'A Modern Raffles'.[17] Selection of cases was key. The specific 'type' of burglary Raffles represented was accomplished using superior physical and mental ability, targeting the property of the wealthier classes, without using excessive violence towards victims. With as broad a license as possible, journalists stuck to these criteria when applying the fictional epithet to real crimes. It also helped if the criminals had an attractive appearance or manner. The way in which this new 'brand' of criminal evolved into a definitive category outside the artistic arena of

[13] See for example Gill Plain, *Twentieth-Century Crime Fiction: Gender, Sexuality and the Body* (Edinburgh: Edinburgh University Press, 2001); Lawrence Frank, *Victorian Detective Fiction and the Nature of Evidence: The Scientific Investigations of Poe, Dickens, and Doyle* (Basingstoke: Palgrave MacMillan, 2003); Simon Joyce, *Capital Offences: Geographies of Class and Crime in Victorian London* (London: University of Virginia Press, 2003); Shani D'Cruze, ' "Dad's Back": Mapping Masculinities, Moralities, and the Law in the Novels of Margery Allingham', *Cultural and Social History* 1 (2004), pp. 256–79.

[14] Christine Grandy, ' "Avarice" and "Evil Doers": Profiteers, Politicians, and Popular Fiction in the 1920s', *Journal of British Studies* 50 (2011), pp. 667–89.

[15] Ireland, 'Criminology, Class, and Cricket', p. 84.

[16] As James Chapman and Matthew Hilton argue, all 'popular fictions', which they distinguish by commercial success, 'both reflect dominant values and serve to construct and reinforce them'. James Chapman and Matthew Hilton, 'From Sherlock Holmes to James Bond: Masculinity and National Identity in British Popular Fiction', in Stephen Caunce, Ewa Mazierska, Susan Sidney-Smith, and John K. Walton (eds.), *Relocating Britishness* (Manchester: Manchester University Press, 2004), p. 127.

[17] 'A Modern Raffles', *Scotsman* (25 Sept. 1928), p. 10.

fiction, theatre, and film did more than accelerate Raffles' commercial currency. Bleeding into criminological texts and police memoirs, it epitomized 'the subjective appropriation of fiction into individual and shared cultural imaginaries' that historian Shani D'Cruze suggests was characteristic of early detective fiction.[18] Fact gave way to fiction, and the infiltration of Raffles into the lexicon of criminals used by highest echelons of state machinery was complete. Burglars also saw the advantage, dubbing themselves 'Real-life Raffles' when the opportunity arose in order to gain a more sympathetic hearing in court or build a new life for themselves as 'true crime' writers after leaving prison.[19]

Although scholars in criminology and history have identified shared international stereotypes of criminal behaviour in scientific discourse during the early twentieth century (particularly in relation to the ideas of Italian criminologist Cesare Lombroso), there have as yet been no similar studies made of a 'popular' criminal attaining such extensive recognition.[20] Fictional worlds collided more publicly, by contrast, when in 1905 in France a new gentleman *'cambrioleur'* (burglar), Arsène Lupin, was presented as the protagonist of a new set of stories by author Maurice LeBlanc. Bearing many of the same personality traits as Raffles, Lupin even faced off against Sherlock Holmes (renamed 'Herlock Sholmes') in a story of 1908, although LeBlanc never acknowledged his character's debt to Hornung's creation.[21] Again, such levels of *homage* to Raffles internationally and intertextually richly suggest the exceptional resonance of the glamorous villain during the turbulent opening decades of the twentieth century. This chapter delves deeper into the burglar's complex cultural meanings.

*   *   *

Stories glamorizing criminals have a long tradition in Britain. Gillian Spraggs has described 'the cult of the robber' in England stemming from fictional and biographical tales of notorious thieves such as Robin Hood, Jack Sheppard, and Dick Turpin, tales sustained by a popularity that straddled the distance between the Middle Ages and the early nineteenth century.[22] Whereas the 'activities' of Robin Hood could be virtuous—the legend's theme of robbing-from-the-rich-to-give-to-the-poor was linked with organized charity in plays as early as the 1470s—the renown of figures such as Sheppard and Turpin grew despite the fact that neither had any similar redeeming virtues.[23] Real-life highwaymen, housebreakers, burglars,

---

[18] D'Cruze, '"Dad's Back"', p. 257.

[19] Ireland's work mentions briefly to the phenomenon of criminals appropriating the appellation 'Raffles in real life', which I have expanded upon significantly in this chapter. Ireland, 'Class, Criminology, and Cricket', p. 81.

[20] See for example Nicole Hahn Rafter, 'Criminal Anthropology: Its Reception in the United States and the Nature of its Appeal', in Peter Becker and Richard F. Wetzell (eds.), *Criminals and their Scientists: The History of Criminology in International Perspective* (Cambridge: Cambridge University Press, 2006), pp. 150–81.

[21] David Drake, 'Crime Fiction at the Time of the Exhibition: The Case of Sherlock Holmes and Arsène Lupin', *Synergies Royaume-Uni et Irlande* 2 (2009), pp. 105–17; also cited in Ireland, 'Criminology, Class, and Cricket', p. 82.

[22] Spraggs, *Outlaws and Highwaymen.*   [23] Ibid., pp. 53–4.

and sometimes murderers, Sheppard and Turpin's literary heroization played upon their working-class origins, 'daring', and 'skill', and made no apologies for their attempts to retain their ill-gotten gains for themselves.[24] Eighteenth-century highwaymen were, in fact, harbingers of Raffles in more ways than one, since the historian Andrea McKenzie describes how their coverage in press and pamphlets rendered highwaymen 'media personalities whose currency transcended class lines', and whose exploits, in the retelling, were used 'as a mouthpiece to denounce the hypocrisy and corruption' of society.[25]

A precedent undoubtedly existed in Britain for the lasting commercial success of narratives of crime that encouraged readers to take pleasure in the extraordinary feats and character of the criminal rather than the law-enforcer. So-called 'gentlemen' highwaymen, who affected respectable manners and dress, were likewise heralded as 'social climbers' whose thefts were 'insignificant compared to those of the country's governors' until the late eighteenth century, when such controversial views fell out of fashion (among middle- and upper-class readers at least).[26] Ultimately, however, all these highwaymen were captured and executed, restoring society to a state of order. But something was about to change. Against a late Victorian proliferation of fiction targeted specifically at the middle- and upper-classes through more upmarket periodicals, *Cassell's Magazine* chose to publish Ernest Hornung's mischievous new story. Raffles was an upper-class socialite par excellence, the sort of man *Cassell's* readers might have known among their close circle of acquaintance. Educated at a public school, resident of London's exclusive bachelor quarters The Albany (a famous private residence off Piccadilly frequented by Oscar Wilde and pals), and member of various unidentified gentlemen's clubs, Raffles was an intimate friend of the fictional aristocracy Hornung created.[27] His closest brush with the law came when his identity as 'The Amateur Cracksman' was unmasked at the end of the first series of stories, forcing Raffles to jump overboard from a cruise ship into the Mediterranean to escape the clutches of Inspector Mackenzie.[28] This was a far cry from the executions that dramatically extinguished the lives of characters such as Sheppard and Turpin, denying the usual triumph of the state's disciplinary procedures over crime.

Raffles' plunge into the Mediterranean at the close of *The Amateur Cracksman* signalled a decisive break from his literary antecedents. Kissing a recent flirtation, Miss Werner, a hasty farewell, and ordering Bunny to restrain the approaching detective, Raffles was described heading to the ship's rail and jumping, 'his lithe,

---

[24] Ibid., pp. 252–4.

[25] Andrea McKenzie, 'The Real Macheath: Social Satire, Appropriation, and Eighteenth-Century Criminal Biography', *Huntington Library Quarterly* 69:4 (2006), pp. 583–4, 587.

[26] Robert Shoemaker, 'The Street Robber and the Gentleman Highwayman: Changing Representations and Perceptions of Robbery in London, 1690–1800', *Cultural and Social History* 3:4 (2006), pp. 389–402. In my earlier article on Raffles, I observed that 'Before Raffles, however, their [crime authors'] protagonists did not cross boundaries of class, rarely venturing out of a working-class lifestyle to adopt an upper-class persona', a view I have since revised in response to the greatly valued guidance of the anonymous reviewer who highlighted McKenzie and Shoemaker's works on the subject of highwaymen.

[27] Hornung, *Amateur*, pp. 41, 45, 76–93; Hornung, *A Thief in the Night*, pp. 386–404.

[28] Hornung, *Amateur*, pp. 173–5.

spare body cut[ting] the sunset as cleanly and precisely as though he had plunged at his leisure from a diver's board!'[29] Raffles' escape chimed well with the escapist fantasies *Cassell's* was fond of publishing, as well as the lifestyle its features evoked. Costing one shilling an issue and consistently valorizing upper-class gentlemen protagonists in a mixture of adventure, romance, and true crime stories by authors such as Rudyard Kipling, its features were juxtaposed against adverts for expensive tailor-made clothes, home decorations, and special edition encyclopaedias.[30] Celebrating the 'adventure culture' to which upper-middle-class men aspired, the magazine's rhetoric embraced themes of British imperial domination and racial strength which, as John Tosh asserts, required men who might be depended upon for 'struggle, duty, action, will, and "character"'.[31] Raffles' abandonment of his sweetheart and accomplice might not have seemed to appeal to those values, but the reader was assured by Raffles' parting words that Bunny at least would be repaid for his loyalty: 'You were a good pal always when it came to the scratch; some day or other you mayn't be so sorry to remember you were a good pal at the last!'[32]

Raffles' care for Bunny bespoke a male comradeship inherited from their public school days, established by Hornung in his first story about Raffles when Bunny recounts how he served as the burglar's adoring 'fag' (a junior who performs errands for a senior). Developing into an adulthood of shared club memberships, cricket tournaments, luxury apartments at The Albany, their homosociability finally found them engaged in the 'joint venture' of burglaries.[33] Hornung wrote about a world he knew. Born to a wealthy merchant in 1866 and educated for several years at private, all-boys' Uppingham School in Leicestershire, he was an enthusiastic cricketer whose early days as a writer were spent in lodgings in west London in close proximity to Oscar Wilde, holding membership of Pall Mall's elite Reform Club.[34] Scandal was becoming familiar to Hornung's circle. They were first rocked in 1885 by the *Pall Mall Gazette*'s 'Maiden Tribute of Modern Babylon' exposé of certain wealthy men's involvement in London's child prostitution racket.[35] Politicians Charles Dilke and Charles Stewart Parnell, and Hornung's friend H. G. Wells, were all immersed in sensational, and publicly ruinous, divorce cases of 1886, 1889, and 1895 respectively.[36] Wells' was made rather worse by his swift remarriage to Amy Catherine Robbins, formerly his student.[37] Yet these

---

[29] Ibid., p. 174.   [30] See for example *Cassell's Magazine* (Dec. 1900), pp. xviii–xxii.

[31] Francis, 'The Domestication of the Male?', p. 643; Tosh, *Manliness and Masculinities*, p. 193.

[32] Hornung, *Amateur*, p. 174.   [33] Hornung, 'In the Chains of Crime', p. 3.

[34] Rowland, Peter, 'Hornung, Ernest William (1866–1921)', *Oxford Dictionary of National Biography*, http://www.oxforddnb.com/view/10.1093/ref:odnb/9780198614128.001.0001/odnb-9780198614128-e-37572 (accessed 29 Dec. 2012); Library of the Reform Club, 104 Pall Mall, London: Unknown Author, *The Rules and Regulations with an Alphabetical List of the Members of the Reform Club* (London, 1896), p. 56.

[35] Walkowitz, *City of Dreadful Delight*, p. 126.

[36] John B. Thompson, *Political Scandal: Power and Visibility in the Media Age* (Cambridge: Cambridge University Press, 2000), p. 15.

[37] Hornung's holiday with Wells documented in photograph by George Gissing, in *The Collected Letters of George Gissing, Vol. 7*, ed. Paul F. Matthiesen, Arthur C. Young, and Pierre Coustillas (1897–9; reprinted Ohio, 1997), 196–9; Parrinder, Patrick, 'Wells, Herbert George (1866–1946)', *Oxford Dictionary of National Biography*, http://www.oxforddnb.com/view/10.1093/ref:odnb/9780198614128.001.0001/odnb-9780198614128-e-36831 (accessed 29 Dec. 2012).

troubles appeared nothing against the infamous libel trial that exposed Wilde's homosexuality in 1895. Suddenly, the public and private personas of Hornung's literary milieu seemed more distant than ever before.[38]

Press reports of the crimes and indiscretions of the upper classes gave Hornung license to create a burglar in their image, as well as the ability to portray them as 'legitimate' victims of Raffles' crimes. Even the few literary critics who reviewed the Raffles novels unfavourably had no quibble with *who* he burgled.[39] Raffles' defence of his cricketing alter-ego, espoused to Bunny in third short story 'Gentlemen and Players', freely ridiculed the idea that moral calibre could be judged by the appearance of social or professional respectability:

> To follow crime with reasonable impunity you simply must have a parallel ostensible career—the more public the better....Mr. Peace [a notorious burglar], of pious memory, disarmed suspicion by acquiring a local reputation for playing the fiddle and taming animals, and it's my profound conviction that Jack the Ripper was a really eminent public man, whose speeches were very likely reported alongside his atrocities. Fill the bill in some prominent part, and you'll never be suspected of doubling it with another of equal prominence.[40]

Using the real examples of Charles Peace and Jack the Ripper reinforced the probability of someone like Raffles existing, eliciting humour whilst subtly forcing middle- and upper-class readers to reflect on the morality of the economic and social privileges the wealthy enjoyed. The relationship between cohorts Raffles and Bunny can also be regarded as appealing to a contemporary reassessment of social and gendered identities. Never explicitly romantic or venturing into the terrain of sexual intimacy that had so compromised Wilde, *The Amateur Cracksman* and its sequels nonetheless crafted a highly intense, emotionally intimate friendship between the two burglars that can be aligned with what Harry Cocks has described as an ideal of 'the true love of comrades' articulated among other groups of male literary critics and thinkers in Britain during the 1890s (groups that Hornung, through his friendship with Ives, was on the fringe of).[41]

Occasionally venturing towards homoerotic desire, this ethos of comradeship was heightened by Raffles' role as 'leader', the veneration of which appeared in Bunny's first, reflective description of Raffles:

[38] Hornung knew Wilde via his friendship with George Ives, with whom Wilde was romantically involved; for the friendship between Horning and Ives, see HRC, George Ives Papers, letters from E. W. Hornung to George Ives, 2 May 1906, and 18 May 1903; HRC, British Sexological Society, Miscellaneous Series, letters from E. W. Hornung to George Ives, postmarked 18 April 1904, 13 May 1904, and 28 May 1907. For Ives' relationship with Wilde see Cook, *London and the Culture of Homosexuality*, pp. 145–7. Matt Cook, 'Law', in H. G. Cocks and Matt Houlbrook (eds.), *The Palgrave Modern History of Sexuality* (Basingstoke: Palgrave MacMillan, 2006), pp. 74–5.

[39] 'Notes on Novels', *Academy* (12 Oct. 1901), p. 342; 'A Thief in the Night', *Bookman*, no. 29 (Nov. 1905), p. 90.

[40] Hornung, *Amateur*, pp. 76–7.

[41] Harry Cocks, 'Calamus in Bolton: Spirituality and Homosexual Desire in Late Victorian England', *Gender and History* 13 (2001), pp. 191–223, 199.

Again...I see his indolent, athletic figure; his pale, sharp, clean-shaven features; his curly black hair; his strong unscrupulous mouth. And again I feel the clear beam of his wonderful eye, cold and luminous as a star, shining into my brain—sifting the very secrets of my heart.[42]

Whilst reminiscent of a romantic ode, the attributes that qualified Bunny's appreciation of Raffles' physique—the athleticism of his figure even when in a casual attitude, or the 'strength' of the mouth that had been used to persuade him to act as accomplice—suggests a reverence for these contemporary markers of leadership and 'character'. Comparable traits were recalled in nearly identical language in press memorialization of Edwardian explorer Captain Scott, who had 'strength and vigour and quickness' and 'clear-cut features'.[43] Yet one cannot exclude the possibility of some readers identifying the relationship between Raffles and Bunny in a tangibly homosexual framework of intimacy. Even The Albany residence, which featured as backdrop to the stories, had a reputation as a hub of the 'homosexual circuit' at the fin de siècle.[44] Whether readers chose to invest in this version of their relationship or not, the bond between the two burglars, centring upon motifs of love and loyalty whilst punctuated by a frisson of sexual charge, offered them a secure masculine friendship weathered by the extraordinary criminal adventures in which they took part.[45]

Raffles' physical attractiveness, athleticism, and ability not only enhanced the tenor of his association with Bunny, but also enabled Hornung to cast him as a cricketing legend in the same mould as some of the most admired sportsmen of the day.[46] Raffles' cricketing career, as well as sustaining the duality of his life, was an important element of the stories' commercial success in other ways. Imbuing the stories with the excitement of reference to a popular sport, it also served as the perfect analogy to the *modus operandi* of Raffles' burglaries; throughout the stories, the 'gentleman thief' used his skill and wits to achieve his ends, rarely employing violence against a homeowner and adamantly declaring that 'violence is a confession of terrible incompetence'.[47] It was a distinction to which reviewers of *The Amateur Cracksman* clung when attempting to justify their enjoyment of the criminal's escape from the law. As one critic noted, Raffles 'had a code of honour, and stuck to it; otherwise he would have been impossible as a hero'.[48] Other critics, by contrast, simply condemned the moral content of the novel, describing Raffles and Bunny as 'weak-minded' and 'evil' (*Glasgow Herald*), 'nefarious' (*Daily Telegraph*), and 'a heresy' (*Windsor Magazine*).[49]

---

[42] Hornung, *Amateur*, p. 45.

[43] Max Jones, *The Last Great Quest: Captain Scott's Antarctic Sacrifice* (Oxford: Oxford University Press, 2003), p. 216.

[44] Cook, *London*, pp. 31, 142.   [45] Ibid., pp. 103–16.

[46] Richard Holt, 'Cricket and Englishness: The Batsman as Hero', in Richard Holt, J. A. Mangan, and Pierre Lanfranchi (eds.), *European Heroes: Myth, Identity, Sport* (London: Frank Cass, 1996), pp. 48–70.

[47] Hornung, *Amateur*, p. 165.   [48] 'Fiction', *Academy* (22 Apr. 1899), p. 458.

[49] 'Literature', *Glasgow Herald* (20 Mar. 1899), p. 11; 'New Novels', *Daily Telegraph* (24 Mar. 1899), p. 5; Edmund B. V. Christian, 'Recent Cricket Matches in Fiction', *Windsor Magazine* (Aug. 1899), p. 280.

Such comments were not without justification. Raffles' 'philosophy' encouraged workers to disregard their worries altogether:

> Why should I work when I could steal? Why settle down to some humdrum uncongenial billet, when excitement, romance, danger, and a decent living were all going begging together? Of course, it's very wrong, but we can't all be moralists, and the distribution of wealth is very wrong to begin with.[50]

Burglary offered an alternative 'career', one in which a would-be thief could realize all the pleasures of a luxurious living, propel oneself into the upper echelons of British society, and fulfil contemporary ideals of masculine endeavour, while taking revenge upon an unrelenting class system with impunity. It was also a sensory experience. Regaling Bunny with a story of how he nearly got caught during his first attempt at burglary in *The Amateur Cracksman*, Raffles swoons,

> Bunny, if you ask me what was the most thrilling moment of my infamous career, that was it. There I stood at the bottom of those narrow stone stairs, inside the strongroom, with the door a good foot open, and I didn't know whether it would creak or not. The light was coming nearer—and I didn't know![51]

The story concluded with just a hint of sexual metaphor, as Raffles, trying to avoid being recognized, explained: 'I used to have a rather heavy moustache...but I lost it the day after I lost my innocence.'[52] Small wonder that as sequels *The Black Mask* and *A Thief in the Night* found their way into print reviewers began to voice fears that such books were 'not...for an unbalanced juvenile, but all right for a policeman or a J.P.', or '...may become actually dangerous...a novel which leaves a scientific and cold-blooded criminal triumphant and unrepentant, may be really harmful to immature and ill-balanced minds'.[53]

Already, then, critics were wary of the potential of Raffles to transcend the boundaries of fiction and infiltrate readers' perceptions of the reality of crime, to an extent that would romanticize popular discourse of crime and, correspondingly, denigrate the law. By the late nineteenth century the reading habits of the British public were coming under increasing scrutiny, now in explicitly psychological terms that 'dismissed engagement with popular fiction as irrational, hysterical, fantastical, or even childlike'.[54] But how to fight moral degradation when it flourished in the pages of elite and middlebrow fiction? After all, its readership encompassed the classes upon whom the future intellectual, racial, and economic strength of the nation was popularly assumed to depend. Unfortunately for those worried about their flagrant celebration of criminality, by 1901 the stories' commercial currency had proven itself in triplicate. Hornung, in collusion with theatre and film producers, now moved to test the allure of the narrative to an even broader audience.

*　＊　＊　＊*

---

[50] Hornung, *Amateur*, p. 58.　　　[51] Ibid., p. 106.　　　[52] Ibid., p. 108.
[53] 'Notes on Novels', *Academy* (12 Oct. 1901), p. 342; 'A Thief in the Night', *Bookman* 29 (Nov. 1905), p. 90.
[54] Houlbrook, '"A Pin to See the Peepshow"', p. 218.

America became the testing-ground for the first theatre adaptation of Hornung's Raffles stories. In September 1903, with a script co-authored by Hornung and Eugene Presbrey (of whom little is known), *Raffles: The Amateur Cracksman* premiered at the Garrick Theatre, Philadelphia. English actor Kyrle Bellew was in the lead role, perhaps in a nod to the story's origins.[55] The play was a runaway success, proceeding to be staged at the National Theatre, Washington, and the Princess Theatre, New York, in October and November that year.[56] American audiences had already proved receptive to Raffles. *The Amateur Cracksman* was reprinted in New York with the title *Raffles* by publishing firm Charles Scribner's Sons in 1901, and one theatre reviewer for the *Washington Times* confidently assumed a broad familiarity with Raffles' fictional origins, noting that '[The play] is based, as almost every one knows, upon the fascinating sketches of the first-named dramatist [Hornung]'.[57] American reviewers explained that the burglar was 'Eton bred, a mighty cricketer in county matches', and 'a gentleman received in the highest social circles in London', illustrating not only that American audiences were conversant with the structure, dynamics, and pastimes of Britain's upper classes, but also that Raffles' characterization and crimes were inextricable from them.[58] In one important respect, though, the play witnessed a decisive departure from the novels.[59]

Abandoning Raffles' cosy homosociability with Bunny, the play (according to the surviving 1906 script) revolved entirely around Raffles' attempts to win Gwendoline Conran, cousin of the Earl of Amersteth. Initially determining to give up crime for Gwen's love, Raffles finds it impossible, as he is firstly threatened with having his true identity revealed by a covetous former lover, Mrs Vidal (nee Miss Werner, formerly abandoned at sea), and finally unmasked by the detective on his heels, Curtis Bedford. Despite these disasters, Raffles escapes the clutches of Scotland Yard with Gwen's help after she declares her love despite his being a thief.[60] Preserving the original tropes that popularized Raffles in fiction—his gentlemanly persona, adventurousness, illicitly earned lifestyle, and ability to evade police—the theme of heterosexual courtly love indicates Hornung and Presbrey's desire to cater for mixed audiences of men and women at the theatre. Raffles' 'appeal' to women took on new meaning when the play transferred to London's Comedy Theatre in 1906. With heartthrob Gerald du Maurier replacing Bellew in the title role, the audience were presented with a Raffles who, as *The Athenaeum*'s reviewer described, was 'a lady-killer'.[61]

Du Maurier offered an elegant, handsome, commanding lead, photographed surrounded by doting women in the play in publicity shots for highbrow periodical

---

[55] 'At the Theatres', *Washington Times* (11 Oct. 1903), p. 2.

[56] Ibid.; 'Raffles and Redwood', *New York Times* (28 Oct. 1903), p. 7; 'New Plays in Gotham', *Washington Post* (1 Nov. 1903), p. 4.

[57] E. W. Hornung, *Raffles* (New York, 1901); 'At the Theatres', *Washington Times* (11 Oct. 1903), p. 2.

[58] 'Raffles and Redwood', *New York Times* (28 Oct. 1903), p. 7; 'At the Theatres', *Washington Times* (11 Oct. 1903), p. 2.

[59] E. W. Hornung and Eugene Presbrey, *Raffles, The Amateur Cracksman* (1906), reprinted in E. W. Hornung, *The A. J. Raffles Omnibus* (Ontario: Battered Silicon Dispatch Box, 2000), pp. 137–84.

[60] Ibid.   [61] 'Drama', *Athenaeum* (19 May 1906), p. 619.

Fig. 2.1. 'Raffles, The Amateur Cracksman, at the Comedy', *Sketch* (30 May 1906), p. 4. Victoria and Albert Museum Theatre and Performance Collections [VAM] (cutting in file Comedy: Raffles 12 May 1906). Reproduced by kind permission, @ Victoria and Albert Museum, London.

The Sketch (Fig. 2.1). The Comedy Theatre was located on Panton Street in the heart of London's West End where middle-class women regularly attended the theatre in the Edwardian period, albeit in the company of an escort to maintain their respectability.[62] Supplying female viewers with Maurier as 'eye candy', as well as the spark of romance and someone with whom to identify in the form of glamorous female accomplice Gwen, the 1906 *Raffles* gave a strong reflection of changing cultural attitudes towards women's agency in British social, political, and domestic life.

Travelling to London to warn Raffles that Detective Bedford was on the trail, and facilitating the burglar's escape by helping him get out of a window and use the carriage in which she arrived, Gwen encouraged women viewers to envision collaboration with the gentleman-burglar as synonymous with wealth, love, and excitement.[63] Though never committing burglary herself (which would have been unthinkable—see Chapter 3), Gwen's role was nevertheless evocative of women's gradually improving autonomy in a period that saw both the intensification of the campaign for women's suffrage and changing ideals of women's employment in the

---

[62] Tracy C. Davis, *Actresses as Working Women: Their Social Identity in Victorian Culture* (London: Routledge, 1991), pp. 137–81; Viv Gardner, 'The Invisible Spectatrice: Gender, Geography and Theatrical Space', in Maggie B. Gale and Viv Gardner (eds.), *Women, Theatre and Performance: New Histories, New Historiographies* (Manchester: Manchester University Press, 2000), pp. 25–45.

[63] Hornung and Presbrey, *Raffles*, pp. 180–3.

labour force as 'liberating'.[64] Women also wielded increasing power as consumers, notably in the emergent market for romance fiction heralded by the arrival of publishing phenomenon Mills and Boon, from which vogue the introduction of Gwen's character clearly sought to profit.[65] This impression can only have been compounded for audiences by casting Jessie Bateman in the role of Gwen. A woman so beautiful she featured in *Strand Magazine*'s list of the one hundred most beautiful women of the previous century in December 1906, Bateman was described as an 'accomplished actress' who had 'scored many successes at the Haymarket and other theatres'.[66] Again playing with the boundaries between fact and fiction, the allure of the character was enhanced by a famous beauty whose publicized personality and lifestyle held comparable motifs of glamour and independence.

Gerald du Maurier, as his daughter Daphne later recorded, similarly embodied Raffles in a way that maximized the audience's emotional investment in his fate. In his first big stage success, du Maurier

> brought something to it that was personal and unique—a suggestion of extreme tension masked by casual gaiety—making of Raffles someone highly strung, nervous, and finely drawn, yet fearless and full of a reckless and rather desperate indifference, someone who by the force of his high spirits had developed a kink in his nature.[67]

This technique, along with du Maurier's good looks, proved a hit with theatregoers and critics alike. 'In the warmth of his love-making and the coolness he displayed in the presence of danger Mr. Du Maurier is equally admirable, and to him the popularity of the whole is mainly due', approved *The Athenaeum*, reflected in the year-long run of the play at The Comedy.[68] It was the making of the actor's career. By December 1914, when du Maurier chose to revive and star again as Raffles at Wyndham's Theatre on Leicester Square (which he managed), reviewers felt him necessary to cope with Raffles' moral and legal deficiencies, and make them attractive. As *Play Pictorial*'s theatre critic B. W. Findon wrote,

> the gracious personality of Mr. Gerald du Maurier is a most admirable cloak for any villainy that might be attempted and carried out . . . as [Raffles] is presented by Mr. du Maurier we cannot but feel a sneaking regard for the man who so wantonly and treacherously betrays the generous hospitality of his host.[69]

Here, Findon not only applauded du Maurier's ability to ameliorate the burglar's 'villainous' character but also his portrayal of the crime itself, suggesting, somewhat shockingly, that audiences had enjoyed watching how the burglary was effected as much as they had admired the acting. Findon's expression for this—'a sneaking regard'—exposes his awareness of having participated in an experience

---

[64] Joyce Senders Pederson, 'Victorian Liberal Feminism and the "Idea" of Work', in Krista Cowman and Louise Jackson (eds.), *Women and Work Culture: Britain c.1850–1950* (Aldershot: Ashgate Publishing, 2005), pp. 27–47.   [65] Dixon, *Romance Fiction*.

[66] 'Our "100 Picture Gallery"', *Strand Magazine* (Dec. 1906), pp. 680–1.

[67] Daphne du Maurier, *Gerald: A Portrait* (1934: reprinted London: Virago, 2004), p. 90.

[68] 'Drama', *Athenaeum* (19 May 1906), p. 619; du Maurier, *Gerald*, p. 92.

[69] B. W. Findon, 'Raffles', *Play Pictorial* 25 (Nov. 1914), p. 88.

which, though staged for the purposes of entertainment, served to legitimize the glorification of crime.[70]

Certainly, when the story was revived again in 1914 for the theatre it marked an important moment at which Raffles could (perhaps should?) feasibly have been rejected by both the state and the theatregoing public. During the intervening years after the play's 1906 success Prime Minister Herbert Asquith set up a Joint Committee to review the laws guiding theatre censorship, in 1909 deciding that the Lord Chamberlain should reject any play 'calculated to conduce to crime or vice'.[71] The Lord Chamberlain's permission for the 1906 play had already been criticized in some quarters as 'inconsistent'.[72] *Academy* reported that in a 1907 debate about censorship at the liberal Playgoer's Club in London its chair, Marshall Hall, K.C., opined that 'the undoubtedly amusing play of *Raffles* (which throws a halo of romance round crime) did far more harm than a work dealing seriously with the problems of sex'.[73] One might have expected that the international situation would have exerted its own subduing influence. After war broke out in August 1914, British theatre, as historian Gordon Williams remarks, 'became concerned not just to entertain but to mobilise; and theatre-goers were invited to drop their inhibitions and submit to the great swelling mood of national solidarity'.[74] What place had a figure like Raffles among plays encouraging national solidarity?

Quite simply, he didn't. On the front cover of a programme issued for the 1914 production at Wyndham's, Raffles remained a literally 'dark' presence in the spectrum of central protagonists (Fig. 2.2). Silhouetted in black against the yellow light of a presumably domestic interior, the sinister aspect of his intrusion into the home is magnified by the obscuration of his face and hands, intimating that the burglar's very flesh is consonant with the shadow that fails to engulf his shirt, bowtie, and sleeve-cuffs. Picked out in contrastingly lurid white, these details of Raffles' attire serve to visually reiterate the paradox at the heart of the criminal's narrative: his gentlemanly alter-ego. With the names of Wyndham's, du Maurier, and Raffles a slick blood-red, nothing in the image suggested a redemptive theme, nor diminished the glamour associated with the character and his crimes against property and privilege.

Maintaining Raffles' glamorous criminality during this period of international crisis denotes the middle classes' continued enthrallment with 'exciting' forms of burglary in this era. As an ideological position it seems somewhat ironic given that the Edwardian period saw a progressively more economically stable, prosperous middle class for whom the security of the domestic space and the accumulation of valuable possessions were paramount.[75] Suburban bliss in practice meant stressful

[70] This evokes Anna Clark's metaphor of 'twilight moments' to describe instances in history when people have engaged in sexual acts deemed 'deviant' and afterwards excused their behaviour on the grounds that it was 'temporary; they returned to their everyday lives, and evaded a stigmatised identity'. Anna Clark, *Desire: A History of European Sexuality* (London: Routledge, 2008), pp. 6–7.

[71] David Thomas, David Carlton, and Anne Etienne, *Theatre Censorship from Walpole to Wilson* (Oxford: Oxford University Press, 2007), pp. 92–6.

[72] 'Life and Letters', *Academy* (14 Dec. 1907), p. 236.   [73] Ibid.

[74] Williams, *British Theatre in the Great War*, p. 13.

[75] Cohen, *Household Gods*, pp. 122–44.

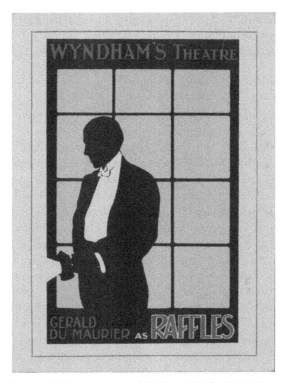

Fig. 2.2. 'Wyndham's 1915', programme (23 Dec. 1914). VAM. Reproduced by kind permission, @ Victoria and Albert Museum, London.

competition for social enhancement, however. Homeowners vied ceaselessly to acquire material belongings and decorations that would suitably equal, or better, those of their neighbours.[76] Burglary may well have seemed like a good solution in this context, and the continuing existence of an audience for the Raffles narrative was confidently assumed by interwar film distributors, who cheerfully marketed six successive films about Raffles made between 1917 and 1939.[77]

Cinema was a more 'democratic' form of entertainment, attracting large working-class audiences of mixed gender from its inception in the early 1900s.[78] Perhaps in response to cinemas' larger audience, Raffles' moral compass was tempered in films made during the immediate post-war years, with the burglar using the profits of his burglaries to make philanthropic 'donations' to the poor and deserving. At the close of *Raffles* (King Bagot, 1925) starring House Peters, Raffles returned Lady Amersteth's pearl necklace to police with strict instructions

[76] Ibid., p. 133.

[77] *Raffles, The Amateur Cracksman* (1917), *Mr Justice Raffles* (1921), *Raffles* (1925), *Raffles* (1930), *The Return of Raffles* (1932), and *Raffles* (1939).

[78] Annette Kuhn, *An Everyday Magic: Cinema and Cultural Memory* (London: I.B. Taurus, 2002), pp. 1–2; Elizabeth Carolyn Miller, *Framed: The New Woman Criminal in British Culture at the Fin-de-Siècle* (Michigan: University of Michigan Press, 2008), pp. 104–5.

that the reward be sent to the Soldiers' Fund.[79] Promoting national unity around the common cause of disabled veterans was canny in a period when political commentators feared the working classes, suffering from the economic depression, would turn to Fascist or Communist political factions finding popularity on the continent. Even criminals, it suggested, recognized their responsibilities towards the poor.[80]

Yet public consumption of these films in Britain (measured in the duration of their cinema screenings in London) suggests that socially conscious alterations to the narrative were not well received. Later films, that allowed Raffles to make off with the loot for his own, self-interested motives, enjoyed greater commercial success.[81] Gwen's diminished participation in Raffles' escape from the law was also a marked feature of less profitable early interwar films. Her role (played by little-known actresses Christine Mayo (1917), Eileen Dennes (1921), and 'Miss DuPont' (1925)) was reduced to a swooning love interest whose sensibilities were shocked by the revelation of her hero's criminal career. Instead of warning Raffles of the detectives' arrival, or assisting his flight, Gwen stood by silently and watched. Burglary was the ultimate threat to domestic harmony, representing a loss of security both physical and symbolic, as well as an attack on material possessions, from which 'respectable' middle-class women should recoil in horror. In reality, this revulsion seemed far from the feelings of a new generation of female cinema-goers: financially independent working-class women, whose expanding opportunities for employment in shops, factories, and offices established them as 'breadwinners' in the home, with all the pressures that entailed.[82] Recycling the lovers into law-abiding citizens meant the failure of these early films, which ignored (at their peril) the anti-authoritarian sensibilities and desire to be freed from everyday stresses and strains of a largely working-class audience.[83]

The phenomenal box-office success of Samuel Goldwyn's 1930 'talking' film *Raffles*, starring English actor Ronald Colman, proved the rule. No penitent speeches or charitable 'donations' redeemed this version. Two burglary scenes saw Raffles procure a bracelet for fiancé Gwen and a diamond necklace to ease Bunny's debts, before escaping justice through a secret passage in a grandfather clock. Indeed, the film's approval by the British Board of Film Censors was surprising, since it so flagrantly challenged their remit to prevent the 'demoralization' of the British viewing public.[84] With a 'record-breaking' eleven-week run at London's

[79] *Raffles* (1925).

[80] Paul Ward, *Britishness since 1870* (London: Routledge, 2004), pp. 102–3; Roper, *The Secret Battle*, pp. 286–9.

[81] Irving's film was screened from 23–27 Sept. 1918; Hepworth's *Mr Justice Raffles* (1921) ran from 24–25 July 1922; and King Bagot's film ran from 18–26 May 1925. 'Entertainments', *Daily Mail* (23 Sept. 1918), 2; 'Entertainments', *Daily Mail* (27 Sept. 1918), 2; 'Entertainments', *The Times* (24 July 1922), 10; 'Entertainments', *The Times* (25 July 1922), 12; 'Entertainments', *Daily Mail* (18 May 1925), 8; 'Entertainments', *Evening Standard* (26 May 1925), 10.

[82] Selina Todd, 'Young Women, Work, and Leisure in Interwar England', *Historical Journal* 48 (2005), pp. 789–809.

[83] Miller, *Framed*, pp. 114–15.

[84] *Raffles* (1930); Jeffrey Richards, 'The British Board of Film Censors and Content Control in the 1930s: Images of Britain', *Historical Journal of Film, Radio and Television* 1 (1981), p. 96.

Tivoli cinema on the Strand, the film critics showered it with praise, declaring that *Raffles* 'catches the real spirit of E.W. Hornung's famous stories', and comparing Colman's portrayal to that of du Maurier's.[85] Like du Maurier, Colman's matinee-idol looks played no small part in *Raffles*' commercial success. Among a series of adverts featured in popular newspapers the *Evening Standard*, *Daily Mirror*, and *Daily Express*, one (Fig. 2.3) was dominated entirely by Colman's brooding visage, positioned above the tagline 'Wanted for Robbery of Safes and Women's Hearts'.[86] Another advert featured in the *Evening Standard* on 29 August 1930 read simply 'Scoundrel! But you can't help liking him', permitting audiences to suspend their morals literally 'in the face' of the gorgeous Colman.[87]

Gwen (played by Kay Francis) also regained some of the autonomy she had lost since theatrical versions, calmly assisting Raffles' escape at the film's conclusion. Francis was voted America's best-dressed woman that year, daringly sporting cropped black hair which, as the magazine *Picture Show* noted, almost cost her a career in cinema due to the demand for blondes. Newly emboldened Gwen was a perfect fit for the actress, hailed by the magazine as a woman who 'gets her own way'.[88] *Raffles*' gleeful return to the handsome burglar and his beautiful lover purloining riches from wealthy victims reflected how closely filmmakers were attuned to their audience, whose economic fortunes were taking a nosedive during the early 1930s. After the global depression caused by the Wall Street Crash of 1929, cinema made a concerted effort to identify with (and cater to the fantasies of) audiences struggling to make ends meet, including working-class unemployed seeking cheap entertainment.[89] Not everyone may have been pleased with the latest celebration of Raffles' misadventures, however. As the Home Office's annual *Judicial Statistics* reports of the incidence of crime in England and Wales asserted, burglary had, on average, experienced a statistical increase over the interwar period.[90] Some were sufficiently perturbed to publicly question police efficiency, with one M.P. asking the House of Commons in April 1931 whether 'for the better protection of the public' they could 'arrange that the police pay less attention to motor cars [referring to a spate of driving offences] and more attention to burglars?'[91]

Domestic crime rates had little effect on filmmakers' desire to appease audiences' fantasies of rebellion. Global warfare was another matter. In 1939, on the eve of the Second World War, the last *Raffles* film was made. Produced again by Samuel Goldwyn, the plot closely imitated its predecessor until the ending, which witnessed

---

[85] R. H., 'New Films', *Manchester Guardian* (12 July 1930), p. 15; 'Tivoli Cinema: Mr. Ronald Colman in "Raffles"', *The Times* (5 Aug. 1930), p. 8; 'Ronald as "Raffles"', *News of the World* (13 July 1930), p. 5.

[86] *Evening Standard* (10 Sept. 1930), p. 4; *Evening Standard* (27 Aug. 1930), p. 4; *Evening Standard* (17 Sept. 1930), 4; *Daily Mirror* (6 Aug. 1930), p. 17; *Daily Mirror* (1 Sept. 1930), p. 21; *Daily Express* (2 Oct. 1930), p. 10.

[87] *Evening Standard* (29 July 1930), p. 4.

[88] 'Kay Francis', *Picture Show Supplement* (5 July 1930), p. 14.

[89] Dan LeMahieu, *A Culture for Democracy: Mass Communication and the Cultivated Mind in Britain between the Wars* (Oxford: Oxford University Press, 1988), pp. 236–53, 243.

[90] HCPP, Cmd. 6167, *Judicial Statistics, England and Wales* (London, 1938), p. 16.

[91] HCPP, *Hansard*, 5th ser., 15 Apr. 31, vol. 251, p. 181.

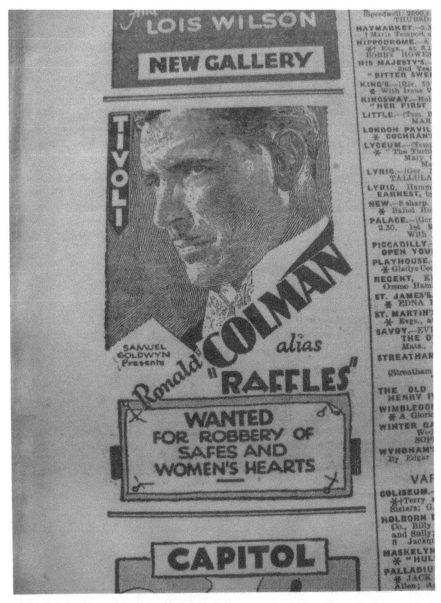

Fig. 2.3. Display Advertising, *Evening Standard* (10 Sept. 1930), p. 4. Reproduced by kind permission © The British Library Board.

a dramatic turn of events. Raffles, now played by English actor David Niven, disappeared into the London fog with the stated intention of turning himself in to Inspector Mackenzie. The modified ending resulted from pressure on Goldwyn by American censors in the Hays Office to display the moral standards appropriate to the international situation. Bunny's character also fell foul of their moralizing, which transformed him from loyal accomplice into a young army officer who blatantly disapproved of Raffles' activities.[92] With the heroic Niven in the lead, whose duty to country was indisputable after he left filming to join the Rifle Brigade before *Raffles* completed, the menace to public virtue represented by the 1939 film seemed fairly tame.[93] Yet for British audiences, as the *Daily Mirror*'s film critic Reginald Whitley observed, Niven's war service served to compound the moral ambiguity of Raffles: 'I am afraid this picture will have a devastating moral effect, for what chance does law and order have when a criminal is portrayed by a handsome young man who in real life sacrifices fame and fortune to fight for his country.'[94]

The moral implications of *Raffles*' conclusion were also complex. Reviewers in magazines *Picture Show* and *Picturegoer and Film Weekly* highlighted how Raffles' surrender to Mackenzie was the result of his love for Gwen (played by *Gone with the Wind* actress Olivia de Havilland), in no measure enhancing the stature or efficacy of the police, or thereby, the supremacy of the state.[95] The *Daily Mail*'s film critic—whose conservative reaction against the film might usually have been taken for granted—pooh-poohed censors' fears, groaning 'I could not fathom the Hollywooden ending which makes Raffles surrender to Scotland Yard. This business of sending heroes and heroines off to serve a prison sentence is becoming positively monotonous.'[96] Gracing London's Regal Cinema Theatre at Marble Arch for a respectable three and a half weeks from 25 March to 19 April 1940, *Raffles* neither obliterated the reckless allure of the gentleman-thief nor fully embraced it; neither capitulated to the law, nor undermined its orchestration.[97] As the farewell appearance of the burglar, who would not be given dramatic life in Britain for another thirty years, *Raffles* betrayed tensions between American and British filmmakers' and censors' ideas about the relationship between popular depictions of criminality and British national values. Although Raffles drew attention to Britain's inequalities of wealth and social status, few would wish to see him captured, a feature of British national identity that was unchanged in the face of international threat.

There were real, criminal implications to Raffles' popularity, though. It started with the press. Converting the name 'Raffles' into a label which connoted the character's skilful and predominantly non-violent *modus operandi*, penchant for stealing from the wealthy, and enjoyment of his victims' lifestyle, the British press used it as a synonym for real-life burglars in forty-seven instances I have discovered throughout the period 1905–39.[98] Headlines such as 'Raffles of the Paintpot'

---

[92] *Raffles* (1939); Sheridan Morley, *David Niven: The Other Side of the Moon* (Sevenoaks: Hodder and Stoughton, 1986), p. 144.

[93] 'David Niven is a Subaltern', *Evening Standard* (4 Mar. 1940), p. 5; 'Easter Egg Films', *Daily Mirror* (21 Mar. 1940), p. 17.

[94] Reginald Whitley, 'He Puts Army before Films', *Daily Mirror* (20 Mar. 1940), p. 7.

[95] Ibid.; 'Raffles', *Picture Show* (4 May 1940), p. 13; Lionel Collier, 'Reviews', *Picturegoer and Film Weekly* (4 May 1940), p. 10.

[96] 'Raffles—Regal', *Daily Mail* (23 Mar. 1940), p. 10.

[97] 'Picture Theatres', *Evening Standard* (25 Mar. 1940), p. 10; 'Picture Theatres', *Evening Standard* (19 Apr. 1940), p. 10.

[98] '"Raffles" and his Valet', *News of the World* (22 Oct. 1905), p. 5; 'Gentleman Burglar', *Daily Express* (13 Feb. 1906), p. 5; 'Parisian Raffles', *Daily Express* (6 Aug. 1906), p. 1; 'Raffles of the Paintpot', *Daily Mirror* (2 Jan. 1907), p. 4; '"Raffles" in Real Life', *Daily Express* (30 Mar. 1907), p. 1; 'Another Paris Raffles', *Daily Express* (30 Sept. 1907), p. 1; 'Raffles in Real Life', *Daily Express* (27 June

(a decorator turned thief, *Daily Mirror*, 1907); 'An Office Boy as Raffles' (*Daily Express*, 1908); or 'Disciples of Raffles' (*Scotsman*, 1926), 'Raffles' was used within a range of newspapers encompassing the *Daily Express*, *Daily Mirror*, *Daily Telegraph*, *News of the World*, *The Times*, *Manchester Guardian*, *Daily Mail*, *Scotsman*, *Observer*, *John Bull*, and the *Evening Standard*. Commonly enthusing about burglars' 'daring' and skill, the sheer variety of newspapers in which this occurred indicates the cross-class imagining of Raffles both as a figure of popular entertainment and as criminal 'type'.

Newspapers also applied the epithet liberally. 'Raffles of the Paintpot' demonstrated how a working-class tradesman became an acceptable candidate for the name. Class and race were no barriers to 'achievement' in the sphere of criminal activity. In nine reports the burglars referred to operated in countries outside Britain, including France, Switzerland, Germany, Serbia, and America. Internationally, newspapers picked up on the name. Disseminated with the same usage throughout press reports in Ireland, France, Holland, Australia, and America, Raffles became an internationally recognized persona, from whose attractive reputation burglars could acquire a more forgiving public identity.[99] It was a dangerous trend. In 1916, American penal reformer Lewis Edward MacBrayne, writing collaboratively with former Massachusetts probation officer James Petrie Ramsay, authored a treatise on first offenders' motives that directly blamed the Raffles phenomenon for legitimizing burglary among the poor. The pair described the moment when one young

---

1908), p. 5; 'An Office Boy as Raffles', *Daily Express* (7 Nov. 1908), p. 5; 'Memoirs of a Real Raffles', *Daily Mirror* (28 Apr. 1909), p. 5; 'A Swiss Raffles', *Daily Express* (20 Apr. 1914), p. 1; '"Old Man" with Four Legs', *Daily Express* (12 Jan. 1916), p. 7; 'Raffles in Real Life', *Daily Express* (14 June 1919), p. 6; 'Gentleman Cracksman', *Daily Telegraph* (11 Dec. 1921), p. 1; 'Gentleman Cracksman', *News of the World* (11 Dec. 1921), p. 1; 'Gentleman Burglar's Smart Clientele', *The Times* (17 Jan. 1922), p. 10; 'Raffles as Art Connoisseur', *Daily Express* (19 Jan. 1922), p. 9; 'Jewel Thieves Busy', *The Times* (8 Feb. 1922), p. 7; 'Berlin "Raffles"', *The Times* (17 June 1922), p. 7; '"Gentleman" Burglar's Astounding Career', *Daily Express* (4 Dec. 1922), p. 2; 'A French "Raffles"', *The Times* (22 Jan. 1923), p. 9; 'A Paris "Raffles"', *Manchester Guardian* (23 Jan. 1923), p. 9; 'Burglar's £1,200 Haul', *Daily Mirror* (9 Jan. 1924), p. 3; '"Raffles" in the Box', *News of the World* (16 Mar. 1924), p. 3; 'A Modern Raffles', *Daily Herald* (30 July 1924), p. 6; '"Raffles" Story in Court', *Daily Herald* (23 Aug. 1924), p. 5; 'Sword of "Bobs"', *News of the World* (31 May 1925), p. 14; 'Clergyman's Son as Raffles', *Glasgow Weekly News* (13 June 1925), p. 7; 'Copying "Raffles"', *Daily Mail* (17 Aug. 1926), p. 5; 'Disciples of Raffles', *Scotsman* (15 Oct. 1926), p. 3; 'Two Young Fools', *Daily Mirror* (15 Oct. 1926), p. 2; 'Exploit of a "Raffles"', *Daily Herald* (3 Feb. 1927), p. 2; 'Courteous Thief Surrenders', *Daily Express* (14 Apr. 1927), p. 9; 'Raffles the Second', *John Bull* (2 July 1927), p. 13; 'Raffles in Belgrade', *Observer* (10 July 1927), p. 12; 'A Plum-Coloured Plunderer', *John Bull* (24 Dec. 1927), p. 11; 'Beware the Motor Raffles', *Evening Standard* (15 Nov. 1927), p. 5; 'A Modern Raffles', *Scotsman* (25 Sept. 1928), p. 10; 'Capture of U.S. "Raffles"', *Daily Express* (23 Oct. 1929), p. 8; '"Raffles" as a Knight Errant', *Daily Express* (28 Aug. 1930), p. 1; 'London Hunt for a "Raffles"', *Daily Express* (3 Sept. 1930), p. 9; 'Armed Burglar in a Bedroom', *The Times* (10 July 1931), p. 8; 'Hunt for a "Raffles"', *Daily Mirror* (5 Nov. 1931), p. 3; 'Beauty and the Burglar', *Daily Express* (22 Apr. 1932), p. 3; 'Prison for Student', *Scotsman* (12 June 1932), p. 14; 'Burglary in the Grand Manner', *News of the World* (9 Oct. 1932), p. 17; '"Life's Grand" Says Convict', *Daily Express* (9 Mar. 1936), p. 11; 'Guest of Star He Robbed', *Daily Mirror* (28 Mar. 1939), p. 3.

[99] See 'A Criminal Prodigy', *Irish Times* (7 Nov. 1934), p. 13; 'Une Etrange Figure', *Le Figaro* (27 Feb. 1925), p. 1 [my thanks to Olivia Luce for translating this]; 'De bankierszoon als inbreker', *Het Nieuws Van Den Dag Voor Nederlandsch-Indië* (21 Aug. 1911), p. 6 [my thanks to Sebastiaan van Shaik for translating this]; '"Cat" Burglar: A Modern Raffles', *Brisbane Courier* (11 Nov. 1927), p. 8; 'Feminine Raffles Comes to Grief', *Los Angeles Times* (23 June 1927), p. 7.

clerk-turned-burglar, unemployed due to the changing 'business conditions' of the company he worked for, read Hornung's *The Amateur Cracksman*: 'The ingenious, cynical appeal of the apparently respectable Raffles got him as though the amateur cracksman had been in the room talking to him.'[100]

In Britain, such was the concern these reports generated within the Home Office that in 1909 they attributed the increase in burglary during the previous decade to press and fiction 'beguiling the lieges with fantastic pictures of a Raffles or Arsène Lupin [the French equivalent of Raffles]...the modern criminal is vested with some of the romance that with more reason belonged to the highwayman of old'.[101] Over time, 'Raffles' was embraced as a synonym for certain categories of burglar within the criminological lexicon. Describing the techniques of the 'modern burglar' in his 1923 book *Sidelights on Criminal Matters*, scientific criminologist John Goodwin explained that 'If the door is locked, and should its key not remain in the lock the modern Raffles tries his skeleton keys'.[102] Comparably, in 1926 ex-Chief Inspector of the Criminal Investigation Department at Scotland Yard Charles Arrow wrote in his memoirs that 'There are cracksmen of the Raffles type, who do not jeopardise their liberty every week or every month', going on to add that these 'first grade' burglars led 'a gentlemanly existence'.[103] Although Goodwin and Arrow's intentions may well have been to engage a popular readership for their accounts, their affirmation of Raffles as a 'type' of burglar authorized the idea of an attractive criminal, challenging the moral premise of the judicial code upon which, ironically, their careers depended.

Astute burglars perceived the sentimental and financial gains to be made by drawing comparisons between themselves and Raffles. On his release from prison in 1929 George Smithson, a burglar active in London and the south-east counties between the years 1910 and 1923, wrote an autobiography entitled *Raffles in Real Life*, published in 1930.[104] Basing himself in a 'luxurious flat in Kensington', Smithson, in his own words, 'graduated from a middle-class cracksman to a Raffles of the gentleman type. My methods, like those of most burglars, were ruthless yet genteel, unscrupulous but discriminating.'[105] In keeping with these claims, the convicted criminal was at pains to emphasize that he only stole from the rich, 'perusing the Society columns of *The Times* seeking news of their movements', and numbering published lists of the wealthy in *Debrett's* and *Burke's Landed Gentry* amongst his 'most treasured possessions'.[106] His description stands in stark contrast to that dealt out by the Chief of the Criminal Records Office, who pronounced Smithson as having 'remarkable impudence' and as being a 'persistent and troublesome burglar'.[107]

---

[100] Lewis E. MacBrayne and James E. Ramsay, *One More Chance: An Experiment in Human Salvage* (Boston: Small, Maynard and Co., 1916), p. 44.

[101] HCPP, Cd. 5473, 5501, *Judicial Statistics, England and Wales* (London, 1909), pp. 10–11.

[102] John Goodwin, *Sidelights on Criminal Matters* (London: Hutchinson and Co., 1923), p. 66.

[103] Charles Arrow, *Rogues and Others* (London: Duckworth Press, 1926), p. 44.

[104] TNA, HO 144/11473, document 254.529/30, 'Convict Report on Completion of 4 Years' (1 Aug. 1927); Smithson, *Raffles in Real Life*.

[105] Smithson, *Raffle in Real Life*, pp. 17–18.   [106] Ibid., p. 17.

[107] TNA, HO 144/11473, Letter stamped 'HOME OFFICE—7 JAN. 1930. RECEIVED, numbered 254.529/33'.

Smithson's motives, at first glance, appear purely commercial. But transforming himself into Raffles afforded him a vital source of income after a life of crime, and gave him a means to reassert, for public and private absolution, a more attractive alter-ego in the grim aftermath of his fall from grace. As he commented forlornly in the concluding paragraph recalling his final entry into prison, 'No longer was I Gentleman George, the modern Raffles. I had now become a marked, tabulated, and registered unit in one of His Majesty's prisons.'[108] Smithson's ability to slip between real-life and fictional personas gave him a chance to adopt the fictive Raffles as a narrative that offered him 'composure'; a version of his life with which he could be reconciled, and comfortably offer up to public scrutiny.[109] Luckily, the interwar period witnessed a number of these 'slippages'.[110] Just as Sherlock Holmes was sometimes thought to be a real person (more so than his author) in this era, Raffles' fame, and appropriation by press and criminologists as a new 'category' of criminal, made such imaginative leaps possible.[111] Moving beyond the culture of pleasure that Hornung's creation drew to burglary, Raffles became an icon in the purest sense: one whose 'life' resonated with the needs, experiences, and identities of generations.

*   *   *

Reminiscing in 1975 about first reading Hornung's Raffles stories as a boy, playwright Graham Greene (born 1904), asserted how he had 'loved the books' but admitted in the same breath 'these men were criminals—they should not be glorified'.[112] Pressed by BBC Radio Four interviewer Ronald Harwood about whether Greene 'had gone on to compound the felony' by making Raffles the star of his own new play *The Return of A. J. Raffles*, premiered at the Aldwych Theatre, London on 4 December 1975, Greene hastily demurred 'Well I've adapted very very loosely—this is not an adventure of Raffles which Hornung wrote'.[113] Seventy-seven years after 'The Ides of March' first appeared in *Cassell's Magazine*, Greene was more confident discussing how his play brought out the 'latent homo-sexuality' he perceived in the original characters of Raffles and Bunny than explor-ing Raffles' unrepentant criminality.[114]

That same year, Yorkshire Television Ltd produced a pilot episode of a new TV dramatization of Raffles starring Anthony Valentine, aired on BBC One. Leading to two series that ran for fourteen episodes from 1975–7, this production cloaked its villainy in a strictly Edwardian historical setting rather than updating the char-acters for a 1970s context. Consequently, as the *Guardian*'s reviewer opined, 'It is

---

[108] Smithson, *Raffles*, p. 242.

[109] Penny Summerfield, 'Culture and Composure: Creating Narratives of the Gendered Self in Oral History Interviews', *Cultural and Social History* 1:1 (2004), pp. 65–93.

[110] Houlbrook, 'A Pin to See the Peepshow', p. 223.

[111] Saler, 'Clap if You Believe in Sherlock Holmes'.

[112] BBC, TX 03/12/1975, Script of interview 'Kaleidoscope Special: Graham Greene in con-versation with Ronald Harwood the day before the world premiere of his play THE RETURN OF A. J. RAFFLES', BBC Radio 4 (3 Dec. 1975), p. 2.

[113] Ibid.   [114] Ibid., pp. 2–3.

all very relaxing and that turn-of-the-century setting has that lushness which is so soothing to the threadbare viewer'.[115] Just as Greene reconciled himself to resurrecting Raffles by fashioning an entirely new plot around the emerging gay civil rights movement, Yorkshire Television ensured the 'distance' between viewers and Raffles through their temporal setting. Neither were willing to fully revive the burglar's uniquely pleasurable criminality, or run the same risks of inspiring viewers that Hornung, filmmakers, and the press had run before the Second World War.

Their reluctance graces the preceding period 1898–1939 with a particular mischievousness, a time when Ernest Hornung's creation was afforded a license to flirt with dangerous, glamorized representations of burglary that anticipated the country's nervous awareness of festering social and economic inequality. Acting as a conduit through which increasingly heterogeneous audiences could vicariously enjoy illicit material gain and the lifestyle of the upper classes, the commercial success of Raffles underpinned this broader challenge. Raffles' acceptability was, however, predicated upon his romantic characterization, gentlemanly persona, and refusal to employ violence. These 'virtues' facilitated a culture of pleasure around the burglar that could be reconciled within a more fluid moral spectrum within public attitudes towards crime than historians commonly assume existed.

Because of this, Raffles provides a unique figure whose various incarnations allow historians to examine the historically specific relationship between factual and fictional accounts of crime. Lover and (sometimes unwitting) accomplice Gwen significantly enhanced Raffles' appeal, bringing forth the romance and mitigating the homosocial, public school boys' vibe of earlier renditions of the story for women audiences. Her involvement was always heavily constrained; Gwen's test of loyalty, love, and morality was a snap decision at the close, a statement of a woman's devotion rather than a wholehearted embrace of burglary. Many audience members may have wondered why, for after all, women criminals certainly existed. Yet in the eyes of novelists, playwrights, film directors, and judges, women were *not* burglars, criminals who made the ultimate affront to the sanctity of homes and who dominated the night-time city with such panache. Could women be burglars? It is this question that the next chapter explores.

---

[115] *Raffles* (United Kingdom: Yorkshire Television Ltd, dirs. Christopher Hodson, David Cunliffe, and Alan Gibson, aired 1975–7); Nancy Banks-Smith, 'Raffles and Bunny', *Guardian* (26 Feb. 1977), p. 8.

3

Marvellous Mrs Raffles?
The Implausible Woman Burglar

It wasn't at all what Mrs Edith Herbert, or Police Sergeant Jackson, expected to find. Glancing out of the rear window of her house in Wealdstone, north London, one April evening in 1938, Edith spotted an unfamiliar shadow among the hedges in her garden. We can imagine the alarm bells sounding in her mind. She may even have detected signs of a sudden movement as the stranger slunk into a crouching position to better conceal themselves. Either way, it was enough to send Edith running swiftly to her telephone to dial 999 for the police. Jackson was first on the scene. Hauling the unknown intruder out from the hedgerow, he would have felt some satisfaction at hearing the tell-tale jangle from their pockets, as a set of sixteen skeleton keys clashed together with the would-be burglar's electric torch, table knife, and pair of scissors. Possession of these tools alone was enough for a judge to sentence someone to ten years in prison, since the Larceny Act of 1916 had made evidence of intention to commit burglary tantamount to getting caught in the act.[1] Yet something about the prisoner was different from the run-of-the-mill burglar. First, she wore her hair fashionably bobbed. And second, she was a woman.[2]

The very idea, it seemed, was ridiculous. During Sally Nolan's trial for attempted burglary a few days later, the prosecuting counsel reportedly declared that 'She [Nolan] is in almost the unique position of being a genuine woman burglar. She acts by herself on these occasions.'[3] The incredulity implied in his description of Nolan as a 'genuine' woman burglar was only qualified by counsel's suggestion she was 'unique'; apparently, women did not commit burglary. Even more damning was her determination. Nolan had a number of previous convictions, including time spent in prison for a series of burglaries in 1932 and 1935 in the nearby districts of Willesden and Hampstead.[4] Plugging the novelty value for all it was worth (and making a specific appeal to their primarily middle-class female readership), the

---

[1] Anyone discovered carrying such tools at night was required to prove that they had a 'lawful excuse' for it, or their 'intent to commit felony' (whether a robbery or burglary) would be assumed, resulting in a sentence of up to ten years' imprisonment. Larceny Act 1916, Geo. V, ch. 50. ss. 6 & 7.

[2] Narrative compiled from: 'Housemaid "Raffles" Goes Back to Gaol', *Daily Mirror* (8 Apr. 1938), p. 13; 'Woman Burglar's Fifth Conviction', *Daily Telegraph* (10 Mar. 1938), p. 11; 'Woman Burglar', *Daily Mail* (8 Apr. 1938), p. 11.

[3] 'Housemaid "Raffles"', p. 13.

[4] For further details of Nolan's previous convictions, see 'A Woman's Exploits', *News of the World* (25 Sept. 1932), p. 8; LMA, CLA/003/PR/02/20, Convict Nominal Register, Holloway Prison (Mar. 1935—Dec. 1935), entry for Sally Nolan dated 16 Apr. 1935.

Daily Mirror entitled their report on events 'Housemaid "Raffles" Goes Back to Gaol'.[5] Since the working-class housemaid and the gentlemanly 'Raffles' were oxymoronic in terms of both gender and class, and in the servile nature of the maid's relationship to the home, the *Mirror's* headline was delivered with a touch of humour. The juxtaposition was evidently ludicrous; this was not a hardened criminal, but a woman who had overstepped her boundaries. Readers could be reassured that Nolan was a freak.

Women burglars certainly weren't 'the norm', but the suggestion that Nolan was 'unique' was a little excessive. On average, women were defendants in fifteen burglary trials per year in England and Wales during the period 1860 to 1938 (4 per cent of all cases), in contrast with 407 trials of men. Statistics for the gendered composition of crime in London ceased in 1931, but until then indicated that ratio was even lower. Three women were tried for every 120 cases against men over the period in the capital (2 per cent of cases).[6] Burgling alone wasn't unusual. Solo female burglars graced the pages of courtroom testimony from the Old Bailey and occupied the cells of London's all-female Holloway Prison alongside suffragettes.[7] Nearly a quarter of all burglaries committed by women took place in London, suggesting the capital held the same attractions of wealth, opportunity, and anonymity that drew male burglars to its bright lights. Managing independently, in teams of men and women, or as accomplices, women *were* involved in burglary.

Except that they were not. Adamantly refusing to engage with the concept of the woman burglar, commentators dismissed them as rarities, a 'new' phenomenon in the annals of crime (every time one was caught). Trespassing on a domain of crime almost universally regarded as 'masculine', women burglars were thought to have betrayed their nature by undermining the sanctity of 'home'. They needed to be explained away, and, seeking to maintain the traditional ideal of women's heightened emotional investment in the home, middle-class novelists, journalists, playwrights, and filmmakers, as well as police, criminologists, and courtroom officials found reasons to suit. Women burglars had 'troubled' childhoods in 'atypical' family circumstances that had alienated them from a 'normal' appreciation of home. Or, they were tricked or seduced into burglary by the immoral men with whom they had fallen in love. Otherwise, maternal instincts, as well as physical and mental attributes thought to be particularly suited to domestic life, would 'naturally' have prevented them from imperilling the home's security, or the safety of other families.[8]

---

[5] 'Housemaid "Raffles" Goes Back to Gaol', *Daily Mirror* (8 Apr. 1938), p. 13; Adrian Bingham, *Gender, Modernity, and the Popular Press in Interwar Britain* (Oxford: Oxford University Press, 2004), pp. 34–6.

[6] Of 32,896 defendants tried for burglary in England and Wales during the period 1860–1939, 31,802 were men and 1,184 were women. Of 8,744 defendants tried for burglary in the Metropolitan Police District and City of London Jurisdiction during the period 1860–1939, 8,522 were men and 252 women. Data gleaned from House of Commons Parliamentary Papers, annual series *Judicial Statistics for England and Wales* and *Report of the Commissioner of Police of the Metropolis*. For full tables and data, see Eloise Moss, Unpublished D.Phil Thesis, 'Cracking Cribs; Representations of Burglars and Burglary in London, 1860–1939', University of Oxford, 2013.

[7] See full list of Calendars of Prisoners consulted from H.M.P. Holloway, Appendix.

[8] Vickery discusses middle-class attitudes to the woman as 'angel in the home' in prescriptive texts at length: Vickery, 'Golden Age to Separate Spheres', pp. 384–7; see also Joanna Bourke's account of

It was a reasoning that stayed remarkably static over the late nineteenth and early twentieth century. For some, it was a convenient excuse. Decades before Nolan's exploits were revealed to the nation, Sarah Hooper stood on trial with her husband Charles for a burglary at Leyton, east London, in May 1882. With proceedings drawing to a close, her statement to the court was simply to claim 'All that I have done has been under my husband's instructions'. This was despite witness testimony of her pawning stolen goods, and a contradictory account of her movements.[9] Sarah's instincts won through.[10] Charles was sentenced to five years in prison; Sarah to six months' hard labour. It is hard not to admire her perspicacity. Denial about women's participation in burglary formed part of a reaction against the changing landscape of women's increasing social, sexual, and political agency. During the 1880s, movements had grown demanding women's equal right to own property within marriage, women's right to enhanced school education and ability to take and be awarded degrees, women's right to a minimum wage, and women's access to a wider range of employment opportunities. These campaigns, along with agitation to repeal the controversial Contagious Diseases Acts (allowing police to forcibly remove prostitutes from the street and medically inspect them for venereal disease), eventually grew into the women's suffrage movement.[11] The refusal of many in positions of authority to countenance this ferocious slew of women's demands bled into their judgements in the juvenile courts, where young girls showing signs of criminal activity were met with welfare-oriented solutions such as sending them to rescue homes, thereby enabling the state to police the 'morals' of young women under the guise of liberal attitudes.[12] They extended the same approach to women burglars. Trying desperately to arrest the speed at which women seemed to be relinquishing domesticity, courtroom dialogue and sentencing patterns were an important facet of a broader discourse that sought to minimize or obscure women's involvement in the crime. This not only occurred in London and across England and Wales, but also influenced legal practices in British colonial territories such as Australia, where women's involvement in burglary was likewise blamed on men, as

---

working-class women's resistance to these tropes: Joanna Bourke, 'Housewifery in Working-Class England, 1860–1914', *Past and Present* 143 (1994), pp. 167–97.

[9] OBP, 22 May 1882 (t18820522–602).

[10] Although the excuse 'my husband told me to do it' wasn't new, as many other cases attest, its success was particularly distinctive in relation to burglary charges in this period when juxtaposed against women's involvement in other forms of theft (which the courts seem to have been happy to convict them on). Shani D'Cruze and Louise Jackson, *Women, Crime and Justice in England Since 1660* (Basingstoke: Palgrave MacMillan, 2009), ch. 2.

[11] There are many fantastic works on this era of women's history, so I offer just a selection here: Judith R. Walkowitz, *Prostitution and Victorian Society: Women, Class, and the State* (Cambridge: Cambridge University Press, 1982); Susan Kingsley Kent, *Sex and Suffrage in Britain, 1860–1914* (Princeton: Princeton University Press, 1987); Gillian Scott, *Feminism, Femininity and the Politics of Working Women: The Women's Co-Operative Guild, 1880s to the Second World War* (London: Routledge, 2005); Julia Bush, ' "Special Strengths for their Own Special Duties": Women, Higher Education and Gender Conservatism in Late Victorian Britain', *History of Education* 34:4 (2005), pp. 387–405; Krista Cowman, *Women in British Politics, c.1689–1979* (Basingstoke: Palgrave MacMillan, 2010).

[12] Pam Cox, *Bad Girls in Britain: Gender, Justice and Welfare, 1900–1950* (Basingstoke: Palgrave MacMillan, 2002).

historian Alana Piper writes (corresponding with the global nature of the burgeoning women's movement).[13]

Impassioned speeches by suffrage activists such as Emmeline Pankhurst and Millicent Garrett Fawcett had, by the end of the nineteenth century, already made many women question the 'allure' of home and family life. Domesticity frequently offered insufficient reward for a lifetime of sexual obligation, successive and unwanted pregnancies, unrecognized domestic and emotional labour, and restricted opportunities for education and employment. After enduring rallies and hunger strikes followed by force-feeding and violence from police and prison officers, suffragettes and the non-violent suffragists alike had demonstrated that they were more than willing to give up such domestic 'comforts' for their freedom.[14] Finally gaining the right to vote on the same terms as men in 1928 after their partial enfranchisement in 1918, women continued to make gains, becoming members of parliament, removing gender barriers to certain occupations, and choosing to have smaller families. These developments did not sit well with many contemporaries, who thought that women would destabilize political life and the economy, and literally 'de-moralize' the nation through renouncing family values.[15] Extolling the rarity, 'misguidedness' and 'failures' of the female burglar was another means for them to critique perceived changes in women's 'natural' sphere of labour. Narratives about women burglars therefore ironically formed part of a conservative rhetoric that tried to moderate the pace of change in how women's lives, and abilities, were being viewed, rather than becoming a product of these broader shifts.

Accordingly, economic destitution and a misguided love of adventure, or their male cohorts, were far oftener supposed to lie at the heart of female burglars' actions than pure greed.[16] An orgiastic need to revel in the pleasures of luxury goods— 'kleptomania'—was as completely absent from discussions of burglary as it pervaded analyses of the psyches of nineteenth-century women shoplifters.[17] Class underpinned this absence. When female defendants for burglary gave their occupation

---

[13] Alana Piper's excellent recent work on burglary in nineteenth- and twentieth-century Australia demonstrates striking similarities in attitudes towards gender and burglary as those prevailing in Britain, highlighting that although burglary 'was the fourth most common activity for which women were indicted in Melbourne' in this era, 'women who did commit burglaries were strongly presumed to have been acting under male coercion'. Alana Piper, 'Victimization Narratives and Courtroom Sexual Politics: Prosecuting Male Burglars and Female Pickpockets in Melbourne, 1860–1921', *Journal of Social History* (2018), p. 5.

[14] C. J. Bearman, 'An Examination of Suffragette Violence', *English Historical Review* 120:486 (2005), pp. 365–97; Angela John, " 'Behind the Locked Door": Evelyn Sharp, Suffragette and Rebel Journalist', *Women's History Review* 12:1 (2003), pp. 5–13.

[15] Adrian Bingham, 'An Era of Domesticity? Histories of Women and Gender in Interwar Britain', *Cultural and Social History* 1:2 (2004), pp. 225–33.

[16] My assessment of how female burglars' motivations were perceived contrasts with William Meier's examination of the impetus of working-class female shoplifters in London *c.*1890–1940, which shows their economic interests were considered to fall into the realm of social mobility and the acquisition of the material markers of 'modern, independent womanhood'. Meier, *Property Crime in London*, pp. 67–84.

[17] Angus McLaren, *Sexual Blackmail: A Modern History* (Cambridge, Massachusetts: Harvard University Press, 2002), pp. 164–91; Tammy C. Whitlock, *Crime, Gender, and Consumer Culture in Nineteenth-Century England* (Aldershot: Ashgate Publishing, 2005).

in trial testimony they were found to be overwhelmingly unemployed or destitute. Shoplifting, by contrast, was aligned statistically and imaginatively with women of the middle classes, suffering from constant temptation by their proximity to expensive clothes when employed as shop assistants and laundresses.[18] Making off with gorgeous clothes and jewellery was certainly a recognized impetus for women to burgle, and, when these items were stolen, 'lady' burglars' enjoyment of wearing the goods afterwards was a recurrent motif in both fictional and journalistic tales and in trial transcripts. Yet these delights were usually framed as their having the ability to finally replace old, worn-out garments for new, as opposed to these women hankering after the latest fashions.

Women burglars were thought of differently to other female criminals in Britain in this era. They were not the 'admirable' and elusive creatures that historian Elizabeth Carolyn Miller identifies in turn-of-the-century crime fiction, wherein female criminals tended to be 'altogether less prone to containment and arrest than male criminals'.[19] Offering readers heroines whose intelligence and beauty were venerated as much as their disdain for the law, Miller's heroines might even be suffragettes. They were followed by 'Miss Moriarty' in the 1920s, a label applied by the press and popular criminologists to describe any flapper-esque offender using robbery to achieve social mobility. One such example was Lillian Bernstein, a getaway driver in smash-and-grab robberies during the 1920s who was thought peculiarly 'modern' in her 'enterprising' use of the car for crime. Anxieties about women's greater social freedom and ambition coalesced on 'Miss Moriarty', who embodied the worst fears about the results of women's political emancipation and economic ambition, and was thought on occasion to burgle as well.[20] Fearlessly independent, and using their sexuality as a powerful tool in manipulating others, these criminals were drastically unlike women burglars, who were portrayed haphazardly attempting to commit a crime for which they had neither the skill, athleticism, nor inclination. Sexual attractiveness, as far as women burglars were concerned, led only to marriage once they had realized the error of their ways, drawing them irresistibly towards a reconciliation with domestic life.

Enduring associations between women and home, and the horror that greeted the possibility of female burglars' disregard for these, were not especially surprising in an era when gender relations were undergoing a constant process of renegotiation. The running battle for women's suffrage followed by women's entry into new, 'masculine' occupations such as munitions work during the war destabilized gender roles in ways that each generation wrestled to accept. Combined efforts to frustrate women's links with burglary simply echoed that struggle. Prostitution, shoplifting, and poisoning: these were 'women's crimes', with reassuringly obvious connections to women's uncontrollable sexuality, love of dresses, and diminished capacity for physical violence. Occasional petty thefts and robberies offered little disturbance

---

[18] Meier, *Property Crime in London*, pp. 67–84.   [19] Miller, *Framed*, p. 5.
[20] Charlotte Wildman, 'Miss Moriarty, the Adventuress and the Crime Queen: The Rise of the Modern Female Criminal in Britain, 1918–1939', *Contemporary British History* 30:1 (2016), pp. 73–98.

to the overall pattern.[21] Statistics alone could not account for the tendency to treat every woman burglar as a 'freak', nor could they explain away cultural discourse and sentencing practices that obscured the true extent of women's culpability. Burglars were supposed to be male; clever, strong, athletic, and virile, sometimes sexually predatory or violent. For them, homes were lucrative economic units rather than ideological bastions. These men took ownership of the night-time and the city-scape with a confidence thought alien to women, whose mobility at night had been subject to censure and regulation for centuries. Countenancing the idea that women were just as capable of crossing these lines was a step too far. This chapter histori-cizes the strength of that denial.

*   *   *

On 30 January 1865, Ellen Harrington stood in the dock at the Old Bailey. At just 18 years old, she was accused with John Gavin and Henry Montague of breaking into a house in the salubrious district of St. James's in Westminster. Together the trio had burgled four coats, four pairs of trousers, and other articles valued at £30 (a small fortune roughly equivalent to a year's wages for a street vendor or 'coster-monger' at that time).[22] Ellen had been arrested by a policeman whilst carrying part of the proceeds under her cloak. There were also witnesses to testify that she had been at the scene of the crime; Henry Hart, the victim's neighbour, had observed her accompanying Gavin and Montague leaving the house with a suspicious-looking bundle on the night of 7 January. Still, she didn't concede defeat lightly. Ellen's excuse for being found with the loot was relayed to the court by policeman Henry Dawson: 'Going to the station she said that a young man gave them to her to carry, and was going to give her a shilling, and he ran away just as she came out, and she did not know his name'.[23]

Unable to offer a description of this mystery man, and with her accomplices found guilty and sentenced to seven and ten years respectively, Ellen Harrington's fate looked sealed. Yet, weak as her testimony appeared, for the jury it was compelling. Perhaps in part because of her youth, they were happy to accept the possibility that she had been taken advantage of by Gavin and Montague. Surely only the direst form of poverty—or stupidity—would have made her risk walking about with unknown items for a mere shilling. Ellen was found guilty on a lesser charge of receiving stolen goods. She had even softened the opinion of the prosecutor, who recommended her to mercy. The judge granted his wish, giving her a suspended sentence.

---

[21] William Meier, 'Going on the Hoist: Women, Work, and Shoplifting in London, ca. 1890–1940', *Journal of British Studies* 50:2 (2011), pp. 410–33; Larry Wolff, "'The Boys are Pickpockets, and the Girl is a Prostitute": Gender and Juvenile Criminality in Early Victorian England from *Oliver Twist* to *London Labour*', *New Literary History* 27 (1996), pp. 227–49; Lucia Zedner, *Women, Crime, and Custody in Victorian England* (Oxford: Oxford University Press, 1991); Whitlock, *Crime, Gender, and Consumer Culture*; Katherine Watson, *Poisoned Lives: English Poisoners and their Victims* (London: Hambledon and London, 2004); Walkowitz, *Prostitution and Victorian Society*; Julia Laite, *Common Prostitutes and Ordinary Citizens: Commercial Sex in London, 1885–1960* (Basingstoke: Palgrave MacMillan, 2011).

[22] Earnings calculated from Henry Mayhew's estimate that the average costermonger earned 10 shillings per week, taking account of periods of low trade, ill-health, and bad weather. Henry Mayhew, *London Labour and the London Poor, Vol. 4* (London: Charles Griffin, 1861).

[23] OBP, 30 Jan. 1865 (t18650130–259).

Ellen's lucky escape coincided with a key moment at which the state was making aggressive strides to contain or eradicate the behaviour of those who threatened the middle-class ideology of home, characterized by economic stability, family, religious faith, and monogamy.[24] Prostitutes were their primary target. Legislation introduced by both Liberal and Tory governments during the 1860s enabled police to forcibly remove prostitutes to lock hospitals, where they would have to undergo invasive medical examinations. Designed to prevent the spread of venereal disease to soldiers and members of the navy, the Contagious Diseases Acts of 1864, 1866, and 1869 also punished women for 'facilitating' the satisfaction of men's sexual desires outside the confines of marriage.[25] Incarcerating prostitutes and allowing Ellen to go free were decisions that had similar principles at stake, enacted through different methods. Both prostitutes and female burglars weakened the ideal of women as mothers and wives, fragmenting women's 'inherent' links to domesticity. Just as the prostitute being treated for venereal disease was temporarily absent from the street and posed less 'danger', so the reframing of Ellen's actions as a lesser crime than burglary diminished her scope for embodying a greater threat to the fabric of society. Ellen was reportedly referred by the judge to the 'Ladies Committee of the prison to take steps for her reclamation', suggesting hers was a mere slip-up that could be resolved by more time spent with (middle-class) women.[26]

Denial, containment, and suppression: these were the pillars on which the law chose to treat the 'problem' of women burglars. Cases like Ellen Harrington's were not uncommon, nor was the alibi she gave, which also saved the following women from a burglary charge:

'A man asked me to go and pledge them [the stolen goods].' Mary Ann Chescow, sentenced to four months for receiving (8 April 1861).

'I know nothing about it being stolen property. A man offered me 6d. to carry it, and I thought it no harm.' Catherine Rennie, sentenced to two years imprisonment for receiving (5 May 1873).

'The prisoner in her defence stated that a man stopped her and asked her to take the articles to the Barbican and sell them for old silver.' Caroline Carter, found not guilty of burglary (27 June 1881).[27]

Chescow was accused of a burglary in Clerkenwell, Rennie in King's Cross, and Carter in Islington. These were all wealthy central London areas and well-known burglary 'hot-spots', where the incidence of the crime was common. Only the sex of the defendants threw their guilt into doubt. Victorian courtrooms welcomed 'recognisably stereotyped characters', encouraging witnesses and defendants alike to give an account of themselves that resonated with the dominant model of gender

---

[24] The same reasoning also applied to homosexuals, whose behaviours and desires were viewed as 'anti-domestic' in the same manner as prostitutes, as Matt Cook has described. Cook, *London and the Culture of Homosexuality*, pp. 17–18.

[25] Walkowitz, *City of Dreadful Delight*, pp. 91–3.

[26] 'Central Criminal Court', *Morning Post* (2 Feb. 1865), p. 7.

[27] OBP, 8 Apr. 1861 (t18610408–328); OBP, 5 May 1873 (t18730505–360); OBP, 27 June 1881 (t18810627–636).

relations, or chimed with sympathetic figures from contemporary fiction (in this instance, the 'wronged' heroine).[28] Women's accounts of being propositioned by men on the street fit this mould, since unchaperoned women pedestrians were viewed as being especially vulnerable to sexualized forms of attack.[29] Sometimes this was outlined explicitly in the testimony. In May 1885, Ellen O'Donnell alleged that she had been 'dragged' from a doorway and 'ill-used' by the man who was now prosecuting her for the burglary of his trousers.[30] It might also be inscribed on a woman's body. The clerk of the court made a telling annotation in November 1895, when Marie Stuart Nicholson pleaded that she was only responsible for pawning goods her male partner, Thomas Murray, had burgled: 'This is what he gave me for not getting more than 5s. for it (*pointing to a black eye*)'.[31]

Subtle gradations in the legal treatment of women accused of burglary suggest that their culpability was mapped sensitively onto contemporary understandings of the emotional and social dilemma faced by those 'living in sin' with a man who either couldn't or wouldn't marry.[32] Such women were already 'fallen'. Having lost their virginity outside of marriage, their reputations were already in tatters and, although not quite social outcasts, few options remained but to stay in the relationship whether they wanted to or not.[33] Accordingly, doubts over a woman's guilt in trials for burglary were more pronounced in cases where a lover emerged as a likely suspect. Visibly beaten Marie Stuart Nicholson was discharged from the court after 'The jury recommended her to mercy as they believed she had been very much under Murray's power', having heard testimony that she had been living with Murray since he 'picked her up helpless in Piccadilly'.[34] Similarly, in March 1895 Annie Pearson was given the lighter sentence of four months' hard labour for receiving because the jury declared that 'they believed she was under the influence' of her two male accomplices, Thomas Gannaway and Henry Mahoney, the former with whom she had been cohabiting.[35] Although neither woman was married, judge and jury disregarded their sexual impropriety. Paradoxically, these women being forced into burglary was, it seemed, a greater injury to the courtroom's sensibilities than the absence of a legally defined relationship.

Courtroom judgements that diminished or marginalized women's involvement in burglary increasingly took place alongside debates about their agency as citizens, generated by the emerging women's movement. Control over one's body, sexual relationships, and ability to acquire income independently of men were underlying themes of the campaign to repeal the Contagious Diseases Acts from the mid-1860s. Led by educated and predominantly upper middle-class women philanthropists and charity workers (who would later join the campaign for women's suffrage), this was a landmark moment when women's flair for organizing high-profile petitions and rallies brought visibility to their activity outside the home. Intelligence, organization,

---

[28] D'Cruze, *Crimes of Outrage*, p.149.   [29] Nead, *Victorian Babylon*, pp. 62–73.
[30] OBP, 18 May 1885 (t18850518–375).   [31] OBP, 18 Nov. 1895 (t18951118–16).
[32] Ginger Frost, *Living in Sin: Cohabiting as Husband and Wife in Nineteenth-Century England* (Manchester: Manchester University Press, 2008), p. 23.
[33] Ibid.   [34] OBP, 18 Nov. 1895 (t18951118–16).
[35] OBP, 25 Mar. 1895 (t18950325–320).

and 'daring' were qualities in abundant display among the leaders of this campaign. Yet these characteristics did not translate into questioning women's ability to commit criminal acts that also 'required' these attributes.

Solo women burglars were not 'dangerous', 'daring', or 'independent', like their male counterparts; they were drunk. Mary Buck, found guilty in November 1895 of the burglary of three wooden stands and other goods at a house in Kensington, stated that she had been so drunk she did not remember anything of the incident, and got off with a sentence of three months' hard labour. Typically, there was evidence to contradict Buck's statement. Arresting officer William Guise testified that Buck 'was not drunk at the time—she appeared to know what she had been doing—she could walk straight and speak distinctly'.[36] Nonetheless, Buck's sentence held, mimicking those of two other women burglars who offered the same excuse.[37] While these cases represent a small sample of the whole, they illustrate the mentality of a legal system that preferred to dismiss women's first forays into burglary as uncharacteristic acts stemming from inebriation rather than treat their cases seriously.

Admittedly, there were exceptions. In 1879 Lydia Lloyd was sentenced to ten years for burgling a shawl at a house in Finchley, north London, an unusually severe punishment given the small monetary value of what was stolen. Lloyd was no ordinary criminal, though. Four previous sentences of between twenty-one days and seven years' incarceration for theft since 1867 cast doubt on her claim that she had woken up in the victim's house after a young man had tried to get her drunk. At the age of 36, she no longer 'fit' the idea of the naive, sexually vulnerable 'heroine', and the suggestion of this liaison subverted, rather than reinforced, gender norms.[38] The judge and jury's credulity had run out.

Burglary had been overwhelmingly determined by the media's portrayal of crime and criminal since the era of Charles Peace. Courtroom dialogue and sentencing practices distancing women from burglary conveniently upheld the media's lucrative, cherished version of London's 'professional' male burglars, as well as reflecting the inherent conservatism of the legal system. Newspaper editors made their decision. As long as women only acted as cohorts, their presence in press articles went unremarked other than listing their names among the accused.[39] Lone female burglars were harder to ignore. Thinking strategically, however, journalists allied their newsworthiness to their rarity. Allotting these reports a separate paragraph or column distinguishing them from other police news, editors deployed headings that focused on the sex of the culprit, including 'A Girl Burglar' (1880), 'A Female Burglar' (1889), or 'Woman Accused of Burglary' (1912).[40]

[36] OBP, 18 Nov. 1895 (t18951118–14).
[37] OBP, 13 July 1874 (t18740713–455); OBP, 23 Mar. 1885 (t18850323–432).
[38] TNA, PCOM 4/71/6, 'License Number: 7574. Name: Lydia Lloyd (4 Dec. 1886)', Penal Record 286/79: Lydia Lloyd (27 Feb. 1879). This is the only surviving record of a woman convicted of burglary prior to 1939 in the National Archives.
[39] See for example 'Worship Street: Burglary', *News of the World* (8 Sept. 1867), p. 7; 'Police', *The Times* (9 Apr. 1877), p. 11; 'Central Criminal Court', *The Times* (23 Mar. 1883), p. 8.
[40] See for example 'A Girl Burglar', *Evening Standard* (27 Oct. 1880), p. 6; 'A Female Burglar', *Morning Post* (28 Nov. 1889), p. 6; 'Woman Accused of Burglary', *Daily Mirror* (25 Oct. 1912), p. 4.

Femininity also provided a weapon to attack the credibility of women burglars. Dress, (im)mobility, and youthful beauty were all lampooned successfully in the image of a woman burglar that dominated the front page of the *Illustrated Police News* on 2 April 1898 (Fig. 3.1). Entitled 'A New Thing in Burglary: Women Have Started "Cracking Cribs" ', it not only deliberately misled readers about the 'newness' of women burglars but also made it sound as though such crimes were the result of a passing fancy. Synthesizing two separate reports of women charged with burglaries in Harlesden, north-west London, and Clapham in the south of the capital, the portrait robbed both defendants of gravitas by showing a tightly corseted figure clambering through a window, one shapely leg exposed to reveal billowing layers of frilly lace petticoats.

This was magnified within the accompanying article, where each was described as 'prettily and stylishly dressed' and 'a well-dressed woman'.[41] Vanity not only impeded these women's athleticism, but proved a distraction to the male detective, who was drawn hiding beneath the kitchen table, poised to perform an arrest. Comically, his walking stick—the weapon he would have used to 'subdue' a male burglar— was cast to one side as he ogled, astonished, the burglar's legs. Looking ready to pounce on her unawares, the detective's demeanour gave the scene the impression of a trap, skewing viewers' perception of from whom the danger emanated. In a clever role reversal, the gendered locus of power in the picture by no means resided with the burglar.

The message was clear. Women were both psychologically and physically unfit to succeed in this highly skilled, highly professionalized, 'masculine' arena of crime. Unlike the glamorous, seductive femininity that Miller argues formed part of fictional female criminals' ability to escape justice, female burglars' attempts to use femininity-as-disguise were often shown to backfire.[42] Vera Calvert, charged with burglary at a house in Shepherd's Bush in July 1897, was reportedly dragged to the police station carrying a silver-mounted umbrella and wearing a belt and cape stolen from a house nearby.[43] Stories like these emphasized the alertness of the police to the supposedly clumsy attempts of female burglars to mask their crimes through sartorial bravura, foolishly exhibiting stolen clothes on their person.

Likewise Minnie Pheby, also convicted of burglary in Shepherd's Bush the previous year, was the subject of an opinion piece in the *Daily News* which commented witheringly that 'her booty was no doubt in reels of cotton and slices of jam tart, and her jemmy was probably a knitting needle'. Suggesting that male burglars would be relieved to hear of Pheby's arrest, the article further remarked:

She must have spoiled a whole neighbourhood for larger operations by putting it on the alert... In a healthier state of society a hard-working burglar would have offered her marriage, and she would have been content to leave the struggle for existence to his care.[44]

---

[41] 'A New Thing in Burglary', *Illustrated Police News* (2 Apr. 1898), p. 3.
[42] Miller, *Framed*, p. 48.
[43] 'Alleged Female Burglar', *Lloyd's Weekly Newspaper* (11 July 1897), p. 10.
[44] *Daily News* (26 Feb. 1896), 5. See also OBP, 24 Feb. 1896 (t18960224–243).

A NEW THING IN BURGLARY.
WOMEN HAVE STARTED "CRACKING CRIBS."

Fig. 3.1. *Illustrated Police News* (2 Apr. 1898), p. 1. Reproduced by kind permission © The British Library Board.

Blaming Pheby's burglaries on her unmarried state, the *News* implied that these were the actions of a 'frustrated spinster', a much more comfortable archetype for middle-class readers to rationalize her existence. 'Frustrated spinsters' were, in fact, becoming legion at the fin de siècle, offering an easy explanation for the behaviour of any woman who openly challenged the alignment of their sex with domestic life. The term would later become practically synonymous with the suffragettes, characterized as 'hysterical' women whose rationality was overwhelmed by their menstrual cycles and lack of children to care for (the same reasons given for refusing women the right to vote).[45] The problem was not the crime, but who perpetrated it. Burglary should be returned to the province of its 'rightful' perpetrators: men. Order restored, police and criminals could go back to working—in their respective ways—on 'serious' criminal enterprise, curtailing burglary from becoming another marker of women's intellect and ambition.

THE LADY BURGLAR: A FARCICAL PROBLEM?

During the early months of 1897, little-known playwrights E. J. Malyon and Charles James were faced with a dilemma. Trying to make their names in London's competitive West End theatre scene, they had been given an opportunity to write and produce a short one-act play at the suburban Theatre Royal in Kilburn, on the outskirts of Westminster. It was to be a prelude to a romantic comedy called *Cupid from the Jewry*, which was being received with moderate interest by critics.[46] If successful, Malyon and James would have a foothold in theatreland and might receive an offer to write a bigger production, achieving fame and the sort of easy access to wealthy theatre patrons that few could dream of. But what they needed was a story, something original and light-hearted to set the tone for the main event, and humorous enough to keep audiences in their seats while the show's main actors prepared.

Malyon and James could hardly have anticipated the scale of their triumph. Their play *The Lady Burglar, A Farcical Problem*, was staged not only at the Theatre Royal, but also at the New Queen's Theatre in Crouch End, finally graduating to the West End's Avenue Theatre at Charing Cross after running throughout 1897–8.[47] *The Lady Burglar* garnered extensive praise from critics, who vaunted it as more 'amusing' than the main entertainment that followed it.[48] The source of their amusement could easily be guessed from the title. The story offered a comedy of errors, as a wealthy gentleman, George Slumleigh, was confronted at his Mayfair

---

[45] Bland, *Banishing the Beast*, pp. 162–82.
[46] 'Theatre Royal, Kilburn', *Financial Times* (3 May 1897), p. 2.
[47] Performances ran at the Theatre Royal Kilburn from 3–24 May 1897, at the New Queen's Theatre, Crouch End on 9 August 1897, and at the Avenue Theatre from 20 Oct. 1897–26 Mar. 1898; *Morning Post* (24 May 1897), p. 2; 'The Theatres', *Daily News* (9 Aug. 1897), p. 5; 'The London Theatres', *Era* (26 Mar. 1898), p. 10.
[48] 'Kilburn Theatre', *Lloyd's Weekly Newspaper* (9 May 1897), p. 6; 'The Avenue', *Era* (23 Oct. 1897), p. 10.

residence by 'lady' burglar Mrs Marshall, who had coaxed the details of his wealth and lack of security arrangements from him at a ball. Initially flattering himself that Mrs Marshall sought a romantic assignation, Slumleigh's realization that she was actually there to rob him was written as a comeuppance, he having gloated that her visit coincided with his wife's absence from the house. Marshall then turned burglary to blackmail after a family friend, Mr Fluffington, found her to his horror in Slumleigh's bedroom.[49]

Threatening Slumleigh with the loss of 'domestic bliss' with his wife, as well as his reputation were she to tell others of their 'affair', in earlier versions of the play Marshall escaped in a taxi with a cheque and stolen goods.[50] Press reviews show, however, that by the time it was staged at the Avenue the ending had been changed to offer a more conservative resolution, wherein Marshall's *coup de grâce* was to tell Slumleigh that his wife had engineered the whole encounter to test his loyalty. She thereby showed that she was not, in fact, a burglar at all, an alteration that highlights West End producers' concern for the commerciality of depicting a woman committing this crime.[51] This was indeed 'A Farcical Problem', and the actress Julie Ring, who was cast as Marshall at the Avenue, provided a 'pretty and graceful and refined' presence (according to the *Era*) to ensure an inoffensive on-stage persona for the controversial role.[52] As such, 'the lady burglar' of Malyon and James' creation was a pale shadow of theatrical male counterparts such as Raffles, ultimately finding herself 'fleeced' of the criminal identity with which her sex and femininity had been deemed irreconcilable by playwrights and critics.

Cultural resistance to the idea of women as burglars took many forms, and appeared to intensify with the introduction of militant tactics within the suffragette movement. Suffragettes were sometimes compared to 'terrorists' in the decade before the First World War broke out in 1914.[53] Window-breaking and slashing portraits in the National Gallery with razors were among the more moderate acts of protest by the Pankhursts' Women's Social and Political Union (W.S.P.U.); firebombing the house of Chancellor of the Exchequer David Lloyd George in 1913 was more extreme.[54] However, in 1911 the *Daily Mail* reported on one suffragette seemingly caught in the act of committing burglary whose charge was swiftly dismissed as 'a remarkable comedy of errors'. The court was far more interested in the W.S.P.U. badges she was carrying in her satchel, while 'laughter' greeted the

[49] E. J. Malyon and Charles James, *The Lady Burglar, A Farcical Problem: French's Acting Edition* (London: Lacy's Acting Edition of Plays, 1897).

[50] Ibid.

[51] The review of the play when staged at the Kilburn in *Lloyd's Weekly Newspaper* recounts its resolution as following the original script, whereas comments about the ending shown at the Avenue by reviewers for the *Guardian* and the *Era* describe the role of the wife in Marshall's actions. 'Kilburn Theatre', *Lloyd's Weekly Newspaper* (9 May 1897), p. 6; 'Our London Correspondence', *Guardian* (18 Oct. 1897), p. 5; 'The Avenue', *Era* (23 Oct. 1897), p. 10.

[52] The Gnat (pseud.), 'At the Play', *Judy, or the London Serio-Comic Journal* (18 Apr. 1900), p. 189.

[53] Sandra Adickes, 'Sisters, Not Demons: The Influence of British Suffragists on the American Suffrage Movement', *Women's History Review* 11:4 (2002), pp. 675–90.

[54] Laura E. Nym Mayhall, *The Militant Suffrage Movement: Citizenship and Resistance in Britain, 1860–1930* (Oxford: Oxford University Press, 2003).

description of her capture by a 'frightened' 16-year-old shop assistant.[55] Like *The Lady Burglar*, suffragettes were often met with ridicule, presumably to offset fears that they might actually achieve their goal. H. G. Wells' 1909 novel *Ann Veronica*, about a young woman who is briefly imprisoned for participating in a suffrage rally (largely because she is scorned in love), famously caricatured suffragettes' 'speeches that were partly egotistical displays, partly artful manoeuvres, and partly incoherent cries for unsoundly ends'.[56]

'Unsoundly ends'—for women burglars, this was carrying off a successful heist and gaining economic independence. These outcomes were inconceivable for Edwardian novelists, who turned their craft to resolving burglars' unwanted achievements safely into marriage. Such was the goal of *The Crackswoman* (1914) by Carlton Dawe, an Australian author who published prolifically when resident in England through stories dealing with themes of crime and romance, often incorporating a moral lesson.[57] *The Crackswoman* detailed the exploits of Nora Steyning, an impoverished upper middle-class woman whose plans of marrying handsome, church-going hero Mr Clarendon are ruined when he catches her burgling a safe at a Mayfair mansion (the discovery signalling Steyning's ineptitude to readers). Heartbroken, Clarendon allows Steyning to go free and joins the army, but losing his love sends her life spiralling out of control. Involved in attempting to burgle an East End jewellery shop with a local man, Steyning's cohort tries to rape her, and she manages to flee just as the police arrive. Reuniting with Clarendon in a battlefield hospital in France, Steyning nurses him back to health from injury and they finally marry.[58]

Ironically, the 'crackswoman' never 'cracked' a safe during the course of the novel, instead relying on her male accomplice to drill through the outer casing.[59] This alone might have made readers question the seriousness with which Dawes had contemplated breathing life into the fictional woman burglar, who was hardly going to break the mould without wielding a blowtorch. Real-life female munitions workers may well have rolled their eyes at the omission, as they skilfully welded missiles together in the wartime factories springing up around the country after Dawe's latest novel entered circulation.[60] Others might have guessed the author's intention from the novel's geographical journey. Shifting the terrain of Steyning's crimes from West End to East End echoed the trajectory of her depleting 'class' of burglaries, from upper-class mansions to residential shops. Barely managing to escape from this inexorable decline without losing both moral and sexual integrity,

---

[55] 'Suffragette's Adventure', *Daily Mail* (5 Apr. 1911), p. 8.

[56] H. G. Wells, *Ann Veronica* (London, 1909), p. 131.

[57] As Sandra Kemp, Charlotte Mitchell, and David Trotter note, earlier novels *A Morganatic Marriage* (1906) and *The Plotters of Peking* (1907) also provided resolutions that followed this trend. 'Dawe, Carlton', in Kemp, Mitchell, and Trotter, *The Oxford Companion to Edwardian Fiction* (Oxford: Oxford University Press, 1997), p. 81.

[58] Carlton Dawe, *The Crackswoman* (London: Ward, Lock, and Co., 1914).

[59] Ibid., p. 191.

[60] Susan Grayzel, 'Liberating Women? Examining Gender, Morality and Sexuality in First World War Britain and France', in Gail Braybon (ed.), *Evidence, History and the Great War: Historians and the Impact of 1914–18* (London: Berghahn Books, 2003), pp. 113–34.

Dawe's heroine had little in common with the 'liberated' female experience-seekers then populating Edwardian modernist fiction. She would have been greeted with sneers by characters such as Rachel Vinrace, the protagonist of Virginia Woolf's novel *The Voyage Out* (1915) whose journey of exploration and self-discovery (albeit doomed) saw her venturing across to South America.[61] By contrast, the resolution offered to *The Crackswoman* suggested a quasi-biblical, Victorian narrative of redemption, Steyning having proven her resistance to temptation and her innate inability to imperil the homes and livelihoods of others, receiving the 'reward' of marriage.

Steyning was also a pale relation of the women criminals of Edwardian film. Her counterpart was 'Three-fingered Kate', the brazen criminal heroine of a series of films directed by Oceano Martinek for the British and Colonial Kinematograph Company between 1909 and 1912.[62] Flicking 'V' signs at the camera, Kate was regularly shown escaping the clutches of the law, leaving notes for the hapless detective on her trail reading 'Compliments to Detective Sheerluck from Three fingered Kate'.[63] Still, even the marvellous Kate could not commit a burglary single-handed. In *Kate Purloins the Wedding Presents* (1912), the physical 'breaking' into the property, using hammers to smash through the brickwork of a fireplace offering a communicating passage between two buildings, was accomplished by Kate's two male cohorts, while Kate and another female accomplice stood idly nearby. As historian Gerry Turvey notes, *Kate Purloins the Wedding Presents* was created at a time when Martinek was contemplating Kate making a transition to the forces of law and order in the next instalment of the films, a move which may have reflected the burgeoning threat of censorship (the British Board of Film Censors was finally established, with Home Office approval, in November 1912).[64] Prevarication over the extent of Kate's involvement in the burglary made for an unusually ambiguous comment on her inherent 'badness', as did her escape from justice, laughing boldly at the camera, at the end. Hence, by the end of the Edwardian period, women's relationship to burglary was increasingly viewed by contemporaries as at worst a passing phase on the road to redemption, never acquiring the status of a 'profession' or 'disease' as had kleptomania or prostitution.

THE LAST OF MRS CHEYNEY

Heterosexual love, Christine Grandy writes, was the goal for which women were encouraged to 'give it all up' (jobs, ambition, independence) repeatedly in films

[61] Virginia Woolf, *The Voyage Out* (London: Hogarth Press, 1915).

[62] Marlow-Mann, Alex, 'Exploits of Three-Fingered Kate, The (1912)', *British Film Institute Online*, http://www.screenonline.org.uk/film/id/727128/index.html (accessed 16 Oct. 2012); Miller, *Framed*, pp. 116–28.

[63] *Kate Purloins the Wedding Presents* (Great Britain: British and Colonial Kinematograph Co., dirs. H. O. Martinek and Charles Raymond, 1912), BFI online, http://www.screenonline.org.uk/film/id/727128/index.html (accessed 4 Sept. 2012).

[64] Gerry Turvey, 'Three-Fingered Kate: Celebrating Womanly Cunning and Successful Female Criminal Enterprise', *Journal of British Cinema and Television* 7 (2010), p. 209; James C. Robertson, *The British Board of Film Censors: Film Censorship in Britain, 1896–1950* (London: Croom Helm, 1985), p. 4.

and fiction produced after the First World War. Returning to domestic bliss meant attaining a full sense of 'selfhood' for women, which, of course, they couldn't possibly realize on their own. Handily, this would also restore the gender balance of the workplace after the dislocation of women's employment in the wartime economy, providing men with their former occupations.[65] Innocent and criminal alike were to suffer the same fate. Women burglars were once again drawn irresistibly to renounce burglary (which they were supposedly never much good at anyway) for a comfortably wedded 'happy ending'.

This was the story of *The Last of Mrs Cheyney*, a new play written in 1925 by former army officer-turned-playwright Frederick Lonsdale. Produced at St. James's Theatre, London, it enjoyed a phenomenal run of 518 shows between 22 September 1925 and 18 December 1926, and then was made twice into films by American company Metro Goldwyn Mayer, with leading ladies Norma Shearer (a Canadian actress) in 1929 and Joan Crawford in 1937.[66] Fay Cheyney, a beautiful young woman purportedly travelling to England from Australia as a wealthy widow, befriends a group of fellow aristocrats and joins their London 'set'. It soon transpires that the whole thing is planned, with Fay, her butler Charles, the footman, and the page boy in league to burgle hostess Mrs Ebley of her pearls. Indeed, professional burglar Charles has groomed Fay for the task since he met her working as a shop girl, suggesting her status as burglar is both recent and temporary. Caught in the act by handsome rake Lord Arthur Dilling, with whom Fay is secretly in love, she is faced with a choice: spend the night with him or have her identity revealed. Fay rings the servants' bell instead, showing Arthur that she would rather be known as a burglar than lose her virtue. Arthur and Fay get married, she having been declared 'too decent' to be a burglar by Charles and having proven that she is a 'good woman' in the most important—i.e. sexual—sense.[67]

Sounds familiar? Women's partial acquisition of the right to vote in 1918 may have stoked a newly confident generation of 'Miss Moriarty's in other arenas of crime, but as far as burglary was concerned the gendering of domestic ideology pulled strongly in the other direction. Figure 3.2 shows a scene of the play in which Fay (played by Gladys Cooper) was discovered stealing the pearls by Arthur (played by Gerald du Maurier, of *Raffles* fame). Refusing to lose her virginity to him while unmarried through an act she compares to 'robbery with violence', the imagined integrity of her body becomes, like the house, the terrain upon which her guilt is decided. In the image of the scene, masculine aggression contrasts with Fay's

---

[65] Christine Grandy, 'Paying for Love: Women's Work and Love in Popular Film in Interwar Britain', *Journal of the History of Sexuality* 19 (Sept. 2010), p. 486.

[66] Dates of its run at St. James's Theatre from 'The Last of Mrs. Cheyney', *Play Pictorial* (Oct. 1925), p. 82; 'Dramatis Personae: Diary of the Week', *Observer* (28 Nov. 1926), p. 15; *The Last of Mrs Cheyney* (United States of America: Metro Goldwyn Mayer, dir. Sydney Franklin, 1929); *The Last of Mrs Cheyney* (United States of America: Metro Goldwyn Mayer, dir. Richard Boleslawski, 1937). There was also a much more loosely based version entitled *The Lady and the Law*, starring Greer Garson, in 1951, although the plot and setting was so considerably changed that it bears little relation to these earlier versions.

[67] Frederick Lonsdale, *The Last of Mrs Cheyney: A Comedy in Three Acts* (London: W. Collins Sons and Co., 1925), p. 48.

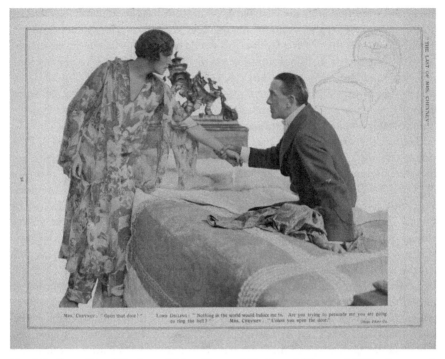

Fig. 3.2. Scene from 'The Last of Mrs. Cheyney' (St. James's Theatre, 1925), photograph featured in the *Play Pictorial* (Oct. 1925), p. 91. Reproduced by kind permission © The British Library Board.

physical fragility and femininity, as she struggles against him wearing a loose, yet materially dense, set of pyjamas with an elaborate floral design.[68] Impractical outfits became par for the course in subsequent films. Shearer wore similarly ostentatious, monochrome kimono-style pyjamas for her stint as Fay, while Crawford dispensed with utilitarianism altogether and wore a romantic, sweeping satin nightgown over a dress festooned with buttons and embroidery. Having a long train that audibly 'swooshed' as she walked—highly problematic for a burglar—her capture was hardly surprising, but then none of the 'Fays' showed great commitment to their profession. Reviewers recognized this, and showed their appreciation. *Play Pictorial* announced that the 1925 play featured a 'beautiful burglar... I am sure you will not be surprised to hear that the last of Mrs. Cheyney is the first of Lady Dilling', while the *Monthly Film Bulletin* commented of the 1937 film that Fay was 'an adventuress with the heart of a respectable woman'.[69]

[68] Katina Bill, 'Attitudes towards Women's Trousers: Britain in the 1930s', *Journal of Design History* 6 (1993), pp. 45–54.

[69] 'St. James's Theatre', *The Times* (23 Sept. 1925), p. 10; B. W. Findon, 'The Last of Mrs. Cheyney', *Play Pictorial* (Oct. 1925), p. 82; 'The Last of Mrs. Cheyney', *Kinematograph Weekly* (12 Sept. 1929), p. 53; 'Last of Mrs. Cheyney, The', *Monthly Film Bulletin* (Apr. 1937), pp. 58–9.

Denial of the female burglar was so powerful that for some (male) criminals, it presented an opportunity for disguise. In two unrelated incidents in 1925 and 1932, the *News of the World* and *Glasgow Weekly News* reported on court cases in which men had dressed up as women, assisting them to commit burglaries at, respectively, Kensington Palace Gardens, and hotels around London and on the south coast of England.[70] Rather than questioning the logic by which the men involved had chosen to wear women's clothes, journalists drew readers' attention to the fact that the ruse had almost worked—despite the culprits' obviously masculine physique. Interviewing witnesses to the 1925 crime in which 'Alice O'Reilly' had stolen £500 in jewellery, police reported that 'From the description they gathered there was a curious blueness about Alice's chin the day after which she was engaged [as servant at the house she burgled], which suggested that "she" had forgotten to shave'.[71] Cross-dressing was a staple of concerns surrounding 'queer' sexualities in interwar Britain, subject to several high-profile scandals of people living for years with alternative identities. Challenging sexual 'norms', these cases also uncomfortably highlighted the 'performative' nature of the behaviours and professions associated with either sex, which were clearly fluid.[72] For the two burglars, anxieties turned more on women's dress as a form of masquerade than the full adoption of a differently gendered identity, yet by playing with their victims' expectations of the sex of burglars the thieves touched a nerve, exploiting the vulnerabilities of retaining such rigid alignments between sex and crime.

Nonetheless, it was a sentiment that the most senior detectives in interwar London clung to when dismissing women's involvement in burglary. As famed Detective Frederick Porter Wensley, one of Scotland Yard's 'Big Four' investigators, reflected in 1931,

> Women are seldom master-minds in crime … In most phases of professional crime in which women engage, they work in some sort of collaboration with men. They act as decoys for blackmailers and tricksters; in some cases get jobs as servants or as casual help and secure information for burglars.[73]

Comparable views were advanced by Cecil Bishop, also a former officer in the C.I.D. and later, a prolific crime writer. In his book *Women and Crime* (1931), he wrote of the (male) burglar's 'woman decoy' whose charm was used to infiltrate homes, and of 'his girl companion' (an accomplice), but not of women burglars.[74] Burglary was thought to require a degree of emotional and physical detachment

---

[70] 'Mysterious Robberies Solved by Arrest of Daring Burglar', *Glasgow Weekly News* (8 Aug. 1925), p. 10; 'Thief in Woman's Garb', *News of the World* (24 Jan. 1932), p. 6.

[71] 'Mysterious Robberies Solved by Arrest of Daring Burglar', *Glasgow Weekly News* (8 Aug. 1925), p. 10.

[72] James Vernon, "'For Some Queer Reason": The Trials and Tribulations of Colonel Barker's Masquerade in Interwar Britain', *Signs* 26:1 (2000), pp. 37–62; Alison Oram, 'Cross-dressing and Transgender', in Matt Houlbrook and Harry Cocks (eds.), *Palgrave Advances in the Modern History of Sexuality* (Basingstoke: Palgrave MacMillan, 2006), pp. 256–85; Matt Houlbrook, "'The Man with the Powder Puff" in Interwar London', *Historical Journal* 50:1 (2007), pp. 145–71.

[73] Frederick Porter Wensley, *Detective Days: The Record of Forty-Two Years' Service in the Criminal Investigation Department* (London: Cassell and Co., 1931), p. 143.

[74] Cecil Bishop, *Women and Crime* (London: Chatto and Windus, 1931), pp. 10–11.

from the home in order to complete the job and disappear. Servants *were* becoming less invested in their work, which by the interwar period was viewed as more of an occupation than a 'lifestyle', as opposed to previous decades, when they tended to live with employers and endure long working hours and 'nosy' mistresses who interfered with their private lives. Greater detachment to service as a profession did not translate into an easy pathway to criminality, however. Especially since there were now easier and more attractive ways for women to make money in mills, factories, and shops.[75] Social freedoms accompanied financial independence. Young lower middle-class women living in the city might go dancing at a nightclub, or meet their sweethearts at the cinema, their hair fashionably bobbed. London's night life would be in full swing, accompanied by the wild jazz rhythms brought over from America and for some young women, an often fatal dabble with popular drugs such as cocaine.[76] But the idea that burglary might become another 'fad' among the 'bright young things' of the age satirized so evocatively by novelist Evelyn Waugh seemed unlikely, if leisure and fun were the ultimate goals.

Unlike the exploits of Raffles, women burglars' (attempted) adventures in this era were described as much less exciting, pleasurable, or successful. In March 1933 the *Glasgow Weekly News*, a publication whose offices were based in Dundee, Scotland, but whose circulation extended across Britain, published a series of articles entitled 'Confessions of a Girl Cat Burglar' under the name 'Estelle Graham'.[77] The first instalment, subtitled 'My Night of Terror on a West End Roof', recounted Graham being coerced by a gang of male burglars to climb onto the roof of a West End mansion from an adjacent rooftop, involving a jump between the two buildings accomplished 'with my heart in my mouth'. Her function would then be to let 'Screwsman Bob', the male safe-breaker, into the house by climbing through the attic window. Her 'teeth chattering with fright', she pulled herself between the two rooftops along a rope which in its swaying motion 'banged me against the opposite wall . . . leaving a trail of blood all the way'. Having reached the opposite side, 'reaction set in and I burst into tears. Once again I sat down to recover my nerve. My hands were badly hurt and I had nothing to stop the bleeding'. Although succeeding in letting her comrades inside to burgle the contents of the safe, 'Graham' was then cautioned by master-burglar Roy that she had left so many clues behind in the form of bloody fingerprints the police were already on her trail, forcing her to flee the country and live in exile.[78]

[75] Selina Todd, 'Domestic Service and Class Relations in Britain, 1900–1950', *Past and Present* 203 (2009), pp. 181–204.

[76] Walkowitz, *Nights Out*; Lucy Bland, *Modern Women on Trial: Sexual Transgression in the Age of the Flapper* (Manchester: Manchester University Press, 2013).

[77] For background on the establishment and circulation of the GWN, see D. C. Thomson & Co., Ltd, *The D. C. Thomson Bumper Fun Book: An Account of the Activities of D. C. Thomson & Co.* (Edinburgh: P. Harris Publications, 1977); Estelle Graham (pseud.), 'Confessions of a Girl Cat Burglar', *Glasgow Weekly News* (11 Mar. 1933), p. 13; Estelle Graham (pseud.), 'Confessions of a Girl Cat Burglar', *Glasgow Weekly News* (18 Mar. 1933), p. 13.

[78] Estelle Graham (pseud.), 'Confessions of a Girl Cat Burglar', *Glasgow Weekly News* (11 Mar. 1933), p. 13.

'Estelle' was depicted as an emotionally fragile woman whose professional incompetence—however illegal or extraordinary that profession happened to be—incorporated a basic lack of common sense in forgetting to wear gloves. Scotland Yard had been tracing fingerprints since the early 1900s, even opening a bureau dedicated to the task in 1901.[79] Her ignorance aside, it is unlikely that 'Estelle Graham' was real. The name appears nowhere in the legal record, and pictures of her posing on the rooftop only added to the implausibility of the account (Fig. 3.3).

The *Weekly News* published several other stories of beautiful, aristocratic, and conveniently untraceable women 'drawn into' crime between 1925 and 1933, including 'The Truth about My Double Life', by 'Blonde Alice' (1926) and 'My Thrilling Time as a Dope Dealer', by 'Eleanor Graham' (1928). All were written so similarly as to be likely to have had the same author.[80] If this wasn't enough to make the historian sceptical, D. C. Thomson, the Scottish newspaper magnate who owned the *Weekly News*, was successfully sued for libel in 1919, 1927, and 1932, suggesting that truth was at a premium in his publications.[81] So what was the point of the article? Refusing to grant 'Estelle' agency within the burglary and emphasizing her fright distanced her from skills and attributes demonstrated on a daily basis in the working and personal lives of 'ordinary' women of all classes and ages, lives that were an increasing source of worry to middle-class traditionalists (the likely readers of this newspaper). Juxtaposed on the page against stories about a young girl sacrificing herself to save a child in a fire and a new recipe for teacakes, the *Weekly News* situated the burglary as a cautionary tale against abandoning one's morality and losing all life's comforts. Only by casting burglary as a highway to misery, embodied in Estelle's clumsy scramble over the rooftops and bloodied, beaten body afterwards, could women's ambitions in this regard be contained and prevented.

As if to hammer the final nail in the coffin, interwar journalists did describe some women burglars as 'Raffles'—but with the addendum 'Raffles in Petticoats' or 'Petticoat Raffles'.[82] One such story, featured in the *News of the World* in August 1924, subtitled its article 'Sex Equality in a New Sphere', joking that women's emancipation 'is being carried into realms which its supporters hardly thought of'. Detailing the lengthy criminal history of Mary Robson, including burglaries of

[79] Simon Cole, *Suspect Identities: A History of Fingerprinting and Criminal Identification* (Cambridge, Massachusetts: Harvard University Press, 2001), pp. 93–4.

[80] See for example: Eleanor Graham (pseud.), 'My Thrilling Time as a Dope Dealer', *Glasgow Weekly News* (24 June 1928), p. 3; 'Lady' Margaret Marcelin (pseud.), 'Confessions of a Society Decoy, *Glasgow Weekly News* (16 May 1925), p. 3; Mrs Muriel Raymond (pseud.), 'Society Lady Acts as Spy for Burgling Gang', *Glasgow Weekly News* (18 Dec. 1926), p. 11; Annie Gleason (pseud.), 'My Life as the Queen of Crooks', *Glasgow Weekly News* (15 Aug. 1925), p. 3; Ada Tatley (pseud.), 'How I Ruined my Life', *Glasgow Weekly News* (8 Apr. 1933), p. 13.

[81] NAS, CS253/2151, Summons at the instance of Mrs Mary Moscrop (with consent) against D. C. Thomson & Company Limited, 4 July 1919: Damages; NAS, CS254/2161 Summons: The Right Honourable The Earl of Carnarvon against D. C. Thomson & Company Limited, 19 Dec. 1927: Damages; NAS, CS257/3650, Second Division, Open Record in Causa Mrs Olga Cook-Holmes against D. C. Thomson & Company Limited, 14 June 1932: Damages.

[82] 'Amazing Double Life', *News of the World* (3 Aug. 1924), p. 4; 'Petticoat Raffles', *News of the World* (17 Aug. 1924), p. 6; 'Auburn-haired "Raffles"', *News of the World* (12 Oct. 1924), p. 1.

Fig. 3.3. 'Estelle Graham (pseud.), 'Confessions of a Girl Cat Burglar', *Glasgow Weekly News* (11 Mar. 1933), p. 13. Used by kind permission of D. C. Thomson & Co Ltd.

jewellery from houses near Waterloo in South East London, the article still managed to efface comparisons with the elegant male 'Raffles' by describing Robson as 'this little woman', and 'though small in stature, she is inclined to be stout'. Robson was 'one of the gentler sex' who had taken up burglary as an 'occupation', and there certainly seemed little cause for readers to concern themselves unduly, since despite her long list of crimes she received just twelve months' imprisonment.[83] 'Petticoat Raffles' here served as a perfect nexus of ill-disguised condescension. Forcing readers to envisage a ludicrous scenario of a woman burgling in her underwear, the juxtaposition infantilized the behaviour and motives of the criminal whilst reclaiming her for a purely sexual, reproductive purpose. At a juncture when women were still agitating for the right to vote on equal terms as men (which would not be gained until 1928), and with unemployment high, these articles used Raffles as a 'hero' once again; this time, as the embodiment of everything that women could never aspire to achieve in the field of criminal enterprise.

* * *

Could women commit burglary? Previous chapters have explored how masculinity and its affirmation lay at the heart of the contest between burglar and police, defined in both popular culture and through the institutions responsible for regulating crime. Accordingly, the 'expert' and 'professional' burglar was popularly and officially designated male. Even when 'assisted' by a woman accomplice, if guilt were proven, the lion's share of the blame would be directed at the man. The gendered portrayal of burglars evolved in the first instance through the connection between the professional burglar and the 'masculinized' traits of athleticism, mechanical knowledge, and adventure; in the second instance, by refusing to countenance the idea that a woman would—or could—perpetrate an attack on the sanctity of homes and families. Moreover, when women occasionally appeared to go off-script by demonstrating their ability not only to commit burglary, but to perform several before getting caught, writers deflected their agency towards familial problems, the influence of male accomplices, and economic destitution. Alternatively, commentators simply ridiculed their efforts, seeming willing to accept the continuance of burglary so long as men perpetrated it.

Constraining women's criminal agency was also about constraining the pace of their advancing citizenship. It is easy to map the heightening antagonism towards, and ridicule of, women burglars onto women's increasing involvement in the political, economic, and social life of the nation. Significantly, the same interchange between media, state, and market that made the (male) burglar a focus for 'pleasurable' versions of crime and criminal acted to dampen and curtail women's efforts in the same arena. Historians have shown that this was not the case in relation to other women criminals, wherein glamorous, sexy, and elusive appear to have been the adjectives signifying the qualities on display. Yet the spatial and temporal contexts of burglary—the night-time home—formed impermeable physical

[83] 'Petticoat Raffles', *News of the World* (17 Aug. 1924), p. 6.

and ideological boundaries, from which women were thought naturally to recoil against trespassing. The following chapters intensify the focus on these contexts, moving our gaze upwards to the rooftops, where, during the interwar years, the 'cat' burglar was believed to dwell, redrawing the city afresh as an unregulated skyline paradise.

4

The Cat Burglar as London's Rooftop Threat

The burglar was dressed in black. Perched precariously on a ledge several stories above the ground, with one arm reaching out tentatively to unhook a window catch, he peered cautiously through the curtains to see if anyone was awake nearby, and what treasures might be located within grasping distance. His swift, silent movements were lost in shadows. As the photograph showed, he had cleverly avoided mounting the wall on the side of the house adjacent to a street lamp, the surroundings of which were bathed in light. Instead, he had negotiated his way up a stack pipe, conveniently installed in a dark little alley tucked away from the visible spaces of the street. Indeed, the image bespoke not only the journey just begun, but also the journey overcome, bringing the burglar to this point of access. Navigating across acres of smooth brickwork devoid of easy footholds, he—for one presumed it was a 'he'—was a gravity-defying pedestrian crawling along a perilous 'road' in the sky, comprised of the city's vertical spatial planes. Passing a thorough-fare of jutting angles and intricate cornices, the athletic criminal turned these unfamiliar edges into ramparts for both building and burglar, now threatening to consume the extant spaces of the photo frame.

Published in *The Times* on 28 April 1926, the photograph (Fig. 4.1) was used to illustrate an article warning homeowners of the new 'risks' posed by burglars to their property. Foremost of these, according to the report, was the 'cat burglar'. A so-called 'professional' among thieves, this type of burglar was also 'more daring and enterprising than [burglars] in the past', a development accounting for the 'rich harvest' of property they had purportedly 'reaped during the past few years'.[1] By presenting crime and criminal thus, the article cautioned readers to be aware of burglars' superior physical strength, through the possession of which they had out-lined a pathway through the city's domestic residences that was negotiated via win-dow, roof, and wall as opposed to pavement, road, or lane. In so doing, the image conceptualized an alternative cityscape seemingly independent from the 'regulated', ordered spaces familiar at street-level; an environment uncharted by maps, unlit by electric lighting systems, and largely unpopulated and un-policed.[2] Devoid of these technologies of seeing and knowing, this rooftop paradise was a neglected oasis of relatively unprotected access points to homes, where burglars (rather than police)

---

[1] 'Burglary Risks', *The Times* (26 Apr. 1926), p. xxv.

[2] I have put the word 'regulated' in quotation marks here to indicate that this was an idealization of streetlife and the function of lighting systems; later in this chapter I discuss the resistance of pedes-trians to state efforts at governance over street mobility. On the use of street lighting as a feature of policing by the end of the nineteenth century, see Chris Otter, *The Victorian Eye: A Political History of Light and Vision in Britain, 1800–1910* (Chicago: University of Chicago Press, 2008), pp. 173–213.

THE "CAT" BURGLAR.—A picture illustrating the methods of the modern "cat" burglar.

Fig. 4.1. 'Burglary Risks', *The Times* (28 Apr. 1926), p. 15.

were the true masters of the landscape. Here, they were impervious to the liberal systems of governance that historian Patrick Joyce has argued were fundamental in ensuring the moral, social, and political regimen of urban space by the end of the nineteenth century.[3]

In this imaginary restructuring of London's modes of traverse, the inviolability of buildings' external facades—comprising the barriers offered by doors, gates, or fences—was rendered impotent by burglars' easy invasion via broken roof tiles, bedroom windows prised ajar, or skylights left on the latch. Just as this landscape facilitated the actions of cat burglars, the cat burglars' physical strength, visual acuity, and mental discipline was inextricable from this alternative geography. Burglars' 'daring' in clambering across the city's heights after dark was requisite to their successful execution of the crime, and subsequent escape from capture. Space, time, and identity thus coincided to sustain the formation of a distinct category of crime, operating as mutually constitutive elements in the manner suggested by spatial and social theorists David Harvey and Henri Lefebvre, among others.[4]

---

[3] Patrick Joyce, *The Rule of Freedom: Liberalism and the Modern City* (London: Verso, 2003).

[4] Lefebvre, *The Production of Space*; Harvey, *The Condition of Postmodernity*; see also discussion in Houlbrook, *Queer London*, pp. 4–5.

Analysing the evolution of cat burglars from the 'climbing burglars' and 'portico thieves' of the late nineteenth century, in this chapter I chart how this version of burglary disposed police and public to think about the cityscape in drastically altered ways. With street-maps defunct, attention turned to the material traces of burglars' escapades to register their presence, comprising broken tiles and drainpipes, soil-marks on walls, and footprints on window-ledges. London's 'dark' geography became legible through this shift, which not only moved the collective focus onto the city's material composition, but also informed the evolution of new modes of policing and regulation based on the emerging techniques offered by forensic science. Consequently, while cat burglars' actions changed the methods and organization of policing, police officers themselves were required to adapt physically to these new demands. During the 1930s, the Force became subject to a fresh wave of legislation, making youth and fitness requisites for the job. Public admiration of the athleticism and sheer nerve necessary to scale the city's heights was fed by the press, as journalists hastened to report every encounter featuring this exciting development in the great 'game' between law-enforcers and burglars. Complicating notions of 'valorous' versus 'daring' masculinity, the lines between popular approbation of police and criminals became blurred. Leading to eroticized accounts of lithe, handsome young cat burglars stealing into women's bedrooms in newspaper articles and fiction, these narratives ensured that the pleasure culture of crime found purchase in yet another key criminal icon of the interwar decades.

Cat burglars were not solely harbingers of criminal fantasy, however. They were also subjects of a concurrent set of fears, located around the relationship between criminals' use of London's skyline geography and the collapse of broader distinctions between the wealth, class, and relative physical isolation of the city's home-owners. After the First World War, the Housing Act of 1919 instigated the building of vast numbers of suburban houses designed to accommodate a growing population of upper working- and middle-class families. The working classes were no longer 'contained' within East End slum areas; they joined millions of others leaving the dirty, overcrowded inner city for new-build council estates on the commutable periphery. These long rows of terraced and semi-detached houses have since been much-maligned for their monotonous uniformity and unimaginative architecture, but for their inhabitants they offered undreamt-of peace and quiet, a small garden, and access to the city for work and leisure.[5] Driving made this easier. As an increasingly affordable domestic 'must' by the 1930s, cars accelerated the mobility of urban residents and collapsed the distance between social groups and areas in ways that shook up wealthier urbanites.[6] London's size and shape was changing. Accordingly, interwar discourse about cat burglars' exploitation of the physical proximity of suburban roofs channelled fears over the worrying depletion of distance

[5] Mark Clapson, 'The Suburban Aspiration in England Since 1919', *Contemporary British History* 14:1 (2000), pp. 152–4.

[6] Michael John Law, ' "The Car Indispensable": The Hidden Influence of the Car in Inter-War Suburban London', *Journal of Historical Geography* 38 (2012), pp. 425–8; Ben Jones, 'Slum Clearance, Privatization and Residualization: The Practices and Politics of Council Housing in Mid-Twentieth Century England', *Twentieth Century British History* 21:4 (2010), pp. 510–39.

and privacy between different social classes.[7] Criminality was supposed to cling to the working classes like a disease, and cat burglars were its latest mutation.

Mobility, materiality, and time thereby surfaced as the factors by which cat burglars were identified, and through which attempts to regulate the crime were ultimately based alongside traditional methods of mapping crime.[8] This adds both to our understanding of histories of crime, and histories of urban modernity. Sociologists and historians have long considered the street a site where the regulation of criminals and 'legitimate' pedestrians alike was most pronounced, yet have attached less significance to the movement of people on alternative surfaces and spatial planes.[9] Recent studies by 'environmental' criminologists have offered a purely cursory discussion of burglars' climbing tactics, dismissing their import as a 'fallacy' propounded as part of the media's toolkit for crafting a good story.[10] This is true, in part. But history teaches us that by rejecting the preferred system of traverse through the streets, or more scandalously, the street itself, burglars' modes of traverse drew attention to the ways in which unpredictable or accelerated travel was viewed as threatening social stability.[11] Worse still, burglars became symbolically and literally associated with an assault on the Metropolis' built architecture, in which, as architectural historian Dana Arnold notes, there was intense emotional investment both locally and nationally. As Arnold writes:

> [London] is not...just a set of buildings in a specific geographical location—the dialectic between architecture and the city and their interrelation is an indicator of

[7] Homeowners' right to privacy in late nineteenth- and early twentieth-century Britain, enshrined, as Sharon Marcus notes, through the 'chief tenet' of contemporary British domestic architecture 'that different households be separated into non-communicating buildings'. Sharon Marcus, *Apartment Stories: City and Home in Nineteenth-Century Paris and London* (Berkeley: University of California Press, 1999), p. 84.

[8] For the period under discussion here, police methods of analysing crime geographically were oriented around statistical indices of crime per area/assigned police district, and first-hand experiences (and preconceptions) of patrolling officers on their respective beats. See for example Walkowitz, *City of Dreadful Delight*, pp. 22–3, 212–13; Houlbrook, *Queer London*, pp. 21–31; Louise Jackson, *Women Police: Gender, Welfare and Surveillance in the Twentieth Century* (Manchester: Manchester University Press, 2006), pp. 80–106; Clive Emsley, *Crime, Police and Penal Policy: European Experiences, 1750–1940* (Oxford: Oxford University Press, 2007), pp. 135–59; Philip Howell, *Geographies of Regulation: Policing Prostitution in Nineteenth-Century Britain and the Empire* (Cambridge: Cambridge University Press, 2009), pp. 76–112. Judith Walkowitz and Simon Joyce's respective analyses of the press coverage of the Jack the Ripper murders in 1888 and the representation of crime in Victorian fiction have shown how popular understanding of the loci of crime in London were constructed through the contemporary media. See Walkowitz, *City of Dreadful Delight*, pp. 191–228; Joyce, *Capital Offences*.

[9] For influential sociological and historiographical perspectives on the disciplining of the street, see Michel Foucault, *Discipline and Punish: The Birth of the Prison*, trans. Allen Lane (London, 1977), pp. 195–228; de Certeau, *The Practice of Everyday Life*, pp. 91–110; Miles Ogborn, *Spaces of Modernity: London's Geographies 1680–1780* (London, 1998), pp. 75–115. Leif Jerram has recently argued that the street functioned as the central site for contesting dominant social, cultural, political, racial, and gendered ideologies across Europe throughout the twentieth century. See Leif Jerram, *Streetlife: The Untold Story of Europe's Twentieth Century* (Oxford: Oxford University Press, 2011).

[10] William M. Rhodes and Catherine Conly, 'Crime and Mobility: An Empirical Study', in Paul J. Brantingham and Patricia L. Brantingham (eds.), *Environmental Criminology* (London: Sage, 1981), pp. 167–88; Marcus Felson and Rachel Boba, *Crime and Everyday Life* (fourth edn., London, Sage, 2010), pp. 10–79.

[11] For other examples of unpredictable mobility as social 'threat', see Tim Cresswell, *The Tramp in America* (London: Reaktion, 2001), and Laura Doan, 'Primum Mobile: Women and Auto/mobility in the Era of the Great War', *Women: A Cultural Review* 17:1 (2006), pp. 26–41.

metropolitan identity which is an agglomeration of histories, geographies, social relationships, production, consumption and governmental institutions. In this way the city becomes a representation of an imagined community or environment which encompasses the symbol or metaphor and the discourses through which notions of modernity and urban experience can be expressed and explored.[12]

Historic understandings of city, crime, and criminal were fundamentally challenged by burglars' mobility, sustaining the formation of a distinct category of crime. Provoking popular and institutional reflections about the impact of environment on everyday life, cat burglars' movements highlighted the emotional and conceptual relationship between residents, their homes, and their city. Fostering new methods of policing through behavioural and material signifiers, as well as erotically charged fantasies of criminal encounters, the cat burglar embodied the tensions and fears of a city recovering from the aftermath of war and in the grip of rapid social change. Perched among the rooftops, these criminals watched for opportunities as a new world emerged.

*   *   *

Beginning to detail his observations on London's burglars in earnest, John Binny, the journalist colleague of social surveyor Henry Mayhew, wrote in 1861 that

> *Breaking into houses, shops, and warehouses* is accomplished in various ways, such as picking the locks with skeleton keys; inserting a thin instrument between the sashes and undoing the catch of windows, which enables the thieves to lift up the under sash; getting over the walls at the back, and breaking open a door or window which is out of sight of the street, or other public place; lifting the cellar-flap or area-grating; getting into an empty house next door, or a few doors off, and passing from the roof to that of the house they intend to rob; entering by an attic-window, or trap-door, and if there are neither window nor door on the roof, taking off some of the tiles and entering the house.... These are the general modes of breaking into houses.[13]

Long before the 'cat burglar' first skulked across the pages of the popular press, Binny's description of burglary took shape within a three-dimensional appraisal of London's built environment. Scaling walls to enter houses via windows, or sailing along the skyline to cross the city from roof to roof to reach adjacent properties, burglars journeyed along invisible pathways leading to vulnerable points in buildings' external skeletons. Invisibility, in this sense, was not just about eluding police. Travelling 'out of sight' of any 'other public place', burglars avoided occupying the same physical space as the 'public', whose lives and mobilities remained wedded to the directions and velocities imposed by the state. Instead, burglars frequented a landscape unused and unknown to pedestrians and the police; a hidden city forming a literal 'overworld' inhabited by the criminal 'underworld'.[14]

---

[12] Dana Arnold, *Re-Presenting the Metropolis: Architecture, Urban Experience and Social Life in London 1800–1840* (Aldershot: Ashgate Publishing, 2000), p. xix.

[13] Binny, 'Thieves and Swindlers', pp. 209–10.

[14] The persistence of the 'underworld' as a geographical metaphor for criminality throughout the eighteenth, nineteenth, and twentieth century has recently been explored in detail by Heather Shore.

Divorcing burglars' movements from the same sphere as those of the public, Binny exposed these criminals' failure to embrace those behavioural patterns considered to be the hallmarks of civilized society. Blankly refusing to circulate through urban space in the manner ordained by those elected to govern, their mobility was tantamount to a renunciation of citizenship before a crime was ever committed. Burglars' athleticism also made a mockery of the class distinctions embedded in the physical environment. Discovered frequently on the roofs of West End mansions, such burglars afforded the press particular delight through establishing a narrative binding their movements to the homes of the super-rich. In April 1885, the *Borough of Marylebone Mercury* devoted half an entire page to reporting a burglary from a local residence in the salubrious Cavendish Square, during which one of those charged, Walter Banton, leapt from the window of the house onto the roof of an adjacent flat.[15] This 'daring' burglar gang, whose attempts at the crime were largely unsuccessful, had presumably travelled from the crime-ridden slums of the East End—although who could be sure if they could move like that? The East End/West End dichotomy between London's poor and wealthy was already a fairly fragile boundary. Journalists, social investigators, and philanthropists were prone to invading the East End, sometimes in disguise, to 'expose' the evils of poverty to public consciousness. Less innocently, those looking for prostitutes similarly crossed freely between the two regions.[16] Burglars' athleticism might fragment these lines of direction even further, polluting the entire city with the fear of crime.

Burglars seemed to revel in muddying the waters, disregarding the aversion of the Victorian middle and upper classes to mingling with the poor or those considered 'degenerate'. This aversion had led them to fence off their gardens, and to attempt to exclude the working classes from communal parks and playgrounds by concentrating them in the West End, leaving the creation of new parks in the province of bureaucratic local authorities.[17] Alas, such measures offered scant defence against the determined criminal. The movement of burglars upon, between, and over houses and areas designated private recurred with monotonous regularity in testimony given during trials for burglary at the Old Bailey. Policemen apprehended suspects found running across a series of roofs between a cowshed and a pub (trial transcript of Thomas Reeves, John Williams, and John Doherty, 17 September 1860), and clambering over advertising hoardings affixed to houses (George Ireson, 29 May 1876). They caught burglars jumping from a building onto a ten-foot-high gate, and then onto the pavement (Edward Wiggins, 25 February 1884), and they followed boot-marks across the rooftops of a school, a penny bazaar, and a church after being alerted to footprints in the garden of a victim (the path identified

Heather Shore, *London's Criminal Underworlds, c.1720–c.1930: A Social and Cultural History* (Basingstoke: Palgrave MacMillan, 2015).

[15] 'Daring Burglaries at the West End', *Borough of Marylebone Mercury* (18 Apr. 1885), p. 3.
[16] Koven, *Slumming*; Walkowitz, *City of Dreadful Delight*.
[17] Peter Thorsheim, 'Green Space and Class in Imperial London', in Andrew C. Isenberg (ed.), *The Nature of Cities: Culture, Landscape, and Urban Space* (New York: University of Rochester Press, 2006), pp. 27, 31–3; H. L. Malchow, 'Public Gardens and Social Action in Late Victorian London', *Victorian Studies* 29:1 (1985), pp. 97–124.

in the trial of Arthur Coombes, Gilbert and Norman Murphy, and Herbert Smith, 10 September 1907).[18] No building was sacred when required to act as stepping-stones to the burglar's escape.

The preoccupation with as-yet-unnamed burglars' mobility festered with police, whose concerns emerged within *Report of the Commissioner of Metropolitan Police* delivered to the House of Commons in 1889. Its author, Colonel Sir Edward Bradford, included for the first time a table devoted solely to the incidence of burglary, as opposed to burglary and housebreaking. Disregarding older templates wherein the incidence of crime was broken down according to police district, the Commissioner focussed upon the means by which entry to houses had been effected.[19] Ranging from the use of false keys (featured in twenty-two cases) to entry gained by forcing the bars or shutters of a closed window (ninety-nine cases), the table suggested that regardless of wealth of area or its inhabitants, one home was just as vulnerable as the next. Furthermore, out of the twelve 'known' techniques of breaking-in listed in the table, four clearly involved some unusual athletic ability on the part of the burglar, who broke in via 'fanlight over the door left open', 'attic windows through empty houses', 'ladders from adjoining buildings', or by 'climbing portico'. The most dangerous period of night was also the darkest. As the table identified, most burglaries were perpetrated between 2 a.m. and 4 a.m., an arena in which one's 'topographical anchorage' in the daytime city dissolved and became the criminal's 'natural' terrain.[20]

The table was clear: police officers must be alive to the movements around, upon, over, and between buildings which appeared to denote suspicious behaviour. Now, micro-spatial frameworks of understanding crime—the broken splinters of a forced window, the very minutiae of burglary's material residue—were elevated to the status of clues, sketching in a detailed picture of the crime and its particular 'dark' geography. Newspapers began to catch on. Experimenting with a name for these erstwhile 'climbing' or 'portico' burglars, the *Daily Chronicle* first coined the term 'cat burglar' for one such thief in 1907 'owing to his skill in climbing'.[21] Three years later, in 1910 the *Daily Mirror* reported how Albert Young, famed for his 'extraordinary climbing powers' when effecting burglaries, was known as 'The Cat', presenting its story to readers with the headline ' "Cat" Burglar'.[22] Yet, whilst the meaning of the term was already in currency, equating the stealthy acrobatic movements of the animal with that of the criminal took longer to gain widespread popularity.

Meanwhile, the police began instituting a new set of directives for officers to deal with the issue. Making sure officers were aware of the legal grounds upon

---

[18] OBP, 17 Sept. 1860 (t18600917–771); OBP, 29 May 1876 (t18760529–394); OBP, 25 Feb. 1884 (t18840225–365); OBP, 10 Sept. 1907 (t19070910–46).
[19] HCPP, Cmd.6164, *Judicial Statistics, England and Wales, 1889. Part I. Police—Criminal Proceedings—Prisons* (London, 1890), pp. 82–7.
[20] Schlör, *Nights in the Big City*, pp. 120–1, 134–5.
[21] ' "Cat burglar" der. of "Cat" n.', *Oxford English Dictionary*, http://www.oed.com (accessed 16 September 2011).
[22] ' "Cat" Burglar', *Daily Mirror* (18 Mar. 1910), p. 5.

which a theft could be termed 'burglary', an instruction manual issued to the
Metropolitan Police in 1912 emphasized that:

> There must be a "*breaking*," i.e., some part of the building must be broken, or some
> door, shutter, window, or other covering must be opened. It is burglary if the thief
> opens the window, but not if he gets in through a window left open. Coming down
> the chimney is burglary. If entry is obtained by force or fraud, or by collusion with
> somebody inside, it is deemed to be a breaking.[23]

Conning their way into a property might well be an easier path for a burglar, but
the manual's concentration on the integrity of a house's structure pushed police to
look first to windows, doors, and shutters. Traces of ash and soot should also trigger
alarm bells, since they were likely left from burglars 'coming down the chimney'.
An earlier chapter cautioned that burglars might impersonate chimney sweeps as a
means of getting in, neatly cultivating suspicion of *anyone* who appeared to work
comfortably above street-level. Such comments encouraged officers to think of the
city as an agglomeration of surfaces, both visible and hidden, from which elements
burglars were able to forge paths of their own design. Forcing police officers to
observe and interpret movements (or the material remains of movement) on both
vertical and horizontal surfaces, at night, the manual intensified their focus on the
landscape extraneous to streets comprising the 'beats' they patrolled every day.
Policing burglary demanded a complete reassessment of London's material composition and conventional modes of behaviour. With thieves encroaching along
the skyline, officers anticipated the need for a 'panoptic', all-encompassing vision
of the city and its surveillance that would in later decades provoke the installation
of CCTV cameras at elevated heights on residences and shopping centres.[24]

Darkness and mobility afforded burglars anonymity, a feature of London life troub-
ling state and society alike at the fin de siècle. Social diversity and cosmopolitanism
acquired a more sinister aspect in the metropolis in this era. London had always
attracted domestic migrants from the countryside looking for work, joined by citizens
from around the globe drawn to the financial and political centre of Britain's empire.[25]
The sense of not really knowing one's neighbour or their national allegiance fed misplaced anxieties over their displacing locals from jobs, instigating terror plots,
and spying, especially among Indian nationalists and refugees fleeing political
turmoil in Russia.[26] Even London's Jewish population, many of whom occupied
respectable middle- and upper-class professions, became the target of 'racial'
profiling and renewed prejudice during the early 1900s. Their 'integration' now
spawned as great a panic as had their 'difference' previously, since the 'enemy
within' were those whose actions could not easily be detected or monitored.[27]

[23] OU, GB/2315/Police Manuals, *Instruction Book for the Guidance of the Metropolitan Police Force*
(1912), p. 33.
[24] Foucault, *Discipline and Punish*, 195–228; Williams, 'Police Surveillance', pp. 27–37.
[25] Walkowitz, *Nights Out*.
[26] Nicholas Owen, 'The Soft Heart of the British Empire: Indian Radicals in Edwardian London',
Past & Present 220:1 (2013), pp. 143–84; David Stafford, 'Spies and Gentlemen: The Birth of the
British Spy Novel, 1893–1914', *Victorian Studies* (1981), pp. 489–509.
[27] Deborah Cohen, 'Who Was Who? Race and Jews in Turn-of-the-Century Britain', *Journal of
British Studies* 41:4 (2002), pp. 460–83.

H. G. Wells' 1897 novel *The Invisible Man* took inspiration from these fears, betraying the novelist's customary perceptiveness. His protagonist, a scientist who entered London from the provinces to find a cure for the chemical accident that had led to his invisibility, proceeded to use his powers to commit both burglary and murder.[28] Fellow authors followed suit, Joseph Conrad's *The Secret Agent* (1907) turning a London shopkeeper into a Russian terrorist, again using his non-descript appearance and ability to travel inconspicuously through different classes of area for criminal purpose.[29]

Although race and ethnicity did not feature prominently (or even consistently) in Edwardian discussions about burglary, concerns about its perpetrators' elusiveness were magnified by coinciding with a racially charged discourse on fellow transient 'strangers'. Predictably, these fears gained even further traction after the First World War. Emerging in a state of social and cultural upheaval following the catastrophic loss of life sustained in the previous four years, inhabitants of the Metropolis soon became overwhelmed by the rapid expansion of the city's population, its suburbs reaching far into the countryside. The stirrings of this problem had been felt since the 1860s, when the then-Commissioner of Police for the Metropolis, Colonel Sir Edmund Henderson, commented in his 1869 report to the House of Commons: 'The rapid increase both of buildings and population which has taken place in the Metropolitan District of late years has outrun the increase which it has been possible to make to the Police Force'.[30] Since 1849, the report stated, London's population had risen from 2,473,758 to 3,563,410, with 225,322 new houses built to accommodate it, and 1,030 miles of new streets added. By contrast, the number of police officers had increased from 5,195 to just 6,672.[31] The sheer scale of the city was still posing difficulties for police in 1935, when Commissioner Philip Game exhorted residents and architects to shoulder some responsibility themselves for preventing burglaries, asking 'Is it too much to suggest to those who design and build new houses and flats that good quality mortice locks should be regarded as no less a normal requirement than, for instance, fireproof electric equipment?'[32] By this time, the total strength of the force was 19,364 officers to oversee a Metropolitan Police District almost 700 square miles in area.[33]

With the city spawning ever more residential districts and the police hard-pressed to maintain its surveillance, the steady increase in burglaries since 1919 reported in the Home Office's annual *Judicial Statistics* was unsurprising.[34] Coupled with these factors, the first half of the 1920s saw high unemployment and eco-nomic depression in Britain, as the economy failed to adjust to a post-war export market for raw materials dominated by America and Japan.[35] It was against this

[28] H. G. Wells, *The Invisible Man* (London: C. A. Pearson, 1897).

[29] Joseph Conrad, *The Secret Agent* (London: Methuen and Co., 1907).

[30] HCPP, *C.150*, *Report of the Commissioner of Police of the Metropolis for the Year 1869* (London, 1870), p. 2.

[31] Ibid.

[32] HCPP, Cmd. 5165, *Report of the Commissioner of Police of the Metropolis for the year 1935* (London, 1936), p. 8.

[33] Ibid., p. 69.   [34] Charts 1 and 2, Appendix.

[35] Roderick Floud and Paul Johnson (eds.), *The Cambridge Economic History of Great Britain Vol. III: Change and Growth* (Cambridge: Cambridge University Press, 2004), pp. 314–43.

backdrop that, on 9 September 1923, *The Observer* reported the exploits of a criminal known as 'The Cat Burglar'. Charles Cobb, alias Carney, was charged at Westminster Police Court 'with being by night on the roof of Victoria Station with felonious intent'.[36] A relatively short article, it nonetheless contained several matters of interest to readers besides Cobb's intriguing moniker. The charge of being found by night on the station roof was rendered vastly more serious in nature by the fact that 'the station roof by Eccleston bridge...abuts on bedroom windows of the Grosvenor Hotel'.[37] Founded in 1862 and attached to Victoria Station, where the Pimlico Railway formed an artery connecting the West End to England's south coastal leisure resorts, the Grosvenor Hotel was as much a hub for the pleasure-seeking aristocracy as an important site of domestic and international tourism. Cobb's feline athleticism heralded a much more significant attack, one that might repel wealthy visitors and imperil hotels' reputations for security at a juncture when a healthy tourist economy was most needed.

Still, journalists wrestled with their admiration for the burglar's feat. The tone of the article was signally lacking in condemnation, hailing Cobb a 'clever and expert climbing burglar' who had crawled along the station roof 'with remarkable agility'. 'The' cat burglar, as yet a singular phenomenon, sounded more like a contemporary mountaineering hero than a figure of transgression or a social pariah, creating fresh trails through the urban landscape to 'redistribute' the wealth of the propertied class.[38]

* * *

By 1924, cat burglars were everywhere. Newspapers used it to christen burglars operating both in Ilford (East London) and around various wealthy west London mansions during October and November of that year, describing the 'considerable skill' with which one of these had scaled a twenty-foot wall to a bedroom window, his fingerprints marking the trail. Jewel thefts were their specialty. A similar burglary at the house of Lord and Lady Stevenson, in Old Queen Street in the heart of Westminster, cost the pair £1,000 worth of jewellery after 'the "cat"...gain[ed] entrance by leaping from the rails which surround the house to the portico of the first floor. Then he climbed to the next floor and obtained entry to Lady Stevenson's bedroom.'[39] In December, the *Daily Express* held that a ' "cat" burglar gang' based in London was travelling between city and country mansions, targeting the neighbouring counties of Surrey and West Sussex to accomplish their criminal deeds.[40] Notably, as the use of the label began to flourish, there was no perceived geographical constriction between the activities of cat burglars and the West End of London, although it was certainly a favourite target.

Cat burglars' extraordinary and atypical mobility gave them freedom to venture far and wide, stealing indiscriminately. Manipulating vertical planes and adjacent

[36] ' "The Cat Burglar" ', *Observer* (9 Sept. 1923), p. 7.   [37] Ibid.

[38] Paul Readman, 'William Cecil Slingsby, Norway, and British Mountaineering, 1872–1914', *English Historical Review* 129:540 (2014), pp. 1098–1128.

[39] 'Cat Burglar', *Daily Mirror* (17 Oct. 1924), p. 2; 'Acrobatic Thief', *Daily Mirror* (23 Oct. 1924), p. 2; ' "Cat" Burglar Again', *Daily Mirror* (31 Oct. 1924), p. 2; '£3,000 Jewel Robbery', *Observer* (16 Nov. 1924), p. 15.

[40] 'Loot of Country Houses', *Daily Express* (20 Dec. 1924), p. 7.

rooftops, their crimes gave them the added impact of perceptible control over, and ability to orientate themselves within, a skyline landscape of the city. Burglars' apparent confidence in negotiating the city contrasted sharply with the constant changes to interwar systems of transport by which residents' movements were constrained, forcing their adjustment to the designated rhythms and velocities of modern urban life. As historian Richard Hornsey writes, during the interwar decades pedestrians were already struggling to survive crossing roads where there was an 'alarming mismatch between speedy modern motor vehicles and London's antiquated road network'.[41] Similarly, from 1923 the Underground system had now to be negotiated via escalators rather than elevators, adding another new tempo to the task of getting around the city.[42] Although the rhythms of the street had never been fixed, with pedestrians criss-crossing between pavements and roads, pausing to have conversations or gaze at shop windows, and jostling each other within the busier crowds, there was a recognized etiquette to urban mobility. Deviations from this code were expected to help police identify criminal movements, as when pickpockets jostled pedestrians aggressively to distract them from theft.[43] Yet how were police to tackle the kind of mobility that dispensed with the street as a thoroughfare altogether? This issue was brought home to readers of the interwar press by detailed illustrations of cat burglars' climbs (Figures 4.2 and 4.3).

Offering graphic visualizations of the paths across residences to be found when travelling vertically, these diagrams afforded a vision of London's residential areas as an inter-connected mass of stack pipes leading to windows, balconies, and rooftops. Here was a veritable paradise of barely protected entry points for the burglar, bearing little relation to the distinctions of fences, gates and doors separating homes at street-level. Perspective was clearly consonant with power over the city, its inhabitants, and their property. Cat burglars' elevated vantage points, like other viewing platforms historically, created a source of power: 'The impression may have been of a maze of streets and alleys, but by being able to take in the whole at a glance, the viewer had visual control of the city, and visual control fed into the understanding of what sort of place the city was.'[44] With the burglar in charge, crime appeared free to proliferate unchecked. As a journalist in *The Times* put it succinctly in 1925, 'Who'll bell the cat?'[45] Drawing an analogy between police attempts to track down cat burglars with pet-owners' efforts to keep track of their feline friends, the suggestion of tying a bell around burglars' necks intimated that little could realistically stop them if the current state of affairs endured.

Like the London Underground, cat burglars' mode of traverse could be said, to borrow a phrase from Janin Hadlaw, to have ' "consumed" the spatial relations

[41] Richard Hornsey, ' "He Who Thinks, in Modern Traffic, is Lost": Automation and the Pedestrian Rhythms of Interwar London', in Tim Edensor (ed.), *Geographies of Rhythm: Nature, Place, Mobilities, and Bodies* (Aldershot: Ashgate Publishing, 2010), p. 99.

[42] Alan A. Jackson, 'From Street to Train', *Journal of the Railway and Canal Historical Society* 34:1 (2002), p. 36.

[43] Andersson, *Steetlife in Late Victorian London*, pp. 115–19.

[44] Tanis Hinchcliff and Davide Deriu, 'Eyes Over London: Re-Imagining the Metropolis in the Age of Aerial Vision', *The London Journal* 35:3 (2010), p. 221.

[45] 'Who'll Bell the Cat?', *The Times* (19 Jan. 1925), p. 13.

Fig. 4.2. ' "Cat" Burglar's £7,000 Booty', *Daily Mail* (7 Feb. 1925), p. 7. Reproduced by kind permission of Solo Syndication on behalf of the Daily Mail, Associated Newspapers Limited.

which existed before its creation'.[46] Newspapers' mapping of burglars' climbs adopted the simplistic tactic of drawing dotted lines or lines of arrows across the fronts of buildings, occasionally inserting the small figure of a person to communicate the height and scale of the conquest. Such devices intimated that similar lines could be drawn all over the city, linking together people, places, and spaces that would normally be isolated by class and cultural divides. Other imaginary lines were expressed through tales of cat burglars who, for example, 'must have climbed over a wall at the back of the house and reached the roof of the dining room' (*Daily Express*, 1925); or more embarrassingly, who 'first succeeded in climbing over the side gate of No. 2, Addison-road, Mr. Lloyd George's house, and, having proceeded along the garden wall, obtained access to Mr. Bates's house at 88, Holland Park' (*Observer*, 1930).[47] One wonders if the former Prime Minister apologized to his neighbour Mr Bates for having unwittingly built such a useful conduit to his property.

---

[46] Janin Hadlaw, 'The London Underground Map: Imagining Modern Time and Space', *Design Issues* 19:1 (2003), p. 25.

[47] 'Cat Burglar's £7,000 Haul of Platinum and Diamonds', *Daily Express* (7 Feb. 1925), p. 9; ' "Cat" Burglar's Exploit: Mr. Lloyd George's Neighbour Robbed', *Observer* (9 Nov. 1930), p. 22.

Fig. 4.3. 'The Way of the Cat Burglar', *Daily Express* (24 Feb. 1937), p. 1. Reproduced by kind permission of Express Newspapers Syndication.

Consternation at the ease with which cat burglars were moving between the houses of their victims coincided with ongoing concerns about housing. During the interwar years, social reformers and the London County Council's architects were confronted with the expansion of crowded, architecturally uniform suburban districts of London, built to accommodate a growing middle class.[48] Their decision in this period to move towards building spacious, satellite garden cities as the preferred model of town-planning for London's development rested upon a need to address the 'problems' inherent 'in large cities and London in particular'—specifically, the twin evils of poverty and crime.[49] Privacy and social segregation—in terms of both class and race—were inherent to the financing, building, and marketing of new suburban estates.[50] As historical geographer Richard Dennis explains in his fascinating survey of the development of London, New York, and Toronto between 1840 and 1930, 'Perpetuating the tradition of gates and bars that characterised many middle-class estates in London's West End in the mid-nineteenth century, the privatisation of suburbia [in the 1920s] was designed not only to protect private estates from intruders but, in extreme cases, to prevent any contact between adjacent areas of public and private housing or of black and white communities'.[51] As a result, the discovery of London's architectural vulnerabilities provoked a strong public response to the 'cat' burglar threat. One solution posited by a correspondent to *The Times* in 1928 was 'round-shaped houses' with 'discouraging' sloping roofs, as seen in German architectural designs.[52] Designs for 'cat-burglar proof' window catches featured at the Ideal Home Exhibitions of 1925 and 1934, and the International Exhibition of Inventions of 1926, all held in the capital.[53] Not since the great age of Victorian lock-picking competitions had domestic security technologies attracted such fierce interest from inventors.[54] Taking things a step further, in 1926 the *Daily Express* reported the endeavours of architect George Grey Wornum to design a house with internal drainpipes, radically altering homes' drainage and infrastructure to thwart burglars' ascent.[55]

Such cat burglar-proofing innovations found humorous expression in a satirical cartoon of the 'cat-burglar proof house' printed in the *Daily Express* in 1924 (Fig. 4.4). Completely detached, surrounded by a moat and with spikes, alarms, and canons adorning the roof, this imaginary house was the ultimate visual rejection of the long rows of semi-detached houses equated with suburbia. An obviously

---

[48] Philippe Panerai, Jean Castex, Jean Charles DePaule, and Ivor Samuels, *Urban Forms: The Life and Death of the Urban Block* (Oxford: Oxford University Press, 2004), pp. 31–2; see also discussion of visual representation of suburban London in the interwar period in Davide Deriu, 'Capital Views: Interwar London in the Photographs of Aerofilms Ltd', *The London Journal* 35:3 (2010), pp. 266–73.

[49] Panerai, Castex, DePaule, and Samuels, *Urban Forms*, pp. 31–2.

[50] Richard Dennis, *Cities in Modernity: Representations and Productions of Metropolitan Space, 1840–1930* (Cambridge: Cambridge University Press, 2008), p. 189.

[51] Ibid. The interwar emphasis on privacy as a facet of the desire to avoid 'neighbourly gossip and intrusion' in suburbia has also been reinforced by Peter Scott's analysis of suburban family life between the wars. See Peter Scott, *The Making of the Modern British Home: The Suburban Semi and Family Life Between the Wars* (Oxford: Oxford University Press, 2013), pp. 60–1, 138–9.

[52] 'Round Houses', *The Times* (12 June 1928), p. 17.

[53] 'Aladdin's Palace, 1925: Marvels of Ideal Home Exhibition that Appeals to Busy Housewives', *Daily Mirror* (17 Mar. 1925), p. 18; 'The Little Worries of Life: Ingenious Inventions: Making It Hard for Cat Burglars', *Guardian* (14 Oct. 1926), p. 18; 'New Gadgets for New Houses', *Observer* (23 Sept. 1934), p. 28.

[54] David Churchill, 'The Spectacle of Security: Lock-Picking Competitions and the Security Industry in Mid-Victorian Britain', *History Workshop Journal* 80:1 (2015), pp. 52–74.

[55] ' "Cat" Burglar-Proof Houses: Drainpipes to Be Inside', *Daily Express* (16 Dec. 1926), p. 6.

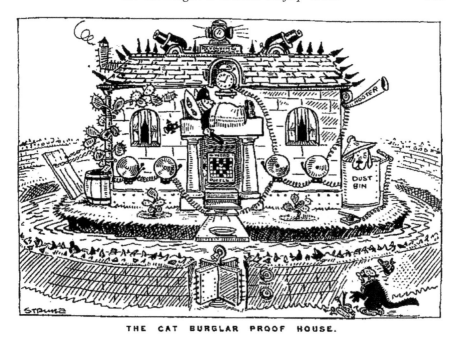

THE CAT BURGLAR PROOF HOUSE.

Fig. 4.4. *Daily Express* (17 Dec. 1924), p. 8. Reproduced by kind permission of Express Newspapers Syndication.

large, wealthy property, this house would be impervious not only to the burglar but also to other, less salubrious social classes and neighbourhoods. Ultimately, this cartoon made a comment both on the methods of the criminal, and on the greater dissatisfaction of the city's residents with the socially and physically compressed topography of its suburbs, which cat burglars' activities had thrown into sharp relief.

There was an undeniable irony, therefore, in the way that cat burglars' identification with climbing gave rise to alluring and even eroticized portrayals of these burglars' physique and character. Popular veneration of masculine beauty overwhelmed concerns about criminality or what was in the national interest, as the veneration of fictional thieves like Raffles had already shown. Perhaps it was fortuitous that the appearance of the cat burglar coincided with a renewed interest in mountaineering as a popular national sport. Its resurgence was led by tragic heroes George Leigh Mallory and Andrew Irvine, who died attempting to reach the summit of Mount Everest in 1924.[56] Since climbers tended to be young, fit, handsome men, it was no surprise that journalists began transferring these traits onto their criminal counterparts. Robert Delaney, sentenced to three-and-a-half

[56] Jones, *The Last Great Quest*, pp. 270–3; Peter Donnelly, 'Social Climbing: A Case Study of the Changing Class Structure of Rock Climbing and Mountaineering in Britain', in Aidan O. Dunleavy, Andrew W. Miracle, and C. Roger Rees (eds.), *Studies in the Sociology of Sport* (Texas: Texas University Press, 1982), pp. 19–22.

years' penal servitude in February 1925 for several burglaries in London, was flatteringly reported as 'a tall, dark, clean-shaven young man with thick brown hair', a 'feline fellow' who had stolen £20,000 from his wife before eloping with her niece.[57] Recaptured for burgling again in 1934, Delaney was accorded the headline 'Cat Burglar Who Holds Women Fascinated' by the *Daily Mirror*.[58]

Even the Home Office file on Delaney, another so-called 'real life Raffles', included a cutting on his exploits as a 'Don Juan' as well.[59] He certainly seemed to have a knack for charming his prison chaplains, who successively described him as 'intelligent and well educated and should have no trouble in keeping out of prison', in 1931, followed by 'quiet, orderly and sensible' in 1939.[60] The Governor of H.M.P. Parkhurst was less sanguine, commenting that he 'should be able to earn an honest living but I doubt if he has any intention of doing so'.[61] Burglary was an alluring career, especially for those whose climbs prospectively offered a glimpse into the bedrooms of the wealthy and beautiful. In 1937 Mark Benney, self-proclaimed architect of one hundred burglaries, authored a series of articles for the *Daily Mirror*, highlights including the theft of 'gossamer' silk underwear while its owner lay sleeping.[62] Since the articles were to mark his supposed retirement from crime, he opined that 'The cat burglar finds at forty, that he no longer possesses the agility required for his predatory excursions; he has put on weight, lost stamina'.[63] By implication, cat burglars were young, slim, athletic men, whose attractions for women might survive even the (creepy) theft of their underwear. The headline of one of Benney's articles—'I Pass by your Window!'—suggested the idea of the cat burglar as a 'peeping tom', a passing male voyeur whose gaze might penetrate into women's bedrooms and espy more than their jewels.

The lurking admiration for cat burglars' athleticism began to encroach on the sentiments of police and other agents of officialdom, including politicians and the army. In 1933, Brigadier Archibald Percival Wavell, delivering a lecture to the Royal United Service Institution on 'The Training of the Army for War', com-mented that in regard to soldiers' skills in battle-craft 'I always feel inclined to put my demands on a lower plane and to say that the qualities of a successful poacher, cat-burglar and gunman would content me'.[64] According to Wavell, soldiers needed to develop 'mobility of mind and mobility of body' in order to win wars.[65] The success cat burglars derived from their mobility seemed to also be exercising the mind of the Home Secretary, Sir John Gilmour. His 1933 White Paper on the

[57] '"Cat" Burglar's Career', *Daily Mail* (6 Feb. 1925), pp. 9–10.

[58] 'Cat Burglar Who Holds Women Fascinated', *Daily Mirror* (20 Dec. 1934), p. 6.

[59] TNA, HO 45/22919, *Robert Delaney: 'Cat Burglar' (1925–1949)*, 'Delaney the Cat: His Full Astonishing Story', *Evening News* (6 Feb. 1925).

[60] TNA, HO 45/22919, *Robert Delaney: 'Cat Burglar' (1925–1949)*, 'Convict Report on Completion of Four Years' (1 Jan. 1939), and 'Convict Report on Completion of Four Years' (1 Nov. 1931).

[61] TNA, HO 45/22919, *Robert Delaney: 'Cat Burglar' (1925–1949)*, 'Convict Report on Completion of Four Years' (1 Nov. 1931).

[62] Mark Benney, 'Stop Thief! Stop Thief!' *Daily Mirror* (28 Jan. 1937), p. 12.

[63] Mark Benney, 'I Pass by your Window!', *Daily Mirror* (17 June 1937), p. 12.

[64] Brigadier A. P. Wavell, 'The Training of the Army for War', *Royal United Service Institution Journal* 78 (Feb. 1933), p. 258.

[65] Ibid., p. 260.

subject of 'certain changes in the organisation and administration of the Metropolitan Police' recommended to Parliament that the police needed 'a younger and more highly trained staff of officers and a more active and energetic body of constables' for fighting crime.[66] In the subsequent debate on this measure held by the House of Commons on 26 June 1933, the antics of cat burglars were raised repeatedly, with M.P. for the London borough of South-West Bethnal Green, Sir Percy Harris, agreeing 'The right hon. Gentleman referred to the necessity for keeping pace with the cunning modern criminals, the cat burglar, the bag snatcher, and so forth. All those cases can be met by giving a preference to young men of good education.'[67] For M.P. Major J. D. Mills (for the New Forest in Hampshire), cat burglars were 'the aristocracy of the profession', lending his support to the recruitment of younger police officers who would be 'alert mentally and bodily'.[68]

Cat burglars were to fundamentally change the shape of the modern police force, as well as reconfiguring the regulation of urban space. In July 1933, the Metropolitan Police Act was passed into law, enabling the Commissioner of Metropolitan Police to 'appoint persons to serve as constables in the metropolitan police force for a fixed period of service, not exceeding ten years', ensuring reductions in the average age of those policing the beat.[69] Older detectives might have recoiled at these developments. In 1931 retired Detective Superintendent Frederick Porter Wensley, once head of the C.I.D., bemoaned the loss of the 'rough and unculti-vated' officers with whom he had worked at the start of his career in the 1880s, who 'never forgot a face or a fact—and seldom had to refer to a notebook'. Younger generations of detectives, according to Wensley, relied too much on the 'machinery' behind them instead of their own initiative.[70] But it was too late to change the direction of travel.

Published by the Home Office and issued to the Metropolitan Police in the late 1930s, a series of pamphlets called 'Forensic Science Circulars' instructed police to attend to the minutiae of material evidence in pursuit of perpetrators, focusing upon burglars' journeys. Using a recent incident of burglary as an example, Forensic Science Circular No. 4 advised officers in May 1938:

> Case No. 13.—It has been emphasised that the examination of lines of approach to the scene of a crime is frequently of greater value than the examination of the actual scene itself. In the following case, entry had been effected after approach to the scene of crime over a roof. Finger-prints were absent, owing to the fact that gloves had been worn. Gloves found in the possession of a suspect were examined and it was established

[66] TNA, CAB/24/241, *Memorandum on the Subject of Certain Changes in the Organisation and Administration of the Metropolitan Police: Draft White Paper* (May 1933), p. 2. Gilmour's ideas were largely informed by the 1932 *Report of the Commissioner of the Metropolitan Police* written by Hugh Trenchard, who had used his first report as new Commissioner to outline a major series of reforms to the service. See HCPP, Cmd. 4292, *Report of the Commissioner of Police of the Metropolis for the Year 1932* (London, 1933); Vincent Orange, 'Trenchard, Hugh Montague, First Viscount Trenchard (1873–1956)', *Oxford Dictionary of National Biography*, http://www.oxforddnb.com/view/10.1093/ref:odnb/9780198614128.001.0001/odnb-9780198614128-e-36552 (accessed 16 Sept. 2011).

[67] *Hansard*, 5th ser. vol. 279, cc. 1297 (26 June 1933).   [68] Ibid., cc. 1250.

[69] 1933 Metropolitan Police Act, 23 & 24 Geo. 5. c. 33.

[70] Wensley, *Detective Days*, pp. 12–13.

that a fragment of slate, soot, fragments of quartz and wheat debris were identical with material from the roofing slates and floor boards of the premises. The case was further strengthened by the identification of jemmy marks on the office door and of paint on the jemmy from the door jamb of the manager's office.[71]

The manner in which the criminal's traverse over rooftops was described as a 'line of approach' offers a glimpse into officers' mental rearrangement of the cityscape to accommodate burglars' tactics. But the text also showed that the nature of 'evidence' was evolving, for which a new breed of officers must be recruited, and re-educated. If culpability could be established from fragments of dust and dirt on a glove, police work now figured as more of a science than a 'regular' job. Henceforth, the judicial process would rely more heavily on physical evidence than witness testimony, and police would have more in common with the members of the community whose property they defended than its poorer citizens.

Forensic science was nothing new, but it was being applied more systematically in response to the cat burglar threat. The devices and processes of scientific investigation with which forensic science is popularly associated even now, including fingerprint technology, forensic profiling, and crime photography, were all inventions of the nineteenth century.[72] Yet it was not until the 1920s that forensic science became fully integrated into the ordinary activities of police investigation, expanding from the original focus on forensic medicine to embrace techniques of analysis in physics and chemistry.[73] Science converted the landscape into a text to be read. Its insights and techniques should complement the close familiarity with their beat and its population that officers were already being asked to acquire, although tracing flickers of movement in the shadows must have been that much harder for police working in the vibrant nocturnal nightlife of interwar London. Cat burglars joined flappers, 'queers', and vamps as creatures of the aftermath, their regulation, like that of prostitutes and homosexuals, requiring attention to subtle cues from modes of dress to making—or avoiding—eye contact.[74] These efforts took on fresh urgency as local London newspapers reported that cat burglars were increasingly roaming far outside the area of the West End. According to them, there were now 'Cat Burglars in Brixton' (*South London Press*, 1925), while a 1932 report exclaimed over cat burglars' theft of clothes from the East Hill Hotel in Wandsworth (*South Western Star*, 1932).[75]

Cat burglars' mobility slowly eroded the utility of older ways of understanding the city. During the 1930s, the Criminal Investigation Department at Scotland Yard contained a 'map room' in which burglaries and other crimes were organized

---

[71] OU, GB/2315/Police Manuals: *Home Office. Scientific Aids to Criminal Investigation. Forensic Science Circulars, No. 4* (London: May 1938), p. 20.

[72] Ronald R. Thomas, *Detective Fiction and the Rise of Forensic Science* (Cambridge: Cambridge University Press, 1999), pp. 3–4.

[73] Frank Smyth, *Cause of Death: The Story of Forensic Science* (London: Orbis Publishing, 1980), pp. 26–7.

[74] Houlbrook, *Queer London*, pp. 21–2.

[75] 'Cat Burglars in Brixton', *South London Press* (2 Jan. 1925), p. 1; 'New Clothes for Old: Cat Burglar's Cool Raid', *South Western Star* (4 Mar. 1932), p. 8.

into differently coloured marks made on maps of the different police districts (Fig. 4.5, Burglary was shown by red markers). Aligning burglary with the entire twenty-six divisions of the Metropolitan Police District, such maps traced simple patterns in the frequency and location of the crime, situating burglary among the broader dispersal of a range of other crimes. By June 1938 the efficacy of this latter system came to be questioned by detectives working in the C.I.D. They suggested that alongside the maps there should be a card index system for officers to consult, detailing crimes committed in much smaller areas *within* individual districts.[76] As Police Constable Gerald Harrison complained of the existing system, 'in some cases the total number of crimes during the period in question cannot be assessed with accuracy owing to the excessive overlapping of the coloured paper marks...apart from showing that crime is either prevalent or not, as the case may be, no information of real value is available from these records'.[77]

Embedded within these suggestions of how burglary could be successfully policed, then, was the presumption that police officers' familiarity with the districts they

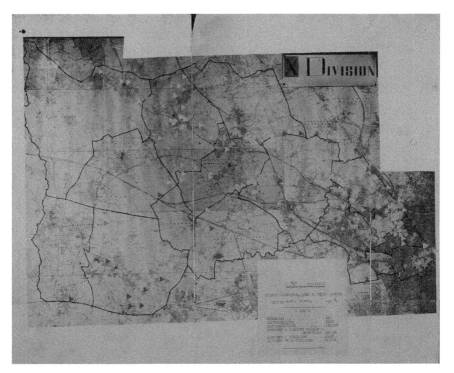

Fig. 4.5. TNA, MEPO 2/5229, Crime Map of 'X' Division (Kilburn) (31 Mar. 1937), p. 218.

---

[76] TNA, MEPO 2/5229, Report to Superintendent, C.I.D., by P. C. Gerald Harrison, dated 2 Mar. 1938, in *Suggested Provision of Card Index System in Map Room* (1938).
   [77] Ibid.

surveyed could, and should, extend to the very fabric of which their surrounds were composed. The interwar police officer's quest to become the nemesis of the cat burglar thus confronted the service with the paradoxical situation that they must evolve as sophisticated a perception of, and ability to manipulate, London's environment as the criminals they tackled. As Forensic Science Circular No. 2 recounted in November 1936, the successful capture of suspected burglars had recently been due

> ... to an observation of the officer of the escort which took them back to the town where the crime was committed. One of the officers, when conveying one of the men in his car, noticed that his boots were very muddy and that the mud appeared to be of the same nature as that which the officer had seen in an old lane, used by cattle, which ran at the back of the house.[78]

The great 'game' of burglar versus police entered a new phase prior to the Second World War. Its 'players' were thought to resemble one another, having youth, fitness, and intelligence, as well as knowledge of their environment that 'ordinary' citizens could only guess at. As Lefebvre writes, journeys via 'holes in the net' of regulated space (e.g. pathways through fields and pastures, or unmarked paths around houses) 'embody the "values" assigned to particular routes: danger, safety, waiting, promise'.[79] The journeys taken by cat burglars and police were likewise fraught with peril, but opened up entirely new vistas onto the city, affording perspectives that augmented the power of both.

* * *

The increasingly high-profile (and approbatory) representations of climbing burglars circulating during the 1860s consolidated into the figure of the cat burglar in the 1920s, a characterization that informed changing practices among, and attitudes towards police, criminals, and the city. Divorced from traditional ideas of the regulated, governed structure of the metropolis' streets, the transgressive nature of burglars' climbs was embedded in the peculiar mobility for which they were famed: their traverse over the rooftops. In the context of the thousands of burglaries in London published annually in Home Office statistics, the proportion of those identified by the press as 'cat' burglars appears miniscule, yet the fact that the 'cat' burglar became the archetype to which burglars in general were referred indicates the widespread appeal of this idea in 1920s and 1930s British culture. As I have shown, discursive and visual portraits of 'cat' burglars and the skyline geography they inhabited functioned as conduits through which issues such as the material and social composition of London and its systems of travel were articulated. Additionally, these portraits augmented glamorous, romanticized versions of burglary and burglars that, as I have argued in Chapters 1 and 2, fostered a pleasure culture of crime about the burglar as a focus for erotic fantasy. These

---

[78] OU, GB/2315/Police Manuals, *Home Office. Scientific Aids to Criminal Investigation. Forensic Science Circulars, No. 2* (Nov. 1936), p. 12.
[79] Lefebvre, *The Production of Space*, p. 118.

figures bore scant relation to the reality of a great mass of burglaries effected on the homes of the poor by working-class men who were largely employed in factories, dockyards, or as various forms of manual labourer. Thus, this research exposes that when interrogating representations of crime and the city in history, scholarly analyses of the specific form of mobility associated with criminals can highlight both alternative negotiations of seemingly static geographies and fragment understandings of how police and criminals were popularly envisaged.

5

Burglary Insurance and
the Culture of Fear

Insurance was no laughing matter in late Victorian Britain. In 1899, the Law Accident Insurance Society of London commissioned a small pamphlet entitled *Burglars and Burgling*. Designed to educate readers in the 'fine art' of burglars' tactics through touring them virtually around the exhibit of burglars' tools in Scotland Yard's 'Black' Museum, the pamphlet warned:

> There is something irresistibly tantalising, yet at the same time fascinating, about your average burglar. Those of nervous temperament may look under their beds for a whole twelvemonth—from the 1st of January to the 31st of December. But he is never there. He is a playful fellow—a merry man; he likes his joke, for on the very night you forget to peep under the couch... he is bound to be there, and the next morning you find all your drawers ransacked.[1]

With masterful creepiness, *Burglars and Burgling* employed an almost fairytale quality to its account of the terrifying possibility of a burglar hiding beneath one's sofa, belying the 'playful' perpetrator who initially seemed a mischievous nuisance at worst. Heightening readers' anxiety by degrees, the pamphlet acquired an increasingly sinister aspect as the reader turned over the pages. Grainy photographs of knives, guns, jemmies, and disguises collected by police from burglaries-past suggested theft would be the least of residents' concerns (Fig. 5.1). Violence and the likelihood of a horrible death were inextricable from the night-time crime, a message that insurers were determined to communicate when evoking the calibre of the menace.[2]

Other images exposed burglars' tenacity and athleticism. The inside cover of *Burglars and Burgling* featured a plate entitled 'A thief climbing a portico', illustrating two thieves scaling the walls of a house after scrambling up its front porch (Fig. 5.2).[3] Penetrating a house that boasted Grecian-style columns adorning its imposing facade, burglars' preferred victims were easily identified from the image as affluent and prosperous. The visible infiltration of this wealthy home therefore implied that burglary was particularly common for the middle and upper classes, incidentally the prospective clientele most lucrative to insurers. As though saving their best weapon for last, renowned burglar and murderer Charles Peace was the

---

[1] CII, 9.94 Box 158, Law Accident Insurance Society, *Burglars and Burgling* (1899), pp. 4–5.
[2] Ibid., pp. 19, 21–2, 25, 27.   [3] Ibid., preface, pp. 7–8, 17–18.

19

this is rarely done now, as an entrance is usually effected through the front door or trap-door in the roof. It is a long time since the police have had a case, however, where the panel of a door has been cut, as it would too readily betray the operation to the passer-by; the more familiar method adopted now is to work through an empty house, and so gain an entrance.

An illustration is given of a lock of a safe cut away by a ratchet. It is an ordinary ratchet about 2 ft. long. It is in reality

REVOLVERS AND DAGGER.

a common workman's tool, and is used every day on palings in the streets. Such an article as this is bought in any ironmonger's shop. No up-to-date safe-breaker would ever think of using such a tool as this. The instrument for cutting through shutters is rather more ingenious. This is evidently a home-made tool. It is a steel-cutter, and can be made any size by moving the centre bit. A knife is at each end, being kept in position by a long screw. A hole is made in the shutter first, the graduated screw

Fig. 5.1. 'Revolvers and daggers', CII, 9.94 Box 158, Law Accident Insurance Society, *Burglars and Burgling* (1899), p. 19. Reproduced by kind permission of the Chartered Insurance Institute Archives.

subject of the latter half of the insurers' pamphlet.[4] Eradicating recent, romanticized versions of Peace's character and crimes, insurers harnessed the nefarious attributes that underscored his 'success', emphasizing Peace's mastery of disguise, 'audaciousness', and the ruthless criminal purpose with which he 'practically killed' the pony he travelled upon through sheer hard work.[5] The notorious burglar was reincarnated

[4] Ibid., p. 25.   [5] CII, 9.94 Box 158, *Burglars and Burgling*, pp. 25–6.

A THIEF CLIMBING A PORTICO.

From " Bye-Ways of Crime."

Fig. 5.2. 'A thief climbing a portico', CII, 9.94 Box 158, Law Accident Insurance Society, *Burglars and Burgling* (1899). Reproduced by kind permission of the Chartered Insurance Institute Archives.

yet again as the ultimate bogeyman, the convicted professional criminal whose invasion into the home was a matter to be treated with preparative action: insurance.

Burglars and Burgling presented burglary insurance as the immediate defensive bastion of a civilization under omnipresent threat of invasion by thieves in the night. While the reference to Peace made it clear that insurers' scaremongering was grounded in fact, the frightening photographs of burglars' tools at Scotland Yard enhanced their threat of violence from which, realistically, insurers could offer little protection. At the same time, their claims would have been familiar to readers used to sensationalist newspaper reportage of burglary, giving the pamphlet some connection with those well-worn narratives of criminal enterprise.[6] Having established these concerns in readers' minds, the pamphlet's final pages suddenly marked a radical change in its discursive tone and textual composition. Offering complex tables with sliding scales of rates and premiums, the pamphlet issued the reader with a set of proposal documents for the Law Accident Insurance Society's new scheme of burglary insurance. After all, channelling these nightmarish scenarios into a practical investment was presumably why they had picked up the pamphlet in the first place.

In these latter pages, readers were invited to complete and submit a legally binding document; one in which burglary turned from the sensational into the scientific and contractually defined. Henceforth insurers demanded highly specific conditions of entry, loss, and culpability, without which they would refuse to reimburse a victim. Following these caveats, only limited cover was offered for those items of property most likely to be stolen, including 'Jewellery, Personal Ornaments, Watches, and Trinkets, and Gold and Plate'.[7] Such items would remain insured during a maximum absence of seven days. A questionnaire asked prospective clients to describe their premises, the length of time they had been occupied, and any previous instances of burglary, as well as any measures taken to prevent future incidences of crime. If a member of the household—especially a servant—were proven to have 'connived' in the burglary the premiums rose sharply. This not only cemented the idea that insurance was primarily a scheme for the wealthy, who were likely to have servants, but also compounded stereotypes of such working-class employees as 'criminal'.[8] What constituted a 'burglary' appeared far more contested in these pages than the pamphlet had earlier suggested, as insurers exhorted homeowners to prove their eligibility to make insurance claims by fulfilling exacting standards of personal wealth and household integrity. Although the spectre of the 'professional' burglar continued to underpin insurers' promise to 'defend' clients against a 'genuine' burglary (i.e. one committed in spite of the security measures specified), burglary was now, by contrast with the pamphlet's earlier pages, eminently within homeowners' capacity to prevent.

Burglars and Burgling encapsulated within its pages the burglary insurance industry's dual representations of the nature and frequency of burglary from the emergence of the industry in the late 1880s. Adopting a sophisticated marketing strategy, insurers deployed letter, newspaper, exhibition, and billboard advertising campaigns with emotionally provocative language and visual devices that sought to maximize an existing culture of fear about the crime, in a calculated bid to attract business. Having acquired an interested clientele on this basis, insurers defined strict legal and contractual conditions of burglary in their proposal documents that were the subject of tense debate in the event of a claim; ironically compounding

---

[6] See Larceny Act 1861, 24 & 25 Vict. c. 96. For analysis of journalistic reportage of crime in London during the 1880s see Walkowitz, *City of Dreadful Delight*, pp. 81–120, 191–214.

[7] Ibid., p. 30.   [8] Ibid., pp. 31–2; Wiener, *Men of Blood*, pp. 28–9.

homeowners' fears of the consequences of getting burgled.[9] This is not to suggest that householders' reactions were irrational. There was every reason to be anxious should an intruder break in at night; yet in this instance, insurers drew both upon realistic and exaggerated reports of burglary circulating through the press when drawing inspiration for their advertising. Assertions of burglars' prevalence and violence were gambits that functioned as psychological tools or 'emotives', propelling future clients towards taking out an insurance contract.[10]

Burglary insurance's appeal was also secured by a subtle shift towards a 'risk society' globally in this era, defined by criminologists as a society which seeks to mitigate the ever greater 'risks' (such as the use of more complex weaponry by criminals) engendered by rapid technological progress.[11] Although burglary insurance was not, nor has it become, a 'preventative' measure in the way that locks or bars on a window could literally thwart burglaries, the rhetoric employed in its marketing positioned insurance in those terms, redefining burglary into a commercial product; a risk that could be alleviated for a certain price. During a period in which home and possessions became architecturally, materially, and ideologically central to the sense of security and identity of an ever-expanding middle class, insurers' emotive advertising strategies successfully fed the burglary insurance sector's extraordinary expansion and prosperity.[12] Even the new security technologies householders were forced to buy to be eligible to contract made no hindrance to the sector, potentially because, as historian Eamonn Carrabine notes, acquiring such technologies 'only serves to heighten our awareness of unforeseen danger lurking around every corner'.[13]

Insurers' advertising strategies were far ahead of their time in their use of psychologically intelligent forms of marketing. Despite the early prominence of psychological theory in the American advertising industry, no similar strategies appeared widespread in British advertising until the 1920s.[14] As *Burglars and Burgling* shows, however, even very early burglary insurance advertising tapped into fears about the danger posed to consumers' physical safety as a result of burglars'

[9] As Judith Rowbotham, Kim Stevenson, and Samantha Pegg assert, the declining comprehension of the workings of the legal system across the late nineteenth and twentieth century, coupled with the rise of sensational crime reporting, contributed greatly to the 'poor management of fear of crime in modern Britain'. Judith Rowbotham, Kim Stevenson, and Samantha Pegg, *Crime News in Modern Britain: Press Reporting and Responsibility, 1820–2010* (Basingstoke: Palgrave MacMillan, 2013), p. 5.

[10] William Reddy, *The Navigation of Feeling: A Framework for the History of Emotions* (Cambridge: Cambridge University Press, 2001), pp. 105–7.

[11] See Ulrich Beck, *Risk Society: Towards a New Modernity* (London: Sage, 1986); Anthony Giddens, *The Consequences of Modernity* (Cambridge: Polity Press, 1990); discussion in Tim Newburn, *Criminology* (Cullompton: Willan, 2007), pp. 329–38.

[12] Marcus, *Apartment Stories*, p. 94; Cohen, *Household Gods*, pp. 136, 122–44; On the historic evolution of the relationship between insurance advertising and combined appeals to fear and prudence, see Geoffrey Clark and Gregory Anderson, 'Introduction', in Geoffrey Clark, Gregory Anderson, Christian Thomann, and J-Matthias Graf von der Schulenburg (eds.), *The Appeal of Insurance* (Toronto: University of Toronto Press, 2010), pp. 3–4.

[13] Eamonn Carrabine, *Crime, Culture and the Media* (Cambridge: Cambridge University Press, 2008), pp. 49–50.

[14] Matthew Thomson, *Psychological Subjects: Identity, Culture and Health in Twentieth-Century Britain* (Oxford: Oxford University Press, 2007), p. 156.

presence within the home, instead of simply relying on criminal statistics to make a 'logical' appeal. In so doing, insurance adverts presaged mainstream advertising strategies by decades. Marketing gurus D. E. Lucas and C. E. Benson exclaimed in their 1930 handbook *Psychology for Advertisers* over the clever 'modern' phenomenon of 'negative' advertising appeals, designed to stimulate readers' repulsion against the 'dangers' in not using an advertised product. This had the dual advantage that after purchase, the product would be associated with the pleasurable sensation of relief.[15] Their estimation of the 'recentness' of this tactic was clearly overstated. Whilst insurance advertisers did not explicitly base their marketing upon psychology, a discipline that only became popular during the interwar period, their campaigns indisputably show that psychologically attuned advertising was present in Britain from the late nineteenth century.

Fear of crime and criminals, and the ways in which their expertise or 'malice' was assessed, have normally been examined by historians in the context of their portrayal in legal testimony, criminological texts, newspapers, and fiction.[16] Whether derived from first-hand experience or a product of 'moral panic' spread by newspapers, historians are agreed on one thing: fear of crime was pervasive in everyday life. What has largely been absent, though, are studies of the commercial machinations through which crime surfaced as the motor of a common household purchase.[17] By placing the market alongside domains of knowledge that historians consider crucial to the formulation of ideas about crime and criminals—social, political, cultural, and legal—we can therefore discover, via burglary insurance, an entirely new set of agents and institutions at work in the cultural landscape of late nineteenth- and twentieth-century Britain.

* * *

The creation of burglary insurance was not without drama. A legend circulated within insurance agents' training books that the idea belonged to a Police Constable Allan, who approached the Mercantile Accident and General Guarantee Corporation after his experience of burglary on the beat in London.[18] This company gleefully laid claim to having innovated the exciting new branch of cover in 1889, but a *Pall Mall Gazette* report of that year made a counter-claim, giving credit to the venerated, centuries-old Lloyd's of London.[19] While insurers scrabbled to be identified with

[15] D. B. Lucas and C. E. Benson, *Psychology for Advertisers* (London: Harper and Brothers, 1930), p. 117.

[16] Wiener, *Reconstructing the Criminal*; Walkowitz, *City*; Frost, *Promises Broken*; D'Cruze, *Crimes of Outrage*; Wiener, *Men of Blood*.

[17] For scholarship on the role of crime in everyday life in this period, see for example: Frost, *Promises Broken*; Heather Shore, *Artful Dodgers: Youth and Crime in Early Nineteenth-Century London* (Woodbridge: Royal Historical Society, 1999), pp. 55–74; collected articles in Shani D'Cruze (ed.), *Everyday Violence in Britain, 1850–1950* (Harlow: Longman, 2000); Louise Jackson, *Child Sexual Abuse in Victorian England* (London: Routledge, 2000).

[18] F. D. McMillan and F. J. Woodroof, *Outlines of Burglary Insurance* (2nd edn, London: C. and E. Layton, 1924), p. 13; C. E. Golding, *Burglary Insurance* (1921: 4th edn, London: Buckley Press, 1949), pp. 2–3.

[19] 'Insurance against Burglary', *Pall Mall Gazette* (31 Oct. 1889), p. 7; F. D. McMillan, 'Burglary Insurance', in Reginald C. Simmonds and Joseph H. Matthews (eds.), *The Insurance Guide and*

this lucrative new line of business, a popular clientele for burglary insurance was swiftly established through invoking the memory of an old nemesis of domestic security. As the *Pall Mall Gazette* article commented, 'The idea of insuring one's goods and chattels against the predatory invasion of artists of the Charles Peace stamp is, to say the least, good'.[20] The commercial value of linking the cover insures' offered to famous instances of crime was thereby deeply rooted in the insurance sector's history, as was the alignment of the birth of burglary insurance with 'active' forms of police protection.

Burglary insurance soon became a common transaction. During the early 1890s, established insurance companies including the General Accident Assurance Corporation, the Law Accident and Contingency Insurance Society, the National Accident Insurance Company, and the Security Company flourished burglary insurance alongside other individual 'general' household risks they would insure against, such as fire.[21] Others took a well-judged gamble, concentrating their services exclusively upon this new branch of business. Specialist burglary insurance companies such as the National Burglary Insurance Corporation, the Fine Art Insurance Company, and the Goldsmiths and General Burglary Insurance Association were founded in 1889, 1890, and 1891 respectively.[22] Considering how recently burglary insurance had been devised, the rapid expansion of the business was a dramatic indicator of its instantaneous popularity, as well as existing levels of anxiety about burglary.

Indeed, the success of burglary insurance can be measured both by commercial prosperity and longevity.[23] By 1907, the National Burglary Insurance Corporation,

---

Handbook Vol. II (6th edn, London: C. and E. Layton, 1922), pp. 248–9; McMillan and Woodroof, *Outlines*, p. 13; 'Burglary Insurance', in J. B. Welson (ed.), *Pitman's Dictionary of Accident Insurance* (2nd edn, London: Sir I. Pitman's Sons, 1938), p. 44; Golding, *Burglary Insurance*, pp. 2–3.

[20] 'Insurance against Burglary', *Pall Mall Gazette* (31 Oct. 1889), p. 7.

[21] CII, 9.701TEKN, file 'Early 1890s Prospectuses of Other Accident Offices', General Accident Assurance Corporation (n.d.); CII, 9.701TEKN, Law Accident and Contingency Insurance Society (n.d.); CII, 9.701TEKN, National Accident Insurance Company (n.d.); CII, 9.701TEKN, Security Company (n.d.).

[22] TNA, BT 31/4674/30757, Certificate of registration 30757—the Burglary Insurance Corporation Ltd (4 Feb. 1889); Robert L. Carter and Peter Falush, *The British Insurance Industry since 1900* (Basingstoke: Palgrave MacMillan, 2009), pp. 7–8.

[23] Although it is difficult to acquire figures on the success of individual branches of the insurance business historically, it is notable that companies offering burglary insurance tended to enjoy longevity, even though ultimately often as part of larger businesses. Following mergers, a number of these insurance companies were absorbed into larger insurance businesses that survive today. The Law Accident and Contingency Society, later the Law Accident Insurance Society of London, merged with the Royal Insurance Group during the 1960s. See 'The Royal Insurance Group', *Financial Times* (25 Nov. 1963), p. 3. The General Accident Assurance Corporation and General Life Assurance Company both survived into the twentieth century, to ultimately be taken over by Aviva, currently one of the largest insurance companies in the UK. See 'General Accident and Employers Liability Assurance Association', https://heritage.aviva.com/our-history/companies/g/general-accident-and-employers-liability-assurance-association-ltd/ (accessed 26 June 2018); 'CGNU Life Assurance Ltd', https://heritage.aviva.com/our-history/companies/c/cgnu-life-assurance-ltd/ (accessed 26 June 2018). Through acquisitions and mergers, Aviva also incorporated the Fine Art Insurance Company (later North British and Mercantile Insurance, then Commercial Union Assurance from 1959), as well as the Ocean Accident Guarantee Corporation in 2005. See 'Fine Art and General Insurance Company', https://heritage.aviva.com/our-history/companies/f/fine-art-and-general-insurance-company-ltd/ (accessed 26 June 2018);

established in 1889, could boast a capital of £100,000 in shares, advertising in the *Daily Mail* that it was expanding to offer insurance against fire damage in consequence.[24] The Law Accident Insurance Society was still proudly offering burglary insurance in 1917, while in 1900 the Ocean Accident and Guarantee Corporation purchased The Security Company specifically to add its burglary insurance business to its own portfolio, worth £30,000 per annum (notably, the Chairman of The Security Company was Sir Howard Vincent, retired Director of the Criminal Investigation Department of the Metropolitan Police, alongside Vice-Chairman Sir George Hayter Chubb, of Chubb and Sons Lock and Safe Co., demonstrating how state and business interests had already intersected around insurance).[25] Following the purchase, in 1925 an advert for 'The Ocean' in the *Daily Telegraph* attested to the success of the merger, claiming that 'the Burglary business has been steadily built up until now it is one of the most important branches of this great office', juxtaposed against the statement (in bold, large letters) that 'A BURGLARY POLICY RELIEVES ANXIETY' for the *Telegraph*'s middle- and upper-class readers to digest.[26] Other companies similarly heralded the success of their burglary insurance schemes decades after they were first introduced. Commemorative books celebrating the history of Lloyd's in 1974 and 1984 singled out burglary insurance as key to the company's endurance.[27] As the later work asserted, 'By the end of the century, no middle-class home was thought safe without burglary insurance', tracing a direct link from this achievement to other forms of 'all-risk' cover against theft.[28]

What accounted for this flourishing new branch of insurance? Burglary was one crime that, against the general trend of decrease in overall crime, had increased or remained stationary in frequency since 1891, as the Home Office's 1894 report on

'Ocean Accident and Guarantee Corporation', https://heritage.aviva.com/our-history/companies/o/ocean-accident-guarantee-corporation-ltd/ (accessed 26 June 2018). Similarly, Eagle Star and British Dominions was absorbed first into Allianz, then Zurich insurance during the 1980s. Nicholas Faith, 'Obituary: Sir Denis Mountain Bt', *Independent* (6 Jan. 2006), https://www.independent.co.uk/news/obituaries/sir-denis-mountain-bt-6112504.html (accessed 26 June 2018). Lloyds and Prudential, of course, continue as established insurers globally today. Only one company featured in this chapter— the Lancashire and General Assurance Co.—did not survive beyond the 1930s in any form. Lancashire and General were forced to liquidate in 1927 after mismanaging a burglary insurance claim, leading to the loss of their reputation and subsequent bankruptcy—again, attesting to the import attached to this form of insurance by the interwar years. 'Special Report: Law Lord's "Unfeigned Regret": Criticism of an Assurance Company', *Daily Telegraph* (5 Nov. 1926), p. 12; 'Risky Business: Failure of an Assurance Company', *Daily Mail* (10 Aug. 1927), p. 5.

[24] 'Chat on "Change": Insurance Company's Expansion', *Daily Telegraph* (22 July 1907), p. 3.
[25] 'Economy in Insurance', *The Times* (10 Dec. 1917), p. 14; The Security Company's burglary insurance portfolio had continued to expand after its purchase of the National Burglary Insurance Corporation in 1893, demonstrating how even smaller specialist burglary insurance companies had generated sufficient business to be vulnerable to takeover bids by the end of the nineteenth century. 'The Security Co. and the Burglary Insurance Corporation', *Financial Times* (8 Feb. 1893), p. 5; 'Ocean Accident and Guarantee Corporation Limited', *The Economist* (3 Mar. 1900), p. 309.
[26] 'Burglary: Necessary Precautions', *Daily Telegraph* (12 Feb. 1925), p. 5.
[27] Raymond Flower and Michael Wynn Jones, *Lloyd's of London: An Illustrated History* (Newton Abbott: David and Charles, 1974), p. 123; Geoffrey Hodgson, *Lloyd's of London: A Reputation at Risk* (London: Penguin. 1984), p. 64.
[28] Hodgson, *Lloyd's of London*, p. 64.

criminal statistics for England and Wales announced gravely.[29] Face-to-face doorstep canvassing between insurers and householders was the earliest means of issuing pamphlets and proposal documents for the new burglary insurance. In pamphlets issued in the 1890s insurers prefaced their tables of rates and premiums with short, sensational statements emphasizing the threat of burglary: as the General Accident Corporation's pamphlet asserted, 'the number of known thieves in Great Britain is estimated at over 70,000, and no class of the community...is free from risk', whilst the Security Company's literature talked of the 'depredations' and 'real danger' of burglars that had resulted in a 'general feeling of insecurity'.[30] Confronted on one's doorstep by myriad, unverifiable assertions about the likelihood of getting burgled, the homeowner's concerns were cleverly vindicated by the suggestion that their 'feeling of insecurity' was shared with others.[31] The use of statistics additionally lent authenticity to insurers' claims, quantifying the threat of burglary in a manner that gave credence to insurers' emotionally charged warnings by mimicking tropes familiar in government publications about crime.[32]

Other companies were less subtle. The Goldsmith's and General Burglary Insurance Association's advert brandished the tagline 'Locks, Bolts and Bars, Soon fly asunder' on the cover of its leaflets.[33] There was a certain irony to this claim. Bemoaning the speed and success of burglars implicitly attacked the competence of the police, upon whose cooperation insurers relied when investigating claims. Insurers also insisted upon homeowners' use of safes and locks as part of their contractual obligations.[34] By positioning their policies as safeguards against loss where the police had failed, insurers promoted burglary insurance as a form of quasi-police protection against the crime. Here was a type of 'security' that would, unlike mere bolts, bars, or policemen, guarantee that the loss suffered to burglary would be minimal. Translating burglary into a phenomenon of intimidating proportions, and suggesting burglars' expertise could overcome the most advanced security appliances, insurers offered their services as the solution to a loosely defined imagining of crime and criminal in which thieves' skill and success were conceived as uniform, and universal.[35]

---

[29] HCPP, C.8072, *Judicial statistics, England and Wales, 1894. Part I.—Criminal Statistics* (London, 1896), p. 14.

[30] CII, 9.701TEKN, General Accident Corporation (189?), p. 28; CII, 9.701TEKN, Security Company (189?), p. 89.

[31] Insurers here employed what Reddy has called a 'third-person emotion claim' whereby conveying the emotional state of others acts as a trigger for eliciting that feeling in the audience. Reddy, *Navigation*, p. 107.

[32] See for example estimations of statistical indices of crimes against property in HCPP, C.7725, *Judicial statistics, England and Wales, 1893. Part I. Criminal statistics* (London, 1894), p. 108.

[33] CII, 9.701TEKN, Goldsmiths and General Burglary Insurance Association, Ltd (189?), p. 33.

[34] TNA, MEPO 3/1211, 'Imparting information to insurance companies where fraud suspected', *Home Office Observations on Correct Police Procedure* (1937).

[35] I use the term 'translation' here in the sense ascribed to it by Reddy; as a twofold process of the identification and selection of the desired language by the author and the internalized emotional response the use of a term such as 'insecurity' was intended to elicit. Reddy, *Navigation*, pp. 78–9, 110–11.

'Locks, Bolts and Bars, Soon fly asunder' also sought to undermine upper- and middle class clients' belief in the impregnability of their homes. Historian Sharon Marcus describes how, 'throughout the nineteenth century, architectural discourse defined the [middle class] house as an impenetrable, self-contained structure with distinct and specialised rooms'.[36] Such domestic strongholds were incompatible with insurers' aims, and the sense of burglars' easy ability to effect entry into the readers' home they tried to convey. Homes' vulnerabilities underpinned the very format of proposal documents. Questionnaires at the back grilled clients on issues such as 'Are the premises Brick or Stone Built, and Tilled or Slated?' and 'How are Windows on the Ground Floor protected?', suggesting that, regardless of when they were built, or whether or not houses were detached, properties were ripe for invasion at every point not composed solidly of bricks and mortar.[37] Ordinary houses' structural and material fragility was further denigrated by images of contrastingly fortress-like edifices of insurance companies' offices, featured as watermarks and headers emblazoned with company names on pamphlets, proposal documents, and general correspondence.[38] By implication, nothing short of the most advanced commercial security could offer the same protection to residential homes that insurance offices enjoyed.

Correspondence was another tool for insurers to hammer home the immediate threat of burglary, writing letters that conflated local incidences of crime into the imminent prospect of personal, individual attack. From July 1904 and throughout the rest of the year, London insurance brokers R. P. Walker and Son sent out 116 copies of a letter to clients in Kent, stating:

> You are doubtless aware that a burglary was recently committed at the Red Cottage, Orchard Road, Bromley, when a considerable quantity of silver plate was stolen. We have Mr. Corfield's permission to say that he was insured through us with the Guardian Assurance Co. and that he is well satisfied with the manner in which his claim has been settled. In case you are not insured against Burglary we take this opportunity of sending you a prospectus of the policy issued by this old established Company, and trust we may be favored with instructions to effect an insurance in your behalf.[39]

Pointing to a specific, well-known local burglary (which had occurred on 26 May 1904 and was reported in local newspaper the *Bromley District Times*), the letter embedded the activities of burglars in the minds of readers not only as prevalent, but nearby, fashioning a highly localized climate of fear towards crime and criminal.[40] Although it is difficult to trace who received these letters, and consequently, at whom they were targeted, the fact that most pamphlets of the 1890s and early

[36] Marcus, *Apartment*, p. 94.
[37] LMA, MS15048, 'Miscellaneous Burglary Insurance Policy Documents', Army, Navy and General Assurance Association Limited (190?); CII, 9.701TEKN, General Accident Corporation (189?), p. 28.
[38] See for example LMA, MS15048, The National General Insurance Company Limited (1907); The Alliance Assurance Company Limited (190?).
[39] CII, 9.701 CN 8CHW9, 'Correspondence and directory of clients: R. P. Walker & Son', letter to F. G. Cubitt Esq. from R. P. Walker and Son (14 July 1904), p. 796.
[40] 'District Courts', *Bromley District Times* (10 June 1904), p. 5.

1900s offered insurance only for total household contents worth more than £100 suggests they were intended for middle- and upper-class clients.[41] Their story thus sought to trigger the emotions of a clientele that considered the home and its furnishings as 'the crucible for the self' in late Victorian and Edwardian Britain. As a space that reflected one's personality and values, the home's violation would have constituted a trespass into the very soul of the owner.[42] Reading this letter in conjunction with the enclosed insurance pamphlet describing thousands of burglaries occurring on a national scale, clients would have been increasingly sensitive to the realistic danger of burglars pilfering the possessions they treasured.

Advertising was not the only means by which insurance companies gathered their clientele. R. P. Walker and Sons canvassed potential clients through their own social networks, spreading the word through their contacts through personal and written introductions.[43] Loyalties generated through this practice were both personal and professional. Like doorstep canvassing, these interactions required judgements of character as well as performative elements, like emotive appeals, from canvasser to canvassed, as well as customers' realistic assessments of the affordability and prudence of an investment.[44] Indeed, in an early *c.*1900 training booklet entitled *How to Train a Young Agent*, insurance canvassers were instructed to be 'ready with sympathy to those in trouble, in sorrow, and endeavour to be the friend of every person, avoiding on all occasions giving offence to anyone'.[45] Insurance salesmen's personal demeanour and emotional sensitivity to the common concerns of prospective clients were seen as integral to acquiring the business, and trust, of customers. Burglary insurance might also be purchased on the advice of friends, or after personal or second-hand experience of burglary, or when buying other forms of insurance to ensure that properties were, in some measure, safeguarded. Whilst it is difficult for the historian to recover these processes of reasoning, the emphasis placed by R. P. Walker and Sons upon cultivating business with clients via word-of-mouth reflects their reliance on the affective network of friends and close associations in generating custom.

Newspapers were perhaps the most obvious way to popularize burglary insurance, yet insurers made relatively little use of it between 1890 and 1914, inserting dull, textually driven adverts listing clauses and premiums into a wide range

[41] CII, *Burglars and Burgling*, p. 31; CII: 9.701TEKN, General Accident Corporation, pp. 30, 28; CII, 9.701TEKN, Goldsmiths and General Burglary Insurance Association Ltd, p. 33; CII, 9.701TEKN, Ocean Accident and Guarantee Corporation Ltd, pp. 43, 58; CII, 9.701TEKN, Security Company Limited, n.d., p. 89; LMA, MS15048, Post Office Employees' Mutual Guarantee Association Limited (12 July 1893); LMA, MS15048, Fine Art Insurance Company Limited (189?); LMA, MS15048, Army, Navy and General Assurance Association, Limited (190?).

[42] Cohen, *Household*, pp. 136, 122–44.

[43] See for example: CII, 9.701 CN 8CHW9, Letter to D. Mason, Esq. from R. P. Walker and Son (26 Mar. 1901), p. 16; CII, 9.701 CN 8CHW9, Letter to Col. A. W. Chambers from R. P. Walker and Son (13 May 1902), p. 231; CII, 9.701 CN 8CHW9, Letter to Mrs Abbott from R. P. Walker and Son (9 June 1902), p. 256.

[44] Sean O'Connell, *Credit and Community: Working-Class Debt in the UK Since 1880* (Oxford: Oxford University Press, 2009), pp. 26–7.

[45] CII: 9.94 box 138 item 1, O. Buttifant, untitled article, in *How to Train a Young Agent, Written by 20 Successful Insurance Men* (London: 190?), p. 9.

of national and local newspapers with none of the flair or menacing imagery of their pamphlets. The First World War inspired insurers to concentrate fully on this media, however. Tapping into what Nicoletta Gullace has called the 'atrocity propaganda' about German war crimes then saturating the British press that encouraged men to protect their homes and families by volunteering to serve in the army, insurers began to produce adverts which offered coverage for burglary alongside cover against *specific* wartime risks (like damage from Zeppelin bombs).[46] As a 1918 advert in the *British Citizen and Empire Worker* pleaded, 'In these days of War worries, the average householder should welcome any proposition likely to remove any part of the responsibilities of life from his shoulders', directing the reader to 'All In' cover for fire, burglary, and other risks.[47] In *The Gentlewoman and Modern Life* the same year, the gendering of the advert was reversed whilst still appealing to the idea of men as 'natural' protectors of the home, whose absence might make a burglary, or other disaster, more likely:

> Now that most of our men folk are at the front—or at least serving in one section or other of our fighting forces—it devolves upon the women who are carrying on to attend to all those many business matters in connection with the home which, in the happy pre-war days, were outside the province of her domestic duties. One of the most important is that of renewing at the proper date the policies in respect of fire, burglary, accidents to servants, and other matters in connection with the home. All this is very confusing to the average woman, and it is not surprising to find that in many instances the omission to pay the premiums in time and the consequent lapse of policies have resulted in very serious losses and in some instances disaster.[48]

Patronizing as this direction might appear, it underscored insurers' core intention of inserting burglary insurance among other wartime concerns affecting the 'average' family. In this instance, they benefitted incalculably from the ability to target appeals at specific sexes and classes, through attuning adverts to the publication's defined audience of 'gentlewomen'. Insurers also situated their new burglary policy as contributing to the war effort through generating insights into the enemy. The *Sunday Times*' report on 'The Week in Germany' in June 1918 offered 'Amazing Burglary Statistics…Insurance Companies' returns show that between March 15 and April 15 there were 405 burglaries of insured premises in Berlin. From January 1 to April 15 the number of burglaries of insured premises amounted to 1,811, at a rate of 520 per month'.[49] Cleverly highlighting the international scope of the burglary insurance business, this article served to promote British morale through suggesting their wartime rival was losing its grip on domestic crime rates.

As insurers transferred the success of this formula onto their representation of domestic risks after the war, one company in particular—Eagle Star and British Dominions Insurance Co., Ltd—produced a press campaign for burglary insurance

---

[46] Nicoletta Gullace, *The Blood of our Sons: Men, Women, and the Renegotiation of British Citizenship during the Great War* (Basingstoke: Palgrave MacMillan, 2002), pp. 2–3.
[47] 'An Alluring Proposal', *British Citizen and Empire Worker* (12 Oct. 1918), p. 127.
[48] 'An All-embracing Insurance for the Home', *Gentlewoman and Modern Life* (2 June 1918), p. 852.
[49] 'Week in Germany', *Sunday Times* (16 June 1918), p. 2.

10 BURGLARIES
in one district in 12 hours

Fig. 5.3. '10 Burglaries in One District in 12 Hours', *Scotsman*, (15 Dec. 1920), p. 7. As published in *The Scotsman* on 15 Dec. 1920 and reproduced with their kind permission.

between the years 1920 and 1927 that exemplified these influences. In 1920, Eagle Star published an advert in the *Scotsman* entitled '10 Burglaries in One District in 12 Hours' (Fig. 5.3).[50] Depicting a couple exclaiming over the disarray of the woman's dressing table in the aftermath of a burglary, the advert visualized the burglar's penetration into one's most intimate possessions and domestic space. As historian Amanda Vickery notes, privacy was a value entrenched in western European ideology about the preferred nature of domestic life by the late eighteenth century, becoming a central tenet of the internal architectural and lived dynamics of the home from the nineteenth century onwards.[51] The violently shattered mirror and the nightgown wrenched into public view from the drawer presented burglary as the horrifying sensation of being forcibly divested of privacy.[52] The premonition of this should then, by implication, induce one to purchase the requisite insurance.

The image of the horrified couple offers a fascinating insight into the specific version of gender relations with which Eagle Star thought readers of the *Scotsman* would identify. Moulding its motifs around a traditional discourse about masculine responsibilities towards women, the advert stated 'Since these depredations cannot be prevented, the wise businessman and householder will insure against such

[50] '10 Burglaries in One District in 12 Hours', *Scotsman* (15 Dec. 1920), p. 7.
[51] Vickery, 'An Englishman's Home Is his Castle?', p. 149.   [52] Reddy, *Navigation*, p. 106.

contingencies by effecting a Burglary...Insurance'.[53] This was a perceptive model for insurers to play upon in a post-war context in which the home was culturally re-established as central to the stability of relations between the sexes—and consequently, the nation—after the upheaval occasioned by women's wartime involvement in the labour force and subsequent political gains.[54] Located on the same page as news from the international markets and law-courts, the use of a statistic as the headline of this advert couched the threat of burglary in a factual, legal, and scientific discourse that was both authoritative and, in this era, predominantly masculine. The home was again presented as a space that was ultimately in the safe-guarding of the man, who stands in the foreground of the image as though attempting to shield his wife's possessions from further intrusion by the readers' gaze.

Eagle Star continued to nourish anxieties about the sanctity of the domestic space. In an advert entitled 'What's Happening at Home?', published in *The Times* in July 1921, they warned 'The holiday season is the Burglar's busy period. Unoccupied homes are his special study', intimating a 'spoilt' holiday and money worries should the burglar strike when the family were absent *and* uninsured. By contrast, another advert issued by the company in *The Times* in May 1923, entitled 'Bolts and Locks offer very little resistance to the modern burglar' suggested that regardless of homeowners' presence or absence the 'modern' burglar was so skilled in picking locks and bolts that the home would inevitably be invaded.[55] Maintaining that stance without reference to possible police intervention, these adverts ingrained a rhetoric of constant danger of burglary from which only insurance could offer recompense. Burglary in these adverts was, curiously, a crime depicted as being entirely beyond the abilities of homeowners to defend against, obscuring the finer details of circumstance and security measures against burglary insurers required when agreeing their contracts.

Eagle Star's adverts appeared in *The Times*, the *Morning Post*, the *People*, and the *Daily Telegraph*, as well as the *Scotsman*, the *Daily Mail*, and the *Daily Express*.[56] The dispersal of burglary insurance adverts across a broad spectrum of newspapers clearly sought to democratize insurers' clientele. In 'What's Happening at Home?' the company were keen to stress that 'The risk of loss from Burglary is covered at rates to suit all classes'.[57] This simultaneously highlighted burglary as a universal threat to homes of all classes, and presented insurance as the available solution. Middle-class expansion from the late nineteenth century marked a corresponding expenditure on domestic goods that would communicate subtle signs of status. This development ensured the threat of burglary appeared of likely concern to

---

[53] '10 Burglaries in One District in 12 Hours', *Scotsman* (15 Dec. 1920), p. 7.

[54] Susan Kingsley-Kent, *Gender and Power in Britain, 1640–1990* (London: Routledge, 1999), pp. 287–310.

[55] 'Bolts and Locks Offer Very Little Resistance to the Modern Burglar', *The Times* (23 May 1923), p. 14.

[56] Headline Advert, *Morning Post* (7 July 1921), p. 1; Headline Advert, *People* (20 June 1920), p. 1; *Daily Telegraph* (5 July 1921), p. 2; see for example *Scotsman* (15 Dec. 1920), p. 7; *Daily Mail* (29 Jan. 1920), p. 3; *Daily Express* (14 Dec. 1920), p. 1.

[57] 'What's Happening at Home?', *The Times* (8 July 1921), p. 13.

more people than ever before.[58] Eagle Star took this a step further by collaborating with the *Daily Express* in 1921 to offer free insurance to regular readers, enhancing the newspaper's circulation figures whilst also, as the Prudential Company's bulletin noted, making people '*accustomed to feeling* insured'.[59] The juxtaposition of the words 'feeling' and 'insured' in relation to a campaign that drew upon legal discourse and journalistic prose perfectly demonstrates how insurance advertising drew media, state, and market representations of burglary into conversation. Delivering the information as a personal, emotional experience to which readers/viewers were entreated to respond, insurers also normalized the transaction, shifting burglary insurance from a new 'specialist' branch of cover to one all householders should expect to purchase.

Through consistently depicting the burglar as a male interloper and by emphasizing the 'thousands' of burglars at large in Britain at any given time, insurers used the experience they had gained in advertising during the war, borrowing from comparable descriptions of the invading German army in the British press in August 1914.[60] Identical themes could still be found in Eagle Star adverts in 1927, illustrating how insurers successfully positioned burglary as a threat equivalent to foreign invasion in the public mind.[61] Eagle Star was not the only company to deploy a sophisticated marketing strategy, though, nor unique in evoking the war as an analogy for burglary. Figure 5.4 shows a toy handed out by the Prudential Insurance Company at the British Empire Exhibition of 1924, a public celebration of imperial rule held in Wembley, north London. In the company bulletin of July 1924, those operating Prudential's kiosk explained the toy, reporting that'

> We have a number of advertising devices which appeal especially to children... there is great demand for a picture of a gentleman with bricks falling on his head (fire, burglary, etc.) who has an anxious-looking face in consequence. By pulling a tag a Prudential helmet comes over his head and his face is wreathed in smiles. The youngsters' faces are also wreathed in smiles in witnessing this remarkable transformation and... "That's Daddy looking worried" is a fairly common remark, and Daddy has to read the advertisement intended for him before he goes away.[62]

Visually comparing the threat of burglary to bricks threatening the homeowner's head, the appropriate emotional response—anxiety—was spelled out in emphatic black capitals beneath, as well as in the character's fearful expression (left). Pulling the tab (right) introduced Prudential Insurance with the visual metaphor of a military-style helmet, framing the company and its clients as combatants in a war

[58] Joanne Hollows, 'The Science of Spells: Cooking, Lifestyle and Domestic Femininities in British Good Housekeeping in the Interwar Period', in David Bell and Joanne Hollows (eds.), *Historicising Lifestyle: Mediating Taste, Consumption and Identity from the 1900s to 1970s* (Aldershot: Ashgate Publishing, 2006), pp. 21–39.

[59] PGA, Joseph Burn, 'Newspaper Insurance', *Prudential Bulletin*, no. 3 (Dec. 1922), p. 379.

[60] Gullace, *Blood of our Sons*, p. 2; see also Susan Kingsley Kent, *Aftershocks: Politics and Trauma in Britain, 1918–1931* (Basingstoke: Palgrave MacMillan, 2009).

[61] See for example 'Recent Burglaries', *The Times* (1 Jan. 1927), p. 12.

[62] PGA, 'The Kiosk at the British Empire Exhibition', *Prudential Bulletin*, no. 5 (July 1924), p. 641.

Fig. 5.4. 1924 British Empire Exhibition artefact. On the left, before pulling tag; on the right, after pulling tag. Reproduced by kind permission of Prudential Group Archives.

against burglary, fire, and accidents. Created so that the threat would be identified and communicated by a child and issued to people enjoying a family day out at the exhibition, the toy sought to reinforce the masculine and familial responsibilities of male homeowners. As the text on the reverse asserted, burglary was a 'big risk' present on a 'daily' basis, yet again quantifying burglary in a language that echoed official publications on crime. The intersection between state and market was also apparent in the context of the toy's dissemination, since the Empire Exhibition was a showcase in which 'Imperial rule could be portrayed as having made significant advances'.[63] Burglary insurance was therefore placed within the broader civilizing narrative of British Imperial 'progress', as another facet of a purportedly secure and enlightened existence.

By the 1930s newspaper adverts issued specifically to market burglary insurance largely disappeared, as the majority of insurers offered it as part of comprehensive household insurance policies. Burglary continued to be identified as a distinct branch of the business in such adverts, however, demonstrating the popularity of the insurance and the effectiveness of its original marketing.[64] The prominence of the 'burglary business' was visibly thrust at prospective clients as they passed insurance offices' London headquarters. As the Prudential Company's bulletin of April 1932 reported, a fifteen-foot-long by ten-foot-high billboard displaying two burglars cracking a safe covered the front of their offices facing Brooke Street.[65] Similarly, the General Life Assurance Company's centenary book of 1937 included an illustration of their chief offices at Aldwych, London, showing the word 'BURGLARY' displayed over the building's front door.[66] Insurers also found complementary marketing outlets through their relationships with safe companies, with whom they forged mutually profitable endorsement contracts (see Chapter 6).[67] The 1930s might therefore be seen as a period when the culture of fear about burglary had become so firmly entrenched in public perception that burglary insurance—initially, a marginal branch of business—had become a common household purchase. Strikingly, against the trend of declining prosperity of other industries during the economic downturn of the late 1920s and 1930s, the insurance industry 'expanded greatly and diversified widely'.[68] Despite the relatively modest increases in recorded burglaries at this time, burglary insurance's success within this unusually stable industry shows the strength of its popular demand.

* * *

In March 1923, Samuel Edward Knight, a sub-postmaster in Wimbledon, southwest London, was burgled. Breaking through a window-shutter at the rear of the

---

[63] J. M. Mackenzie, 'The Popular Culture of Empire in Britain', in Judith Brown and W. M. Roger Louis (eds.), *The Oxford History of the British Empire: The Twentieth Century* (Oxford: Oxford University Press, 1999), p. 214.

[64] See for example 'Royal London Mutual Insurance', *Evening Standard* (8 Jan. 1930), p. 7; 'Norwich Union insurance society', *Daily Mirror* (1 Oct. 1931), p. 6; 'Hackney', *John Bull* (3 Oct. 1931), p. 23; 'Your Best Free Insurance', *Daily Mail* (1 Jan. 1934), p. 11; 'It's Different—and It's Free', *Daily Mirror* (22 Jan. 1935), p. 12; 'Epidemic of Robberies', *Ideal Home* (Apr. 1935), p. lxv; 'News Chronicle Free Insurance', *Daily Chronicle* (1 Jan. 1936), p. 6; 'Over £500,000 to Registered Readers', *John Bull* (22 Aug. 1936), p. 4; 'Atlas Assurance Company Limited', *Daily Express* (24 June 1937), p. 24; 'Alliance Assurance Company Limited', *The Times* (14 July 1937), p. 19; 'Atlas Assurance Company Limited', *The Times* (16 Mar. 1938), p. 17; 'Royal London Mutual Insurance', *Daily Mirror* (26 Apr. 1939), p. 22.

[65] PGA, 'Our Picture Gallery', *Prudential Bulletin*, no. 13 (Apr. 1932), p. 1992.

[66] Arthur Champness, *A Century of Progress: The General Life Assurance Company* (London: The Company, 1937), p. 36.

[67] See for example 'Safes Should Be Thief-Resisting', *The Times* (23 Sept. 1932), p. 14.

[68] John Butt, 'Life Assurance in War and Depression: The Standard Life Assurance Company and its Environment, 1914–39', in Oliver M. Westall (ed.), *The Historian and the Business of Insurance* (Manchester: Manchester University Press, 1984), p. 156.

Post Office, the thief stole an entire safe and its contents (comprising both personal and Post Office property) from the bedroom. The *Daily Express* outlined the scene of devastation when Knight returned a few hours later: 'Ornaments and furniture were broken, rugs torn up, and groceries scattered about. The safe had been wheeled away on a hand-barrow, and stamps and money orders were gone. The loss is between £900 and £1,000.' As the reporter commented evocatively, 'the shop looked like the playground of a poltergeist', intimating the sheer scale of the mess and the ghost-like elusiveness of the criminals who had created it.[69] Applying to the Fine Art and General Insurance Company for remuneration, Knight was to face further disappointment. The insurer's assessors, Messrs. Francis Dod and Company, informed him bluntly that the claim would be refused. In a personal call to the Post Office's Investigation Branch on 27 July to explain why,

> Mr. Dod stated that under the terms of the Policy issued to Mr. Knight there was no legal liability on the Company to pay any part of the value of the stolen property inasmuch as more than one of the additional provisos typed upon the policy had not been complied with by the Sub Postmaster's failure to comply with the proviso (1) [stating that the policy holder must be above the age of 25 years] upon the copy of the Policy at page 71 and his alleged failure to provide some of the fastenings, especially the Hobbs padlock mentioned in proviso 4 (b).[70]

Despite Knight's protestations that the burglary insurance policy had been issued to him after a thorough inspection of the property and its security by the insurance agent, and that neither he nor his wife were asked their age (both were 21), the insurance company refused to pay. In further correspondence, it emerged that Knight had been asked to buy a 'Hobbs Hart close shackle padlock' for the side gate, but being unable to find that specific brand, affixed an identical, unbranded lock from the blacksmith. This, however, Knight judged irrelevant, as the burglar had entered through the window-shutter. Fine Art and General disagreed. Knight had failed to meet their conditions, and in regard to the Sub-Postmaster's age, they insisted 'The original contract was issued by us with the express condition that a responsible and capable person of not less than 25 years of age shall at all times of the day and night be actually present in and upon the premises'.[71] The Post Office's solicitor pronounced the claim impossible to recover, waspishly commenting that 'if a man does not read his policy he has only himself to blame'.[72] Knight tendered his resignation on the grounds of ill health shortly afterwards.

Was Knight's treatment fair? Fine Art and General's policy against burglary carefully weighed the likely level of burglars' skills against specific expectations

[69] 'Telephone Aids a Burglary', *Daily Express* (31 Mar. 1923), p. 6.
[70] RMA, POST 33/149A, 'File no. 35, 14 June 1923–15 Oct. 1925', memo. (1 Nov. 1923) and minute (14 June 1923); Letter from S. E. Knight (19 June 1923); 'Further statement of Mr. S. E. Knight made at the investigation branch' (16 Nov. 1923).
[71] RMA, POST 33/149A, Letter to S. E. Knight from the Fine Art and General Insurance Company Limited (3 Dec. 1923); Letter to the secretary, Fine Art and General Insurance Company from S. E. Knight (27 Nov. 1923).
[72] RMA, POST 33/149A, Letter to the secretary, Fine Art and General Insurance Company from D. A. Stroud (8 Nov. 1923).

of homeowners' personal levels of responsibility. These were embodied in requiring homeowners' ages to be suitably advanced—assuming 25 years old constituted a 'responsible and capable person'—and their implementation of appropriate security technologies. Questioning homeowners' vigilance in protecting their properties implicitly gradated responsibility for a burglary, suggesting that homeowners could easily fend off most 'ordinary' thieves and, therefore, that 'real' burglaries should involve the demonstration of uncommon skill by the criminal. Specifying the 'Hobbs Hart close shackle padlock' as the only mechanism to pose a truly adequate obstacle to prospective thieves (by no means a unique insistence upon branded products to emerge in a claims dispute) distinguished the type of burglar against whose crimes insurers would recompense as 'professional': one who could defeat the most well-known, successful makers of safes and locks.[73] Fine Art and General's good will may have also been eroded by circumstances beyond Knight's control. Prior to arriving at the post office, the burglars telephoned a neighbouring post office in Clapham to ask if the Wimbledon post office was open that day. Clapham duly responded that there was 'No reply' from Wimbledon, effectively giving the green light to the burglars to proceed.[74] Taken as a whole, responsibility for the burglary increasingly turned against the actions of Post Office employees, and Knight bore the brunt. This marked a clear departure from insurers' adverts, and their promises to bring 'relief' to clients by guarding against hordes of burglars of all levels of ability.

Negotiating a claim shifted insurers' definition of burglars towards the much more commercially useful notion of the 'recidivist' or 'professional' criminal, one who persistently reoffended, and was believed to be genetically predisposed to a life of crime. The recidivist was a key figure in official, criminological, and medical thought about crime in Britain between 1865 and 1918.[75] It was also a feature of the transatlantic conversation about crime and punishment, with American criminologists Edwin Sutherland, and Sheldon and Eleanor Glueck, offering highly influential theories about the nature of criminals in the 1930s that revolved around identifying the persistent 'professional' offender.[76] Under criminal law, the distinction between one-time, opportunistic offenders and repeat offenders was recognized by harsher punishments for those with previous convictions.[77] Nonetheless, these distinctions constituted far more generalized analytical frameworks than those suggested by insurers' insistence that a 'real' burglar be defined by their skill in overcoming certain brands of security measures. Here, the commercial dimension of insurance companies' input into contemporary discourse about crime was magnified, as clients were forced to purchase those branded locks and safes insurers

[73] RMA: POST 33/148, 'File no. 22, 17 Mar.–26 Aug. 1916', letter from C. A. Comber, postmaster, to 'The Controller', 17 Mar. 1916; memo. 'B.H.A' to the staff branch (8 May 1916).

[74] 'Telephone Aids a Burglary', *Daily Express* (31 Mar. 1923), p. 6.

[75] Neil Davie, 'Criminal Man Revisited? Continuity and Change in British Criminology, c.1865–1918', *Journal of Victorian Culture* 8 (2003), pp. 1–32.

[76] John H. Laub and Robert J. Sampson, 'The Sutherland-Glueck Debate: On the Sociology of Criminal Knowledge', *American Journal of Sociology* 96 (1991), pp. 1402–40.

[77] Larceny Act 1916, Geo. V, c. 50. ss. 6 & 7, 28:4 (a).

had chosen for their presumed or proven ability to withstand the efforts of potentially highly skilled criminals.

The age of the homeowner, and its implications upon their ability to effectively guard against burglary, were conspicuously absent from burglary insurance adverts. Still bruised from Fine Art and General's dismissal of his claim on those grounds, Samuel Knight launched an appeal against the company's verdict in November 1923, asserting that

> I understand that as the matter now stands the Insurance Company do not appear to be legally liable for any claim under the Policy but as in my opinion they are morally or equitably liable to some extent I propose to write them again asking them to make some payment in the circumstances described.[78]

Knight's proposition that the insurer was 'morally' liable (and failure to recognize the constrained terms of the civil law contract to which he had agreed) exposed his conceptual conflation of insurers' business tactics with a betrayal of an assumed code of ethical conduct. His incredulity at their refusal to pay out after the burglary underlined the disparity between claim negotiations and the emotionally supportive relationship insurers promulgated in their advertising. Indeed, Knight's complaint, and the language of betrayal in which he articulated it, recurred periodically in newspaper reports of insurers' refusal to meet claims between 1900 and 1939. As early as 1904, the *Daily Mirror* published an article entitled 'Is Insurance a Real Safeguard?', in which 'a high authority' was quoted warning that 'In the case of burglary policies particularly, I should advise the public to be very careful as to the wording, the tendency of those issued by many companies being to practically exempt the company from all liability'.[79] Comparably, in 1926 *John Bull* reported a court dispute arising from the refusal of the Lancashire and General Assurance Co. to make good a burglary insurance claim in which the judge, Lord Wrenbury, remarked 'that he thought it a mean and contemptible policy on the part of the company to take the premiums and then refuse to pay by availing themselves of a technical excuse'.[80]

However, insurers were also highly justified in maintaining strict codes of business conduct. Repeated attempts to swindle insurers through faked or 'bogus' burglaries recurred, the reports of these scams providing a telling juxtaposition to press critiques of insurance companies' refusal to make good burglary claims.[81] In April 1923 *The Times* reported the case of Mrs Annie Fletcher, at that time styling herself the 'Countess Wrateslaw' in order to avoid her debtors. Fletcher/Wrateslaw lost her claim against the Traders and General Insurance Association, Ltd for remuneration of a burglary insurance policy to the value of £1,500. The money was to compensate her for the loss of a picture supposedly painted by Rembrandt,

---

[78] RMA, POST 33/149A, 'Further statement of Mr. S. E. Knight' (16 Nov. 1923).
[79] 'Is Insurance a Real Safeguard?', *Daily Mirror* (18 Apr. 1906), p. 4.
[80] 'Insurance Co.'s Strange Methods', *John Bull* (27 Nov. 1926), p. 15.
[81] 'Great Art Robbery', *Daily Mirror* (28 Feb. 1907), p. 4; 'Burgled by Consent', *Daily Mirror* (26 July 1913), p. 13; 'Sham Burglary Case', *Daily Express* (24 Apr. 1923), p. 5; 'Famous Folk Who Swindle', *John Bull* (16 Oct. 1926), p. 24; 'Bogus Burglary Allegation', *Daily Express* (27 June 1933), p. 9.

stolen in a 'burglary' on 22 October 1921.[82] Summing up the evidence for the jury at the High Court of Justice in London, Mr Justice Swift found himself unable to state with certainty that the burglary from Fletcher's mansion at Bryant-Square in London's wealthy West End was real, despite the police having clearly identified the marks of a forcible entry made through a window at night whilst Fletcher was at the theatre.[83] Revelations during the course of the trial, though, drew attention to Fletcher's alleged association with known thieves and drug-dealers, and damning testimony was offered by Sidney Jackson (a former inmate of a Borstal institution for young offenders) that he had received a £10 cheque signed by Fletcher as an incentive to commit a proposed burglary of the picture in February 1921. This forced Swift to ask the jury to assess 'whether a person of the character, disposition, and mode of life of the plaintiff ought to be believed'.[84] Finding in favour of the insurance company, the jury affirmed that burglary was defined against the actions and behaviour of the homeowner as much as the criminal during insurance claims.

Notably, when burglary insurance frauds were reported in the press, they situated insurers as victims of theft through recalling a similar sense of personal loss and betrayal as homeowners felt, and used the same language to emphasize the danger posed by thousands of burglars purportedly at large. As an exposé in newspaper *John Bull* claimed on 19 September 1931, there was an 'army' of 'phantom burglars' targeting insurance companies, numbering in the thousands.[85] Comparably, insurance expert C. E. Golding recycled the discourse used by angry claimants for the benefit of insurers when talking of such frauds: 'As we have seen, an insurance policy is a contract of the utmost good faith, and the least amount of fraud or untruth will render it void'.[86] Insurers' contestation of burglary claims, and their precise lists of clauses for the crime's identification, were therefore both legitimized and recognized within a context of the 'risks' under which they also laboured, manifested in clients' potential attempts at fraud. It was widely recognized by the press, police, and government that the claim became the site at which the emotionally supportive relationship between clients and insurers, carefully crafted through their adverts, collapsed, and commercial imperatives took over. Accordingly, the burglar changed too, measured by insurers against the 'professional' skill of the criminal, who should commonly be defeated by branded security devices, and the character and dependability of homeowners.

*   *   *

The period following 1889 proved fertile ground for the consolidation of several commercially lucrative definitions of burglary and burglars by insurance companies. Insurers proved remarkably adept at deploying marketing that successfully manipulated contextually sensitive emotional 'triggers'—emotives—with which to extol the threat of burglary. The growth of the burglary insurance sector indicates

---

[82] 'Law Report, April 20', *The Times* (21 Apr. 1923), p. 5.   [83] Ibid.
[84] 'High Court of Justice', *The Times* (24 Apr. 1923), p. 5.
[85] 'An Army of Bogus Bankrupts', *John Bull* (19 Sept. 1931), pp. 18–19.
[86] Golding, *Burglary*, p. 35.

the receptivity of consumers to these influences, and the successful integration of state, media, and (most importantly) market representations of crime upon which insurers built their sector. Additionally, the expansion of the middle classes, which increasingly brought domestic concerns to the forefront, as well as innovations in printing and the growth of newspaper advertising, furnished the perfect conditions to cultivate a mass audience for the consumption of burglary insurance. Remaining sensitive to the complexity of this audience, insurers operated within the overlapping frameworks provided by ideas about domestic life and homeowners' responsibilities. By marketing towards the protective presence of a male owner, but practising a more realistic daily interchange with homeowners of both sexes, insurance companies exploited the tensions between public and private models of everyday life to their best advantage.

Insurers also successfully negotiated the divide between marketing towards versions of crime and criminal defined under criminal law and adopting more specific definitions within their contractual agreements. Establishing standards by which a burglar could be measured, such as extraordinary skill at safe-breaking or lock-picking, insurers were able to retain profits in the face of challenges by honest claimants and swindlers alike. Strikingly, in borrowing the category of 'professional' burglar from criminological and legal discourse and integrating it into their contracts, insurers exploited strategies they had successfully used for the purposes of marketing. Arguably, it is this aspect of insurers' involvement in the promulgation of ideas about burglary and burglars in early twentieth-century Britain that is most compelling. Illustrating the agency of commerce in the formulation of cultural, social, and political responses to crime and criminals, burglary insurance literature confounds the historiographical convention of treating these domains in isolation. It shows how crime shaped relatively mediocre decisions regarding domestic arrangements on an everyday basis. Security technologies took this a step further. Through applying the requisite safes, locks, and alarms requested by insurers, householders changed the very fabric and organization of their homes to render them 'burglar proof'. As the next chapter shows, however, designing the perfect burglar-proof home was less easy than it seemed. Barriers would need not only to be impenetrable, but, to see off the phantom-like burglar, *invisible* as well . . . .

6

Designing the Burglar-Proof Home

GOING TO THE THEATRE

She had kissed the baby for the last time—until she returned and kissed him again. She had carefully locked every door in the house and all the windows. She had turned the gas to the exact point at which it was to be left until her return. She had attended to the grate, and warned Bridget not to meddle with it for fear of fire. She had explained to that functionary the use of the burglar alarm, the fire alarm, and the policeman's whistle. She had put the cat and dog in the cellar, and had wrapped a newspaper around the canary's cage. And then she was ready.

She locked the inside door and tried it. Then she locked the outside door and tried it. Then she opened the outside door and tried the inside door again. Then she locked the outside door again, tried it, and they started. They had proceeded two streets, and her husband had just begun to congratulate himself that she really was ready, when she suddenly stopped.

'John', she said, 'I must go back and tell Bridget to be sure not to wake the baby up unless he wakes himself.'

London Journal (8 December 1900), p. 496

'Going to the Theatre' was a story about fear. Checking and re-checking an elaborate array of security technologies, the worried young mother, watched by her exasperated husband, could only enjoy her night out after ensuring that both baby and nurse were ensconced within a fortress of locked windows, doors, and alarms. Ironically locking *in* both child and employee, her anxiety seemed to extend to a lack of trust in her own employee, as Bridget's presence was ignored as a potential safeguard from fire or someone who might discourage a burglar's attack. Forced to trail behind as the protagonist painstakingly works through her sequence of domestic locks, we (the readers) vicariously experience the home as a set of obstacles. Living rooms, bedrooms, cellar, and entrance hall are suddenly transformed into discreet confined spaces and safe havens. Hidden by myriad doors preventing any glimpse of the interior, the secrets within these spaces are lost to snooping readers, who act as a proxy for the prying eyes of a potential burglar.

The sheer range of technologies mentioned in this story reflects how the domestic security industry had prospered, and specialized, in Britain over the course of the nineteenth century. Historian Amanda Vickery has described how domestic locks became *de rigour* in wealthy London homes during the eighteenth century, their use serving to deter thieves (including burglars), encourage privacy, and create boundaries between rooms that maintained the gendered division of labour.[1] Lock-makers' craftsmanship had evolved still further by the late Victorian period, intensifying their (lucrative) efforts in the fight against crime by creating devices whose appearances mimicked the latest interior designs, cunningly camouflaging their technologies. Security companies including famous names such as Chubb's, Milners' Safe Co., Chatwood's Safe Co., Hobbs & Co., and John Tann Safes Co. thereby designed products to meet the technological expertise of burglars *and* consumer demand for a home decorated to 'fashionable' tastes. In the case of locks and safes, this involved designing them with decorative patterns on the surface that blended with the latest furnishings through elegant floral designs (Fig. 6.1).

Burglar alarms then gave properties an added layer of impregnability. Inventions of the 1890s, these experimental products of specialist companies and inventors were designed from the outset to be placed around the home where burglars would not notice, at least until the devices were triggered. From the 1920s some favoured a silent device, marketed as sending an instantaneous electrical signal to the nearest local police station once its sensors detected a burglar's presence, usually by touch or footfall.[2] Light, sound, and pressure thereby furnished homes with an array of invisible, mostly intangible boundaries. New routines were added to domestic occupants' everyday security checks, as switches to activate the alarms had to be turned off or on to mark the household's retirement to bed or leaving the house in the morning. Such innovations redefined the domestic interior, modelling it for use as both home and well-disguised burglar trap. They also reflected the slow shift towards more companionate forms of marriage, as responsibility for safeguarding the home from danger was visualized as something that either men or women could ensure, simply by flicking a switch.[3]

This chapter explores how security devices not only shaped the behaviours of residents—how they moved around and used different rooms of the house—but also where they kept their possessions, and latterly how burglar alarms and other devices shaped the relationship between citizen and state. Historians of domestic space have treated decoration and security separately, highlighting the architectural boundaries created by locks and bolts but disregarding their effect on the visual appearance of homes or the psychology of their inhabitants.[4] Locks, safes, and alarms made certain locations in the house more secure, where household 'treasures' such as jewellery would live depending upon their monetary or emotional value.

---

[1] Vickery, 'An Englishman's Home Is his Castle?', pp. 147–73.

[2] BTA, POST 33/1332, 'Use of Telephone Circuit in Connection with Burglar and Fire Alarms: Adams Silent Burglar Alarm, 1921–1927', letter from S. G. Adams to the Rt. Hon. A. H. Illingsworth M.P., H.M. Postmaster General (13 Jan. 1921).

[3] Marcus Collins, *Modern Love: An Intimate History of Men and Women in Twentieth-Century Britain* (London: Atlantic Books, 2003).

[4] Vickery, 'An Englishman's Home Is his Castle?', pp. 147–73; Hamlett, *Material Relations*, pp. 29–71. See also Inga Bryden and Janet Floyd, 'Introduction', in Inga Bryden and Janet Floyd (eds.), *Domestic Space: Reading the Nineteenth-Century Interior* (Manchester: Manchester University Press, 1999), pp. 1–17; Stefan Muthesius, *The Poetic Home: Designing the 19th Century Domestic Interior* (London: Thames and Hudson, 2009), pp. 16–17.

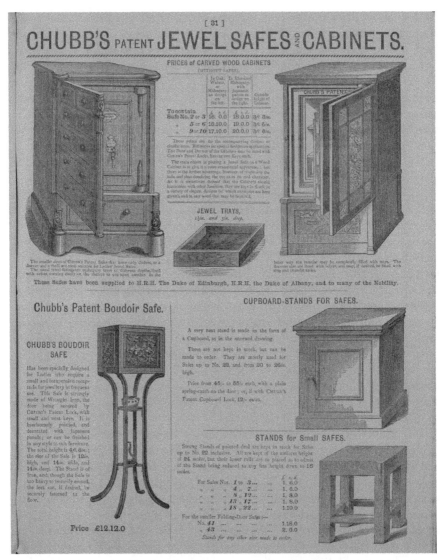

Fig. 6.1. LMA, CLC/B/002, Box 264, *Illustrated Price List of Chubb & Son's Patent Locks and Safes* (Oct. 1882), p. 31. Reproduced by kind permission of London Metropolitan Archives (City of London).

Mirroring the acutely gendered nature of interior design in the late Victorian and Edwardian periods, locks and safes incorporated gendered notions of style that reflected their use protecting rooms and objects associated with either male or female householders. These patterns combined to reinforce and shape contemporary imaginings of the emotional and sexual organization of the home, and where burglars were more likely to target, enhancing the sense of violation. Burglars' attempts to penetrate into certain (predominantly 'feminized') rooms were continually encoded in certain press reports, fiction, and security company advertising as a form of pseudo-sexual assault. Criminologists have long recognized the psychological association of burglary with rape, stemming from identifying the physical security of one's home with that of one's body and mind.[5] Actual rape did not feature in any of the recorded burglaries in this book, but the marketing of security technologies certainly profited from the association, and cultivated it actively, again forming part of the 'culture of fear' surrounding the crime.

Burglar-proofing the home was the obvious solution, a process that, in turn, created new social networks. Whether through the use of a branded lock to frustrate a burglar—the breaking of which would have to be examined—or by the 'ring' of an alarm, a home's inhabitants summonsed police, insurers, and security company agents to investigate. Neighbours and passers-by would also be expected to help. Connecting the home imperceptibly to the outside world, locks and alarms collapsed the putative public/private divide between domestic and exterior worlds. In the case of alarms, this meant quite literally 'calling' into being networks of social reciprocity and regulatory action against crime that drew these groups into the same physical and imaginative space (the home), uniting them in a common resistance to burglary.[6] Yet sometimes people refused. As alarms became commonplace, local residents gradually ignored their ringing in the assumption that others would help, or through increasing annoyance at the sound.[7] Noise acts 'as a register of the *intensity* of relationships', because it is both welcomed and resisted, depending upon the level of intrusion into 'peaceful' silence it represents. It also denotes the attempt of someone to make contact with others, which may not be desirable.[8] Reciprocity in offering and receiving help between citizens, as well as neighbourly codes of friendship, were tested by burglar alarms, shedding light on local and class-based tensions in London during this era.

Privacy was also imperilled by these devices. Burglars' attempts to break a lock or safe, or the accidental triggering of an alarm, briefly rendered the home a site of consensual surveillance.[9] Contrary to prevailing ideals of domestic isolation—'a

[5] See for example criminologist Mike Maguire's classic study of this: Mike Maguire, 'The Impact of Burglary upon Victims', *British Journal of Criminology* 20 (July 1980), pp. 265–6; see also Eamonn Carrabine's discussion of the visual security devices of the home as a physical manifestation of 'risk society': Carrabine, *Crime, Culture, and the Media*, pp. 48–9.

[6] Anti-burglar devices thus arguably occupied the role of 'actants': what sociologist Bruno Latour, expounding the idea of 'actor-network theory', defines as any things that are 'participants in a course of action...In addition to "determining" and serving as a "backdrop for human action", things might authorise, allow, afford, encourage, permit, suggest, influence, block, render possible, forbid, and so on'. Bruno Latour, *Reassembling the Social: An Introduction to Actor-Network Theory* (Oxford: Oxford University Press, 2005), pp. 71–2.

[7] TNA, HO 45/20369, 'Burglar Alarms 1920–1945', Folder 398952, 'Electric Alarm Bells, Continuous Ringing Of' (4 Dec. 1928), cover flap.

[8] Hillel Schwartz, *Making Noise: From Babel to the Big Bang and Beyond* (New York: Zone Books, 2011), pp. 20–1.

[9] This ideal was embodied in legislation such as the 1861 Offences Against the Person Act requiring police officers in Britain to obtain search warrants from a Justice of the Peace before they could enter houses, as well as the architectural preference for houses built to stand separately from one another (itself progressively rare as the city's population expanded, resulting in a greater number of

man's home is his castle'—security devices, when activated, legitimized the presence of outside observers within the home, and made it knowable in ways that anticipated the development of CCTV cameras within gated communities later in the twentieth century.[10] In July 1920, for example, the *Daily Express* reported on a recent invention called the 'Buzzer-Light-Shriek Alarm' by a Mr Braun of Caledonian Road, north London. This device would not only communicate precisely where the property's perimeter had been breached through the noise of the alarm, but would also bathe the interior in light for all to witness. As the report stated, the invention 'renders it impossible for a burglar to enter premises by door, window, skylight, or chimney without raising an alarm. Not only do bells ring, but the premises become lit up inside, and a red sign outside blazes forth "Police" in large letters.'[11] Whilst the report presented this as appealing, the number of false alarms causing problems in this period may have made it less so. In 1929, a memorandum to the Metropolitan Police observed that during the previous year, 4,171 alarm bells had rung throughout London of which only six were found to be the result of legitimate burglaries. As the report noted, 'this evil is a greater one than has been realised'.[12] One suspects sales of Mr Braun's invention, which disappeared quickly from the market, were correspondingly slow.

The 'Buzzer-Light-Shriek Alarm' may not have proved the commercial success its inventor hoped, but its aggressive demand for police attention revealed a commercial truth: alarm creators expected police to respond. The purchase and use of 'burglar-proof' locks, safes, and alarms in this period, at prices affordable only to the more prosperous classes of society, therefore meant that protecting the home from criminals depended upon economically driven forms of consent and cooperation among citizens, state, and business. State services, including the water supply and sanitary agencies, were already a source of conflict among citizens over how much they should pay in the 'rates' for their personal, domestic use.[13] Under the Liberal governments of late Victorian Britain, citizens treated their 'entitlement' to these services much as though consumers, forging 'a crucial dynamic of flux, agency and contestation in everyday material politics'.[14] The emergency services of police, fire, and ambulance provision became subject to similar forms of competition, with security companies' promises to provide accelerated access to police via burglar alarms exacerbating tensions around access. What customers were really 'buying' was the assurance of security companies that either the police

---

semi-detached properties). Public General Acts 44 and 45 Vict., 1861, c. 100 ss. 65; Marcus, *Apartment Stories*, p. 94.

[10] See Rowland Atkinson, Sarah Blandy, John Flint, and Diane Lister, 'Gated Cities of Today? Barricaded Residential Development in England', *Town Planning Review* 76 (Oct. 2005), pp. 401–22.

[11] TNA, HO 45/20369, clipping in file *Burglar Alarms 1920–1945*: 'Unemployment for Burglars', *Daily Express* (24 July 1920), p. 5.

[12] TNA, MEPO 2/8345, *Burglar Alarm Bells: Annoyance Caused by Continuous Ringing—Introduction of Bye-Law, 1928–43*, 'Memorandum: Burglar Alarm Bells: False Calls' (16 Dec. 1929).

[13] Vanessa Taylor and Frank Trentmann, 'Liquid Politics: Water and the Politics of Everyday Life in the Modern City', *Past and Present* 211 (2011), p. 203.

[14] Ibid., pp. 202–3.

or their own agents, working in a quasi-judicial role, would commit to defending the material interests of the middle and upper classes. Once more, the market proved effective at interfering with state regulatory machinery, with security companies working hand-in-hand with the burglary insurance industry.

Locks, safes, and alarms provided another dimension to the material culture of police prevention in this period, offering physical, aural, and electrical 'boundaries' around the home in addition to street lighting and other municipal improvements designed to enforce morality through environmental change.[15] Burglar-proofing the home thus brought a new set of visible and invisible defences into the armoury of those fighting the war against thieves in the night. Although they had little tangible success, these technologies nonetheless transformed domestic space and the nature of surveillance within wealthy urban neighbourhoods. In addition, they drove forward a worrying new question: should protection from burglars be guaranteed, or bought—and who was willing to protect whom?

* * *

'Inside of the house and out of it, people who wish to be safe, must look to their locks'.

Henry W. Holland, 'The Art of Self Protection Against Thieves and Robbers', *Good Words* (1 December 1865), 848

The aesthetic appearance of domestic locks and safes, as against their purely mechanical functioning, was of greater concern to their manufacturers in the 1860s than it had been in any previous decade. In 1862 the International Exhibition was held at South Kensington, organized with an even greater emphasis on the arts in the context of industrial manufacturing than the preceding Great Exhibition of 1851. Now, the decorative properties of locks and safes were presented alongside the mechanism of the lock itself as commercially desirable.[16] Chubb's were one company that did particularly well at this challenge. Awarded a prize medal in the category of Iron and General Hardware, Chubb's designs were praised 'For the perfection of workmanship and construction of Locks, also for the manufacture of Iron Safes'.[17] Figures 6.2 and 6.3 show the products for which they won the award. Beautiful decorative surfaces adorned both locks and jewellery safes, which the pamphlet described as being of 'an elaborate medieval design' and 'ornamental'. In the same paragraphs, they also assured customers that they were 'gunpowder-proof' and therefore 'thief-proof'.[18] Chubb's acclaim for counteracting burglars' latest techniques of 'cracking' safes using explosives (a method attracting considerable

[15] Joyce, *The Rule of Freedom*, pp. 144–71; Otter, *The Victorian Eye*, pp. 193–6; Mark Neocleous, 'Social Police and the Mechanisms of Prevention', *British Journal of Criminology* 40 (2000), pp. 710–26.
[16] Jeffrey Auerbach, *The Great Exhibition of 1851: A Nation on Display* (London and New Haven: Yale University Press, 1999), pp. 216–17.
[17] Advertisement, *Examiner* (2 Aug. 1862), p. 494.
[18] LMA, CLC/B/002/10/01/008, Exhibition booklet *Chubb's Patent Locks and Safes. International Exhibition, 1862. Class XXXI. No. 6017* (1862), pp. 2–3.

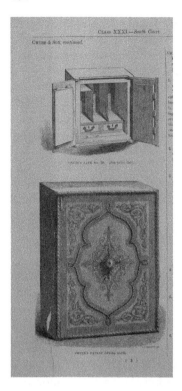

Fig. 6.2. LMA, CLC/B/002/10/01/008, Jewel safe featured in exhibition booklet *Chubb's Patent Locks and Safes, International Exhibition, 1862. Class XXXI. No. 6017* (1862), p. 3. Reproduced by kind permission of London Metropolitan Archives (City of London).

attention in the press) was thus significantly enhanced by their incorporation of the latest styles in furnishings.[19] Naturalistic floral patterns and intricate scrolls and leaf shapes chimed perfectly with the Gothic Revival, popularizing cabinets and bureaus for middle-class homes that evoked a 'medieval' spirit, with a romantic 'natural' harmony.[20]

Using 'nature' to disguise a set of ingenious mechanical locks wrought entirely through the scientific and steel-making advancements of the industrial revolution forged an elegant dialectic, linking the protection of the 'natural' family unit

---

[19] Documents kept by the Chubb Co. from this period include a letter of thanks from a Mr John Ellison regarding a burglary in which there was a 'desperate attempt made with Gunpowder drills and picklocks to open the Safe which was purchased from you...but we are happy to say that it withstood all their efforts'. LMA, CLC/B/002/10/01/009, *Chubb Collectanea Vol. 3 Part 3*: letter to Messrs. Chubb and Son from Mr John Ellison (3 March 1863). The governments of the 1860s instituted both a Special Committee on Gunpowder (1858–66) and subsequent Committee on Gunpowder and Explosives (1869–81) in order to investigate the legitimacy and extent of its usage in Britain. Seymour H. Mauskopf, 'Pellets, Pebbles, and Prisms: British Munitions for Larger Guns, 1860–1885', in Brenda J. Buchanan (ed.), *Gunpowder, Explosives and the State: A Technological History* (Aldershot: Ashgate Publishing, 2006), p. 304.

[20] Judith A. Neiswander, *The Cosmopolitan Interior: Liberalism and the British Home, 1870–1914* (London and New Haven: Yale University Press, 2008); Lesley Jackson, *Twentieth Century Pattern Design* (London: Mitchell Beazley, 2002), pp. 6–13.

Fig. 6.3. LMA, CLC/B/002/10/01/008, Door Lock featured in exhibition booklet *Chubb's Patent Locks and Safes, International Exhibition, 1862. Class XXXI. No. 6017* (1862), p. 2. Reproduced by kind permission of London Metropolitan Archives (City of London).

against the depredations of the technologically adept 'modern' burglar. Ornate designs for locks, and particularly safes, subsequently began to feature in the sales catalogues and marketing material of companies including Hobbs & Co., Milner's Safes, and the Chatwood Safe Co. Ltd throughout the late Victorian and early Edwardian period (Fig. 6.4).[21] Brochures organized products into two sections. Using the opening pages to advertise different sizes and technological grades of fire- and burglar-proof safes without accompanying cabinets, they then gave illustrations of safes within furniture to highlight the successful camouflage their designs afforded. In the first section, illustrations showing the thickness of steel used in the walls and the different models of locks that could be affixed to each design demonstrated safes' scientific security against burglars' efforts. Heightening consumer anxiety, manufacturers asserted that their opponents were 'burglars of exceptional skill' (Chatwood's, 1900), 'scientific cracksmen' possessed of 'daring' as well as 'the most powerful liquid explosives...[and] the deadly Blowpipe' (Milner's,

---

[21] LMA, CLC/B, Box 72/1, 1999/007, *Descriptive and Illustrative Price List of 'Hobbs & Co'.s' Series of Locks and Lock Furniture* (1 May 1884), pp. 44, 50–2; LMA, CLC/B, Box 72/1, 1999/007 'Milner-Sales Catalogues', *Milner's Safes* (1900), pp. 40–2; LMA, CLC/B, Box 72/1, 1999/007 'Milner-Sales Catalogues', *Milner's Safes* (1907), pp. 40–2; LMA, CLC/B, Box 72/1, 1999/007 'Milner-Sales Catalogues', *Milner's Hold-Fast and Fire Resisting Safes, Chests, Strong Rooms, Strong Room Doors, Powder Magazines, &c.* (c.1880), pp. 24–7; LMA, CLC/B, Box 72/1, 1999/007 'Milner-Sales Catalogues', *Milners' Safe Co.* (1915), pp. 33–9; LMA, CLC/B, Box 72/1, 1999/007 'Milner-Sales Catalogues', *Milner's Safes* (1911), pp. 25; LMA, CLC/B, 1999/007 'Chatwood Printed Items', *The Chatwood Safe Co. Ltd* (1912), pp. 28–31.

MILNERS' JEWELLERY SAFE CABINETS.

Made in any kind of wood, to suit other furniture.

Prices from **£14 10 0** to **£25 0 0**

Exclusive of Safe.

For cost of Safes, see Price List.

Manufactory: PHŒNIX SAFE WORKS, LIVERPOOL.

LONDON: Milners' Buildings (opposite Moorgate-street Station), City, E.C.

LIVERPOOL: 8, Lord Street.

MANCHESTER: 28, Market Street.

Fig. 6.4. LMA, CLC/B, file 1999/007, 'Milner's Jewellery Safe Cabinets', in *Milner's Hold-Fast and Fire Resisting Safes, Chests, Strong Rooms, Strong Room Doors, Powder Magazines, &c.* (*c.*1880), p. 24. Reproduced by kind permission of London Metropolitan Archives (City of London).

1915).[22] Providing readers were able to move past their shock at being informed of the prospect of a small explosion taking place in their house at night, the second section then invited them to register the way in which the highly finished surfaces would 'fit' within their homes. Visually juxtaposing safes within these cabinets (instead of just showing the exterior designs), served as the ultimate 'revelation' of their effective disguise, bringing home to customers the marriage between safety and beauty of design.

Some companies went further than others. In June 1880, George Hayter Chubb (grandson of Charles, the original founder) involved his company with the Arts and Crafts Movement, co-founding the Art Furnishers Alliance. As 'one of the first interior decorating firms in the modern sense and covered virtually all fields of design', the Arts Furnishers Alliance employed Christopher Dresser, the designer famous globally for his application of decorative art onto domestic industrial goods.[23] Chubb's 1882 catalogue betrayed this influence, offering locks and safes designed to suit individual rooms and pieces of furniture. Among a series of designs for door-locks were a 'drawer lock', 'cupboard lock', and 'wardrobe lock', as well as a 'Two-bolt Mortise Lock for Dining and Drawing Rooms' that had a 'reversible Latch-bolt to suit either hand, best Brass furniture, and self-adjusting spindle for any thickness of door'.[24] These products were advertised for sale repeatedly in catalogues of 1893, 1894, 1905, 1906, and 1907, indicating their commercial success.[25] Flattering customers by implying that their homes were decorated throughout in the latest styles with expensive brass furniture to match—something that was rarely the case in this period—Chubb's also impressed clients with the fragility of their wealth.[26] Only by fixing locks on myriad rooms, doors, bureaus, chests, and drawers, the brochures warned, could the burglar be thwarted.

Competitors followed suit. Hobbs Co., advertising their wares in a 1905 trades book of domestic hardware, presented 'detector' locks for nursery gates and to affix to bureaus, cupboards, and letter- and cash-boxes, either in brass or finished in a japanned style to suit furniture.[27] Recalling the narrative of 'Going to the Theatre', the nursery gate locks equated familial safety with the safety of possessions, offering mechanical devices as the solution to both sources of worry. Appeals to parental instincts drew force from a conservative set of expectations about the heteronormative composition of middle-class households, expectations that found similar form in other, explicitly gendered inventions (Fig. 6.5). Chubb's 1882 'Boudoir

---

[22] LMA, CLC/B, 1999/007 'Chatwood Printed Items', *Chatwood's Patent 'Solid' Steel Safes* (1900), p. 4; LMA, CLC/B, Box 72/1, 1999/007 'Milner-Sales Catalogues', *Milners' Safe Co.* (1915), p. 3.

[23] Widar Halén, *Christopher Dresser: A Pioneer of Modern Design* (London, 1990), pp. 9, 18, 46.

[24] LMA, CLC/B/002, Box 264, *Illustrated Price List of Chubb & Son's Patent Locks and Safes* (Oct. 1882), pp. 4–5.

[25] LMA, CLC/B/002 Box 264, *Illustrated Price List of Chubb's New Patent Fire and Thief Resisting Safes, Vault Doors, Grilles, Strong Rooms, &c., Detector Locks, Japanned Boxes, &c.* (Oct. 1893), pp. 4–5; LMA, CLC/B/002 Box 264, *Chubb's Locks, Door, and Window Fittings* (1 June 1894), pp. 3–4; LMA, CLC/B/002 Box 264, *Chubb's Steel Strong Room and Party Wall Doors* (June 1905); LMA, CLC/B/002 Box 264, *Chubb's Price List of Locks and Safes* (Oct. 1906), pp. 8–11; LMA, CLC/B/002 Box 264, *Chubb's List of Patent Detector Locks* (Nov. 1907), pp. 4–11.

[26] Hamlett, *Material Relations*.

[27] GMA, *G. Harding & Sons Hardware Merchants and Manufacturers* (Sept. 1905), pp. 358–68.

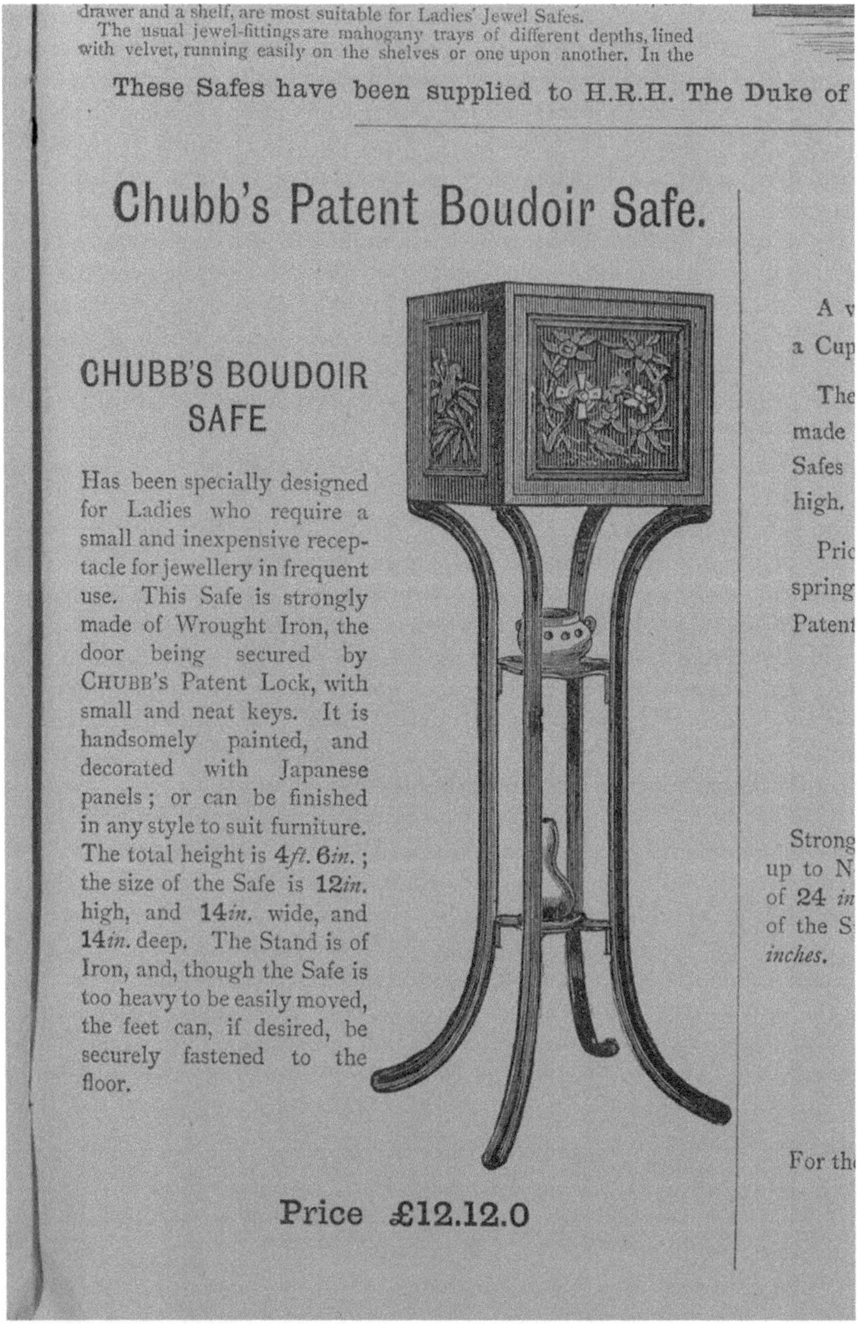

drawer and a shelf, are most suitable for Ladies' Jewel Safes.
The usual jewel-fittings are mahogany trays of different depths, lined
with velvet, running easily on the shelves or one upon another. In the

These Safes have been supplied to H.R.H. The Duke of

Chubb's Patent Boudoir Safe.

CHUBB'S BOUDOIR SAFE

Has been specially designed for Ladies who require a small and inexpensive receptacle for jewellery in frequent use. This Safe is strongly made of Wrought Iron, the door being secured by CHUBB'S Patent Lock, with small and neat keys. It is handsomely painted, and decorated with Japanese panels ; or can be finished in any style to suit furniture. The total height is 4*ft.* 6*in.* ; the size of the Safe is 12*in.* high, and 14*in.* wide, and 14*in.* deep. The Stand is of Iron, and, though the Safe is too heavy to be easily moved, the feet can, if desired, be securely fastened to the floor.

A v
a Cup

The
made
Safes
high.

Pric
spring
Patent

Strong
up to N
of 24 *in*
of the S
inches.

For th

Price £12.12.0

Fig. 6.5. LMA, CLC/B/002, Box 264, *Illustrated Price List of Chubb & Son's Patent Locks and Safes* (Oct. 1882), p. 31. Reproduced by kind permission of London Metropolitan Archives (City of London).

Safe' (reissued in successive years and updated decorative styles until 1939) was annotated with the description,

> Has been specially designed for Ladies who require a small and inexpensive receptacle for jewellery in frequent use. This Safe is strongly made of Wrought Iron, the door being secured by CHUBB'S Patent Lock, with small and neat keys. It is handsomely painted, and decorated with Japanese panels; or can be finished in any style to suit furniture.[28]

Gorgeously decorated 'boudoir & dressing room jewel safes' also appeared in the Hobbs-Hart catalogue of 1884, suggesting they too saw a market for these designs, and for consigning women's interests close to the bedroom.[29] Boudoirs encapsulated ideals about women's sexual and reproductive roles in the home, to which the middle classes clung throughout the onslaught of campaigns for women's suffrage and right to earn an income autonomously.[30] A gently titillating aspect lurked within interior design manuals for middle-class homes, which envisaged the boudoir as a 'transitional' space leading to the bedroom, where acts of dressing and undressing were carried out among the sensuous comforts of rich draperies and 'soft' furnishings.[31] Although Jane Hamlett's study of Victorian boudoirs has shown they were frequently used by men as well, lock and safe manufacturers were hardly going to engage with these practicalities by dispelling such a commercial fantasy.[32] Besides giving them the chance to create furniture that could be purchased as an exciting indulgence, boudoir safes encouraged customers to imagine the worst when considering which rooms the burglar would target. Companies like Chubb's could profit nimbly from cultivating a sense of prospective violation, all while appearing to maintain romance in the marital bedroom.

They likely took inspiration from fiction. The burglary of a cursed Indian diamond from the boudoir of English heiress Rachel Verinder in her country mansion formed the plot of Wilkie Collins' phenomenally popular sensation novel *The Moonstone* (1868).[33] Its perpetrator was Franklin Blake, the young man with whom Rachel

---

[28] LMA, CLC/B/002, Box 264 *Illustrated Price List of Chubb & Son's Patent Lock's and Safes* (Oct. 1882), pp. 31; Boudoir safes were also featured in the following: LMA, CLC/B/002, Box 264 *Chubb's Locks, Door, and Window Fittings* (1 June 1894), p. 40; LMA, CLC/B/002, Box 264 *Illustrated Price List of Chubb's New Patent Fire and Thief Resisting Safes, Vault Doors, Grilles, Strong Rooms, &c., Detector Locks, Japanned Boxes, &c.* (Oct. 1906), p. 34; LMA, CLC/B/002, Box 309 *Safe as Houses* (1939), p. 11.

[29] LMA, CLC/B, Box 72/1, 1999/007, *Descriptive and Illustrative Price List of 'Hobb's & Co.'s' Series of Locks and Lock Furniture* (1 May 1884), p. 51.

[30] Leonore Davidoff and Catherine Hall, *Family Fortunes: Men and Women of the English Middle Class, 1780–1850* (London: Routledge, 2002).

[31] Anne Troutman, 'The Modernist Boudoir and the Erotics of Space', in Hilde Heynan and Gülsüm Baydar (eds.), *Negotiating Domesticity: Spatial Productions of Gender in Modern Architecture* (London: Routledge, 2005), p. 296.

[32] Jane Hamlett, '"The Dining Room Should Be the Man's Paradise, as the Drawing Room Is the Woman's": Gender and Middle-Class Domestic Space in England, 1850–1910', *Gender and History* 21 (2009), p. 576.

[33] Collins, *The Moonstone* (1868). For analysis of The Moonstone's popularity and literary legacy see Ronald R. Thomas, 'The Moonstone, Detective Fiction, and Forensic Science', in Jenny Bourne Taylor (ed.), *The Cambridge Companion to Wilkie Collins* (Cambridge: Cambridge University Press, 2006), pp. 65–78.

was in love who committed the crime under the influence of hypnotism and drugs.[34] As the plot was gradually unravelled by London detective Sergeant Cuff, his account of the virginal Rachel watching in horrified silence as her diamond was 'snatched' in the middle of the night (and subsequent maintenance of that silence to protect Blake) was rich with suggestions of sexual power, domination, and compromise.[35] Standing 'on the threshold of her bedroom door...almost as white in the face as the white dressing-gown that clothed her', Rachel joined the pantheon of 'wronged' women populating Victorian melodrama.[36] Blake's loss of control as he entered the boudoir to commit the burglary was also tellingly evocative of the sexual act, seeming to chime with broader debates in late Victorian Britain about the 'dissipating' effects of luxury and vice on the morality of the upper classes.[37] In *The Moonstone*, both Blake and his manipulator, Geoffrey Ablewhite, are wealthy gentlemen, but the combined lure of Rachel, the jewel itself, drugs, and the interior geography of the house gives them motive and opportunity to commit crime. Collins thus instituted a narrative of burglary entwined with sexual possibility and danger, charged by the symbolism of a male interloper in the acutely feminized space of the boudoir.

Collins' novel was just the first of several stories to deploy the boudoir as a tantalizing haven for criminals.[38] An 1879 story entitled 'Lady Charmeigh's Diamonds', written anonymously for periodical *London Society*, saw Lady Charmeigh's husband purchase her 'from London a fine ebony strong-box, with the most adorable of gold keys attached as a pendant to a bracelet. This pretty gift quite delighted Lady Charmeigh, who convoked all her acquaintances to [Charmeigh] Hall to see her wonderful anti-burglar safe.'[39] During the inevitable burglary that followed, 'Lady Charmeigh's dressing-room was entered by means of a ladder and the safe, the famous safe, was broken open like a walnut'.[40] In an intimate space containing her most personal possessions, Lady Charmeigh's (apparently rather poor quality) gift from her husband was 'cracked', in a theft loaded with pseudo-sexual and marital implications. So much for the integrity of Charmeigh Hall.

Boudoir safes became so ingrained in the cultural consciousness that in 1903 the *Architects Magazine* published an article on the ideal 'dwelling house' that practically insisted on their presence, and on this gendered arrangement of rooms within the home. Prevailing on its wealthy readers to endorse its designs, the *Magazine* ordered 'There should also be two other small rooms, one for the master's

---

[34] Collins, *Moonstone*, pp. 450–1.

[35] Lewis Roberts, 'The "Shivering Sands" of Reality: Narration and Knowledge in Wilkie Collins' *The Moonstone*', *Victorian Review* 23 (1997), pp. 171–2.

[36] Collins, *Moonstone*, p. 87; D'Cruze, *Crimes of Outrage*, p. 149.

[37] Lisa Rodensky, *The Crime in Mind: Criminal Responsibility and the Victorian Novel* (Oxford: Oxford University Press, 2003), pp. 3–34; Wiener, *Reconstructing the Criminal*, pp. 244–56.

[38] Charles Gervase, 'Maurice Durant', *London Reader of Literature, Science, Art, and General Information* (Jan. 1873), pp. 241–4; Jewel safes in the boudoir were featured explicitly in the following: Unknown Author, 'Lady Charmeigh's Diamonds', *London Society* (Jan. 1879), pp. 1–16; Unknown Author, 'Diana's Diamonds', *London Reader of Literature, Science, Art, and General Information* (Nov. 1886), pp. 97–101; John Paslew, 'No Robbery', *Belgravia: A London Magazine* (June 1889), pp. 465–80; Arthur Stringer, 'The Button Thief', *Pall Mall Magazine* (Oct. 1911), pp. 611–24.

[39] 'Lady Charmeigh's Diamonds', p. 1.   [40] Ibid., p. 3.

studio and to hold his deed safe, and the other for the mistress's boudoir and the jewellery safe'.[41] The *Architects Magazine* was the organ of the Society of Architects, established in 1884 as an offshoot of the Royal Institute of British Architects.[42] The inclusion of 'boudoir safes' in this publication showed their phenomenal commercial ascent, the expectation of the 'burglar in the boudoir' gaining credence among some of the most revered architectural designers of the period.

Court and police reports detailing the goods burglars had stolen from London homes did little to dispel these ideas. Across London as a whole the most commonly stolen items were jewellery, clothes, and cash, all easily portable, their conventional location in wardrobes and compartments within the bedroom aggravating readers' fears of being physically near an intruder whilst asleep.[43] Burglaries of jewellery might additionally represent the loss of possessions that had intense emotional associations.[44] Reading through the weekly reports of the *Police Gazette*, a publication issued by the Metropolitan Police to circulate useful information about ongoing investigations, there are striking fragments of personal history that enliven the long lists of jewellery, watches, clothes, and other ornaments purloined. On 21 June 1878, the Metropolitan Police's 'T' division recorded the burglary of rings from a house in South Kensington, among them 'one mourning ("In memory of Ann Pickett, died 1842", engraved inside)' and 'a large plain gold Locket, raised monogram "A.M.P.", portraits of two children inside'. Time had no effect on the hurt that burglars inflicted. Years later, in January 1890 the C.I.D. reported that they were searching for '1 gentleman's very thick gold ring, with black enamelled edges (enamel partly worn), hair inside, with inscription, "God love you, my darling."'[45] Desire and death, the unending cycle of everyday life, left their marks on absent treasures.

Besides revealing moving insights into the domestic lives and affections of families long since departed, these reports tell us about a crucial feature of the 'security' companies such as Chubb offered to provide. Theirs was not simply an offer of economic resistance to burglary. Locks and safes also promised to alleviate emotional pain, safeguarding priceless artefacts of clients' emotional and familial histories. Security was, however, an exclusionary business. Innumerable thefts of miscellaneous goods valued at less than ten pounds highlighted the reality of a majority of burglaries happening in working-class homes, whose occupants could scarcely afford locks or other devices. Indeed, 'moveable' goods—such as clothes for Sunday best, and small decorative ornaments to cloak a front parlour in an aura of respectability—were regarded as important status symbols in the better-off working-class households, commensurately making them prime targets

---

[41] 'Dwelling Houses', *Architects Magazine* (Oct. 1903), p. 252.

[42] C. McArthur Butler, 'The Society of Architects, 1884–1913', *Journal of the Society of Architects* (Mar. 1914), pp. 184–95.

[43] Table 1, Appendix.

[44] See analysis of the emotional symbolism of Victorian jewellery in Charlotte Gere and Judy Rudoe, *Jewellery in the Age of Queen Victoria: A Mirror to the World* (London: British Museum, 2010), pp. 176–81.

[45] 'Burglary and Housebreaking', *Police Gazette* (21 June 1878), p. 1; 'Property Stolen', *Police Gazette* (17 Jan. 1890), p. 4.

for burglars.[46] Yet their owners were simply disregarded as target clientele for security firms, an exclusionary practice that shaped relationships between citizens and state. Customers, security companies, insurers, and police were brought into contact with one another through the integration of security technologies into the home, especially for those who held insurance contracts specifying the use of branded locks and safes.[47] 'Transacting' security based on patterns of social exclusion (i.e. the inability of the poor to afford security devices), these groups legitimized a hierarchy of state- and market-sponsored regulation against burglary that eroded the idea of policing based upon democratic rights to state surveillance. Alarms formed the next phase of security, in their turn, exacerbating the atomization of urban neighbourhoods through a whole new feature: sheer annoyance.

*   *   *

During the 1870s and 1880s, while lock and safe manufacturers sought ways to make their devices 'blend in' with domestic furnishings, inventors on both sides of the Atlantic were looking to go one better by creating burglar alarms that would be imperceptible to residents and criminal until triggered. Burglar alarms were being used in America as early as 1853. Yet these early prototypes only caught the attention of the British press when, in 1870, the *Morning Post* noted that a 'burglar alarm' had been exhibited in Cincinnati 'which not only rings a bell and indicates the window or door attacked, but also turns on and lights the gas'.[48] Delight at this ingenious invention seems to have been surprisingly muted. In Britain, it was not until 1876 that a report in the *Western Mail* declared that a Mr W. R. Lake had secured a patent for 'transmitting and registering fire and burglar alarm and other signals', although what became of his invention was unclear. Indeed, only during the 1880s were burglar alarms finally being mass-produced.[49] Perusing the Trades Section of the *Post Office London Directory*, readers of its 1882 issue were suddenly presented with no less than four businesses in London advertising 'burglar' or 'thief' alarms, fresh additions to their range of electric bells for use in the home.[50]

Technologically, a revolution had occurred in the interval between the Cincinnati alarm and the later inventions featured in the *Post Office London Directory*: the use of gas in the former, and electricity in the latter. London emerged as Britain's 'urban laboratory' for electric lighting in these decades, finally catching up to the transition from gas-powered forms of lighting in homes and cities that had long been

---

[46] Paul Johnson, 'Conspicuous Consumption and Working-Class Culture in Late Victorian and Edwardian Britain', *Transactions of the Royal Historical Society* 38 (1988), pp. 35–7.

[47] See Chapter 5.   [48] Schwartz, *Making Noise*, 339; *Morning Post* (26 Nov. 1870), p. 7.

[49] 'New Patents', *Western Mail* (4 Aug. 1876), p. 7.

[50] *The Post Office London Directory for 1882* (London, 1882), p. 1585. The businesses listed were: 'Koeber, John Adam, 44 Frith street, Soho W; electrician to Her Majesty's Government, telegraphic engineer &c; manufacturer of…thief detectors'; Markham, Thomas Thornhill, 102 Potter la EC…fire and thief alarms'; Sax, Julius, 108 Great Russell street, Bloomsbury and Morwell at WC; patentee & manufacturer of the best kind of electric bells, fire and thief alarms'; 'ELECTRIC FIRE AND BURGLAR ALARM MANUFACTURERS AND FITTERS. Johnston & Co. 189 Wardour street W'.

accomplished in other cities across Europe and America.[51] Electricity, though ultimately viewed as a safer alternative to gas power given the propensity of gas to leak in houses and cause explosions, was greeted initially with some suspicion due to its 'invisible and inodorous' nature. Unlike gas, there would be no forewarning should a short-circuit occur and spark a fire; fire being the only thing worse than burglary in most homeowners' estimations.[52]

These concerns soon disappeared, though, in the face of press articles and advertisements hailing the arrival of burglar alarms. The Electric Fire and Signals Alarm Co. Ltd even gestured that its devices could defend against both fire and burglary, in November 1882 trumpeting its alarms' ability to send 'calls for messengers, cabs, police &c. . . . at will'. Pressing the point home, it added 'The great increase in the number of attacks on property by armed burglars throughout the country will doubtless commend the simple self-acting burglar alarms to the attention of all householders'.[53] Comparably the 1888 'Automatic Burglar Alarm', invented by former Inspector of the C.I.D Maurice Moser, sought to calm potential detractors by explaining that it had 'a bell similar to that used with the ordinary electric apparatus'. Attached to a cord 'drawn across such places as it is thought desirable to guard', when cut or loosened this 'immediately causes the bell to ring loud enough to attract notice throughout the house and even in the adjoining street'.[54] Anticipating that burglars would look for an alarm, this device cleverly made sabotaging it the trigger that would set it off, perhaps reflecting Moser's knowledge from years of service.

Efficient communication with others was prioritized in these adverts. Alarms with the power to issue alerts 'at will' or 'immediately' collapsed the spatial and temporal distances between resident, neighbours, and police. Alarm manufacturers, perhaps disingenuously, articulated such innovations in terms of safety rather than intrusion, assumptions that gave little heed to Londoners' existing distaste for interference. Yet from complaints about overhearing noisy neighbours due to the thinness of walls in newly built houses, to fears that one's most intimate secrets might be heard by eavesdroppers monitoring the wires of telephones and wireless radios, contemporaries were incessantly conscious that privacy, and physical barriers between classes, were becoming rarer.[55] Early reports of burglar alarms suggested that resistance to burglary would override such anxieties, reconciling citizens with the surrounding community and agents of the state to enter homes through extending an audible invitation. Moser's invention, especially, assumed that all those who heard the burglar alarm would respond to it, relying upon neighbourhoods behaving as an active and engaged citizenry bound by reciprocal forms of sociability. Some were not so sure.

---

[51] Otter, *Victorian Eye*, pp. 230–45.   [52] Ibid., p. 240.
[53] 'The Electric Fire Alarm and Signals Company (Limited)', *Morning Post* (30 Nov. 1882), p. 1.
[54] 'Automatic Burglar Alarm', *Morning Post* (21 Jan. 1888), p. 2.
[55] Marcus, *Apartment Stories*, pp. 124–5; Richard Menke, *Telegraphic Realism: Victorian Fiction and Other Information Systems* (Stanford: Stanford University Press, 2008), pp. 222–3.

Household pets were more popular as burglar alarms than mechanical inventions at the fin de siècle. As Mrs C. E. Humphry, editor of *The Book of the Home* recommended in 1909, 'A small indoor dog is a great safeguard [against burglars], from its habit of barking at the slightest noises'.[56] Certainly this seemed a more effective plan than the 'make your own' alarms recommended to families in other domestic manuals, involving the rigging up of various wires and bells with directions that, to the modern reader, make the worst DIY instructions seem fairly legible.[57] Jokes were made about the ineffectiveness of burglar alarms, such as the following in the *London Journal* of 1910:

> GRIMES: 'We had a burglar alarm put into the house; but it didn't work.'
> WILLIS: 'Didn't go off, you mean?'
> GRIMES: 'Oh, it went off all right. But it didn't alarm the burglar in the slightest.
>   It only frightened my wife half out of her wits.'[58]

For all the mockery, the idea of safeguarding the home through the use of alarms was not abandoned—it simply lay dormant until other forms of technology made it possible to construct a more sophisticated device. Michael Egan, author of *The All-Electric Home*, reflected in 1931 that early burglar alarms—a 'couple of cells and a few bits of wire'—were fraught with problems due to batteries running down too quickly, rusty contacts between circuits, and the fact that 'a clever burglar, if he suspects there is an alarm circuit on the inside of the window, may attempt to disconnect this before trying to enter'.[59] Visibility of the wires was a fundamental failure of these devices, as Egan highlighted that these could easily be 'ripped away' once identified.[60] Consumer confidence in the use of electricity in the home also remained uncertain. Not until the years immediately preceding the outset of the First World War did middle-class consumers believe in electricity's 'reliability and economy in the home', having only recently grown accustomed to gas power.[61]

Thankfully, the 1920s witnessed the start of the 'Electric Age'; admittedly, a claim most prominently espoused by electricity suppliers.[62] Their vision proved true in the case of burglar alarms, whose inventors surmounted the issues surrounding the integrity of wires and their contact with the mechanism, and progressively made the wires themselves sensitive to interference. Consequently, they could boast that the lightest touch would be capable of triggering the alarm.[63] What this meant for both burglars and homeowners were visualized most clearly in the advertising leaflet of the convincingly named 'Rely-a-Bell Company' in 1936 (Fig. 6.6).

[56] MODA, Mrs C. E. Humphry (ed.), *The Book of the Home* (London, 1909), pp. 26–7.
[57] MODA, *Harmsworth's Household Encyclopaedia* (London, *c*.1900), pp. 579–82.
[58] 'Might Have Known', *London Journal* (10 Dec. 1910), p. 154.
[59] MODA, Michael Egan, *The All-Electric Home* (London, 1931), pp. 76–7.
[60] Ibid., p. 77.
[61] David Jeremiah, *Architecture and Design for the Family in Britain, 1900–70* (Manchester: Manchester University Press, 2000), pp. 19–20.
[62] Ibid., p. 56.   [63] Egan, *All-Electric*, p. 77.

Fig. 6.6. TNA, MEPO 3/2026, Front Cover of Rely-a-Bell pamphlet, in *Burglar Alarms Connected to Police Stations: Policy, 1934–1947* (1936).

Scrambling to maintain his hold on the drainpipe after being startled by the alarm, the burglar finds himself unable to even enter the window of a property having triggered it, catastrophically causing him to drop his jemmy: the symbol of burglars' ability to break into homes and 'crack' safes. Thrown into sharp relief by the light and floundering in response to the noise, the burglar is represented here as a figure of ridicule. His menace, despite the mask, is eradicated by his look of comical bewilderment and exclamation 'Wot with bells aringin' and lights aflashin' anyone would fink it was my birfday!'[64]

The working-class cockney accent of the burglar mimicked in this advert echoed still-prevailing associations of criminality with London's working-classes. Rely-a-Bell's alarm was clearly aimed at protecting the confines of the middle- and upper-class interior, eradicating the threat of both skilled and—worse—lower-class burglars penetrating its confines.[65] No burglar would be able to lay a finger beyond the exterior perimeter when the mechanisms used would be intangible. In 1930, the Radiovisor Company's 'Invisible Ray' alarm—its trigger based on the interruption of infra-red lights in this case—suggested that the very air within the home would be saturated with the means of rendering its occupants safe.[66] This was not always found to be the case, however. As minutes from a consultation between Superintendent Best of the Metropolitan Police's 'D' Division and Mr Gunn and Mr Tibbles of the Rely-a-Bell Company revealed in 1936, 'I extracted from Mr. Gunn the information that there was at least one authentic case in which thieves took half an hour to load up and remove the property and were not disturbed in the slightest by the fact that the alarm bell was ringing continuously during this period'.[67] A working alarm was not necessarily, on its own, the last word in safety.

The noise of alarm bells ringing, paradoxically, even contributed to the erosion of neighbourly goodwill and police attention. Newly sensitive alarm bells were found to be prone to being triggered accidentally, underpinning the process of atomization and privatization of homes in the city that alarm-makers had sought to arrest. In 1932 the London County Council, in correspondence with the Home Office and the Metropolitan Police, were forced to issue a 'By-Law as to the Ringing of Alarm Bells' for the city ordering that

> If any alarm bell…causes a prolonged ringing or continuous noise so as to occasion annoyance to the inhabitants of the neighbourhood, the occupier, tenant, or lessee of such house, building, or premises shall be guilty of an offence and liable on conviction to a penalty not exceeding £5.[68]

---

[64] TNA, MEPO 3/2026, *Burglar Alarms Connected to Police Stations: Policy, 1934–1947*, Rely-a-Bell (1936).

[65] See Chapter 1.

[66] BTA, POST 33/1332, *Use of T.P. Circuits in Connection with Burglar & Fire Alarms: Radiovisor Parent Ltd, 31 October–19 December 1930: Radiovisor: The Invisible Ray* (1930).

[67] TNA, MEPO 3/2026, *Burglar Alarms Connected to Police Stations: Policy, 1934–1947*: Superintendent K. B. Best, Communications, 'D1', Report on Interview with Rely-a-Bell, Limited (27 July 1936).

[68] TNA, MEPO 2/8345, *Burglar alarm bells: annoyance caused by continuous ringing—introduction of bye-law, 1928–43*: London County Council: By-Law as to the Ringing of Alarm Bells (1 Sept. 1932).

Describing the 'serious annoyance' this had caused to 'poor [i.e. unfortunate] residents', the report offered the opinion that 'warning lights might be found more effective in securing the detection of thieves'. Even this was queried, for the reason that 'the same mechanical defects may develop in any "lights" and these may become invisible and found entirely useless in foggy weather'.[69] Light and sound were therefore negotiated as different kinds of intrusion onto the urban environment. Sound, unlike its alternative, connoted a trespass into the 'calm' of urban residents that, as historian Hillel Schwartz argues was, in the case of burglar alarms, a derivative of the 'tone of urgency that was being culturally fixed to the *brrrang* of electric gongs and bells'.[70]

Ridding the city completely of this disturbance was found to be more difficult than either the police or government anticipated. Revealed in the minutes of the 1936 meeting with the Rely-a-Bell Company were the details of insurance companies' interest in maintaining the use of noisy electric bells. Without them, insurers unanimously refused to contract with alarm companies, despite Rely-a-Bell's plans to integrate a silent alarm device using a wire transmission to local police stations. As Messrs Gunn and Tibbles explained, 'In every case the insurance company continued to insist on the inclusion of the bell, their point of view being that they wished to frighten off the intruder wherever possible, and that they were not interested in the fact that he might possibly break into other premises later since this would be the affair of some other company'.[71] Insurers thereby orchestrated, through industrial channels adjacent to their own, further control over the domestic security of their upper- and middle-class client-base. Independently instituting an idea of the defences needed to combat the technological expertise and skill of burglars, they stubbornly promoted prevention over detection; a move that further mitigated the chances of their having to compensate a claim.

Burglar alarm inventors, however, progressively sought other ways to integrate their devices into existing forms of police surveillance through competing to intersect their systems with the telephone lines connecting police stations in the capital. Between 1921 and 1936, the General Post Office [GPO], the government department controlling the telephone lines, received twelve requests from alarm manufacturers both in Britain and internationally to be allowed to appropriate or monopolize the telephone lines connected to London's police stations, in the event of an alarm being triggered.[72] The earliest of these applications, sent from Mr S. G. Adams of the London-based Adams Silent Burglar Alarm Company in

---

[69] Ibid.   [70] Schwartz, *Making Noise*, pp. 338–9.

[71] TNA, MEPO 3/2026, *Burglar Alarms Connected to Police Stations: Policy, 1934–1947*: Superintendent K. B. Best, Communications, 'D1', Report on Interview with Rely-a-Bell, Limited (27 July 1936).

[72] BTA, POST 33/1332, *Use of Telephone Circuit in Connection with Burglar and Fire Alarms, 1921–1934*: applications received by British companies: Adams Silent Burglar Alarm Co. (1927), J. L. Barry (1924); J. J. Daniels (1933); John Donald (1934); Radiovisor Alarm Co. (1931); W. C. Kent (1934); BTA, POST 33/4902, *Telephone apparatus. Burglar, Fire alarms. Devices attached to subscribers' lines. Conditional permission, 1930s*: applications from H. Birenberg (1935); Mr J. A. Smith (Copenhagen, 1938); Burgot Burglar and Fire Alarm Device (France, 1934–6); Signaphone Alarm Co. (Paris/America, 1936).

January 1921, couched his bid in political and economic terms, both as an innovation to state regulation of burglary and as a lucrative means of getting more people to embrace having telephones in their homes:

> Sir,
>
> I submit for your consideration a device the adoption of which by the Post Office would undoubtedly reduce to a minimum the present opposition to the new scale of charges to telephone users and favourably impress the public—and the House of Commons—as a whole....
>
> I patented (No. 33839) on 30th November last a system by which all telephone subscribers can be provided (without alteration to the existing telephone system) with a secret, silent, instantaneous burglar alarm to the Police. This system merely requires the fitting of any type of electrical contacts at all or any doors, windows, safes etc. at Subscribers' premises, and their connections, by means of a switch or other suitable device with the Subscribers' telephone Exchange lines.[73]

As with burglar alarms of the 1880s, Adams sought to popularize his system on the grounds of its efficiency of communication, this time exclusively with the police. Crucially, though, the ability of Adams' alarm to be 'secret, silent, instantaneous' would delay burglars' realization they had been detected until it was too late.[74] Intimating that burglars had been too fast, or intelligent, to be caught out by previous alarms, the 'secretive' nature of Adams' device also implied that his alarm would serve as an invisible presence in the household, providing security without disrupting the existing internal organization or appearance of the home, unlike locks and safes. Indeed, besides looking for ways to eradicate the 'annoyance' associated with the ringing of alarms, over the course of the interwar period several other London burglar alarm manufacturers—including J. Fraser & Son's 'Electric Burglar Alarm' (1920), Mr D. Nightingale's 'Silent Burglar Alarm' (1922), the Radiovisor Company's 'Invisible Ray Device' (1930), and Rely-a-Bell's burglar alarm (1936)—developed 'silent' devices explicitly using an intangible signal to communicate for help.[75]

This process of attempting to embed security seamlessly into the home in the immediate post-war period chimed with other designs for household appliances that were 'labour-saving' and 'efficient'. Supporting the ethos of home as a 'refuge', makers of appliances such as washing machines and hoovers recognized that their machines reflected women's desire for greater freedom from household chores,

---

[73] BTA, POST 33/1332, *Use of Telephone Circuit in Connection with Burglar and Fire Alarms: Adams Silent Burglar Alarm, 1921–1927*: letter from S.G. Adams to the Rt. Hon. A.H. Illingsworth M.P., H.M. Postmaster General (13 Jan. 1921).

[74] Ibid.

[75] TNA, HO 45/20369, *Burglar Alarms, 1920–1946*: letter to the Home Secretary from T. Fraser & Son (24 Jan. 1920), and letter to the Ministry of Health from D. Nightingale (22 Aug. 1922); BTA, POST 33/1332, *Use of T.P. Circuits in Connection with Burglar & Fire Alarms: Radiovisor Parent Ltd, 31 Oct.–19 Dec. 1930: Radiovisor: The Invisible Ray* (1930); TNA, MEPO 3/2026, *Burglar Alarms Connected to Police Stations: Policy, 1934–1947*: Superintendent K. B. Best, Communications, 'D1', Report on Interview with Rely-a-Bell, Limited (27 July 1936).

assisting them to pursue new professional opportunities available after the war.[76] Indeed, the relative lack of technical skill needed by residents to operate burglar alarms was a recurrent feature of their marketing during the interwar period, with the 1930 leaflet for the Radiovisor company's 'Invisible Ray Burglar Alarm' assuring readers 'The switching on and switching off is of the simplest form and requires no technical knowledge', whilst the 1936 leaflet of the Rely-a-Bell burglar alarm company extolled that 'The mechanism is very simple and light'.[77]

Gadgets that ensured the smooth running of the home but required little effort to use gradually freed up women's time for paid work and leisure. 'Unchaining' women from the kitchen sink gestured at the ideal of companionate marriage gathering strength during the 1920s, wherein women were 'managers' of the home, whose labour was recognized as such by their husbands, rather than domestic 'slaves' (this transition was, unfortunately, more of an ideal than a reality, since the declining numbers of domestic servants forced many women to perform household cleaning tasks and for working-class women, little changed in terms of domestic chores).[78] New visions of more equitable gender relations were reflected in the ways that safes conformed to interior design. A 1936 leaflet for Hobb's & Co.'s products revealed the company had abandoned the heavily feminized boudoir safes in favour of 'wall safes' that, embedded within the walls of homes, were advertised simply as offering 'protection against theft'.[79] Chubb's 1939 brochure for homeowners, entitled *Safe as Houses*, carefully avoided marketing its anti-burglar devices specifically towards male or female occupants in almost every respect, arguing instead that 'Everyone has some sentimental token to be cherished in secret. That is where the Chubb Deed Box comes in...or the Cash Box.'[80] Such advertising suggested that male and female householders' treasures might be found within the same, shared space. Safes' new 'modernist' aesthetic subtly upheld the demands for interior designs that privileged functionality and fewer distinctions between men's and women's lives and work.[81] The security they offered was now directed towards possessions earned through jointly valued incomes, 'securing' harmony between husbands and wives, sons and daughters, during the upheaval of the interwar decades.

The value placed on the safety of the home also functioned as the commercial motor for Adams and other alarm inventors to try to construct a technologically

[76] Deborah Ryan, '"All the World and her Husband": The *Daily Mail* Ideal Home Exhibition 1908–39', in Maggie Andrews and Mary M. Talbot (eds.), *All the World and her Husband: Women in Twentieth-Century Consumer Culture* (London: Cassell, 2000), pp. 12, 16–17; Jeremiah, *Architecture*, pp. 70–1.

[77] BTA, POST 33/1332, *Use of T.P. Circuits in Connection with Burglar & Fire Alarms: Radiovisor Parent Ltd, 31 Oct.–19 Dec. 1930*: *Radiovisor: The Invisible Ray* (1930); TNA, MEPO 3/2026, *Burglar Alarms Connected to Police Stations: Policy, 1934–1947*: *Rely-a-Bell* (1936).

[78] Ryan, 'All the World and her Husband'; Todd, 'Domestic Service and Class Relations in Britain 1900–1950', pp. 181–204.

[79] LMA, CLC/B, Box 72/2, file 1999/007, 'Hobbs & Co.'s Wall Safes for Protection against Theft' (London: 1936).

[80] LMA, CLC/B/002, Box 309, *Safe as Houses* (London: 1939), p. 3.

[81] Vicky Long, 'Industrial Homes, Domestic Factories: The Convergence of Public and Private in Interwar Britain', *Journal of British Studies* 50 (2011), pp. 438–9.

defined relationship between alarm-owner and police via business arrangement with the GPO and their telephone lines. In attempting to integrate alarm systems with the telephone circuit, burglar alarm manufacturers recognized a way to exploit the economically driven, unequally class-based hierarchies of access to the police. Before, the absence of telephone lines meant that the ringing of alarms attracted police on duty patrolling the streets, an attention that was predicated on the ability of someone to purchase a device in the first place.[82] Adams' 1921 application imagined an intensification of that precedent, the medium of telephone lines enabling those with alarms to call police discreetly and exert an 'instantaneous' monopoly over police attention that would summon officers immediately to the home in question. State surveillance of the city would re-orientate onto particular properties (and wealthier classes of people) for the duration of the alarm. The volume of requests from alarm manufacturers to the GPO to use the telephone system this way shows that Adams was not the only one to envisage the commercial opportunities of formalizing the hierarchy of surveillance. As alarm inventor J. L. Barry wrote to the Postmaster General on 13 January 1934 requesting to link his own 'silent' burglar alarm to the telephone system,

> Even if people are asleep when burglars enter they are not, as with ordinary burglar alarms, open to any bodily injury by challenging the intruders, because until the arrival of the Police they would be unaware that anything unusual was happening. I suggest that the Post Office Telephones could exploit this system, charging the subscribers an extra rental fee on their telephone accounts.[83]

In August of the same year, inventor John Donald wrote to the GPO to proffer an identical plan for his own alarm, with the added inducement 'The selling of such devices might prove profitable and be an added inducement for the adoption of the telephone by the public'.[84] In principle, such schemes met with no objections and were even accorded the support of the police and the LCC. When the Radiovisor Company applied in 1931 to set up 'Tell-tale Centres' at Police stations which would connect their alarms through the use of private telephone wires, it was noted in GPO files that Radiovisor 'have the continued good-will of the Police Authorities (both the Metropolitan and City Police)'.[85] Yet these Centres were not established. Their failure to be realized was explained when the Rely-a-Bell Co. attempted to do the same in 1936 and was rejected by the Metropolitan Police on the grounds

---

[82] In 1893, burglar alarms advertised by O'Brien, Thomas & Company in their *Illustrated Catalogue of Builders Goods* offered devices for doors and windows costing between one shilling and sixpence and two shillings and eightpence each, or twenty-nine shillings and threepence for a dozen. MODA, O'Brien, Thomas & Company, *Illustrated Catalogue of Builders Goods* (Jan. 1893), p. 833.

[83] BTA, POST 33/1332, *Use of Telephone Circuit in Connection with Burglar and Fire Alarms: Mr J. L. Barry, 13 Jan.–4 May 1934*: letter to the Postmaster General from J. L. Barry (13 Jan. 1934).

[84] BTA, POST 33/1332, *Use of Telephone Circuit in Connection with Burglar and Fire Alarms: Awards Case No. 45,868, 13–17 Aug. 1934*: GPO, 'Awards Form A' (13 Aug. 1934).

[85] BTA, POST 33/1332, *Use of Telephone Circuit in Connection with Burglar and Fire Alarms: Radiovisor, 1931*: letter from Controller, L.T.S. [London Telephone System] to The Secretary, GPO (24 Jan. 1931).

that police headquarters might be inundated by as many false alarm signals as real ones, all to which they would have to respond.[86]

It was not the end of the story. Letters sent from Rely-a-Bell to the Metropolitan Police during their negotiations detailed how they and other burglar alarm companies maintained business in the meantime by fielding alarm calls through a switchboard (or 'exchange' system) to police via company operators on duty at their offices, who 'immediately' telephoned the Information Room at Scotland Yard.[87] As the Deputy Assistant Commissioner commented, 'Action by Police naturally follows the receipt of information from this company in exactly the same way as it would follow the receipt of similar information from any other source'.[88] Burglar alarm manufacturers thereby used their products to establish themselves as intermediaries between clients and police, situating themselves in a quasi-judicial role by determining whose alarms would merit police attention and organizing the speed of the response, compromising the statist nature of its disciplinary and regulatory arms. The existence of this two-tier system of policing, based on the economics of who owned certain brands of burglar alarms and how those companies were organized, illustrates the contested nature of the 'material politics of the home' between citizen, state, and businesses in this era. Burglar alarms informed the rise of 'material civilization', directing public sensibilities about how society was structured and organized at its most fundamental levels (in this instance, the regulation of crime) through a dialectics of ownership of goods and rights of access to state services.[89]

Perhaps conscious that they were losing power, this arrangement was not found wholly satisfactory by the Metropolitan and City Police forces. During the late 1930s they began working with the GPO to democratize access to the police through the telephone system independent of alarm inventors. Inspiration eventually struck following a horrific house fire at Westminster in 1935, in which several people died and witnesses trying to call the fire brigade were frustrated by the telephone lines being jammed.[90] The resulting product was the 999 Emergency Calls System, by which those who dialled the number '999' on a telephone would circumvent the operators employed in directing the traffic of calls at London's Telephone Exchanges and be connected directly with operators at a switchboard for one of three emergency services—police, fire brigade, or ambulance. As the press release for the new system issued by the GPO on 16 February, 1937, stated,

London's emergency telephone calls in case of fire, crime, or accident are to be considerably speeded up. Soon two of the most efficient telephone rings will encircle inner and outer London. Police stations, fire brigades and ambulance services will be

---

[86] TNA, MEPO 3/2026, *Burglar Alarms Connected to Police Stations: Policy, 1934–1947*: Superintendent K. B. Best, Communications, 'D1', Report on Interview with Rely-a-Bell, Limited (27 July 1936).

[87] TNA, MEPO 3/2026, *Burglar Alarms Connected to Police Stations: Policy, 1934–1947*: letter from the Deputy Assistant Commissioner, Metropolitan Police, to Messrs Wilson & Gill (10 Sept. 1936).

[88] Ibid.   [89] Trentmann and Taylor, 'Liquid Politics', pp. 210–11.

[90] Eloise Moss, '"Dial 999 for Help!" The Three-Digit Emergency Number and the Transnational Politics of Welfare Activism, 1937–1979', *Journal of Social History* (2017).

linked up with them. The system devised is the most advanced of any previous design and it will reduce the operation of making emergency calls to seconds. Both the inner and outer London rings of the Metropolitan Police Force are to be so equipped.[91]

Visions of the police and other emergency services 'encircling' London to act at speed gave new meaning to 'panoptic' forms of surveillance that residents of the metropolis could expect, being purportedly surrounded at all times by the agents of the state and only seconds from encountering them should a problem arise. At its crux, however, the 999 emergency system sought to address economic inequality. By providing brightly coloured blue telephone boxes on street corners from which residents could exclusively place 'emergency' calls without charge, those who did not yet own telephones in their homes could (supposedly) acquire the same level of state intervention as those wealthier residents should they demand it.

As chance would have it, the very first call using this service was made to inform police of a burglary. On 7 July 1937 at 4.20 a.m., a Mrs Beard, of Elsworthy Road in Hampstead, north London, dialled 999 on the house telephone at the instruction of her husband. Woken by the sound of someone moving on the terrace outside his window, Mr Beard faced a horror by then familiar to London householders expecting the invasion of a cat burglar in their bedroom any minute. Apparently 'within five minutes', the police arrived and captured a man named Thomas Duffy, who was charged that afternoon at Marylebone Police Court with attempting to commit burglary. Newspapers, predictably, made much of this event, with headlines focusing particularly on the 'under five minutes' in which it had taken police to reach the scene.[92] Of greater interest, however, was a quote by Mr Beard that recurred in press reports in the *Star*, *Evening News*, *Daily Telegraph*, *Evening Gazette*, *Morning Post*, *News Chronicle*, and *The Times*, praising the new service in economic terms:

> As a result of using that signal almost instantaneous connexion was made with the police station, and in less than five minutes this man was arrested. It struck me as a householder and a fairly large taxpayer that we were getting something for our money, and I was very much impressed by it.[93]

Despite the seemingly unlimited expansion of police services into the lives of Londoners that had accompanied the 999 service, therefore, the policing of burglary was still articulated as a product of monetary exchange between state and society, inflecting the prevention of crime with the influences of class and wealth. Besides the question of how far taxes were viewed as 'payment' for police response, the first call made in response to a burglary from a prosperous home in the salubrious area

---

[91] BTA, *999 Emergency Calls*: 'Post-Office Speed-Up of London's Emergency Services' (16 Feb. 1937).

[92] See for example BTA, *999 Emergency Calls*: press cutting '999 Led to Arrest: Five Minutes after Wife Dialled', *Star* (7 July 1937).

[93] BTA, *999 Emergency Calls*: '999 Led to Arrest: Five Minutes after Wife Dialled', *Star* (7 July 1937); 'Tribute in Court: Dial 999: Accused Man Detained within Five Minutes', *Evening News* (7 July 1937); 'Success of 999 Signal: Man Arrested within Five Minutes', *The Times* (8 July 1937); '999: Arrest in Four Minutes', *News Chronicle* (8 July 1937); 'Success of 999 Signal: Police Make Arrest in Five Minutes', *Morning Post* (8 July 1937); ' "999" Makes Good', *Evening Gazette* (8 July 1937); 'Tribute to 999 Phone Call: Arrest within Five Minutes', *Daily Telegraph* (8 July 1937).

of Hampstead demonstrated vividly how those capable of subscribing to private telephone lines retained a privileged position in relation to the state. Appended to the article was an image of Mrs Beard making the famous call from within her home, as against calling from one of the public phone boxes located on street corners across the city. The 'less than five minutes' in which the emergency services arrived made no mention of the comparable time it would have taken to reach the nearest phone box, nor did it factor in the additional cost of telephone subscription— estimated as equivalent to the cost of hiring a maid in a publicity film issued by the General Post Office in 1934.[94] Far from ameliorating class tensions over access to the emergency services to report a crime, the 999 system was to prove a defining feature of the distancing of certain citizens from the state.

* * *

Between 1860 and 1939 the security technology industry transformed how middle- and upper-class Londoners conceptualized what it meant to live in a 'burglar-proof' domestic space. By inserting their products, and their agents, as mediators between citizens and state forms of surveillance, the manufacturers of locks, safes, and burglar alarms reconditioned crime prevention into a form of privileged commercial transaction, to which the wealthier classes were more privy than their working- class counterparts. In so doing, manufacturers also collapsed the spatial and temporal distances between people resident within, and external to, the home. Characterizing these networks as a sought-after commodity rather than the unwanted intrusion of public onto private space, security companies capitalized upon the ethos of safety that was fundamental to the organization and gendered dynamics of domesticity, particularly after the First World War. Further, locks and safes took on an aesthetic role in the Victorian and Edwardian home that served to institute a psycho-sexual understanding of the threat posed by burglars. Material culture thereby allows historians to retrieve *both* the economic and emotional dynamics of state surveil- lance historically, and unearth new insights into how different forms of crime were constructed in the popular imagination. In the next chapters, the evidence that burglars had managed to sneak brazenly past security technologies and into the homes of London's most high-profile residents took on an even graver meaning, when burglars seemed to have gained a new occupation as Cold War spies....

---

[94] *Pett and Pott* (United Kingdom: General Post Office Film Unit, 1934), http://www.btplc.com/ Thegroup/BTsHistory/BTfilmarchive/1930s/ (accessed Sept. 2015).

7

Defying the Burglar in Post-War London

A TALE OF TWO BURGLARIES

In September 1948, Cecil Beaton, the celebrated war and portrait photographer, sat at his desk in the beautiful surrounds of his mansion, Reddish House in leafy Wiltshire, to write to his great friend and occasional lover, the Hollywood actress Greta Garbo.[1] Greeting her with his customary 'Darling' and cheerfully recounting the latest news and gossip from their circle of friends, Beaton recalled how he recently suffered a burglary at his London house:

> While the London home was empty thieves tried to break in, & tried a lock on a door, but were disturbed before continuing with their plans. The charwoman passing the house on another occasion saw all the lights burning. Next day when she arrived they were turned off—none of us can fathom the mystery but we have had to have all the keys and locks altered. Meanwhile the original maid has returned from her holiday to look after the house here, the chickens and the geese. The geese are the latest addition & are fed only on apples.... They are excellent burglar alarms as I believe I told you before.[2]

Tales of burglar-alarm-geese aside (they would certainly be shrill), Beaton's flippant tone could not disguise his discomfort at the presence of 'mysterious' intruders in his home. Unable to ascertain what had been stolen until he returned, the artist could count himself fortunate that he was absent when the burglars were inside, and had servants and local employees keeping watch for unusual signs of activity in the house who recognized the criminal significance of the lights. Beaton's financial resources were also apparent. Swiftly directing all the locks and keys to be changed in his second home, Beaton could rest assured that the burglars' skeleton keys, had they been made for purpose, would henceforth be ineffective. With these safeguards in place, and with, perhaps, a dash of extra perspective after his experiences documenting the war, Beaton was able to describe the burglary as a 'mystery' rather than a 'disaster' and return to regaling Garbo with other news.

Compare Beaton's letter with another sent seventeen years later. In 1965, Ruth Arup wrote to her husband Ove, a senior consultant in the engineering firm that carried his name, Ove Arup and Partner. The correspondence between the upper middle-class couple was regular and affectionate. Frequently abroad on business,

---

[1] Hugo Vickers, 'Beaton, Sir Cecil Walter Hardy (1904–1980)', *Oxford Dictionary of National Biography*, http://www.oxforddnb.com/view/article/30801 (accessed 12 Sept. 2017).
[2] CU, St. John's College Library, Letter from Cecil Beaton to Greta Garbo (Sept. 1948).

Ove would soon achieve fame for his work constructing Sydney Opera House, later acquiring a knighthood.[3] Despite his regular absence, however, he was nonetheless 'upset' at the news their house in Highgate had suffered a serious burglary.[4] This was nothing, though, to the couple's concern that a friend and less prosperous neighbour, Grete, had also been burgled:

> They forced the lock off the flat front door. You can imagine she is in rather a state. She is the last person who should have to endure a burglary as she was very nervous about it when she moved in, I remember. I wish some nice chap would marry her, or at least live with her, for I fear she hates to be alone, and this is the last straw.[5]

Thieves had stolen Grete's silver jewellery, a treasured possession purloined when she was out working (according to Ruth) that compounded her distress.[6] Ruth Arup's account of the situation, factoring Grete's lack of relationship and relative isolation in her block of flats into her judgement of the impact of the burglary— 'this is the last straw'—offered a telling insight into her dismissive view of the so-called 'independence' enjoyed by single women after the war, a common strain of conservative thought in this era.[7] It also suggested her hostile impression of the pitfalls and vulnerabilities of modern urban lifestyles. Unlike the burglary at the Arups' or at Beaton's home some years before, Grete had apparently received neither family nor neighbourly assistance, nor were fellow flat-occupiers regarded as her 'community'. She was 'alone'. By contrast, Ruth deployed Ove to communicate with their insurance company, and received help from Mr and Mrs Wancke next door, who noticed a bedroom window open at 11 p.m. on Saturday night when she was out, telephoning the police and burglar alarm company immediately on their friends' behalf. The couple's adult children boarded up the bedroom window to prevent further incursions, while yet another neighbour, Mrs Bradley, helped police begin their investigation.[8] A lesson in contrasts, the Arups' letters reveal how easily their stable family life, class, and social position sustained the same networks of assistance between the state (police), commercial anti-burglary agencies, and local citizens on which Beaton had been able to rely in 1948. Those like Grete, who did not fit that 'model' of traditional heteronormative living nor, as women, were expected to orchestrate their own security as well as successful bachelors like Beaton, were forced to negotiate the effects of crime in relation to the sometimes atomized, lonely experience of newer types of households.[9]

---

[3] Povl Ahm, 'Arup, Sir Ove Nyquist (1895–1988)', *Oxford Dictionary of National Biography*, http://www.oxforddnb.com/view/article/40049 (accessed 12 Sept. 2017).
[4] CU, Churchill College Archives, ARUP 2/108/6: Letter from Ruth Arup to Ove and Li Arup (2 Nov. 1965).
[5] Ibid.   [6] Ibid.
[7] Single women were frequently maligned as unlovable or irresponsible 'spinsters', despite their greater opportunities for employment and the loss of thousands of men's lives during the war. Katherine Holden, *In the Shadow of Marriage: Singleness in England, 1914–1960* (Manchester: Manchester University Press, 2007).
[8] CU, ARUP 2/108/6: Letter from Ruth Arup to Ove Arup (11 Nov. 1965).
[9] Richard Hornsey discusses this in terms of the 'atomization' of urban neighbourhoods in this era as a result of new kinds of housing a post-war dislocation. Richard Hornsey, ' "Everything Is Made of

Burglary tarnished the hopes of those engaged in reconstructing the metropolis during the fragile new era of peace. Its incidence rose sharply at a local and national level. In London, recorded burglaries increased from 222 in 1939 to 1,317 in 1968, with a peak of 1,625 in 1965. In England and Wales, burglaries numbered 1,515 in 1938, soaring to 8,846 in 1968, with a peak of 9,026 in 1966. In reality, burglaries were a mere fraction compared to the number of housebreakings, which peaked at 24,474 in London during 1966 and an astonishing 126,953 in England and Wales during 1968.[10] As before the war, however, it was the increases in the more sinister, night-time crime of burglary that inspired contemporary fears and debate. Organizing homes and belongings to counter the threat was a customary part of everyday life. Ruth Arup described how she routinely hid her son Jonathan's camera from view, after her ten-year award for service at the engineering firm was burgled in the heist at their house. Her agitation was shared by their friends:

> The Rigbys hide their possessions all over the house in countless little hiding places, so that they forget themselves where they are, and have lovely surprises about a couple of years later, when they open the lid of an antique teapot and find a pair of earrings, or a treatise on Greek Iambics and find a few ten pound notes.[11]

Comical as this sounds, it illustrated how futile even upper middle-class house-holders regarded the strategies of police to contain burglary. Despite having the latest technologies, such as the 999 service and radio transmitters, as well as greater speed and mobility through using 'panda' cars to patrol the streets, police were clearly losing the 'war on crime'. Public confidence was ebbing. Ironically, historian Sarah Manwaring White writes, the very technologies on which the Force increas-ingly relied to regulate crime more efficiently after the war were responsible for reducing face-to-face contact with 'beat' officers, diminishing 'bobbies on the beat' to an extent seen as damaging in popular opinion.[12] The harried concealment of belongings was hardly a vote of confidence in commercial security technologies either. Citizens were right to be worried; in 1968, the Home Office Working Party on false alarm calls estimated that nationally, 97 per cent of the burglar alarms to which police had responded in the past year were false.[13] This was a situation

---

Atoms": The Reprogramming of Space and Time in Post-War London', *Journal of Historical Geography* 34:1 (2008), pp. 94–117.

[10] See Charts 3 and 4, Appendix 1; for individual figures, see HCPP: Cmd. 6201, *Report of the Commissioner of Police for the Metropolis for 1939* (London, 1940), p. 48; Cmd. 3052, *Report of the Commissioner of Police for the Metropolis for 1965* (London, 1966), p. 101; Cmd. 4060, *Report of the Commissioner of Police for the Metropolis for the Year 1968* (London, 1969), p. 86; Cmd. 6167: *Criminal Statistics, England and Wales, 1938* (London, 1940), p. 16; Cmd. 3332, *Criminal Statistics, England and Wales, 1966* (London, 1967), p. 1; Cmd. 4098, *Criminal Statistics, England and Wales, 1968* (London, 1969), p. 1.

[11] CU, ARUP 2/108/6: Letter from Ruth Arup to Ove and Li Arup (2 Nov. 1965).

[12] Manwaring-White, *The Policing Revolution*, pp. 17–51; Joanne Klein, 'Traffic, Telephones and Police Boxes: The Deterioration of Beat Policing in Birmingham, Liverpool and Manchester Between the World Wars', in Gerald Blaney (ed.), *Policing Interwar Europe: Continuity, Change, and Crisis, 1918–1940* (Basingstoke, 2007), pp. 215–36.

[13] TNA, HO 287/1676, *Home Office Working Party on False Burglar Alarms, Eighth Meeting* (1968), 'Minutes of the Home Office Standing Committee on Crime Prevention' (20 Sept. 1968), p. 3.

unchanged since the report of a previous working party on the subject in 1946.[14] Given the tens of thousands of alarms represented in each survey, 'If the false alarm call rate was not reduced the volume of false calls would increase, as more alarms were installed, to a point at which...the whole system would break down and alarms would be virtually useless', opined one official.[15] Alarms' ineffectualness could strike in unexpected ways. The burglar alarm system fitted at the Arups' house had failed to ring at all throughout their (very real) burglary. 'The burglar alarm people couldn't give any explanation', noted a justifiably irritated Ruth Arup.[16] As the volume of burglaries in London tested the stretched resources of police and the faulty machinery of security firms, a well-worn set of fears about the crime rapidly crystallized.

Privacy was under siege. The very walls of the city's residences were materially thinner and more compacted, with high-rise blocks of flats and prefabricated houses becoming the norm. Hastily built rows of prefab suburban homes were described by Commissioner of Metropolitan Police Sir Joseph Simpson in 1964 (in his opinion, the 'worst year of the century for crime') as offering 'flimsy defence against intruders' in comparison to their interwar counterparts.[17] People were living in close quarters. Entrances to flats (like Grete's) were easily obtained if a night watchman or porter were not employed; once inside, thieves might try to break into any number of homes, since constables walking 'the beat' were not required to patrol inside such buildings. The greater porousness and proximity of urban living provided burglars with fresh opportunities to penetrate into homes at a moment when, as historian Claire Langhamer describes, 'even within crowded working-class housing, a premium was placed upon the ability to mark out at least some measure of privacy in everyday life'.[18] Burglary rendered privacy a transient and elusive quality, exposing a stranger to the most intimate confines of the home. It also drew the attention of neighbours and police, who would be admitted to the scene of the crime. These successive interventions would especially be felt by the poorest, who remained the most frequently victimized and unable to afford the requisite technologies to counter the threat.

Faced with a spiralling crime rate, police were forced to rely on, and actively urge, neighbours to report any 'unusual' activity to a greater extent than ever before. Residents had to contemplate which was worse: the brief, but possibly devastating intrusion of the criminal, or the well-meaning, albeit prolonged, watchfulness of neighbours. Encouraging 'nosy' neighbours was anathema to a society who distinguished between the 'common' and 'better' elements of the working and lower middle classes by those who 'kept themselves to themselves' versus those who were

[14] TNA, MEPO 2/8798, *Burglar Alarms: General Policy* (1946), Letter from Sir Harold Scott to S. J. Baker, Home Office (5 Dec. 1946).

[15] TNA, HO 287/1676, *Home Office Working Party on False Burglar Alarms, Eighth Meeting* (1968), 'Minutes of the Home Office Standing Committee on Crime Prevention' (20 Sept. 1968), p. 3.

[16] CU, Churchill College Archives, ARUP 2/108/5: Letter from Ruth Arup to Ove Arup (11 Nov. 1965).

[17] HCPP, Cmnd. 2710, *Report of the Commissioner of Police for the Metropolis, 1964* (July 1965), p. 9.

[18] Claire Langhamer, 'The Meanings of Home in Postwar Britain', *Journal of Contemporary History* 40:2 (2005), p. 351.

'gossipy', as a Mass Observation study of conditions in London's new-build flats related in 1943.[19] Mass Observers (a body of middle-class social anthropologists who conducted investigations into everyday life in Britain from 1937) were themselves accused by the press of being 'busybodies' and 'nosy parkers' of whom the public should beware, despite their stated intention to shed light on the conditions of 'ordinary' life, including poverty and its effects.[20] At the heart of such compromises lay the broader stirrings of what would come to be known as the 'surveillance society'. Since criticized as eroding the values of a supposedly liberal state, collective surveillance, whether via the 999 emergency system, CCTV cameras, or later 1980s schemes such as Neighbourhood Watch, tended to be introduced as mechanisms of welfare by safeguarding people from crime or other injury.[21] Yet government injunctions to keep tabs on one's neighbourhood for signs of crime threw a spanner in the works, by provoking a more pressing (financial) question: who should ultimately bear responsibility for the prevention of burglary—citizen or state?

London bore witness to the emergence of this debate in a dazzling public spectacle, when in 1950 the Home Office, police, and insurance companies cooperated to launch the National Crime Prevention Campaign at Selfridges department store on Oxford Street. The first of two concerted anti-burglary initiatives to grace the country over the course of the next two decades, the campaign's dismal effect on the incidence of the crime provoked despair among politicians and police, whose efforts (and money) produced the meagre reward of a brief spike in the purchase of security technologies.[22] In 1967, they redoubled their efforts again with the 'Watch Out! There's a Burglar About!' publicity drive.[23] Significantly, both campaigns deployed a familiar wartime rhetoric of personal 'duty' to protect property and embrace neighbourly 'vigilance' against thieves, casting citizens as 'troops' in the battle to 'beat the burglar', and even using the 'war' on crime as their slogan. This chapter considers how their marketing strategy largely failed through focusing on white, middle-class victims of burglary at the exclusion of others, and by taking little heed of the way security technologies mediated access to the emergency services along lines of class and wealth. In so doing, organizers unwittingly championed

---

[19] MO, *An Enquiry into People's Homes* (London, 1943), pp. 49–51.

[20] 'What Were You Doing at 8:57 Last Night?—You Were Being Watched!', *Daily Mirror* (25 June 1937), p. 12; 'Public Busybody No. 1', *Daily Mirror* (6 Dec. 1938), p. 14; John Baxendale and Chris Pawling, *Narrating the Thirties: A Decade in the Making, 1930–Present* (Basingstoke: Palgrave MacMillan, 1996), pp. 17–45; Peter Gurney, ' "Intersex" and "Dirty Girls": Mass Observation and Working-Class Sexuality in England in the 1930s', *Journal of the History of Sexuality* 8:2 (1997), pp. 256–90; Deborah Cohen's study of citizens' efforts to keep 'family secrets' from neighbours in this period, such as illegitimate children, adoptions, homosexuality, and divorce, also shows how fraught were the boundaries between public and 'private' knowledge of domestic affairs: Deborah Cohen, *Family Secrets: Living with Shame from the Victorians to the Present Day* (London: Viking, 2013).

[21] Williams, 'Police Surveillance and the Emergence of CCTV in the 1960s', pp. 127–37; Chris Moores, 'Thatcher's Troops? Neighbourhood Watch Schemes and the Search for "Ordinary" Thatcherism in 1980s Britain', *Contemporary British History* 31:2 (2017), pp. 230–55; Moss, ' "Dial 999 for Help!" '.

[22] TNA, HO 287/239, *Crime Prevention Campaign: Exhibitions and Displays* (1951–61).

[23] TNA, INF 2/124, *Home Office: Civil Defence and Crime Prevention* (1961–73).

consumer-citizenship over the 'active' forms of citizenship they sought to encourage.[24] Ultimately, these campaigns exposed the growing alienation of officials from the everyday lives of most Londoners, and indeed, urbanites elsewhere. Consequently, relations between police and public gradually deteriorated, while rates of burglary climbed ever further beyond control.

Burglary in London during the decades after the Second World War continued to emblematize the fears, preoccupations, and experiences of 'home' of modern urbanites. Burglars joined, and sometimes overlapped with, the unruly youths and sexual predators roaming the capital's streets in this era of unrest.[25] Their presence was inextricable from the city's national and international reputation, a reality that posed a stark criminal contrast to the refrain of Britons' 'never having it so good', as Prime Minister Harold MacMillan declared in 1957.[26] Violence, especially the spiralling rates of sexual violence that tore apart households attempting to recover from the war, created a more pronounced association between burglary, rape, and other serious crimes (such as murder) than existed before. Embodied in a series of violent burglaries committed during the late 1950s and early 1960s, the details of which were unusually preserved within National Archives files, they revealed the attempts of police officers and criminal psychologists to rationalize the actions of perpetrators in relation to their childhoods, relationships, and family circumstances. Demonstrating how the discipline of criminology evolved to integrate psycho-sexual explanations of criminality, officials' observations largely effaced the broader reality of widespread forms of poverty and precarious employment that drove the crime in reality. As the final section of this chapter explores, burglary thereby drew attention to the enduring fragility, and inflexibility, of concepts of 'home' and family life, with far-reaching social ramifications in personal, local, and national contexts. The metropolis was the unique crucible for these issues to emerge collectively, finding expression in the city's 'most characteristic crime'.[27]

* * *

'Peacetime' was anything but peaceful for the Metropolitan Police and most Londoners. Senior Driver George 'Jack' Frost, a member of the flying squad, recorded in 1950 that the Blitz had offered an early indication of the upsurge in burglary that would accompany the war, as black-outs and disruption to domestic lives created new opportunities to thieve. 'It was a grim wartime jest that some of the "flat busters" could do as much damage in a single night as a "blockbuster" bomb', Frost recalled, drawing a moral and physical equivalence between the actions of the Nazis and burglars, and indicating the profound trauma that victims of burglary experienced.[28] By 1948, the number of property crimes—particularly burglary and its daytime counterpart, housebreaking—had doubled since 1938,

---

[24] On 'active' citizenship see Moores, 'Thatcher's Troops', pp. 230–1.
[25] Mort, *Capital Affairs*.
[26] 'House of Commons: Thursday, July 25', *The Times* (26 July 1957), p. 6.
[27] See Introduction.
[28] George 'Jack' Frost, *Flying Squad* (London: Youth Book Club, 1950), p. 159.

while police were struggling to achieve sufficient recruitment of new officers.[29] Law enforcers were exasperated, and not just with thieves; the *Report of the Commissioner of Police for the Metropolis* for the years 1943, 1945, 1946, and 1948 raged against the public that despite 'advising the public to take reasonable precautions for the protection of their own property, carelessness in this respect continues to be the greatest ally of the thief'.[30] Doors and windows left open, unbolted locks, and valuables left lying around in places visible from outside all contributed to the police's dwindling patience with citizens: 'It is our duty to give our help to such people but they can hardly expect our sympathy', wrote Commissioner Sir Harold Scott in 1946.[31]

The new 999 emergency number, still in the process of being rolled out nationally after a successful trial in London in 1937, was designed to bring police and public into closer proximity to extinguish crime through cooperative forms of local surveillance.[32] However, an Ealing Studios film, box-office hit *The Blue Lamp* (1950), took a playful swipe at it by highlighting its potential to turn neighbour against neighbour. In one sequence, the film showed a gentleman-householder knocked unconscious by burglars in his West London home, witnessed from across the street by an elderly woman from the window of her own home. As the criminals fled and the victim clambered to his feet, the elderly lady burst through the open front door wearing a marvellous tartan nightgown, declaring proudly to the assembled party 'I dialled 999! I dialled 999!' It soon transpired, though, that the victim was anything but pleased at the lady's assistance. His response to his elderly neighbour's 'I dialled 999!' was an angry 'Oh, who asked you to interfere? Go on get on!' a reaction clarified when he was first forced to admit that his wife's stolen pearls were fake, and second that he was living under an assumed name. With the jewellery business of 'Mr. Evans' unveiled as far from legitimate and his wife loudly condemning him as a 'dirty, filthy old liar', the film injected a note of slapstick humour into an otherwise serious ordeal. Yet the joke offered a suggestive commentary on the downside of the emergency number, equipping neighbours with a means of 'interfering' and compromising those about whom they telephoned. The emergency number was also seen to be fallible, as the burglars were only caught much later, after shooting dead the beloved character Police Constable George Dixon, shaking viewers' faith in the imperviousness of police through one of post-war cinema's most shocking and harrowingly violent plot twists.[33]

Produced in close consultation with the Metropolitan Police, *The Blue Lamp* brought to screen the tensions between tradition and change, young and old, order and disorder being negotiated in the streets and homes of the post-war

---

[29] Amy Helen Bell, *Murder Capital: Suspicious Deaths in London, 1933–1953* (Manchester: Manchester University Press, 2015), p. 170.

[30] HCPP, Cmd. 6536, *Report of the Commissioner of Police of the Metropolis for the Year 1943* (London, 1944), p. 5; Cmd. 6871, *Report of the Commissioner of Police for the Metropolis 1945* (London, 1946), pp. 5, 26; Cmd. 7156, *Report of the Commissioner of Police for the Metropolis 1946* (London, 1947), p. 8; Cmd. 7737, *Report of the Commissioner of Police for the Metropolis 1948* (London, 1949), p. 8.

[31] Cmd. 7156, *Report of the Commissioner of Police for the Metropolis 1946* (London, 1947), p. 8.

[32] Moss, ' "Dial 999 for Help!" '.

[33] *The Blue Lamp* (United Kingdom: Ealing Studios, dir. Basil Dearden, 1950).

metropolis. Historian Richard Hornsey writes of the film's formulation of the 'perfect reconstruction citizens', P. C. Dixon and his young colleague P. C. Mitchell, whose 'rhythmic' pacing of the beat accompanied their dutiful assistance in 'helping old ladies cross the road, and apprehending a car driver who ignores a pedestrian crossing'.[34] Their numbers were dwindling, however, both as a result of deaths among Metropolitan Police officers who served during the war, and due to a post-war recruitment crisis wherein the poor rates of pay and the retirement of a large proportion of veteran officers rendered police numbers unstable.[35] As they struggled, burglars and deserters 'preyed on London like wolves, stealing whatever they could' described ex-Chief Superintendent of the C.I.D Peter Beveridge in 1957. He recalled the death of P. C. Nathaniel Edgar on 13 February, 1948, shot while 'on anti-burglar night patrol' after chasing a suspect at Winchmore Hill, north London.[36] The case sparked a high-profile manhunt for the killer, Donald George Thomas, grinding the city to a standstill while police searched taxis, buses, and underground trains.[37] Despite Thomas' eventual capture, the tragedy, which inspired the scene in *The Blue Lamp*, underscored the dangers and accelerating crime rate police were facing.[38] At this critical juncture for the reputation of the Force, Assistant Commissioner of the Criminal Investigation Department Mr R. M. Howe took a fateful trip. To Sweden.

In 1942, Sweden devised an innovative way to deal with its own epidemic of burglaries. Instituting a formal partnership between police and insurance companies named the 'Defying the Burglar Association', the two sectors launched a mass media assault on the public consciousness, educating citizens about domestic security and the need to cooperate with police via a travelling exhibition and films on the subject. They also founded a 'school for burglary prevention' in Stockholm, where 'the public, especially persons from neighbourhoods which have suffered from burglars' depredations...are shown such exhibits as a sample door, the lock of which can be picked with a penknife or opened through the letter box by a piece of wire'. Astoundingly (from the British perspective) insurance companies had footed the bill for all these measures.[39] This seems to have made waves internationally, as one Canadian underwriter, corresponding with the Metropolitan Police in 1946 prior to Howe's visit, exclaimed that 'Sweden, which is first in so many things, has done it again...The thought occurred to us that the insurance companies

---

[34] Richard Hornsey, *The Spiv and the Architect: Unruly Life in Postwar London* (Minneapolis: University of Minnesota Press, 2010), pp. 22–3.

[35] Bell, *Murder Capital*, p. 170; T. A. Critchley, *A History of Police in England and Wales* (2nd edn, London: Constable, 1978), p. 227 (my thanks to the anonymous reviewer who drew my attention to this reference).

[36] Peter Beveridge, *Inside the CID* (London: Evans Brothers, 1957), pp. 73, 140–1. Beveridge's comment about deserters accords with the occupational breakdown of those accused of burglary at London's Magistrates Courts during the period 1940–65. Sampled at five-year intervals, of the 2,006 men and women featured 125 were in the Armed Services, although their numbers were concentrated in the period 1940–55. See Table 3, Appendix.

[37] 'Bandit Kills London P.C.', *Daily Mail* (14 Feb. 1948), p. 1.

[38] Jeffrey Richards and Anthony Aldgate, *Best of British: Cinema and Society from the 1930s to the Present* (London: I.B. Taurus, 1999), p. 130.

[39] TNA, HO 287/239, *Memo re Exhibitions Held in Aid of Crime Prevention* (24 Dec. 1953).

of this country might well gain a lot of kudos and at the same time reduce the spate of burglaries in Canada by emulating the example of the Swedish.'[40] Howe appears to have had the same thought. Returning to London in 1947, he immediately set about contacting colleagues, insurers and security firms to stage a comparable scheme in Britain. Here, it was to be called the National Crime Prevention Campaign (1950–1).

Beyond educating the public about the latest anti-burglary measures, the National Crime Prevention Campaign sought to instil a 'new' model of citizenship—one that, ironically, harked back to the war. Launched at Selfridges department store on 1 May 1950 by Home Secretary James Chuter Ede, he described the remit of the campaign as an opportunity 'to bring home to the public the simple measures they can take to protect their own property, how they can help each other, how they can help the police and how they can help themselves'.[41] Entreating citizens to 'do their bit' by looking beyond their own interests to 'help' neighbour and state (through supporting police to do their job), Ede's rhetoric recalled a national unity of purpose that, as historian Sonya Rose describes, was integral to the conceptualization of British national identity in government propaganda during the war.[42] Actively resisting the growing emphasis on personal privacy and 'home-centredness', Ede continued, 'Perhaps we pride ourselves too much on minding our own business. Instead we should be good neighbours and help each other by keeping an eye on each other's' homes.'[43] Others involved in the campaign mimicked Ede's strategy, some drawing explicitly on the recent experience of war. Sir Harold Scott, Commissioner of Police, wrote the foreword to Captain W. J. Hutchinson's *A Policeman Puts You Wise* (1951). Offering anti-burglary advice to householders and issued by the *Police Journal* in 1951 to accompany the national campaign, the book's foreword proclaimed: 'This is no static war: the troops on either side—criminal and law-abiding—constantly change and the enlistment and instruction of the friends of law and order must keep pace with the regular reinforcement of the forces of the law breakers.'[44]

Burglars were to be the ultimate enemy in the war on crime. 'The Burglar and You' was central to the National Crime Prevention Campaign between Metropolitan Police, Home Office, and the British Insurance Association displayed in Selfridges. On tour around London from October 1950 until June 1951, it showcased panels (Fig. 7.1) depicting the dangerously close proximity of the burglar to a family at night. Modern, insular leisure activities, such as families gathering to watch television in the front room of an evening, were shown leading to carelessness in securing locks and doors in other rooms, allowing thieves to enter. Exhibition-goers were

[40] TNA, MEPO 2/8052, Letter from 'Canadian Underwriter' (1 Apr. 1946).

[41] TNA, MEPO 2/8052, Speech by Sir James Chuter Ede delivered at Selfridges Department Store (1 May 1950).

[42] Sonya O. Rose, *Which People's War? National Identity and Citizenship in Wartime Britain* (Oxford: Oxford University Press, 2003), pp. 2–4.

[43] TNA, MEPO 2/8052, Speech by Sir James Chuter Ede delivered at Selfridges Department Store (1 May 1950).

[44] Sir Harold Scott, 'Foreword', in W. J. Hutchinson, *A Policeman Puts You Wise* (London: The Police Journal, 1951), p. 6.

Fig. 7.1. TNA, MEPO 2/8052, 'Whitehall 1212: Exhibition at Selfridges, taken for Exhibitions Division' (May 1950).

repeatedly told to 'Ring the Police', and to 'check the defences', while being presented with stalls full of security technologies including locks, burglar alarms, and safes.[45]

Neighbourliness and cooperation with police through staying 'vigilant' also created a fresh outlet for the duties of the housewife, a figure to which the campaign frequently referred despite the reality of millions of working- and middle-class women in full or part-time employment.[46] 'The housewife, too, has greater opportunity for observing what goes on in the street and in the houses around', directed Hutchinson in *A Policeman Puts You Wise*. 'She is probably more curious about or interested in other people than her menfolk; and she tends to gather, perhaps

---

[45] TNA, MEPO 2/8052, 'Home Office Circular NO. 55/1950' (17 Mar. 1950).
[46] Dolly Smith Wilson, 'A New Look at the Affluent Worker: The Good Working Mother in Post-War Britain', *Twentieth Century British History* 17:2 (2005), pp. 206–29.

unconsciously, a fund of information. Thus the police ought to be able to look to the women for a good deal of support in the matter of reporting suspicious circumstances.'[47] Hutchinson's advice was accompanied by an illustration showing a housewife leaning out of the window and dialling 999 after espying a burglary.[48] Youthful and attractive, her actions were juxtaposed on the opposite page against an anecdote about her opposite: 'Mrs. B', a single working mother, whose careless-ness of the security around her own home resulted in a burglary.

> Everyone said she should have been more careful. Fancy leaving her back door key like that, and the window open! Fancy the neighbour telling a stranger so much! It was just asking for trouble to leave the bread bag on the door with a note for Tommy [her son] telling the burglar just where to find the key! Of course, you and I would never be *so* stupid.[49]

Flagrantly pitting the levels of common sense and responsibility of the married housewife against that of the lone working mother, Hutchinson's condescension extended to the social milieu of the latter, whose neighbours were apparently more likely to stand around chatting to prospective burglars about the frequently empty house next door. Here, a very fine distinction was drawn between the kinds of neighbours whose interests in each other's business were 'gossipy' and those who kept watch in order to protect each other from crime, a distinction shaped by the class and relationships (social and sexual) of the women involved. The plight of Mrs B was not wholly unsympathetic. It was noted that she had lost her husband during the war, a factor that readers would undoubtedly relate to, and one that suggested Hutchinson's nostalgic appeal to a pre-war era of supposedly 'simpler' and more traditional family models. However, some five years had elapsed since the end of the conflict, and the author's cruel jibe at the 'stupidity' of Mrs B sent a broader indictment of her failure to acquire a new husband and father for her son, and her attempt to be economically independent. Aligning the sympathy of police for victims with those who were seen to be 'responsible' in the choices they made for their private lives, such judgements were surprisingly static, carrying over into the next decade. In 1964, the Commissioner of Metropolitan Police's annual report described a new 'tally of vulnerability' for houses, that included the lack of domestic workers and women's propensity to go out to work, meaning that 'never before have so many dwellings been left unoccupied for so long'.[50] Again, Simpson's comments betokened his nostalgia for a highly upper middle-class lifestyle that, as historian Joe Moran asserts, was associated with prosperous neighbourhoods of London during the 1950s, characterized as the housewife's 'domain ... in an era of high male employment and gendered divisions of labour'.[51]

---

[47] Hutchinson, *A Policeman Puts You Wise*, p. 28.
[48] Ibid. The image has not been reproduced here due to copyright restrictions, but it can be viewed in the copy of this book held in the Bodleian Law Library, Crim 575 H978c (sec coll).
[49] Ibid., p. 29.
[50] HCPP, Cmnd. 2710, *Report of the Commissioner of Police for the Metropolis, 1964* (July 1965), p. 9.
[51] Joe Moran, 'Imagining the Street in Post-War Britain', *Urban History* 39:1 (2012), p. 182.

By promoting traditionally gendered roles within the home, the National Crime Prevention Campaign fused the wartime creed of duty to others with pre-war appeals to middle-class consumer citizenship (and middle-class idealizations of home life) found in insurance and security advertising.[52] These were models of national and personal character that had proven commercial and political success. Yet, as historians have shown, the concept of what it meant to be a 'good citizen' became fundamentally contested in post-war Britain, especially in urban centres.[53] The kinds of middle-class suburban homes that the campaign sought to protect from burglars actively excluded those living in flats, tower blocks, and social housing. Unsurprisingly, they also failed to acknowledge ethnic diversity. Deliberately avoiding having to engage with the cosmopolitanism of a city, and country, that had experienced immigration from around the world for successive decades since the late nineteenth century, campaign strategists also preferred a monolithic class structure.[54] A decision was taken early on by Metropolitan Police that the 'model house' of burglar-proof design the public would be shown 'should be a small semi-detached house, rather above the council-house type'.[55] Flat security was to be wholly avoided.[56] Effectively 'whitewashing' the campaign (the term is Kathleen Paul's helpful synthesis of attitudes towards race in post-war Britain), the reluctance of police, Home Office, and commercial sector to apprehend post-war society and victimization by burglars in relation to broader spectrum of class, race, and gendered experience ultimately looked regressive instead of visionary.[57]

The effects of the campaign's distance from the diverse realities of urban lifestyles was revealed in London perhaps more starkly than elsewhere. Just 48,000 people visited the London exhibition over an eighteen-day period in 1950, as against the attendance figures for cities such as Portsmouth, where 93,000 attended in fourteen days.[58] Excuses were forthcoming; Mr T. S. Lodge of the Metropolitan Police's Statistical Division noted for the record that the Metropolitan Police already provided annual, independent anti-burglary exhibitions at the Ideal Home Show in Olympia.[59] These were certainly popular, and included a demonstration of a 'House that Should Not be Burgled' that attracted royal publicity in March 1951 when Princess Margaret, accompanied by the Duke and Duchess of Kent, visited

[52] See Chapter 4.

[53] See for example: Mort, *Capital Affairs*; Kathleen Paul, *Whitewashing Britain: Race and Citizenship in the Postwar Era* (London: Cornell University Press, 1997); Phil Hubbard, 'Sex Zones: Intimacy, Citizenship and Public Space', *Sexualities* 4:1 (2001), pp. 51–71; Becky Conekin, *The Autobiography of a Nation: The 1951 Exhibition of Britain, Representing Britain in the Post-War World* (Manchester: Manchester University Press, 2003); Helen Meller, 'Urban Renewal and Citizenship: The Quality of Life in British Cities, 1890–1990', *Urban History* 22:1 (1995), pp. 63–84; Matt Houlbrook and Chris Waters, 'The Heart in Exile: Detachment and Desire in 1950s London', *History Workshop Journal* 62:1 (2006), pp. 142–65.

[54] Walkowitz, *Nights Out*.

[55] TNA, MEPO 2/8052, 'Crime Prevention Publicity, 48B' (20 Feb. 1950).

[56] TNA, MEPO 2/8052, Chief Superintendent G. Hatherill to A.C.C., 'Anti-Crime Exhibition' (4 Aug. 1949), p. 2.

[57] Paul, *Whitewashing Britain*.

[58] TNA, HO 287/239, 'Crime Prevention Campaigns: Results' (24 Dec. 1953).

[59] TNA, HO 287/239, CMD Pulling, Metropolitan Police, to C. Parkinson, Home Office, 'Report on the Effect of the Crime Prevention Campaign in the Metropolitan Police District' (16 July 1951).

and gamely allowed themselves to be photographed 'breaking in'.[60] Yet even this could not ameliorate the fact that after a collective spend of £20,000 by government agencies and insurers (comprising the touring exhibition, pamphlets, press coverage, and a publicity film entitled *Help Yourself* charting the day in a life of a burglar), no significant statistical decrease in burglary or housebreaking was recorded in the aftermath. On the contrary, the statistics revealed a slight increase at a local and national level, much to the frustration and bewilderment of organizers.[61] The effect on police-public cooperation was equally dismal, being described by one Chief Constable as purely 'temporary'.[62] Lodge was forced to conclude ruefully that 'We cannot, however, state with any degree of certainty that crime prevention exhibitions have contributed to a reduction in crime....such changes as there are seem to be rather in the wrong direction than the right'.[63]

The disappointing outcome of the National Crime Prevention Campaign of 1950–1 suggested a severe disconnect between police and public. Arousing merely temporary interest, the wan reaction to anti-burglary campaigns indicated that citizens were now more invested in using their purchasing power to resolve problems than taking on another set of 'responsibilities'. Popular appeals that drew upon concepts of national strength, duty, and sacrifice were beginning to founder, especially when concentrating on the experiences of a relatively narrow section of society. This manifested during the mid-1950s in the declining anti-nuclear Civil Defence movement, whose civilian membership were increasingly antagonistic towards active expressions of 'patriotism' as a core value, instead favouring home-based leisure pursuits that were individualistic and nominally 'apolitical'.[64] In fact, the main short-term 'winners' from the campaign were insurers and security technology companies. Sales of locks, bolts, and burglar alarms experienced a sharp increase in the aftermath of the campaign, Lodge conceded.[65] Realistically, commercial interests seemed likely to triumph from the outset, since even the site of the launch—Selfridges—illustrated the campaign's contested ideological aims. When negotiating the use of their floor space in 1949, Metropolitan Police came up against the store's branding imperatives as a family friendly space for leisurely consumption, which swiftly took precedence over the police's desire to exhibit artefacts from its Crime Museum. Selfridges would only allow these in a closed-off area marked 'Adults Only'.[66] Similarly, lock and safe companies pressured police to exhibit their wares

---

[60] VAM, Photograph Album, *Daily Mail Ideal Home Exhibition* (Mar. 1950), images 51/347, 51/333.

[61] TNA, HO 287/239, T. S. Lodge to Miss Logan (21 Jan. 1951); Burglaries increased from 570 to 613 in London between 1951–2, and in England and Wales, from 3,729 to 3,847. HCPP: Cmd. 8944, *Report of the Commissioner of Police for the Metropolis for 1952* (London, 1953), p. 43; HCPP: Cmd. 8941, *Criminal Statistics for England and Wales* (London, 1952), p. 3.

[62] TNA, HO 287/239, T. A. O'Brien to S. J. Baker, 'Crime Prevention Publicity Campaign' (3 Aug. 1951).

[63] TNA, HO 287/239, T. S. Lodge to Miss Logan (21 Jan. 1951).

[64] Matthew Grant, ' "Civil Defence Gives Meaning to your Leisure": Citizenship, Participation, and Cultural Change in Cold War Recruitment Propaganda, 1949–54', *Twentieth Century British History* 22:1 (2011), p. 53.

[65] TNA, HO 287/239, 'Crime Prevention Campaigns: Results' (24 Dec. 1953).

[66] TNA, MEPO 2/8052, 'P.H.F'. Memo to Secretary (no. 83) (13 July 1950).

with labels reading 'as recommended by Scotland Yard', attempting to turn cooperation into lucrative endorsement. Their requests were refused. Nonetheless, officials recognized that the mere presence of these companies at the exhibition, which helped defray costs, implicitly gave them a promotional boost. Making necessary financial choices to get the exhibition running, police hosted rival security companies and their products at the risk of aggravating the Chubb Company, with whom the Metropolitan Police worked most closely in reality.[67] Having to sacrifice their desire to display the most frightening evidence of burglars' crimes or the most effective security products of the time, purely to appease Selfridges and maintain fair competition in the security market, Home Office and police ambitions for the campaign were compromised at the start.

Throughout the 1950s, rates of burglary, housebreaking, and other property crimes continued to climb. They reached their zenith in the 1966, when cases of burglary and housebreaking combined accounted for 92,641 cases of crime in England and Wales, reported in the annual *Judicial Statistics* sent to the House of Commons.[68] The soaring annual statistics made international headlines, with the *New York Times* reporting 'Modern Crime Wave Grips Britain', in December 1965, telling readers to 'forget about Raffles', whose 'old-fashioned, genteel crimes' were eclipsed by those of 'burglars [who] get smarter all the time'.[69] That year, the Home Office sent out a new leaflet and series of posters entitled 'Don't Invite Crime', again charging the public with acts of 'neglect or carelessness which made it easy for the thief'. Urging citizens to help police 'to win, decisively, the war against crime in Britain', they redeployed the wartime rallying cry to be 'vigilant' in equipping houses with locks and bolts, along with informing police of suspicious activity. Exclusively referring to homeowners with the masculine pronouns 'he' and 'his', the leaflet retained a conservative outlook on the 'typical' household.[70] One poster (Fig. 7.2) portrayed a woman idly leaving a window on the latch to go shopping, giving the burglar easy access to the home; while men 'secured' households, the image implied, women were not only callous but dangerously focused on cares beyond the home. The same message was sent out in an advert issued throughout the London newspapers, the headline of which was emblazoned 'I felt sick...they'd wrecked the room—smashed things—torn things—even our wedding photos...and I'd only left the bathroom window open'.[71] Like the interwar burglary insurance adverts of yesteryear, the advert equated the burglar's entry with the destabilization of marital harmony through 'robbing' the couple of a shared history, for which the wife's negligence was blamed.

Burglars' threat to domesticity was emphasized at a time when women's economic, social, and sexual agency was growing stronger. Anti-burglary propaganda

[67] TNA, MEPO 2/8052, 'P.H.F'. Memo to Secretary (no. 83) (13 July 1950); Memo to Commissioner (no. 84) (18 July 1950).
[68] HCPP, Cmnd. 3332, *Criminal Statistics, England and Wales, 1966* (London, 1967), p. 1.
[69] 'Modern Crime Wave Grips Britain', *New York Times* (27 Dec. 1965), p. 3.
[70] TNA, INF 2/124, Home Office, 'Don't Invite Crime' (London 1965).
[71] TNA, INF 2/124, 'Don't Invite Crime' advert (10 Nov. 1965), issued to the *Daily Mail* (18 Nov.); *Daily Express* (20 Nov.); *Sunday Express* (21 Nov.); *News of the World* (23 Nov.); *The People* (5 Dec.).

Fig. 7.2. TNA, INF 2/124, Home Office, 'Don't Invite Crime' (1965).

ventriloquized official fears about these changes, entwining the declining health of marriage and the nation's morality with the threat posed to property. This connection was painted most vividly in the 'Watch Out! There's a Thief About!' campaign begun by the Home Office in 1967, which ran into the early 1970s. Figure 7.3 shows one of the campaign posters, featuring a photograph of a young couple staring in horror at the smashed remains of the dressing table in the bedroom. Foregrounding the woman's stockings strewn casually out of drawers and a framed picture of their wedding day smashed in the foreground, it was uncannily similar to the Eagle Star and British Dominions burglary insurance advert published in *The Scotsman* in 1920 (Fig. 5.3), produced shortly after the First World War when women's recently won ability to vote and incursions into the workforce had provoked comparable social upheaval (accompanied by escalating rates of divorce). The text that accompanied Figure 7.3 declared that an evening out had 'cost' the couple, whose 'most treasured possessions [were] smashed or stolen. Their whole house ransacked. Her favourite picture broken. And all because they left one window open...Insurance can't replace stolen memories.'[72] Resurrecting the motif of the burglar's trespass into the bedroom and proximity to the most intimate, personal possessions of the (female) householder to evoke

[72] TNA, INF 2/124, 'Watch Out! There's a Thief About!' undated, *c.*1968–70.

Fig. 7.3. TNA, INF 2/124, Home Office, 'Watch Out! There's a Thief About!' (*c.*1967).

the crime as a 'rape' of the marital chamber, it again levied responsibility for burglary at the young couple's frivolity, their unaccountable lack of care for preserving the sanctity of home.

Including a dig at insurers by highlighting that they 'can't replace stolen memories', the poster also betrayed irritation at companies' commercial success from campaigns initiated to assist police in preventing burglary. In 1969, Home Office correspondence about insurance companies' contribution (or rather lack thereof) to crime prevention included a press cutting from *The Times* of the previous year, which concluded that 'the bulk of the mass media advertising carried out on behalf of the insurance companies is not preventative...no matter how the insurance industry strives to keep down costs and claims, its ultimate sanction, despite the wishes of the Government, is to raise premiums to match risks and claims'.[73] Too late, politicians realized that the relationship between media, state, and market in defining the risks associated with burglary skewed unevenly in the interests of the commercial sector. Instead of creating 'active' forms of citizenship orientated around reciprocity and personal responsibility to prevent crime, this affiliation had underscored the shift towards consumer-citizenship. Those who could afford anti-burglary technologies and insurance were those who would expect, and receive, the most attention from the state. Officials were doubly thwarted by their own efforts to encourage greater popular engagement with anti-burglar security, proliferating adverts and campaign material that clung to traditional, putatively middle-class family models and gender dynamics. Anti-burglary campaigns underscored the tensions and contradictions of the so-called 'permissive' decades, which historians agree were less 'swinging' than they have since been remembered.[74] The final section of this chapter explores how police, criminologists, and psychologists channelled their fears over the latest gender crisis to proffer fresh understandings of burglars' motives, using the dislocation between 'traditional' and 'modern' families and adolescence to explain thieves' frightening new recourse to violence.

* * *

She woke up covered in blood. Standing over her was the burglar, a man she knew well as a neighbour from across the road. He worked as a carpenter for her father's building and decorating company and lived with his wife and two small children. The scene, in a small house in the suburbs of north-west London, was one from a nightmare; yet the 16-year-old girl, unlike the white-faced burglar and attempted rapist before her, remained calm. With extraordinary presence of mind, she pretended to hear her father returning downstairs, and told the man he should go away at once. Fortunately, her attacker had already lost his nerve at the sight of the blood from the head injury he had struck her. Taking the girl downstairs where she put a wet towel on the wound, he followed her insistent commands to leave and

---

[73] TNA, HO 287/1004, Cutting, Roy Mackie, 'Their Own Worst Enemies', *The Times* (4 Dec. 1968).
[74] Mort, *Capital Affairs*; Nick Thomas, 'Will the Real 1950s Please Stand Up? Views of a Contradictory Decade', *Cultural and Social History* 5:2 (2008), pp. 227–35; Adrian Bingham, *Family Newspapers? Sex, Private Life, and the British Popular Press 1918–1978* (Oxford: Oxford University Press, 2009).

ran out of the house, retreating to his own home. Soon, the girl's parents arrived and brought Bishenden back to talk to the police—along with his wife. Arrest followed swiftly, and in a statement, he pleaded that 'I don't know I was all mixed up, I didn't know what was happening. I am sorry about all this and I am pleased that the sight of all the blood stopped me from raping [her].' The apology was unlikely to have inspired much sympathy from the girl's mother, who grimly helped the police to find the metal poker, discarded in the fireplace, used to hit her daughter. Strands of hair were still attached. The year was 1960. Dennis Bishenden, aged 22, was sentenced to six years for burglary and attempted rape, the leniency of the judgement reflecting the fact that his brother had recently died and it was thought this might have triggered his behaviour.[75] Sympathy was, in this instance, misplaced. Released from prison in 1966, Bishenden raped and attempted to strangle another girl, aged just 13. Passing down a term of life imprisonment, the horrified judge pronounced Bishenden 'a terrible danger to any young girl who crosses your path'.[76]

Violence, particularly domestic abuse and sexual assault, proliferated after the Second World War. Initially, the problem was blamed on deserters and demobbed soldiers returning home 'brutalized' by warfare, venting their frustrations over wives and former girlfriends who were often suspected of cheating as the long years of the war dragged on. Ultimately, though, the association between actual service in war and the new incidence of violence proved to be largely mythical.[77] Juvenile criminality, and gang culture among those too young to have served, festered at the heart of the crime 'wave' of the 1950s and 1960s suffered by residents of the metropolis and other urban centres across Britain. Scholarship by both criminologists and historians portrays this as an era in which law-abiding members of society felt themselves 'under siege' from teenagers and young adults who ran riot unchecked.[78] Members of the 'Teddy Boys', young working-class men dressed sharply in faux-Edwardian suits, were on a fundamental level gangs of thugs engaged in racially targeted fighting and vicious (sometimes fatal) knife attacks over status and girlfriends.[79] Concerns about them circulating in the national media prompted the National Union of Teachers to launch a survey of instances of 'gang culture' in secondary modern schools in England and Wales, although the returns showed these fears to be exaggerated.[80] Harder to ignore were the annual statistics released by the Commissioners of Metropolitan Police indicating that in London, ever increasing numbers of young men under the age of

---

[75] TNA, CRIM 1/3511, *R. v. Dennis Bishenden* (1960).

[76] 'Life Sentence for "Terrible Danger"', *The Times* (13 Dec. 1966), p. 9.

[77] Alan Allport, *Demobbed: Coming Home after World War Two* (London and New Haven: Yale University Press, 2010).

[78] Eugene McLaughlin, 'From Reel to Ideal: *The Blue Lamp* and Popular Cultural Constructions of the English "Bobby"', *Crime, Media, Culture* 1:1 (2005), p. 14; Mort, *Capital Affairs*, pp. 86–9; Abigail Wills, 'Delinquency, Masculinity and Citizenship in England, 1950–1970', *Past and Present* 187 (2005), pp. 157–85.

[79] Mort, *Capital Affairs*, pp. 86–9.

[80] Louise Jackson and Angela Bartie, *Policing Youth: Britain, 1945–70* (Manchester: Manchester University Press, 2014), pp. 89–90.

21 were bypassing petty forms of theft altogether and turning to serious forms of larceny such as burglary.[81]

Violent burglaries, including those with rape and murder or involving the use of explosives, were not recorded separately in criminal statistics for London at the time. We can discover their legacy in files held at the National Archives however, just eleven of which were preserved for the period 1955–68.[82] Modern criminal case files, in the words of ethnographer Alexander Kozin, are 'social texts', boasting a diverse authorship of police, lawyers, and medical professionals to collectively construct a 'narrative' or 'case' about the life and choices of defendants. Marshalling evidence in a 'continuum [that] embraces past acts, present motions, and future consequences', the less active voices are, ironically, defendants and victims, whose thoughts are related through institutional forms and filters over which they have little control.[83] During the mid-twentieth century, at the height of popular concern about the causes of male juvenile violence, this 'continuum' was increasingly informed by psycho-sexual readings of defendants' childhoods and relationships. Bishenden's father, a police officer, was described as 'probably dominant and authoritative'; the death of Bishenden's brother, coupled with a wife just 18 years old and two small children, was thought to have led to his becoming 'mentally disturbed'.[84] Similarly, in February 1959 Thomas Patrick Dumphy (age 20), convicted at the Central Criminal Court of burglary and attempted rape at a flat in East Dulwich, south-east London, was given a detailed psychological profile. Highlighting that he 'sometimes rebelled' against his violent and controlling father, it was recorded that Dumphy's father had 'set about his son' on more than one occasion.[85] This file was particularly noteworthy for the defence team's efforts to determine whether Dumphy's victim, a married woman who met him at a party, had been drunk or tried to seduce him. Prompting one witness to affirm she 'was sober and she had been behaving herself', the strategy makes for unsettling reading in a case where the defendant already had previous convictions for joyriding and shop-breaking.[86]

Male 'delinquency' (particularly juvenile delinquency, for which Bishenden and Dumphy were only just too old to qualify in their early twenties) was blamed on family breakdown and unhelpfully pluralistic standards of masculinity during the

---

[81] HCPP, Cmnd. 2710, *Report of the Commissioner of Police for the Metropolis, 1964* (July 1965), p. 10.

[82] TNA, CRIM 1/3099, *Rex. v. Brian William Smith and Donald William Carter* (1958); CRIM 1/3141: *Rex. v. Thomas Patrick Dumphy* (1959); CRIM 1/3391, *Rex. v. J. Clarke* (1960); CRIM 1/3511, *Rex. v. Dennis Bishenden* (1960); CRIM 1/3883, *Rex. v. James William Ball and Martin Daniel Hayes* (1962); CRIM 1/4362, *Rex. v. Leslie Fitt* (1965); CRIM 1/2646, *Rex. v. James Anderson Leitsch* (1955); CRIM 1/2668, *Rex. v. John Cohen and Two Others* (1955); CRIM 1/2894, *Rex. v. Albert William Pusey* (1958); CRIM 1/3472, *Rex. v. Robert Kenneth Holmes* (1960); CRIM 1/5013, *Rex. v. John William Smith* (1968).

[83] Alexander Kozin, 'Scrapbooking the Criminal Defence File', *Crime, Media, Culture* 4:31 (2008), pp. 49–50.

[84] TNA, CRIM 1/3511, F. H. Brisby, Principal Medical Officer H.M.P. Brixton, to Clerk of the Court, Central Criminal Court (25 Dec. 1960).

[85] TNA, CRIM 1/3141, D. V. Thomas, Probation Officer, to Central Criminal Court (10 Mar. 1959).

[86] TNA, CRIM 1/3141, Statement of the Deponent (9 Feb. 1959).

post-war decades. Swapping the 'martial' masculinity associated with war service for 'domesticated' masculinity in peacetime was no easy task, as those working in borstal and young offenders' institutions testified.[87] Inability to control ones' temper and displays of emotional distress were pathologized, regarded as incompatible with being 'good' (male) citizens; yet emerging youth cultures celebrated rebellion and 'permissiveness'. Women, on the other hand, were handed a mixed bag of legal 'benefits' and cultural stereotypes. Finally gaining the right to abortion and the pill during the 1960s, they also carried the stigma for unwanted pregnancies and had to contend with assumptions of their sexual 'availability' that did *not* necessarily correspond with greater access to contraception.[88] Did violent forms of burglary stem from young men's confusion in the face of these conflicting ideas and realities? The defence team's attempt to cast doubt on the victim in Dumphy's case, despite decades of women being identified as most likely to suffer from burglars' attacks, suggests they were willing to test this rationale. Throwing the blame on the emotional crises wrought by fractured families and changing gender roles repackaged burglaries as another consequence of modern lifestyles and youth. Their assumptions were echoed in at least two other cases. The impact of an 'overbearing father' and a mother characterized as zealously 'overprotective' (*R. v. Robert Kenneth Holmes*, 1960), or the separation of the perpetrator's parents (*R. v. James Anderton Leitsch*, 1965) were key factors offered by professionals in these case files, heightening the danger surrounding intergenerational conflict.[89]

Homosexuality, and associations with 'deviant' sexual actors such as prostitutes, likewise figured among the supposed causes of burglary, phenomena also prominently implicated in familial breakdown in these decades. In December 1955, an armed burglary by a gang of young thieves took place at a residential jeweller's in Earl's Court. Measured by any standard, this was an especially horrific crime. Two of the arresting police officers were shot through the arm and thigh respectively, while a third officer sustained cuts from the shattered glass of the front window of their police car, which came under fire. The burglars, John Cohen and his accomplices Ronald Thomas Parsons, John Robert Cotten, and John James Thomas, all in their twenties with numerous previous convictions, pleaded guilty.[90] Passing down their sentences, including twenty years' imprisonment for ringleader Cohen, Lord Chief Justice Goddard denounced the latter as a 'wild animal'. As the *Daily Telegraph* reported, in its design, the gun the group used was 'contrary to the rules of international warfare', firing bullets with slits to maximize the impact of

---

[87] Wills, 'Delinquency, Masculinity, and Citizenship in England 1950–1970'.

[88] Hera Cook, 'The English Sexual Revolution: Technology and Change', *History Workshop Journal* 59 (2005), pp. 116–20; Marcus Collins, 'The Pornography of Permissiveness: Men's Sexuality and Women's Emancipation in Mid Twentieth-Century Britain', *History Workshop Journal* 47 (1999), pp. 99–120; Harry Cocks, 'Saucy Stories: Pornography, Sexology and the Marketing of Sexual Knowledge in Britain, *c.*1918–70', *Social History* 29:4 (2004), pp. 465–84.

[89] TNA, CRIM 1/3472, Detective Sergeant E. Anning, 'Antecedents of Robert Kenneth Holmes' (9 Aug. 1960); CRIM 1/2646, Detectives G. Hayler and W. Gay, 'Antecedents of James Anderton Leitsch' (10 Oct. 1955).

[90] TNA, CRIM 1/2668, *Rex. v. John Cohen and Two Others* (1955).

shrapnel.[91] War weapons scattering bullets across London's streets was shocking enough. Still worse, as the case file made clear, were the sexual habits of those involved. All were 'associates of homosexuals'. In Cohen's case, this was particularly contrasted with his 'respectable' parents, to whom he had not spoken for several years. Cotten, it was noted, was estranged from his wife and mingled with prostitutes and homosexuals alike, but it was Thomas, 'a self-confessed homosexual', whose influence was thought to be particularly malign:

> Thomas makes no secret of his physical abnormality and says that he is constantly seeking the companionship of persons who are either homosexuals or bi-sexuals. ... He says he has an unnatural affection for both Cohen and Parsons and when either has asked for his assistance, because of his affection he has been unable to refuse.[92]

Connecting homosexuality to other crimes was hardly revolutionary. 'Deviant' sexualities had long been fused with prevailing social ills, especially in an urban context, where anonymity and discreet encounters both sexual and criminal were possible. Drawn to the city and forced to move within the same 'underworld' terrain to avoid surveillance, queer men were frequently ensnared in blackmail and theft, although more often as victims than perpetrators.[93] Burglary was merely the latest offence that homosexuals were linked to. However, what is striking in the account of Thomas's statement is his (apparent) attempt to use the gang's affective ties to excuse his involvement in the crime—'because of his affection he has been unable to refuse'. Thomas' recourse to his sexuality indicates that he thought officials might be sympathetic to his plight, perhaps recognizing that they sought to explain the rising tide of the crime in relation to factors beyond their control, as well as those that handily justified their conservative stance in regard to gender and sexuality. Accepting medical 'treatment' sometimes alleviated prison sentences, as in the case of Alan Turing, convicted for having a relationship with a man in 1951, although the appalling physical and psychological trauma of chemical castration led to the eminent mathematician's suicide in 1954.[94] Thomas' strategy was an extraordinary gamble, if that was indeed his intention. Thomas' and the gang's sexuality was more likely to compound their guilt than mitigate it, being discovered two years before the 1957 Wolfenden Report recommended that homosexual activity be sanctioned between consenting adults in private, and ten years before the 1967 Sexual Offences Act brought this into law.[95] Thus, while Thomas received the lightest sentence of five years' imprisonment, this was more likely due to his lesser involvement in the crime (he was not party to the shooting), rather than for being in love with his accomplices.

---

[91] 'Lord Goddard Gaols a "Wild Animal"', *Daily Telegraph* (9 Dec. 1955), p. 10.

[92] TNA, CRIM 1/2668, 'C.R.O. No. 17210/35, John Cohen' (23 Nov. 1955); 'C.R.O. No. 31657/45, John Robert Cotton' (17 Nov. 1955); 'C.R.O. No. 10283/39, John James Thomas' (21 Nov. 1955).

[93] Houlbrook, *Queer London*, pp. 178–81.

[94] Laura Doan, 'Queer History/Queer Memory: The Case of Alan Turing', *GLQ: A Journal of Lesbian and Gay Studies* 23:1 (2017), pp. 113–36.

[95] Chris Waters, 'The Homosexual as a Social Being in Britain, 1945–1968', *Journal of British Studies* 51:3 (2012), pp. 685–710.

Tensions between old and new versions of masculinity and urban lifestyles found their ultimate expression in the murder and burglary of Frederick Scott, in September 1968. A senseless, impulsive act of violence, it was committed by Edward Hutchinson (age 28) and John William Smith (age 33), although since the jury could not decide which of them had struck the fatal blows they were found guilty of burglary alone.[96] Described by Lord Justice Phillimore as 'a grave miscarriage of justice', there was no avoiding the fact that one of the pair must have been the murderer.[97] Scott, an elderly and frail man in his late seventies who lived with his older sister, Louisa, in a small terraced house at Edmonton in north London, was stabbed several times in the chest with a chisel. He stumbled onto the thieves when he came downstairs in the night. Born in the previous century, Scott was a retired factory worker, and the house he shared with his sister (known affectionately to the neighbours as 'Granny Lil') spoke little of wealth.[98] Crime scene photographs (Figs. 7.4 and 7.5) offer us a glimpse of the life they lived together. A sitting room contained a dresser crammed with teacups and crockery, and a small, ornate china dog. On the mantelpiece, the most prominent photograph was of a cat, positioned above a large electric heater that underlined the siblings' age and infirmity. Two chairs sat side by side, adorned liberally with cushions for comfort. Books were piled next to the forced-open dresser drawers, from whence a sewing kit was on view. The parlour, the entrance to which was now spattered with blood, opened onto a small, faintly ornamented settee where the two could sit beneath calendars depicting the royal family. The first calendar, on the right, showed its younger members, the Queen and Princess Margaret, with their husbands in the state room at Buckingham Palace. The second displayed them waving from the famous balcony, the Queen Mother standing next to Prince Philip, in full military dress, and the young Prince Charles. Domesticity, comfort, and patriotism: these were the hallmarks of the Scotts' retirement. The lack of personal family photographs added a slightly poignant sense of their spending their final days alone-together, neither being married—Louisa was still formally addressed as 'Miss Scott'.[99]

Crime scene photographs laid bare the destruction burglary had wrought in the Scotts' peaceful lives, their clearly modest means emphasizing the futility of the whole episode. The pictures offered a compelling narrative of the contrasting culpability and respectability of victims and perpetrators, a ploy used commonly by police photographers to try to sway the jury's decision, as historian Alexa Neale argues.[100] In this case, the narrative was reinforced by the fact that Scott and his sister were heading to bed at nine p.m., just as the two young burglars made their first, fatal strike of the night. Where Frederick Scott represented the values of patient hard work and commitment to family and nation, signalled by the patriotic

---

[96] TNA, CRIM 1/5013, *Rex. v. John William Smith* (1968).
[97] 'Killer Escaped by Miscarriage of Justice', *Daily Telegraph* (22 Aug. 1969), p. 17.
[98] TNA, CRIM 1/5013, 'Witness Statement of Ronald Brian Goldhawk' (28 Sept. 1968).
[99] Ibid.
[100] Alexa Neale, 'Framing a Murder: Crime Scene Photographs in Mid-Twentieth-Century London', paper delivered to British Crime Historians Symposium, October 2016 (article forthcoming). My warmest thanks to Alexa for allowing me to cite her here.

Fig. 7.4. TNA, CRIM 1/5013, 'Crime Scene Photograph 11', *Rex v. John William Smith* (1968).

calendars, Smith and Hutchinson's actions again invoked the dubious character of modern male youth.[101] Such reservations extended to casual associates and leisure habits. Smith's claim that he was at the 'Cock Pub' over the road during the burglary—although too drunk to recall the details—in his statement drew attention to his reliance on pub clientele and bar staff to offer him an alibi, points underlined in pencil in the case file by officials. Smith did have the sense, in an era still marked by racial tensions (Enoch Powell's 'Rivers of Blood' speech was delivered a few months earlier, in April 1968), to assert that 'There was a load of coloured fellows in there but I don't know them', distancing himself from affiliations with ethnic groups that might be prejudicial to his defence.[102] Yet the file also highlighted that Smith was separated from his wife, by whom he had six children (four of whom were in care homes), and was living with another woman, with whom he had a

---

[101] This was another common narrative in crime scene photographs and case files of this era. See Bell, *Murder Capital*, pp. 182–5.

[102] TNA, CRIM 1/5013, 'Statement of John William Smith' (25 Sept. 1968).

Fig. 7.5. TNA, CRIM 1/5013, 'Crime Scene Photograph 12', *Rex v. John William Smith* (1968).

baby aged just five weeks.[103] As the elder of the two burglars, Smith's drunkenness and promiscuity suggested his longstanding embrace of the worst excesses of 'permissiveness'. His declaration to one police officer that 'I love old people. I wouldn't do that', when accused of Scott's murder, rang hollow in light of his aggressive renunciation of everything Scott's life embodied.[104]

The murder of Frederick Scott did not make front page news. Given the low social status of the victim and his moderate lifestyle, there was no dusting of celebrity stardust to capture journalists' interest; apart from the violence of the crime, here was another 'everyday' tragedy that would soon disappear from popular memory. This burglary was, however, far more emblematic of the kinds of burglaries ordinary people were encouraged to guard against. One did not have to be dazzlingly wealthy (or even marginally well-off) to find a burglar waiting in the living room at night. With this in mind, when reviewing the case files of post-war

[103] TNA, CRIM 1/5013, V. P. Durke, 'Metropolitan Police: Antecedents of John William Smith' (25 Sept. 1968).
[104] TNA, CRIM 1/5013, 'Statement of Witness Harry Tapin' (30 Sept. 1968).

burglaries, it is, perhaps, the references to more obvious reasons for committing burglary (such as poverty) that give the clearest insights into the meanings of the crime in these decades. In 1965, Leslie Fitt (then aged 22) was convicted of burglary, after handing himself in to police custody. His file appears to have been retained at the National Archives because he was also an arsonist, setting fire to his own lodgings as he left in an effort to cover his tracks—fortunately, the fire did not take hold. Fitt was broke, as was his wife. The incident in 1965 was to be the first of a career in burglary that saw him return to prison just three years later, in 1968, for the same crime. When finally asked about his motives, he replied 'We had no money at all and it was the only way out for us'. In the 1968 case, he and his wife complained that they had not eaten for several days when Fitt broke into some flats in Kentish Town, north-west London, to steal jewellery (they were caught attempting to pawn it at a jewellers' in Leicester Square). Unlike other case files, officers seem to have accepted Fitt's reasons for burgling, making fewer observations regarding his childhood and associates. Indeed, his plea had echoes of a response given to the same question ten years earlier, when Brian Smith, tried for burglary in 1958, stated bluntly to police 'For reasons which are quite obvious and having to keep on the move and without occupation and nowhere to sleep—I was in dire need of money'.[105]

Unemployment, or being employed in low-waged, manual forms of labouring on building sites and in factories together accounted for the most frequent occupational backgrounds of burglary defendants at London's magistrates courts during the period 1940–65.[106] Even those brandishing skilled forms of labour, such as carpenters, steel workers, and plumbers, featured prominently in the figures; the other major group were those serving in the armed forces, whose numbers diminished during the mid-1950s after demobilization. The steady stream of burglary defendants whose low or uneven wages saw them living hand to mouth, manifested a continuity of motive between pre- and post-Second World War decades that established poverty as the underlying structural cause. 'Poverty' can be used here to capture both workers in skilled and unskilled forms of labour, for another historian, Selina Todd, comments insightfully that even those working-class families who appeared among the 'better off' could still be living precariously.[107] Periods of unemployment were the norm for most labourers. Projects came and went, and a great deal of working-class 'affluence' was propped up by new systems of credit that masked heavy debts. A single injury might also put paid to the prosperity of families still mostly dependent on a male 'breadwinner'. The increasingly consumer-driven social landscape, of which increasing burglaries were, of course, a symptom, also meant that 'respectability' equated with the ability to purchase items some social surveyors viewed as luxuries—like televisions—that in reality

---

[105] TNA, CRIM 1/3099, 'Statement of Brian William Smith' (6 Dec. 1958).

[106] See Table 3, Appendix 1.

[107] Selina Todd, 'Affluence, Class, and Crown Street: Reinvestigating the Post-War Working Class', *Contemporary British History* 22:4 (2008), pp. 501–18.

functioned as important markers of neighbourhood social 'capital'.[108] Thus despite the shift towards psychologically informed understandings of what prompted burglars to thieve in the remaining archived case files, and the attempt to blame the public for their 'careless' attitude to their properties in the National Crime Prevention Campaign, officials' efforts to discover what lay at the heart of the post-war burglary crisis remained fruitless. Poverty flourished at the root of burglary after the war, ensuring that the crime remained inextricable from urban life for yet more decades to come.

* * *

The physical destruction wrought by the Blitz irrevocably disrupted the social relations and forms of movement and residence that prevailed before the war. Reconstructed London was both ideologically and physically a different space; yet burglary continued to thrive, underlining the types of social instability to which the crime pertained. The enduring relationship between media, state, and market in constructing fears about burglary, directing citizens towards the appropriate security measures to take, failed to keep pace with these profound social changes. Metropolitan Police in particular suffered a catastrophic distancing from the every-day experiences of those they were supposed to serve. By clinging to narratives of the burglar victimizing middle-class, wealthy, suburban couples, even in the face of statistics that showed the steady volume of thefts from poorer homes, and refus-ing to tackle the vulnerabilities faced by those living in social housing or flats, their National Crime Prevention campaigns were doomed to failure. The legacy of this disconnect was felt into the late twentieth century. In 1997, historian and crimin-ologist Ian Loader highlighted that:

> Among some populations (such as young people, or the excluded communities of Britain's inner cities and peripheral estates), the symbols of policing may have precious little appeal, and the police may be as if not more likely to conjure feelings of anxiety and trepidation than they are 'gratifying sensations of order and security'...To speak of a paleo-symbolic attachment to policing may be to refer largely, if not exclusively, to 'middle England'.[109]

'Middle England' had certainly always been those best equipped to take advantage of the anti-burglary technologies on offer, and to number among insurers' clientele. Another resource was 'neighbourliness'—at least the kind that would assist victims of a burglary rather than mark a form of interference. The Home Office and police's inability to effectively recruit citizens into assisting them to tackle the ris-ing numbers of crime unfortunately coincided with tensions over the possibility for neighbourly 'surveillance' to impinge on privacy, offering unwanted additional

---

[108] Todd, 'Affluence'; Avner Offer, 'British Manual Workers: From Producers to Consumers, *c.*1950–2000', *Contemporary British History* 22:4 (2008), pp. 537–71; Becky Taylor and Ben Rogaly, '"Mrs. Fairly Is a Dirty, Lazy Type": Unsatisfactory Households and the Problem of Problem Families in Norwich 1942–1963', *Twentieth Century British History* 18:4 (2007), pp. 429–52.

[109] Ian Loader, 'Policing and the Social: Questions of Symbolic Power', *British Journal of Sociology* 48:1 (1997), p. 9.

stress to already-fraught domestic boundaries. Since technologically driven and citizen-led solutions were continually preferred over examining how structural conditions like poverty informed burglars' motives, it is hard not to conclude that anti-burglary campaigns fed commercial interests at the expense of delivering new forms of cooperation between state and citizen.

Burglary thus continued to define social, political, and economic relationships in the post-war capital, acting as a barometer for changing modes of citizenship, urban lifestyles, and popular concerns. Latterly, the strengthening of commercial agendas in the presentation of the crime to the public also began to destabilize its older association with night-time, as both police and insurers sought ways to energize a 'round-the-clock' interest in security. The epilogue to *Night Raiders* that follows considers the dramatic legislative change marked by the Theft Act of 1968, which eliminated night-time conditions for the crime from the law, even though its association with darkness and shadowy moonlit escapades remained salient in popular culture. The new law also fundamentally impacted on the punishment of burglary, taking fresh account of its effects when coupled with rape or other forms of violence. Beforehand, however, the next and final chapter returns to life in the capital in the immediate aftermath of the Second World War. Burglary would provide the mirror to reflect another, deeper fissure in national and international politics as the war with Germany came to a close, as London's burglars slunk artfully into the first of many diplomatic tussles with the Soviet Union, through flourishing a tool for Cold War spying.

8

Spy-Burglars and Secrets in the Cold War Capital

'There you are', said M. as Bond came up. He waved to the chair that faced him across the card table. 'Just let me finish this. I haven't cracked this man Canfield for months. Drink?'

'No thanks', said Bond. He sat down and lit a cigarette and watched with amusement at the concentration M. was putting into his game.

'Admiral Sir M*** M******—something at the Ministry of Defence'. M. looked like any member of any of the clubs in St. James's Street. Dark grey suit, stiff white collar, the favourite dark blue bow-tie with spots, rather loosely tied, the thin black cord of rimless eyeglass that M. seemed only to use to read menus, the keen sailor's face, with the clear, sharp sailor's eyes. It was difficult to believe that an hour before he had been playing with a thousand live chessmen against the enemies of England: that there might be, this evening, fresh blood on his hands, or a successful burglary…

Ian Fleming, Moonraker (London, 1955)

Poised to embark on the adventure that would pit him against supervillain Sir Hugo Drax, a Nazi-turned-Soviet-spy who planned to destroy London using nuclear 'Moonraker' rockets, British secret agent James Bond met with 'M', head of covert intelligence operations at MI5. Reflecting on his chief's many qualities, Bond mentally listed burglary as second only to M's ability to assassinate.[1] 'His' observation—channelled through the genius of the author, Ian Fleming, a former Naval intelligence officer—suggested to readers the critical role those skilled at burglary might play in the vital work of Cold War espionage.[2] During the tense decades after the Second World War, when hostilities between the Soviet Union and the Western allies escalated towards plausible nuclear attack, those capable of slipping silently into the homes of enemy agents by night to retrieve valuable information had obvious advantages.[3] Burglary made perfect sense as a strategic component of modern conflict waged through 'journeys in shadows'—a scholarly

---

[1] Ian Fleming, *Moonraker* (London: Jonathan Cape, 1955), p. 43.
[2] Andrew Lycett, 'Fleming, Ian Lancaster (1908–1964)', *Oxford Dictionary of National Biography*, http://www.oxforddnb.com/view/article/33168 (accessed 2 Oct. 2017).
[3] Jeremy Black, *The Politics of James Bond: From Fleming's Novels to the Big Screen* (London: Praeger, 2005), pp. 18–19.

phrase applied to diplomatic skirmishes accompanied by acts of espionage.[4] Criminality aside, burglars had long been recognized for their athleticism and technological ability to 'crack' into homes and safes, talents that eclipsed the moral ambiguity of the act.[5] 'M's aptitude for burglary was therefore unsurprising; moreover, the story was laced with a grain of truth. Fleming's career in intelligence during the Second World War gave him extensive experience of covert operations, for which burglary was a credible tactic to acquire information behind enemy lines.[6]

In both real and fictional encounters, spies lurking surreptitiously in London's midst were dragged into the spotlight by a series of Cold War-related burglaries after the Second World War. An incident connecting burglary with espionage in real life had in fact already occurred, discovered by the Foreign Office in April 1946. Dr Józef Retinger, an independent, and sometimes controversial, political advisor to Britain on Polish affairs, reported a burglary at his London flat to the Foreign Office.[7] Deeply embedded in navigating relations between the Soviet Union and other European countries, Retinger was 'convinced that the burglary was the work of Warsaw Polish agents', since 'some of his papers and all of those of his Secretary M. Maciurgyush had been ransacked. They contained material that would incriminate many people in Poland.'[8] He had initially called in Scotland Yard, who the eminent advisor described as 'very helpful', but given the context 'he doubted whether they would find the culprits'. Retinger's claim was treated with some scepticism in the first instance. Although certain key figures in the Foreign Office (including Soviet expert Thomas Brimelow) had already shifted gears from viewing member states of the Soviet Union as allies to considering them enemies by 1946, the direction of their future relations with Britain was still crystallizing. In April they achieved a consensus that the Soviet Union 'was an ideologically driven expansionist power', but it was not until 1947 that the Foreign Office pushed for more explicit anti-Soviet propaganda.[9] Since Retinger was viewed as likely acting in 'connection with an anti-Communist witch-hunt', officials hesitated to respond to his complaint.[10]

After consulting with Secret Service agency MI5, however, officials appear to have decided there was some merit to the story. They sent Retinger to be interviewed by MI5 operatives, chief among them Captain Guy Liddell, who was given a copy of the file (it is worth noting that the file that remains in the National Archives is curiously thin, comprising just five pages of notes and a scrap of paper recording its transfer to Liddell's care, indicating that sensitive material on the case may have been 'pruned'). Liddell was head of B Division at MI5, the department

---

[4] Peter Jackson and L. V. Scott, 'Introduction: Journeys in Shadows', in P. Jackson and L. V. Scott (eds.) *Understanding Intelligence in the Twenty-First Century: Journeys in Shadows* (London: Routledge, 2004), pp. 2–3.

[5] See Chapters 1 and 2.   [6] Lycett, 'Fleming, Ian Lancaster (1908–1964)'.

[7] TNA, FO 371/56654, *Burglary of Dr Retinger's Flat, Code 55 File 6241* (1946); M. B. B. Biskupski, *War and Diplomacy in East and West: A Biography of Józef Retinger* (London: Routledge, 2017).

[8] TNA, FO 371/56654, P. Allen minute to Mr Bromley, cc. M.I.5 (6 May 1946).

[9] John Jenkins, *British Propaganda and News Media in the Cold War* (Edinburgh: Edinburgh University Press, 2006), pp. 32–7.

[10] Ibid.

formerly dealing with 'Doublecross deception' activities against Germany and regarded as the 'cream' of the agency.[11] Claiming direct experience of working with the Polish Secret Service during the war, Liddell was given increasing responsibility for tracking the penetration of Soviet agents into the security services in West Germany during the late 1940s and early 1950s.[12] Despite Liddell's background, it is uncertain, however, whether officials were truly interested in clearing up the Retinger burglary. The file concluded with a note from Liddell that 'Retinger must be in a position to communicate a good deal more information regarding the Polish Embassy and the persons he suspects of having visited his flat'.[13] Here, burglary had created an opportunity to generate new sources of leverage over political friends and opponents alike, demonstrating the complex uses to which such incidents could be turned.

As this chapter explores, during the late 1940s a spate of burglaries from residences attached to the Soviet Embassy afforded an unexpected window onto the activities of those engaged in Cold War espionage, both perpetrated by Russian agents living in London and directed against them by British operatives. The machinations of covert agents, foreign and domestic, surfaced within press reports and Top Secret Foreign Office files in connection with these raids. Thrillingly, they exposed how London's burglary problem offered a convenient cloak to disguise thefts of information more priceless than jewels. The files at times reading more like preparatory notes for a spy novel than the monotonous daily exchange of minutes and memos that have always driven state bureaucracy. Instances of espionage in which burglary featured, whether real or fictive (it is sometimes difficult to discern which) offer an important new insight into how London's distinctive urban character was a factor in shaping international politics in this era. Burglaries were not, of course, confined to London. It is notable that the crime features in contemporary accounts of espionage activity in other countries, including Germany and Canada.[14] Yet these passing mentions cannot compare with the sustained interrelation of burglary and spying in London in popular culture, press stories, and official reports during the period 1946–65.

Tracing how burglary and espionage were linked in the post-war era enhances our understanding of the factors that brought pressure to bear on Whitehall officials in the build-up to negotiations with Russia and France over whether to join the Marshall Plan in 1947.[15] The burglaries of residences attached to the Soviet

[11] Richard D. Aldrich, *The Hidden Hand: Britain, America and Cold War Secret Intelligence* (London: John Murray, 2001), p. 95.

[12] Guy Liddell, *The Guy Liddell Diaries: Vol. II: 1942–1945*, ed. Nigel West (London: Routledge, 2005); Aldrich, *The Hidden Hand*, p. 430.

[13] TNA, FO 371/56654, 'SECRET: G. M. Liddell to T. E. Bromley, Esq.' (6 May 1946).

[14] Bernard Newman, *Epics of Espionage* (London: Werner Laurie, 1950), pp. 199–200; Bernard Newman, *Spy and Counter-Spy* (London: Hale, 1970), pp. 218–19. One of these, a burglary effected by Soviet agents on the flat belonging to defector Igor Gouzenko in Canada in 1946, has since been corroborated; see Aldrich, *The Hidden Hand*, pp. 104–5.

[15] This was a crucial period in the formation of a post-war consensus regarding the Soviet Union's ideological aims and territorial expansion, and has led to scholarly debates regarding Britain's role in 'starting' the Cold War. See William C. Cromwell, 'The Marshall Plan, Britain, and the Cold War', *Review of International Studies* 8:4 (1982), pp. 233–49; Anne Deighton, 'Britain and the Cold War,

Embassy in London, and subsequent wrangling over culpability and evidence of the crimes with those involved, mark a little-known aspect of the escalating tensions between the Soviet Union and the Foreign Office under Ernest Bevin. Later intrigues involving burglary reveal another intersection between espionage and what has been termed the 'cultural' cold war.[16] 'Scholarship in the last decade has confirmed that the Cold War was much more than a diplomatic confrontation and nuclear competition. It pervaded all aspects of life', observes historian Michael Hopkins.[17] Popular culture served as arguably the most effective form of anti-Soviet propaganda in these years, directing the public to stay 'vigilant' against foreign agents attempting to insert themselves inconspicuously into British society or trying to convert others to their cause. As such, it is unsurprising that burglary figured in the hugely popular spy novels of Ian Fleming and John Le Carré, and became a staple topic for authors such as Bernard Newman, whose prolific output of books purporting to give a 'true' history of spying transformed, and rivalled, the true crime genre during these years.[18] Given the high-profile concerns about the volume of regular burglaries circulating through initiatives like the National Crime Prevention Campaign of the 1950–1, as well as in security company advertising (discussed in the previous chapter), it seems inevitable that burglar and spy would become twinned in these ways. As scholars Patrick Major and Rana Mitter explain, 'We are beginning to see how the West constructed its enemy stereotypes [during the Cold War], using a mixture of popular psychology, advertising techniques, and even academic research', listing the same authorities used to cultivate fear of burglary historically.[19]

The burglar—especially the 'spy burglar', a label coined during the early 1960s—was as much a central protagonist on the stage of the post-war metropolis as the suave 'man about town' or the 'spiv'.[20] Above all, however, spy-burglars inhabited a similar imaginative terrain to the homosexual in relation to the 'Soviet threat'. Frank Mort's exhaustive work on post-war London has ably demonstrated how, in the aftermath of the defection of Foreign Office employees Guy Burgess and Donald Maclean to the Soviet Union in 1951, the media forged 'a set of connections between the Establishment world of Whitehall, London's "secret

---

1945–1955', in Anne Deighton (ed.), *Britain and the Cold War* (Basingstoke: Palgrave MacMillan, 1990), pp. 119–23; Michael Hopkins, 'Continuing Debate and New Approaches in Cold War History', *Historical Journal* 50:4 (2007), pp. 916–17; Marc. J. Selverstone, *Constructing the Monolith: The United States, Great Britain, and International Communism 1945–1950* (Cambridge, Massachusetts: Harvard University Press, 2009), pp. 58–65, 73.

[16] Tony Shaw, 'Introduction: Britain and the Cultural Cold War', *Contemporary British History* 19:2 (2005), pp. 109–15.

[17] Hopkins, 'Continuing Debate and New Approaches in Cold War History', pp. 933–4.

[18] Fleming, *Moonraker*; Ian Fleming, *Casino Royale* (1953; reprinted London: Vintage Digital, 2012), p. 8; John Le Carré, *Call for the Dead* (London: Victor Gollancz, 1961); Newman, *Epics of Espionage*; Newman, *Spy and Counter-Spy*; Bernard Newman, *Spies in Britain* (London: Robert Hale, 1964).

[19] Patrick Major and Rana Mitter, 'East is East and West is West? Towards a Comparative Socio-Cultural History of the Cold War', *Cold War History* 4:1 (2006), p. 9.

[20] Newman, *Spies in Britain*, 148–59; on the 'spiv' as an archetype of post-war London, see Mark Roodhouse, *Black Market Britain, 1939–1955* (Oxford: Oxford University Press, 2013), pp. 225–52; Hornsey, *The Spiv and the Architect*, pp. 117–62; on the 'man about town' see Mort, *Capital Affairs*, pp. 55–6.

society" of homosexuality, and Cold War espionage'.[21] Both homosexuals and burglars were thought to occupy the same social venues and milieus, associating freely with prostitutes and other 'shady' urban actors in bars and clubs. Crucially, they were denizens of the night-time, inhabiting the nocturnal city of shadowy meetings in unsupervised corners and parks, though not always by choice.[22] Their supposed 'networks'—encounters with the wealthy and privileged through sex or theft, and with the poor and criminal, whether prostitutes or fences—similarly required both burglars and homosexuals to modify their manners and codes of dress, the *modus operandi* of spying. Being equally at home in West End gentlemen's clubs, mansions, and theatres as in the poorer resorts of the East End required forms of knowledge and movement akin to being 'under cover' in hostile enemy territory. It was therefore unsurprising that some 'true spy' books of the era contained chapters on homosexuality and espionage, and burglary and espionage, in swift succession.[23] However, spy-burglars differed from homosexuals in that, when operating on behalf of British intelligence agencies, they could reclaim the kinds of 'heroic' and 'daring' epithets previously applied to characters like Charles Peace and Raffles, and more recently associated with 'cat' burglars. The regulation of burglary was also feted for providing clues to covert intelligence gathering.

In 1961, the discovery of a suburban spy ring in north London (comprised of Soviet double agents with links to notorious spymaster Colonel Rudolf Ivanovich Abel) was exposed partly via the 'excessive' integration of anti-burglar devices around the household that sparked police suspicion.[24] This was a coup-de-grace that had been anticipated as early as March 1948, when the need for counter-espionage experts to support the policing of burglary was alluded to in a House of Commons debate convened to discuss how to tackle the staggering increase in property crime. Sir Arthur Salter M.P., a former deputy Director General in the United Nations, asserted to the Commons chamber that 'In this war, as in the first war, it was proved that we had a comparatively small but very important number of people who showed a kind of genius in the services of military intelligence, naval intelligence, espionage and counter-espionage work, penetrating the plans of the enemy and discovering their secrets. I suggest that the association of some of the best of these...might be an extremely valuable addition to the police system.' By way of context, Salter outlined that 'in a place like London, for considerable categories of houses it is probably rather the exception not to have been burgled in the last two years than to have been burgled...whatever be the precise reasons, the armies of defence [in the war on crime] are not winning'.[25] His comments were

[21] Mort, *Capital Affairs*, pp. 105, 189.   [22] Houlbrook, *Queer London*, pp. 43–67.

[23] Newman, *Spies in Britain*, pp. 13–14, 122–5; for a scholarly perspective on the perceived predilection of homosexuals towards spying in this period, see Allan Hepburn, *Intrigue: Espionage and Culture* (London and New Haven: Yale University Press, 2005), pp. 117–18.

[24] TNA, J82/163, Lonsdale, G.A. [and others], *Conspiracy to Contravene the Official Secrets Act* (1961); James B. Donovan, *Strangers on a Bridge: The Case of Colonel Abel and Francis Gary Powers* (New York: Secker and Warburg, 1964).

[25] *Hansard*, 5th ser., vol. 448, cc. 2591–2648 (20 Mar. 1948), cc. 2591–2648; Denis Rickett, 'Salter (James) Arthur, Baron Salter (1881–1975)', *Oxford Dictionary of National Biography*, http://www.oxforddnb.com/view/article/31651 (accessed 31 July 2017).

remarkably prescient. Surveillance against burglary was orchestrated with uncanny similarities to surveillance against spying, particularly through encouraging neighbours to keep watch over each other's houses for unusual activity and in the application of technologies that would record the movements of strangers around a home. These tactics not only featured in the 1961 case, involving the capture of Soviet agents Peter and Helen Kroger, but also made their way into other accounts of foiled espionage plots of the time.[26]

Through burglary's new ties to espionage, attention was drawn to the quiet skirmishes of the simmering international conflict to which the metropolis played host. These not only animated debates about the battle of wits and ideologies between the new global superpowers among London's residents, but constituted a source of fascination across the world. At stake, just as with burglary, were shared visions of 'home', and the prospect that a feeling of security would forever disappear should intruders successfully penetrate into its most guarded domains unnoticed. Elevated to a national footing when military secrets were at threat of being lost instead of the usual loot of televisions, cash, or pearls, the relationship between burglary and espionage underpinned some of the most startling developments of Britain's Cold War years.

*   *   *

It was shaping up to be a rough week at the Foreign Office. On 4 June 1947, a letter landed on the desk of Mr Robert Hankey Esq., senior diplomat and administrator, from Mr Saksin of the Soviet Embassy. Having had it translated from the original Russian, Hankey was confronted with the description of two recent crimes that had the potential to destabilize the recently hard-won peace, although the details—who the perpetrators were, what they were looking for, and whether they had found it—were still uncertain. Saksin wrote to complain of two burglaries at the London homes of Soviet Officials affiliated with the Embassy. The first, late in the evening of 23 May, took place at the home of Captain Shandabilov on Porchester Road in west London. 'Unknown persons' had forced the lock of the door, and proceeded to carry out 'a systematic search of the house, showing special interest in books, papers, and personal letters of Captain Shandabilov'. Despite this, Saksin noted that the only thing stolen was 'a lady's gold watch, value £12, whilst other valuables—clothing, furs, etc.—which were lying about were left untouched in the house'.[27] Saksin's careful outline of the elaborate path of searching, rather than simply noting the watch that was ultimately stolen, carried a clear message: this was no 'ordinary' theft, but barely disguised espionage. After all, even if the papers had not been stolen, it did not mean that the 'unknown persons' had not read their contents, or made copies using photography.

---

[26] This reflects the perceptive observation of Patrick Major and Rana Mitter regarding the need to place 'surveillance society' on the research agenda of Cold War scholars. Major and Mitter, 'East is East and West is West?', pp. 12–13.

[27] TNA, FO 371/66453A, *Burglary of Soviet Officials' House in London* (1947), Letter from Soviet Embassy to Mr Hankey, Foreign Office (4 June 1947).

The second incident was notably similar. Boris Karavaev, First Secretary of the Soviet Embassy (among its highest-ranking diplomats) returned home to his house in Powis Square, a leafy residence in the vicinity of Notting Hill, on 2 June to find the lock had been 'smashed'. Again, 'unknown persons' had 'made a thorough search, turning out all the pockets in the clothes and even searching for something or other in the coal scuttle. Some articles belonging to the family of Mr. Karavaev were stolen', although these were unspecified.[28] An accusatory air hung over the two accounts. Had the Foreign Office, or other British government agency, been involved in these crimes, the Soviets were on the alert. Their letter clearly signalled that they were not going to be fooled by any attempt to dismiss such incidents as part of London's international reputation for daring burglaries. If the perpetrators were someone else, it was a problem for both countries, but one for which Whitehall should clearly take responsibility since it happened on domestic turf. The crimes seemed shrouded in mystery. Insofar as Foreign Office files contain all non-verbal discussions related to these events (which the historian cannot verify), officials were apparently no wiser about who had committed the thefts. Annotated on the cover of the file was a comment that 'it may turn out to have been one of their employees; but speculation, though absorbing, is in vain'.[29] As the fatalistic tone of the observation implied, the damage was already done. Regardless of whether the burglar was captured, the situation had generated suspicion between diplomats and British officials that would henceforth be difficult, if not impossible, to assuage.

What did these burglaries signify? By the early months of 1947, peace was beginning to look less secure than it had only a year before. President Truman's speech to Congress ordering military and economic assistance to Greece and Turkey against encroaching communist forces (known thereafter as the 'Truman Doctrine' signalling the start of the Cold War) was delivered in March of that year.[30] The two burglaries, occurring as diplomatic relations between the U.S.S.R., America, and other Western allies took a decisive shift towards antagonism, heralded the manner in which the Cold War would be fought. Information significant to the security of Russia and Britain had possibly exchanged hands; the uncertainty itself was ominous, gesturing towards the existence of an intelligence marketplace with unpredictable (criminal) actors and outcomes. While the burglaries remained unsolved, diplomats working for the two countries would remain entangled in a web of vague threats, accusations, and suspicions, stymying progress in other areas of negotiation. This was quite simply hazardous when the negotiations involved issues such as the sovereignty of East Germany, the Marshall Plan, and trade between the emerging Eastern bloc and the rest of the world.[31] Minutes record that Whitehall officials kept the Treaty Department apprised of the unfolding burglary investigation, warning them 'that it would be impolite to try and rush things through' in early July, just before the negotiations broke down, when an

---

[28] Ibid. [29] TNA, FO 371/66453A, *Burglary of Soviet Officials' House in London* (1947).
[30] Howard Jones, '*A New Kind of War': America's Global Strategy and the Truman Doctrine in Greece* (Oxford: Oxford University Press, 1989), pp. 43–4.
[31] Melvyn P. Leffler, *A Preponderance of Power: National Security, the Truman Administration, and the Cold War* (Stanford: Stanford University Press, 1992), pp. 8–9.

opportunity arose for Karavaev to give evidence in court (which he anyhow refused).[32] As events would show, the burglaries initially proved a useful tool for accruing sympathy towards Soviet officials in the British press, while serving as exciting commercial fodder for newspaper reports. Hence the battle for the security of Londoners' homes from burglary became part of the bigger war for hearts and minds between the two nations, gaining international significance in the post-war era.

For Mr Hankey of the Foreign Office, charged with the task of responding to Saksin's first letter, the worst was yet to come. Having immediately contacted Commissioner of Metropolitan Police Sir Harold Scott to demand an urgent investigation, another letter arrived on Hankey's desk, this time sent from Ambassador Georgiy Nikolaevich Zarubin to Hankey's boss, Secretary of State for Foreign Affairs Ernest Bevin. Written on 30 May, and with time elapsed for it to be translated from Russian into English, it was stamped as having been received by the Foreign Office on 6 June, two days after the first letter arrived. Zarubin described a further series of burglaries which, although less likely to have been committed to steal secrets, still posed the threat of a more sinister form of espionage by menacing the children of Soviet officials. As Zarubin wrote,

> Latterly there have been cases where unknown persons have entered the premises of the Soviet Embassy school during the night. The School is in No. 20 Heath Drive, Hampstead. These persons usually open the front door of the School with tools and keys which they possess, look through the school's rooms, and check over the contents of the desk of the Director of the School. There is obviously nothing for thieves to take in the School and therefore the said unknown persons enter the School with some other purpose in view.[33]

'Some other purpose in view': this could have only one meaning. Successfully breaking into the Soviet Embassy School meant that its students were vulnerable to kidnap. The comment that the thieves had 'looked through the School's rooms' intimated the disturbing scenario of burglars prowling around places children regularly studied and played, gaining familiarity with the building's layout and (lack of) security. The staff of the school, Russian citizens who slept on the premises, were additionally at risk.[34] For the Foreign Office, the letter was another blow to Anglo-Soviet relations in an already-difficult week, and an unwelcome harbinger of the complex dangers, personal and political, that burglary could signal.

Yet all was not as it seemed. Responding to Hankey's request for an investigation to be launched into the first two thefts, and following a supplementary directive from Bevin to look into the burglaries at the school, Commissioner Scott reported that 'no record could be found of the incidents mentioned'. Neither local police stations nor Scotland Yard's Information Room had been alerted.[35] A further

---

[32] TNA, FO 371/66453A, N7734, Minutes sent from Mr H. W. Stotesbury, Home Office, to Mr Brimelow (2 July 1947).

[33] TNA, FO 371/66453A, Letter from D. Zarubin to Secretary of State, dated 30 May 1947 (stamped receipt by FO 6 June 1947).

[34] Ibid.

[35] TNA, FO 371/66453A, Commissioner of Metropolitan Police to Under Secretary of State (13 June 1947).

round of inquiries dredged up a response from Notting Hill Police Station, which noted that Karavaev had in fact reported his flat being broken into during his wife's absence on 2 June. The officers on duty had decided, however, that 'there was nothing to suggest this case was any different from any other case' since bedrooms had been ransacked and jewellery stolen—an assumption they may well have regretted with hindsight. Apparently taking little heed of the status of the victim, their report outlined rather dismissively that they found 'the premises to be a large house which has been converted into eight flats and has a common street door, which is usually open for the convenience of residents. There is no porter or doorman at these premises'.[36] The victim might as well have issued an invitation to burglary with such scant defences, the report implied. Towards the end its author repeated the description 'flat in house, common stairway' when referring to the case as unremarkable, carefully invoking the old insurance emphasis on individuals' and neighbours' responsibility to protect their homes or be deemed in part liable for a crime.[37]

For the Foreign Office, the missed opportunity at Notting Hill Station was merely an unfortunate blip in a bigger mystery of why the other crimes had not been reported. Detectives sent to inspect Shandabylov's flat for evidence discovered an empty apartment in the process of being redecorated. Shandabylov and his family had left suddenly for Russia a week earlier, and the staff who worked at the building expressed themselves unaware that any burglary had recently taken place.[38] Police had slightly better luck at the Embassy School, where the Director, Madame Radionova, explained (in the presence of the private Secretary to the Soviet Ambassador, who was summoned to act as interpreter) that once she had reported the burglaries to the Embassy she had not felt that she needed to inform the police. With nothing stolen from the School, the only task left for the investigating officers was to send a pane of glass from one window off for fingerprint analysis, and to deliver to Radionova a set of strict instructions for calling the police in future.[39]

Were the burglaries real? There was certainly cause for scepticism, after the inexplicable disappearance of Shandabylov and the absence of evidence in the other cases. Creating a political headache for Bevin would, in addition, have been a strong motivation for Soviet officials to fabricate the story. Bevin, 'one of the key architects of the Cold War', had charged America with taking over the mantle of militarily supporting anti-communist forces in Greece and Turkey after Britain withdrew financial aid to those countries in February 1947.[40] Inciting America to take an interventionist stance against the Soviet Union and Communist ideology

---

[36] TNA, FO 371/66453A, Shelley Symes, Detective Inspector 'F', to Divisional Detective Inspector (12 June 1947).

[37] Ibid.

[38] TNA, FO 371/66453A, Divisional Detective Inspector, 'F', to A.C.C. [Assistant Chief Constable] (13 June 1947).

[39] TNA, FO 371/66453A, Detective Inspector E. Davies to A.C.C. (12 June 1947).

[40] Chris Wrigley, 'Bevin, Ernest (1881–1951)', *Oxford Dictionary of National Biography*, http://www.oxforddnb.com/view/article/31872 (accessed 8 Aug. 2017).

spreading across Europe, Bevin, whether acting through premeditated design, financial necessity, or force of political circumstances, was widely regarded as the catalyst for the Truman Doctrine.[41] After steering the course of Britain's post-war anti-Soviet foreign policy, Bevin was vulnerable to political attack both at home and abroad.[42] It descended upon him swiftly. While the Foreign Office and Metropolitan Police were still conducting preliminary interviews in regard to the Soviet Embassy burglaries, trouble arrived in the form of the press. The British Ambassador to Russia, Sir Maurice Peterson, telegraphed on 13 June of reports circulating in Moscow blaming the British authorities for deliberately obstructing a full investigation.[43] Peterson was too late. TASS, the Russian news agency, had already sent a message to British newspapers. From 11 June, articles in national and local newspapers including *The Times*, the *Daily Mail*, and the *Telegraph* repeated TASS's assertion of the 'strange helplessness of British Police' in the face of the crimes.[44] On 12 June 1947, the *Evening Telegraph* ran a story under the headline 'Moscow Complains of Strange Burglars in London',

> A London despatch to the Soviet official news agency, Tass, to-day accused the Metropolitan police of 'strange helplessness' in tracking down intruders who, it said, had on a number of occasions recently broken into premises belonging to the Russian Embassy in London.... 'The strange behaviour of the burglars and the no less strange helplessness of the police prompt one to think that the British authorities are not interested in the capture of the "unknown persons" and the disclosure of their suspicious activity.'[45]

Such articles, intimating a cover-up at the highest levels of government about incursions into the homes of diplomatic representatives of Britain's wartime ally, seemed designed to provoke public questions over the integrity of politicians and officials during the fragile new era of peace. This accords with the argument of historian John Jenkins, who identifies the reluctance of certain quarters of the press to turn against the Soviets during the late-1940s. *The Times*, in particular, had been 'very indulgent' towards the Soviets under the ideological direction of its then-editor, Robin Barrington-Ward and his deputy, historian E. H. Carr. Both embraced *realpolitik* and reasoned that 'either Germany or Russia would dominate Eastern Europe. Germany had failed, and protesting against Russian domination would only antagonize the Soviets and drive them toward rapprochement with

[41] Robert Frazier, 'Did Britain Start the Cold War? Bevin and the Truman Doctrine', *Historical Journal* 27:3 (1984), pp. 715–27.

[42] As recently as November 1946, Bevin's hard-line anti-Communist stance provoked fears about his subservience to America among those on the left within the Labour Party, who moved for a vote of no confidence against Bevin in the House of Commons. Deighton, 'Britain and the Cold War', p. 122.

[43] TNA, FO 371/66453A, Telegram from Sir M. Peterson, Moscow, to Foreign Office (13 June 1947).

[44] 'Moscow Complains of Strange Burglars in London', *Evening Telegraph* (11 June 1947), p. 8; 'Police "Strangely Helpless"', *Gloucester Citizen* (11 June 1947), p. 6; 'Moscow Criticises Our Police', *Nottingham Evening Post* (11 June 1947), p. 5; 'Bevin Told of Burgled Soviet Premises', *Dundee Courier* (12 June 1947), p. 2; 'Soviet Flats Raided', *Daily Mail* (12 June 1947), p. 1; 'Soviet Protest over Burglaries', *The Times* (12 June 1947), p. 3.

[45] 'Moscow Complains of Strange Burglars in London', *Evening Telegraph* (11 June 1947), p. 8.

Germany'.[46] In 1946, attempts by Bevin to interfere with newspaper editors' stance on government policy towards Russia ended badly.[47] It was significant, therefore, that it was not until 20 June 1947 that the crucial nugget of information— that only Karavaev had reported the burglary at his flat to police on the day it occurred, but none of the other 'victims' had come forward until much later— featured in a *Daily Telegraph* follow-up report on the burglaries.[48] The *Daily Telegraph* was the logical publication to point out this disparity, since MI6 agent Malcolm Muggeridge was ensconced there as correspondent, leader writer, and deputy editor, and had been charged with using the newspaper to counter Soviet propaganda.[49] However, this effort could not stem the tide of fury incited at the Home Office by the earlier reports. A memo sent on behalf of Home Secretary James Chuter Ede decried the 'extraordinary' behaviour of the Foreign Office in failing to alert them about the burglaries, which Ede was 'left to find out from the newspapers'. Anticipating that questions would be raised in Parliament, Ede's officials coolly demanded 'comments on the proposed reply', and further warned that 'We shall want to pursue this aspect of the matter'—referring to the silence between the two Offices—'at greater leisure'.[50]

Facing condemnation from press, public, and fellow MPs alike, and with little fresh evidence forthcoming, Bevin's Foreign Office found itself neatly skewered.[51] Their wrong-footedness was all the more inconvenient given the approaching talks at the 'Big Three' Conference in Paris to begin on 27 June, convened for France, Britain, and the Soviet Union to discuss the terms offered by America for economic co-operation under the Marshall Plan.[52] On 2 July, a reprieve finally came; the Metropolitan Police were delighted to report that they had recovered some of the stolen jewellery and arrested three men on suspicion of the burglaries. With a note of relief, Home Office representative Mr Stotesbury commented, 'It is hoped to prefer a charge so that the action of police will receive due publicity', indicating that the barrage of press reports denouncing the deliberate 'helplessness' of police had begun to take their toll.[53] Unfortunately, Karavaev and colleagues at the Soviet Embassy had other ideas. Refusing to co-operate, Karavaev and his wife informed British officials that they would not give evidence in court, and did 'not agree that the police took appropriate measures for the speedy investigation of the burglary and illegal entry'.[54] Frustrated from ever solving the matter, which raised another set of unanswerable questions, the Metropolitan Police managed to secure a conviction for the three men anyway after they admitted guilt. The relatively light sentence—three years' penal servitude for two of the men, and borstal detention

[46] Jenkins, *British Propaganda and the News Media*, p. 33.   [47] Ibid.
[48] 'Embassy Burglaries: Russian Press Reports', *Daily Telegraph* (20 June 1947), p. 3.
[49] Jenkins, *British Propaganda and the News Media*, p. 63.
[50] TNA, FO 371/66453A, Philip Allen, Home Office, to T. Brimelow Esq., Foreign Office (14 June 1947).
[51] 'Embassy Burglaries: Russian Press Reports', *Daily Telegraph* (20 June 1947), p. 3; 'M.P.s' Queries about Burglaries at Soviet Embassy', *Dundee Courier* (20 June 1947), p. 3.
[52] Cromwell, 'The Marshall Plan, Britain and the Cold War'.
[53] TNA, FO 371/66453A, Mr H. W. Stotesbury, Home Office, to Mr Brimelow (2 July 1947).
[54] TNA, FO 371/66453A, Soviet Ambassador to Foreign Office (7 July 1947), Letter 87–A.

for their younger accomplice—showed a level of uncertainty over their culpability, though, and perhaps reflected the lack of witness testimony.[55] It is difficult not to view the timing of Soviet Officials' refusal to cooperate with police as directly related to the breakdown of talks in Paris. Soviet Foreign Minister V. M. Molotov walked out in disgust from the meetings with his British and French counterparts on 2 July, the same day, having rejected the terms of the Marshall agreement and particularly, its aim for European countries to pool information and resources with America.[56] Henceforth, relations between the Foreign Office and the Soviet Embassy would be severely strained. In May 1948, the Soviet Embassy School closed its doors in London and transferred staff and pupils to Russia without explanation.

After the events of 1947 the Soviet Embassy lingered under a cloud of suspicion. In 1954, two of the Embassy's officials, Second Secretary Barabanov and Mr Katasanov, chauffeur and clerk to the Soviet Air Attaché, were respectively discovered to be a member of the Russian Intelligence Service (Barabanov) and caught approaching off-duty British military personnel with bribes for information about the strength of the Armed Forces (Katasanov).[57] Luckily for them, there was little appetite to turn these revelations into a scandal at this juncture. Following the death of Stalin in March 1953, Nikita Khrushchev rose to power, signalling a change in direction for both domestic and foreign affairs (Khrushchev would denounce Stalin at the Twentieth Party Congress in 1956) that had as yet uncertain implications for Britain in 1954.[58] In the file on Barabanov and Katasanov, the Foreign Office thus made clear that 'We do not at present want unnecessary disputes or an exchange of retaliatory expulsions with the Soviet Government'. Proceeding with this line of argument, the author referred to a minute from the Prime Minister, Winston Churchill, that cautioned: 'Is it [not] sometimes better to let a leakage run on so long as you know its dimensions and so long as it does not touch the higher levels? I suggest that neither Mr Barabanov nor Mr Katasanov are sufficiently important for it to be worth our while to expel them'.[59] Indeed, the problem soon solved itself. On 20 April 1955, a confidential memo confirmed that both men were to sail for the Soviet Union within the week accompanied by their families, and using non-return visas.[60]

The burglaries at the Soviet Embassy residences remain a puzzle. They do not feature at all in current histories of the Paris negotiations of 1947, most likely

---

[55] TNA, FO 371/66453A, Detective Sergeant Davison, 'F', to Divisional Detective Inspector (7 Aug. 1947).

[56] Peter G. Boyle, 'The British Foreign Office and American Foreign Policy, 1947–48', *Journal of American Studies* 16:3 (1982), p. 387.

[57] TNA, FO 371/116801, *Submission on the Implication of M. Barabanov of the Soviet Embassy in the Trial of John Clarence* (16 Feb. 1955).

[58] Ted Hopf, *Reconstructing the Cold War: The Early Years* (Oxford: Oxford University Press, 2012), pp. 143, 198–9.

[59] TNA, FO 371/116801, SECRET: H. A. F. Hohler, 'Implication of a Member of the Soviet Embassy in the Clarence Case and an Attempt by Another Member of the Soviet Embassy to Obtain Information from Members of H.M. Forces' (17 Mar. 1955).

[60] TNA, FO 371/116801, CONFIDENTIAL: Memo by A. J. De La Mare (20 Apr. 1955).

because they were not mentioned in Bevin's personal correspondence with Molotov or other officials at the time, although Bevin was certainly aware of the investigation.[61] Given the surveillance of Soviet diplomats working at the London Embassy that followed, however, it is likely that the burglaries brought into focus the problematic ways in which London's reputation for the crime might be used to obscure acts of espionage were officials not keeping close watch. In the early 1960s, the realization of the ways burglary (and defence against it) pertained to spying finally turned to British advantage, in a case known as the 'Portland Spy Ring'.

* * *

The summer of 1960 was unseasonably wet. Storms bringing weeks of rain, thunder, and lightning spoiled holiday plans across the country, and the only inkling of the iconic, 'swinging' label that would henceforth be applied to the decade was found in the unlikely music haunts of Hamburg, where a Liverpudlian band called The Beatles began achieving fame.[62] For officials, the weather may have seemed perfectly apt. Towards the end of 1959, Metropolitan Police and the British Naval intelligence service began tracking the movements of a spy-ring at the naval base in Portland, whose five members converged on London. Criss-crossing the streets around Waterloo Station during walks together that inexplicably led them past each other's cars multiple times, they were observed stealthily exchanging briefcases and envelopes. These receptacles, when finally examined in July 1960, contained damning evidence of Soviet espionage. Copies taken of a book entitled *Particulars of War Vessels* (a classified publication issued by the Admiralty to its officers and civil servants) detailed the Naval building programme and the specifications of H.M.S Dreadnought, the first nuclear submarine. Admiralty Fleet orders, and 310 photographs, documented 'alterations and additions to weapons systems' in a number of navy ships.[63] A Praktina camera—a model manufactured in East Germany from the early 1950s—and reels of undeveloped film, as well as a magnifying glass, suggested the group's methods; letters written in Russian and messages encoded as 'microdots' on tiny pieces of paper indicated their nationalities, and national allegiance.[64] On 7 January 1961, after over a year of carefully orchestrated surveillance, arrests were made.

Spies could flourish in suburbia just as well as in any urban centre. Arguably the most shocking of the group's activities centred on their occupation of what Attorney General Sir Reginald Manningham-Buller called a 'very burgle-proof

---

[61] The burglaries do not receive a mention in the correspondence of Ernest Bevin held at CU, Churchill College Archives, GBR/0014/BEVN.

[62] 'Monthly Weather Report of the Meteorological Office', 77:7 (July 1960), http://www.metoffice.gov.uk/binaries/content/assets/mohippo/pdf/e/n/jul1960.pdf (accessed 16 Aug. 2017); 'Monthly Weather Report of the Meteorological Office', 77:8 (Aug. 1960), http://www.metoffice.gov.uk/binaries/content/assets/mohippo/pdf/e/0/aug1960.pdf (accessed 16 Aug. 2017); Jonathan Gould, *Can't Buy Me Love: The Beatles, Britain and America* (London, 2007).

[63] TNA, J82/163, 'Opening Address of the Attorney General' (13 Mar. 1961), pp. 10–14.

[64] 'Das Praktina-System', http://www.dresdner-kameras.de/praktina-system/praktina-system.html [accessed 16 Aug. 2017]; TNA, J82/163, 'Opening Address' (13 Mar. 1961), p. 9.

house' in Ruislip, west London.[65] Here, along a nondescript road called Cranley Drive adjacent to the wistfully named Willow Gardens, lived married couple Peter and Helen Kroger, aliases of Morris Cohen (then aged 51) and Lorna Pitka (aged 48), erstwhile antiquarian book-sellers. American citizens whose parents had emigrated from Russia and Poland, they had left the United States in the month following the arrest of Julius and Ethel Rosenberg for passing nuclear secrets to the Soviet Union in June 1950.[66] Recalling the search of the house to the jury at their trial in March 1961, the Attorney General recounted that:

> The front door had on it a Yale lock and a Chubb mortice lock, the back door a Chubb mortice lock and bolts. The French windows had four bolts and Chubb locking devices, and there were patent locking devices on all ground floor windows.[67]

The property boasted the unusual accolade of being an insurer's dream. Its ground floor domains seemed impenetrable, equipped with the most expensive, branded locks on the market. The French windows, normally fitted to give the border between house and garden an illusory air, had not one, but *four* bolts in addition to other Chubb devices, securing it to an almost ludicrous extent. There could have been no doubt in the jury's minds that these fortifications were far in excess of requirements for a 'small' and 'innocent-looking suburban house'.[68] So patently were the security measures disproportionate to those necessary to thwart a burglar that Peter Kroger tried to pose as the gullible client of a wily insurance salesman in his testimony. Referring to his erstwhile professional cover as a book salesman, Kroger pleaded, 'My insurance agent at the Alliance Company recommended on a visit to my home that I make it security proof with locks and bolts as a prerequisite for insuring the books', claiming that one rare book in his possession was worth '£900...which I certainly wanted to safeguard'.[69]

The Krogers' burgle-proof house enlivened the courtroom testimony and captured the imaginations of true-crime writers, who produced a number of books about the case. An image of the bungalow the Krogers shared appeared in *Spy Ring: The Full Story of the Naval Secrets Case*, a 1961 work by journalists John Bulloch and Henry Miller, both of whom worked for the *Daily Telegraph* (Fig. 8.1). That newspaper had already drawn readers' attention to the 'noticeable feature' of the house's 'number of security devices to stop any gaining admission' when the point was first raised during the trial.[70] Now, Bulloch and Miller suggested that safeguarding from burglary or other intruders was a kind of mania for Peter Kroger:

    [65] TNA, J82/163, 'Opening Address' (13 Mar. 1961), p. 19.
    [66] TNA, J82/163, Detective Superintendent George Gordon Smith, 'Antecedents', 59; Roger H. Platt has also published a brief account of the case in relation to the prisoner exchange of the Krogers for British lecturer Gerald Brooke in 1969. See Roger H. Platt, 'The Soviet Imprisonment of Gerald Brooke and Subsequent Exchange for the Krogers, 1965–1969', *Contemporary British History* 24:2 (2010), pp. 193–212.
    [67] TNA, J82/163, 'Opening Address' (13 Mar. 1961), p. 19.
    [68] Ibid., pp. 19–25.
    [69] TNA, J82/163, 'Statement of Prisoner Peter Kroger' (21 Mar. 1961), p. 5.
    [70] 'Secrets Court Shown Spy Equipment', *Daily Telegraph* (8 Feb. 1961), p. 20.

Fig. 8.1. 'The Krogers' Bungalow in Ruislip', in John Bulloch and Henry Miller, *Spy Ring: The True Story of the Naval Secrets Case* (London: Secker and Warburg, 1961), p. 65. Reproduced by kind permission of the Press Association.

There was, in fact, one consistent feature in Kroger's book lists. He frequently asked for works on locks and keys and for the objects themselves...But Peter Kroger had another, more personal interest in locks and keys; an interest directly connected with his spying activities. Long before the subject was raised in court, his neighbours at Ruislip knew that he had taken extraordinary precautions to secure the windows and doors of the bungalow. Each window was fitted with its own locking device and every door had an elaborate lock and a double set of bolts. It was the kind of security system that would have been more appropriate in a bank or jeweller's shop.[71]

Bulloch and Miller's account, situated a few pages from the photograph of the comfortable property in Cranley Drive, gave readers a sense of the scale of expense

[71] John Bulloch and Henry Miller, *Spy Ring: The Full Story of the Naval Secrets Case* (London: Secker and Warburg, 1961), p. 28.

required to fully secure a house of this size—not just once over, but with double locks on several points of entry. The authors' subtle jibe at the neighbours having noticed the 'extraordinary precautions' at the Krogers' house also inferred the importance of neighbourly surveillance to guard against spies, extending their defence against burglary. Comer Clarke, an author previously noted for his biography of Nazi war criminal Adolf Eichmann, similarly focussed on the impregnability of the 'white painted bungalow in the sleepy red-bricked suburb', in his book *The War Within: Red Spy Trial—the Frightening Truth*, also published in 1961. Outlining the same series of locks and bolts on windows and doors that made the place 'like a fortress', Clarke sought to relay events from the neighbours' perspective, claiming 'When the visitors did comment, Kroger said: "Protection against burglars. I've got a lot of valuable books in the house, you know." '[72] Here was yet another opportunity for ordinary citizens to have raised the alarm with police—if only they were willing to treat their neighbours' claims with a healthy dose of scepticism, encouraging a climate of suspicion with parallels to local 'witch-hunts' of Communist sympathizers under the shadow of McCarthyism in America.[73]

The significance of the burglar-proofing at Cranley Drive continued to reverberate through popular culture. In 1963 the story was brought onto cinema screens when it was turned into the film *Ring of Spies* starring Bernard Lee, directed by Robert Tronson. Scenes portraying Lonsdale's visit to the Krogers' house showed Helen Kroger, played by well-known character actress Nancy Nevinson, conspicuously locking windows and shutting curtains, joking knowingly that 'We're getting more like Fort Knox every day'. The film was a box office success (except in Ruislip, where as Cold War film scholar Tony Shaw notes, it was diplomatically chosen not to be screened).[74] Writing nearly thirty years later in 1985, Peter Wright, former Assistant Director of MI5 who was actively involved in the capture of the Krogers, also recalled the early impression made by the house's security in his notorious autobiography *SPYCATCHER* (1987).[75] 'We still knew very little about the Krogers, and their house at 45, Cranleigh Gardens [sic], beyond the fact that shortly after Lonsdale went to stay, high-grade Chubbs and window locks were fitted to the house, including the access to the roof', he noted.[76] Books were the least of the reasons for the Krogers' security fetish. As the evidence unfolded, their 'home' was slowly revealed to be none other than 'a high-powered wireless station

[72] Comer Clarke, *The War Within* (London: World Distributors, 1961), p. 91.

[73] Deborah Nelson, *Pursuing Privacy in Cold War America* (New York: Columbia University Press, 2002), pp. 74–111; Robert Corber, 'Resisting History: Rear Window and the Limits of the Postwar Settlement', *Boundary 2* 19:1 (1992), pp. 121–48.

[74] Tony Shaw, *British Cinema and the Cold War: The State, Propaganda and Consensus* (London: I.B. Taurus, 2006), pp. 58–9.

[75] The book gained notoriety primarily for exposing investigations by Wright and others into Harold Wilson's government and for accusing Sir Roger Hollis, then head of MI5, of being a Russian double-agent. See Peter Martland, 'Wright, Peter Maurice (1916–1995), Security Service officer and author', *Oxford Dictionary of National Biography*, http://www.oxforddnb.com/view/10.1093/ref:odnb/9780198614128.001.0001/odnb-9780198614128-e-57934 (accessed 29 June 2018).

[76] Wright's fading memory (he was diagnosed with Alzheimers in 1994) appears to have confused the North London Cranleigh Gardens with Cranley Drive in Ruislip. Peter Wright, *SPYCATCHER: The Candid Autobiography of a Senior Intelligence Officer* (New York: Viking, 1987), p. 135.

capable of transmitting to and receiving messages from Moscow'. In drawers and compartments around the house where neighbours in adjacent houses were concealing jewellery and other valuables from thieves, the Krogers hid radio transmitters, headphones, and unusually long lengths of flex capable of carrying high-frequency band transmissions from around the world. A table in the lounge by the fire held secret compartments with plans and signal frequencies used to communicate, while panels in the bathroom converted it into a dark room for processing photographs.[77]

Above all, however, it was the concentration of evidence of Soviet activity in the bedroom that demonstrated how fundamentally the spy ring subverted domestic 'norms'. The most acutely gendered, feminized space of the home—the space in which victims of burglary were most vulnerable—was transformed into a hive of treasonous operation:

> …in the bedroom there was found a Britex microscope in a blue box by the chest-of-drawers. You will hear that it is a useful instrument for reading micro-dots.…In a clothes basket in that that bedroom was found rather an odd thing to find in a clothes basket— $49\frac{1}{2}$ ft. of white electric flex with a plug on one end and a bulb on the other. Also in that bedroom were found £200 in money, in two bundles of £5 notes in a black handbag, and two New Zealand passports…behind some books. Inside a Bible in this bedroom in a book-case was found a piece of white coated cellophane paper. You will hear it was coated with a light sensitive substance, and you will hear that cellophane paper coated in that way is a type of home-made film used by the Russian Intelligence Service for making micro photographs.[78]

Everyday objects unravelled fresh layers of the spy ring's conspiracy. The (mis)use of the bible, in the room designated the 'hub' of marital harmony, was the perfect allegory for the Russian spies' rejection of Christianity and the conservative model of gender relations on which post-war stability in Britain was pinioned.[79] The Krogers' outward appearance as a middle-aged, happily married middle-class couple reinforced the dualism of their public and private lives. Such 'betrayal' of normative domesticity was also (supposedly) embedded in the delegation of responsibilities within their home. Bulloch and Miller wrote that 'Mrs. Kroger, who was often wearing slacks and an unbecoming jumper, dominated the household'.[80] Condemned for her poor fashion sense as much as for selling state secrets, Joyce Kroger was an affront to what readers were clearly assumed to regard as the appropriate power balance in marriage. Joyce was apparently the one 'to control the purse strings', arrange theatre and dinner plans, organize the itineraries of visiting 'booksellers'

---

[77] TNA, J82/163, 'Opening Address' (13 Mar. 1961), pp. 22–5.

[78] Ibid., pp. 22–3.

[79] Alana Harris, 'Love Divine and Love Sublime: The Catholic Marriage Advisory Council, the Marriage Guidance Movement and the State', in Alana Harris and Timothy Willem Jones (eds.), *Love and Romance in Britain, 1918–1970* (Basingstoke: Palgrave MacMillan, 2015), pp. 188–224; Sam Brewitt-Taylor, 'Christianity and the Invention of the Sexual Revolution in Britain, 1963–1967', *Historical Journal* 60:2 (2017), pp. 519–46; Paul Froese, *The Plot to Kill God: Findings from the Soviet Experiment in Secularization* (Berkeley: University of California Press, 2008); Christopher Marsh, *Religion and the State in Russia and China: Suppression, Survival, and Revival* (London: Continuum, 2011).

[80] Bulloch and Miller, *Spy Ring*, p. 33.

and, damningly, 'Kroger had to rely on her to drive him everywhere'.[81] Targeting Mrs Kroger's financial acumen, intelligence, and independence, the authors drew upon older, pseudo-criminological characterizations of 'deviant' women.[82] Their efforts to render her unattractively 'dominant' also succeeded in emasculating her spouse, suggesting a certain weakness in those who spied for Russia in comparison to the kind of virile masculinity associated with British 'spy-heroes' like James Bond.[83]

Herein was a form of counter-cultural attack on the ways the spy ring subverted prevailing ideals of suburban life. Signally, the Krogers had taken the post-war emphasis on citizens' responsibility for defending their homes and used it for malicious ends. It was unsurprising, then, that in drawing the jury's attention to the finer points of the case, the Attorney General compared the spy ring's conspiracy to the collusion of a gang of burglars rather than other traitors. Appearing on behalf of the prosecution, Manningham-Buller explained:

> If two or more persons are found together committing a burglary it is clearly to be inferred (is it not?) that they have agreed together to commit a burglary, and so are parties to a conspiracy to burgle. So here, if you are satisfied by the evidence we shall call before you as I submit you should be, that these five persons were jointly engaged in spying... then it is clearly to be inferred, in my submission, that they were parties to an agreement to do so and so are guilty of a conspiracy to do so.[84]

Burglary offered more than a convenient explanatory device for this case; it encouraged jurors to draw a direct comparison between the attack on home that this form of theft represented, and the attack on nation constituted by spying. Conversely, the prosecutors' deft use of the Krogers' excessive anti-burglar technologies as a means of confirming their guilt appears to have inspired contemporary writers, who set about rehabilitating both burglary and its detection as tactics that could be used by operators on the British side of the conflict. In 1961, John Le Carré's novel *Call for the Dead*, the prequel to his hugely successful *The Spy Who Came in from the Cold* (1963) featuring cynical secret service agent George Smiley, saw Smiley and his collaborator Inspector Mendel of the C.I.D. concoct a 'burglary' at a house in the Surrey region of the Metropolitan Police District. Putting a trace on the telephone at the house of the 'victim', the so-called-burglary allowed them to monitor the calls of suspected Soviet spy Elsa Fennan, again transforming the crime into a legitimate tactic for British intelligence.[85] Le Carré, who in real life was employed by both the Foreign Office and MI6 during the late 1950s and early

---

[81] Ibid.

[82] Her characterization as 'dominant' is uncannily similar to that accorded by press and police to Edith Thompson, executed as an accomplice to the murder of her husband by younger lover Freddie Bywaters in 1922, despite numerous witnesses her apparent horror and surprise at the stabbing and with only flimsy evidence to connect her to the act itself. Thompson has since been publicly exonerated. See Bland, *Modern Women on Trial*; Houlbrook, 'A Pin to See the Peepshow'.

[83] Christine Bold, '"Under the Very Skirts of Britannia": Re-Reading Women in the James Bond Novels', in Christoph Lindner (ed.), *The James Bond Phenomenon: A Critical Reader* (Manchester: Manchester University Press, 2003), pp. 168–83.

[84] TNA, J82/163, 'Opening Address' (13 Mar. 1961), p. 3.

[85] Le Carré, *Call for the Dead*, p. 31.

1960s, described his own brushes with burglary in an interview with German newspaper *Der Spiegel* in 1989:

> INTERVIEWER: To be an intelligence service agent, does that give you a sense of superiority?
>
> LE CARRÉ: At the time when I was one, it did.... It is the feeling of belonging to an elite that does questionable things so that the average person can sleep in peace. An heroic self-image.
>
> INTERVIEWER: And the questionable things are sanctified...
>
> LE CARRÉ: ...with medals, yes. You are doing the questionable things also because the criminal side of your nature is called upon. It is an enormous pleasure to organize a burglary with the support of your government. A double pleasure.[86]

Whether or not Le Carré was just talking up his experiences for the sake of the publicity afforded by the interview, the author sustained the interrelation between burglary and spying in a manner that repackaged the crime among other 'heroic' acts perpetrated on behalf of one's country. However morally questionable, Le Carré allotted burglars a set of 'British' skills and courage, iconography that could be traced back to Raffles, with comparable motifs of pleasure and excitement surrounding the illicit act. True-crime writer Bernard Newman took this a step further. In 1964, his book *Spies in Britain* (the twenty-eighth book on espionage he had published since 1935) devoted an entire chapter to 'spy-burglary', in addition to a lengthy account of the Portland case. As Newman described,

> One of a spy's most frequent assignments is that of 'borrowing' a top secret document. This may involve burglary. But spy-burglary is a very much more delicate and difficult operation than what we may call private-enterprise-burglary. In the latter operation the burglar breaks in, usually leaving traces such as a broken window or jemmy-marks on the door, and a shambles inside after he has hastily opened drawers and safes, emptied their contents on the floor, and dashed away with the loot. But if it ever becomes known that a document has been borrowed, security precautions can be put into operation which will nullify the spy-burglar's exploit. Not the slightest trace may be left, therefore, to indicate that the spy has ever entered the burgled premises.[87]

Newman's distinction between the 'private-enterprise-burglar' and the 'spy-burglar' honed the skills of the latter to convey the idea that the government employed the ultimate master-thief, placing burglary at the pinnacle of 'transferable' criminal talents. Silence, and an untraceable method of breaking in and exiting were the hallmarks of this agent. Casting back to the earlier burglaries at the Soviet Embassy residences, Newman's description would have ruled out British intelligence officers as the culprits if his assertions were accurate, perhaps retrospectively dismissing the idea that British agents could leave traces of their presence as a form of intimidation

[86] 'What Would I Be Like If I Were He?' *Der Spiegel*, 32 (7 Aug. 1989), p. 143, reprinted in Matthew J. Bruccoli and Judith S. Baughman (eds.), *Conversations with John Le Carré* (Jackson: University Press of Mississippi, 2004), p. 112.

[87] Bernard Newman, *Spies in Britain* (London: Robert Hale, 1964), pp. 148, 115–21, 148–59.

(although this is pure speculation). What is clear is that the 'spy-burglar' was now a brand of criminal/agent with recognized cultural currency. Discussed within the book alongside real events like the Krogers' spy ring, Newman's work sought to make an authoritative stake for the reality of this form of espionage, while claiming it epitomized the skills of British operatives.

In the Kroger case, unsurprisingly, the jury swiftly found the five defendants guilty. Their decision enabled the judge, Lord Chief Justice of England Hubert Lister Parker, to pass sentences of twenty-five years' imprisonment for Lonsdale, twenty years for the Krogers, and fifteen years for Houghton and Gee.[88] In a final twist, however, a press report appeared in the *Daily Mail* on 19 May (the same morning the trial concluded) alleging that 'The Ruislip spy bungalow has been burgled "by someone obviously looking for something"', purportedly according to Special Branch informants.[89] Anthony Cave Brown was the author of the piece, a journalist with a reputation both for his work on the Burgess and McLean spy scandal and for his cavalier methods (such as allowing interviewees to assume he was a member of Special Branch or an aristocrat). Brown described neighbours discovering a broken window giving access to the Krogers' study, and the house in a state of 'disorder'.[90] Speculating on the cause of the theft, he noted the 'apparent intention [of the burglars] of trying to find specific items perhaps overlooked by the police'.[91]

It is impossible to verify this account. No record of the burglary appears in the National Archives files on the case—at least, those currently open to public access. The article managed to ruffle the feathers of the Lord Chief Justice, though, whose concluding comments to the court sent a reprieve to the *Daily Mail* for 'reference [that] is made to a number of matters which go much beyond the evidence in the case....I would like to say, and say strongly, that I deprecate reporting of that character, reporting which might well tend to prejudice the fair trial of the case'.[92] Brown had touched a nerve. Even if the article's information was faked, it successfully used burglary as a hook to reel in readers, and to recount key developments in the Portland spy ring scandal, using column inches to detail key points in the case again at length. Subtitled 'Spy-house riddle', the piece hinted at tantalizing, unfinished business in the case that the 'burglary' might later reveal, creating a legacy of interest for readers should an opportunity arise to revive the story in future. Burglary and espionage would remain twinned in the popular imagination, stealing secrets and spinning lies requiring the same traits of organization, ruthlessness, and 'daring' with which the 'professional' burglar was historically endowed.

*   *   *

[88] TNA, J82/163, Lord Chief Justice, 'Sentences', pp. 70–1.

[89] Anthony Brown, 'Riddle of Raid on the Spies' House', *Daily Mail* (19 May 1961), pp. 1, 15.

[90] Brown, 'Riddle of Raid on the Spies' House', pp. 1, 15; Dan Van Der Vat, 'Obituary: Anthony Cave Brown', *Guardian* (17 Oct. 2006), https://www.theguardian.com/media/2006/oct/17/pressand-publishing.booksobituaries (accessed 16 Aug. 2017); Douglas Martin, 'Anthony Cave Brown, 77, Historian of Espionage, is Dead', *New York Times* (2 Aug. 2006), http://www.nytimes.com/2006/08/02/arts/02brown.html (accessed 16 Aug. 2017).

[91] Brown, 'Riddle of Raid on the Spies' House', p. 15.

[92] TNA, J82/163, Lord Chief Justice, 'Sentences', p. 73.

The media discovered a fresh vein of scandal in the form of espionage stories linked to burglary. Ensuring that London retained its status as the 'hub' of the most daring, intriguing cases of the crime, instances when burglary and spying overlapped also held international ramifications. London became the crucible of a new kind of covert warfare, ultimately spawning an army of its own 'elite' spy-burglars, if the novels of Fleming and Le Carré and the works of Newman are believed. The burglaries of Soviet Embassy residences during 1947 are harder to pin down. While they may either have been orchestrated by the political interests of the Soviet Union or of the British government, there is also a strong possibility that they were just 'regular' burglaries, exaggerated to disproportionate heights of significance by the context of the negotiations in Paris occurring simultaneously. We may never discover the answer, but they certainly offer a unique insight into the frictions between the former allies at the start of the Cold War. They also gesture towards the kinds of covert activity that both sides assumed would take place under the cloak of burglary, given the metropolis' reputation for the crime. Newspapers' reactions to these events, largely reproducing the Soviets' criticism of both Foreign Office and Metropolitan Police, similarly marks a moment of uncertainty in the transition towards a Cold War mentality in British national discourse. For journalists, spy burglars were a gift. Eager to whip up drama for their readers, press articles dealing with burglary-related spy cases maintained the topicality of a crime that had always generated reliable news interest within the Cold War era. When Soviet spies' excessive burglar-proofing was also discovered to be a sign of their activity, burglary offered a convenient subject to discuss how surveillance was linked to citizenship beyond the realm of crime prevention. Once more, burglary scripted the national conversation on the centrality of 'home' as an impermeable space, and as an ideology of belonging that required citizens both to maintain traditionally gendered, heteronormative relationships, and defend each other from 'foreign' interlopers—in this instance, Communists. The epilogue that follows considers how entrenched burglary had become in the national psyche by the mid-1960s. Charting the demise of older versions of burglary through the caveats of the Theft Act 1968, it considers the legacy of the crime in shaping urban life.

Epilogue
'We Are All Burglars'

In 1955, Turkish-Cypriot author Taner Baybars moved to London to begin a career as a novelist and poet.[1] Making ends meet by working for the British Council at the same time, after ten years living in the capital he produced his first book. Entitled *A Trap for the Burglar* (1965), it described a descent into madness:

> After having been burgled three times they decided something must be done about it. Although the insurance had covered the loss, he was aware of the incalculable mental energy that had gone to waste. She, in her own way, wept but wouldn't tell him why. They were certain about one thing: the three burglaries were the work of the same man, whether large or small, who had avoided any kind of deterrent like leaving the hall light on over the week-end when they went away, or putting a live wire into the key hole at night expecting to come down in the morning to find a paralysed second-rate burglar. Burgling them didn't give a good testimonial to the burglar's art. They had no money hidden away, no precious jewellery. Second-rate is not an apt word. A *desperate* burglar who would take away anything, anything that lay about. But he was skilful. They couldn't deny that. He managed, every time, to steal something that even he himself had forgotten he was still hiding; is that why she weeps, too? And doesn't tell me?[2]

John and Jane, the recently married protagonists of the story, had attracted a most unusual burglar. Instead of stealing possessions of financial value, their burglar puzzlingly stole a single shoe, a toothbrush, an old pair of slippers, and a well-worn carpet. Causing their insurers great mirth when the burglaries were reported, the agents' belief in the couple's story rapidly evaporated due to the negligible cost of what was stolen—in a clever dig at real-life burglary insurers' preference towards wealthy clientele. Frightening the couple, who began questioning their own minds, John and Jane became reluctant to make further claims, instead noticing in silence as their belongings slowly vanished around them. Setting nerves on edge, the real burglary crisis was only just unfolding. Some days later, the burglar stole an otherwise innocuous 'jewel': a single flower. The last bloom of Jane's favourite plant, its loss precipitated the disappearance of items that held intrinsic emotional significance. These were possessions that, consciously or otherwise, held the foundations of the couple's relationship. Realization dawned. John and Jane's love

---

[1] The Epilogue subtitle is taken from 'Fiction', *Times Literary Supplement* (24 June 1965), p. 545.
[2] Taner Baybars, *A Trap for the Burglar* (London: Peter Owen, 1965), p. 10.

for each other was the item being 'burgled'. Powerless to stop the thief, they began to suspect each other of being the burglar, instituting a new kind of terror. As Jane reflected, 'To have the fear of a burglar is different from having a husband who is a burglar and after your precious treasure'.[3]

A Trap for the Burglar pushed the idea of losing something precious to a stranger to its farthest limits. Acting as a metaphor for British citizens' relationships and modes of modern urban living during the 1960s, burglary represented the 'theft' of stability in all its forms. In a world where homes could disintegrate so rudely and suddenly, trust in oneself, family, and values were at risk. Once again, burglary emblematized other perceived attacks on the stability of home; indeed, as a recent immigrant, Baybars may well have used the criminal figure to ventriloquize his experiences of being stigmatized as an 'exotic' and 'disruptive' force. Baybars numbered among the millions of 'dark strangers in our midst' to which British journalists, anthropologists, and sociologists of race relations referred during the post-war era.[4] Like the burglar, immigrants were thought to exert a 'dangerous' sexual fascination for women, encouraging a culture of licentiousness and even prostitution.[5] Old secrets, sexual transgressions, and prejudices were dragged into plain sight by the burglaries in the novel. John had affairs, impregnating Jane's friend Valerie. Jane gambled and had long been quietly frustrated by John's sexual selfishness and intellectual manipulation. Husband and wife had already 'burgled' each other many times over during their brief marriage, as the moral of the story made clear. Driving them inexorably towards separation, the novel culminated in an act of murder by the desperate John, whose plan to catch the burglar red-handed fatally backfired.

Baybars' novel suggested burglary was a way of life consonant with metropolitan lifestyles and fears. Although the novel received mixed reviews, it seemed to strike a chord. The *Times Literary Supplement*, that most esteemed of critics, regarded Baybars' work as 'an unusual first novel', demurring that 'It is dangerous to let a metaphor become so much of a presence'. Yet the reviewer conceded that 'Mr. Baybars gets some uncanny effects and some good comedy of the unexpected out of it', and the headline to the review—'We Are All Burglars'—expressed succinctly their recognition of the novel's key achievement: showing how fundamentally burglary had lodged in the cultural imagination.[6] *Night Raiders*, like Baybars' novel, has sought to demonstrate the depths to which burglary penetrated

---

[3] Ibid., p. 27.

[4] Chris Waters, '"Dark Strangers" in our Midst: Discourses of Race and Nation in Britain, 1947–63', *Journal of British Studies* 36 (1997), p. 209; see also James Vernon, *Distant Strangers: How Britain Became Modern* (Berkeley: University of California Press, 2014); Venetia Evergeti, 'Notions of Home and Belonging Among Greeks in the UK', in Louise Ryan and Wendy Webster (eds.), *Gendering Migration: Masculinity, Femininity and Ethnicity in Post-War Britain* (Aldershot: Ashgate Publishing, 2008), pp. 114–16.

[5] Mort, *Capital Affairs*, 226; Elizabeth Buettner, '"Would You Let Your Daughter Marry a Negro?": Race and Sex in 1950s Britain', in Philippa Levine and Susan Grayzel (eds.), *Gender, Labour, War and Empire*, (Basingstoke, 2009), pp. 219–37; James Hampshire, *Citizenship and Belonging: Immigration and the Politics of Demographic Governance in Post-War Britain* (Basingstoke: Palgrave MacMillan, 2005), pp. 79–149.

[6] 'Fiction', *Times Literary Supplement* (24 June 1965), p. 545.

into the everyday lives of Londoners between 1860 and 1968. Even those who had no direct experience of being burgled were touched by the crime, whether through the accumulation of sensational stories of dramatic burglaries in the press, theatre, and on film, or through the integration of anti-burglar technologies around their homes. Walking around the city at night, catching glimpse of a broken rooftile or a sudden movement near the perimeter of a house, both residents and police would have likely turned their thoughts to thieves. The legal definition of burglary, and high-profile criminal cases, were just one dimension of the broader conversation about burglary. Burglary pervaded citizens' lives through an interchange between legal, cultural, and market-driven versions of crime and criminal. Practices of policing and sentencing, as well as the meanings London's residents attached to their homes and the roles of those within them—gendered, sexual, and economic— were shaped to some extent by the desire to defend against these thieves.

Night Raiders has offered a history of a single crime that affords a window onto a period of dramatic social change in London and across Britain. Nonetheless, it has also exposed a rich seam of continuity in relation to three areas: the stereotyping of gender roles in the home, gendered forms of criminality, and hierarchies of state protection against crime structured by class and wealth. Idealizing 'home' as a comfortable middle-class household, the burglar threatened destruction to marriages and property, the twin idols of domestic and national stability. This brand of 'conservative modernity' was rooted in older narratives about crime. Historian Alison Light has shown that the popularity of Agatha Christie's famous crime novels during the interwar years grew from attributing murders and robberies to family breakdown and greed. Accordingly, the capture of the criminal at the resolution saw adulterers punished and 'regular' family life restored.[7] Comparable motifs in anti-burglary campaigns and insurance advertising—charging male householders with protecting the home from thieves, portraying (male) burglars' penetration into bedrooms as a sexualized encounter, and blaming frivolous and absent-minded women for leaving doors and windows unlocked—maintained this moral code into the 1950s and 1960s. Why did these ideas about burglars and burglary emerge during this particular historical period?

First, the period witnessed the 'birth' of the professional burglar.[8] A criminal legend, the professional burglar—the 'aristocrat' of thieves—was called into being by the exacting legal definition of burglary that bestowed their reputation for feats of criminal enterprise conducted by night, in darkness. Professional burglars' cultural currency was enhanced by the media profile of actual and fictional perpetrators, notably Charles Peace and Raffles. In sharp contrast to the vast majority of burglaries recorded in trial reports, which revealed that the crime was typically opportunist, committed by working-class men who were either unemployed or labouring in precarious manual occupations, 'professional' burglaries were thought

---

[7] Light, *Forever England*, pp. 61–112.

[8] See also recent work by Dave Churchill on this subject: David Churchill, 'Security and Visions of the Criminal: Technology, Professional Criminality and Social Change in Victorian and Edwardian Britain', *British Journal of Criminology* 56:5 (2015), pp. 857–76.

to carry greater risks and rewards. Committing several burglaries before getting caught, these criminal 'artists' could thieve from the better-protected homes of the wealthy, displaying unusual athleticism (in the case of the 'cat burglar') or technological knowledge in the process. Their intelligence and skill were supposed to make them socially adaptable as well. Tales of their ability to usurp the class to which they belonged by emulating the mannerisms and dress of prosperous and respectable members of society exploited fears about the accelerating instability of social class, both as a concept and as a set of political and economic relationships.[9] Disruptive and transgressive, burgling 'social climbers' could emerge, apparently, from any background. The slippage between poor and wealthy occasioned by burglars' antics became a standard trope of popular culture. Burglary transformed into a satire on the assumed morality of those possessing material wealth. Stories of professional burglars' lives and criminal escapades thereby appealed to successive generations of audiences, offering a version of criminality that subverted the restrictions experienced in everyday life.

This pleasurable, entertaining category of crime infiltrated into criminological texts, and into police training through methods of surveillance that sought to guard against the 'expert' burglar. Forging a dialogue between police and popular culture about the lifestyle and modus operandi of certain offenders, shared sensibilities about the 'admirable' qualities of burglars exposed how law-enforcers were not immune from enjoying the transgressive. Burglary could be a game, and burglars, worthy opponents. During the Cold War years, this philosophy accounted for the ways that burglary became woven into the fabric of espionage. Masculinity and its affirmation defined the terms of this contest. The 'expert' and 'professional' burglar was popularly and officially designated male, reinforced by statistics that showed the staggering volume of male perpetrators against miniscule numbers of women. This remained the case during the post-war era.[10]

Women's involvement in burglary, when recognized, continued to portray them as less skilled, or as unwitting and unequal accomplices to men. Captain W. J. Hutchinson's *A Policeman Puts You Wise* (1951) described to readers one woman burglar whose selection of victims revealed her lack of professionalism: 'In not a single instance has she been known to enter one of the better class of properties; she confines herself to a working-class district where the habit of leaving

---

[9] This was a system already in flux (though never extinguished) in this period, adjusting to key changes including, to list just a few: expansions to the franchise in 1884 and 1918, the growth of the trade unions, the rise of the Labour party, declining levels of hereditary wealth, and the dismantling of the servant sector. Just some of the many key works on class in nineteenth- and twentieth-century Britain published during the last three decades include: David Cannadine, *Class in Britain* (London: Penguin, 1998); Selina Todd, *The People: The Rise and Fall of the Working Class, 1910–2010* (London: John Murray, 2014); Anna Clark, *The Struggle for the Breeches: Gender and the Making of the British Working Class* (Berkeley: University of California Press, 1995); Jon Lawrence, 'Class, Affluence, and the Study of Everyday Life in Britain, *c.*1930–1964', *Cultural and Social History* 10:2 (2013), pp. 273–99; Ross McKibbin, *Classes and Cultures: England, 1918–51* (Oxford: Oxford University Press, 1998).

[10] A survey of burglaries tried at London's Metropolitan Police Courts, sampled at five-yearly intervals between 1945–65, recorded 1,703 men and just 33 women tried for burglary and/or possession of housebreaking implements by night. See Appendix 1 for survey data and references.

the key on a piece of string is prevalent.'[11] A year earlier, former Flying Squad detective George 'Jack' Frost pondered in his own book why the 'woman flat-breaker' should 'get mixed up with the teams' of burglars, claiming that 'Only too late do they find that a four-way or six-way share of what is left after the receiver has paid, is negligible. But by then these women often feel that they are on the wrong side of the legal fence, so they go on stealing.'[12] Women burglars were trapped into lives of crime that would offer little monetary reward or glamour. At best, women were supposedly prey to the 'devious' schemes of their male counter-parts. Both of these texts were authored by former police officers trying to demystify burglary to the public, encouraging them to improve household security while painting burglary as a futile endeavour that would eventually lead to a lengthy prison sentence. Still, their gendered portrayal of burglars upheld the connection between the professional burglar and the 'masculinized' traits of athleticism, mechanical knowledge, and adventure. By refusing to countenance the idea that a woman would—or could—become proficient at the crime, they retained the asso-ciation between women as natural defenders of the sanctity of homes and families. Constraining women's criminal agency despite their advances in other (legal) areas of national life, these commentators ensured that men continued to be identified with burglary and the qualities needed to police it.[13]

Second, designating the burglar as male enabled the construction of particular fears associated with burglary, especially the analogies to rape or sexual assault it generated.[14] By the 1960s burglary and rape had been imaginatively entwined for nearly a century, through carefully crafted allusions to the nature of the 'violation' felt by the female victim in novels such as Wilkie Collins' *The Moonstone* (1861), and the proliferation of 'boudoir safes' to combat the burglar-in-the-bedroom. Yet inference hardened into political initiative in 1968, when, after several horrifying cases like the Bishenden burglary (see Chapter 7), the Theft Act redefined burglary to encompass 'stealing anything in the building or part of a building in question, of inflicting on any person therein any grievous bodily harm or raping any woman therein'. Henceforth, it was legally possible to describe being 'raped by a burglar' instead of raped by a rapist.[15] Explicitly legislating against the most traumatizing

---

[11] Hutchinson, *A Policeman Puts You Wise*, pp. 18–19.

[12] Frost, *Flying Squad* (1950), p. 139.

[13] My argument here is also informed by the work of Louise Jackson on the 'masculine' culture of policing that women police officers experienced during the 1950s and 1960s, and their relegation to policing family disputes, runaway girls, and other 'welfare' situations rather than 'serious' crimes involving theft or murder. See Jackson, *Women Police*, pp. 47–79; Louise Jackson, '"The Coffee Club Menace": Policing Youth, Leisure and Sexuality in Post-War Manchester', *Cultural and Social History* 5:3 (2008), pp. 289–308. Lizzie Seal's work on the murderess in post-war Britain has similarly high-lighted the conservatism that underpinned ideas about their motives (such as 'transgressive' or frus-trated sexuality, including lesbianism, as well as promiscuity, even where the murders lacked any sexual component). See Lizzie Seal, *Women, Murder, and Femininity* (Basingstoke: Palgrave MacMillan, 2010), pp. 89–105; Lizzie Seal, 'Discourses of Single Women Accused of Murder: Mid-Twentieth Century Constructions of "Lesbians" and "Spinsters"', *Women's Studies International Forum* 32:3 (2009), pp. 209–18.

[14] Men have historically been the aggressors in these cases. See D'Cruze, *Crimes of Outrage*; Gullace, *The Blood of Our Sons*; Bourke, *Rape: A History from 1860 to the Present*.

[15] Theft Act 1968, Elizabeth II. c. 60, ss. 9.

possibilities of burglars' assault, life-long scar tissue in the everyday lives of victims, this clause also sought to address *who* in the home was likely to suffer most from the burglar's incursion. On reflection, though, women may have had little cause to thank the legislators for their consideration. Once again, they were categorized both ideologically and physically as the most vulnerable individuals in the home. To add insult to potential injury, the debate in the House of Lords that preceded the amendment made clear that it was now conceivable that a criminal might end up being sentenced on the lesser charge of burglary, having also committed a rape.[16] Judge and jury would decide which of the two crimes they felt took precedence in the case.

Still more resounding was the change to the legal criteria for burglary, removing the condition that it take place between the 'night-time' hours of nine p.m. and six a.m. Burglary and housebreaking were collapsed together into a single category of offence, henceforth to be known exclusively as burglary. The move had been anticipated during preparations for the National Crime Prevention Campaign in 1949. Minutes of one of the meetings held recorded how Chief Superintendent Hatherill of the Metropolitan Police opined 'The public is inclined to associate burglaries with night, and I stressed the daytime danger, which is of equal, if not greater, importance. I said that afternoons, when the husband is at work and the wife is out shopping, is probably the most favourite time for housebreaking in the suburbs.'[17] Rebranding housebreaking as 'burglary' for the duration of the campaign, the committee sought to encourage people to safeguard homes in the face of both crimes, willingly undoing decades of successful work distinguishing between the two. Adopting marketing tactics for their own use, police were willing to obscure the law to simplify their anti-burglary message in the interests of getting them to fortify their properties 'round the clock'. Choosing burglary—the less statistically significant crime—as the label for both was a clear acknowledgement of the cultural weight the figure of the burglar carried as opposed to the housebreaker, confirmed permanently by the 1968 Act.

Ingrained fear of burglary supplied the logic for this decision. Home Office correspondence about the legislation registered concern that the new law might reduce burglary to a less serious form of theft, prompting officials to order magistrates never to summarily try breaking-in cases that met the conditions supplied by the old criteria for burglary (in a dwelling house, at night). Such cases should continue to be referred upwards by the lower courts, since 'one must consider that the occupants of the house (perhaps a woman alone in the house) may be put in considerable fear', wrote J. A. Howard, attached to 'F' Division.[18] Marginalia on the file suggested this met with general agreement:

many people wd [would] take the view that making any offence of burglary in a dwelling triable summarily (particularly in view of the new proposals on short-term

[16] Hansard, 'Theft Bill', HL Deb 11 Mar. 1968 vol. 290 cc. 78–86.
[17] TNA, MEPO 2/8052, Chief Superintendent G. Hatherill to A.C.C., 'Anti-Crime Exhibition' (4 Aug. 1949), p. 2.
[18] TNA, HO 291/744, *Proposed Amendments under Theft Bill 1968* (1968), J. A. Howard, minute (14 July 1966).

imp!) will tend to diminish the protection due to the public from what can never or very rarely be a trivial offense; if someone is in the house he will always be put in a certain stupor of fear, &... there is still the feeling that a person's innermost security has been broken.[19]

'Tidying up' the larceny laws by creating a single piece of legislation encompassing various types of breakings-in, the conditions of the Theft Act 1968 still had to accommodate the culture of fear specifically associated with burglary. Civil servants' ability to imagine themselves as victims of the burglar, and beyond that, to confidently assume their feelings and reactions during and afterwards, including the fractured emotional ties to the home, confirmed the success of over a century of commercial and cultural psychological conditioning. The comments could, in fact, have been lifted directly from Baybars' *A Trap for the Burglar*, in which Jane, thinking she had stumbled upon the burglar as she returned home, similarly reflected that 'She couldn't see his body in the half dark but only one leg and that emphasized her fear of the bodiless existence of someone who intrudes in your private existence'.[20] This, of course, also strongly recalled motifs from burglary insurance advertising. The affective training in burglary's emotional impact at the highest levels of government underscores how the crime allows historians to move from intimate histories of the home to explore grander narratives of histories of the state, welfare, consumer markets, industrial mass production, and technological change. Propelled by fear, the sensibilities of lawmakers, government officials, insurers, and those embroiled in security industry towards burglary reveals how histories of emotion are also deeply embedded in larger histories of capitalism and liberal democracy.

The gravity of the offence appeared to worsen after the Second World War. Explosives were increasingly used after thieves raided quarries and mines in the provinces, returning to the city to blast open strong-rooms and safes. During 1959, Metropolitan Police reported that enough gelignite had been stolen to open 13,000 safes.[21] The aptly named Chief Superintendent Sparks of the Flying Squad additionally commented that, in a horribly ironic twist, training to use oxygen cylinders as explosives was given in prison and borstal, on courses in industrial manufacture designed for the rehabilitation of offenders.[22] As the Acting Chief Constable of Police bemoaned in July 1966, 'Some criminals now use explosives with the same abandon as their fathers used jemmies. Little expertise is required, and cash rewards are assured.'[23] The explosive age had replaced the electric age, tipping the balance of power once again towards the burglar. The constant see-sawing between burglar, police, and security companies as new technologies gained

---

[19] TNA, HO 291/744, Annotated comments beneath note from J. A. Howard, minute (14 July 1966).

[20] Baybars, *A Trap for the Burglar*, p. 26.

[21] TNA, MEPO 2/10145, *Safe Cracking and Blowing* (1960), Thomas L. White, 'Report from S.2. Map room on safe-blowings', (24 Oct. 1960).

[22] TNA, MEPO 2/10145, Chief Superintendent Sparks, Report to A.C.C. from 'C' Department (21 Mar. 1963).

[23] TNA, MEPO 2/10145, Minute 88 'A.C.C (thro' Commander 'C') (12 July 1966).

prominence was further invigorated by the changing size, scale, and social composition of the city. Creating fresh challenges for regulating London effectively, they ensured that the crime continued to inspire fear. In turn, these factors cultivated new markets and consumers for insurance, lock-and-safe, and burglar alarm companies, allowing them to situate themselves as another branch of state-sponsored regulation of burglary. Forcing us to rethink the power of the state over how crime was defined and contained, governance-by-market may be a more accurate summation of how burglary was regulated in this period.

London was more than a 'backdrop' to these events. The capital's unique composition of people, houses, shops, streets, monuments, and transport, as well as the policing of its districts, informed ideas about the appearance, methods, and movements of burglars. These in turn forced residents to reflect on their own relationship to city and home. London also shaped the market for anti-burglar security technologies and insurance. Locks on windows and doors, alarms affixed to rooftops, burglary insurance, and finally, the 999 emergency number all became recognized features of Londoners' way of life—their absence as well as their presence, especially where poorer residents found themselves excluded or restricted from access to these safety measures. Burglar alarm companies perhaps had the biggest impact on how London was itself altered by the threat of burglary. The noise aggravated residents to the extent that the LCC had to introduce bye-laws curtailing their use. Trialling these and other measures in the metropolis confirms the city's reputation as the crucible for anti-burglar technologies. London's streets were the first to have their telephone lines rewired to bring the emergency number into effect, making London the capsule for techniques of surveillance that remain in use today. As the capital of England, and the financial centre of Britain, London burglaries were elevated from the concerns of the city's residents to an attack on the nation's wealth and social and political integrity. This symbolic resonance meant that versions of burglars and burglary in London acquired international publicity through the press and entertainment media, and fostered a transnational criminological dialogue about the nature of burglary that was informed by popular culture. London is therefore crucial to our understanding of how dominant characterizations of burglary were developed in this period.

Night Raiders has explored the dominant ideas about burglars and burglary, and their relationship to urban space, circulating in the nineteenth and twentieth century. It is crucial to note their historical specificity. The emphasis on rooftop movement seems anachronistic when set against the competing velocities and trajectories of urban life today. The shifting preconceptions of post-war Britain, too, make this a very different world. Late twentieth century versions of Raffles spoke to an audience whose concerns were far removed from those who first encountered the burglar before the war. Graham Greene's 1975 theatre production of Raffles, using the intimacy between Raffles and Bunny to address debates about the gay rights movement, serves as just one example of the radically different agendas to which narratives about burglary have been put to use. *Night Raiders* has sought to emphasize the playful narratives of burglars and burglary that, by their frivolity and pleasurable dangers, allow us to understand the range of responses to burglary in this period. Yet it has chosen to linger on the fear that these thieves inspired, recognizing how fundamentally traumatic the intrusion of burglars into one's home remains to this day, and seeking to help us understand some of the historic sources of that fear. Burglary may have been regarded as an art form by some, but at a terrible cost to property and a sense of personal safety, as well as, occasionally, to life. These reasons explain why, more than any other crime, burglary shaped the everyday rhythms, purchases, and organization of modern urban life, a legacy that continues into the twenty-first century.

Appendix

NOTE TO TABLES AND CHARTS

Data on defendants tried for burglary at the Old Bailey (Central Criminal Court) retrieved from <https://www.oldbaileyonline.org/>, sampled at five-yearly intervals from 1860–1910 (years 1860, 1865, 1870, 1875, 1880, 1885, 1890, 1895, 1900, 1905, and 1910). Total Old Bailey sample comprised 371 cases; where duplicates between these cases and defendants featured in the Magistrates' Courts were encountered, data was entered only once. For full list of Old Bailey references, see Eloise Moss, Unpublished D.Phil Thesis, 'Cracking Cribs: Representations of Burglars and Burglary in London, 1860–1939,' University of Oxford, 2013. Court registers of Metropolitan Magistrates Courts and City of London Justice Rooms sampled at five-year intervals, 1880–1965 (with one four-year interval sample for the years 1935–9). References consisting of date ranges in brackets denote that the original label had fallen off the document, leaving the dates. All registers held at the London Metropolitan Archives [LMA]:

Bow Street: PS/BOW/A/01: 001–002; 010–013; 022–025; 037–041; 058–061; 075–080; 095–102; 125–132; 157–163; 182–187; 211–215; 280–288; 327–331; 366–369; 283; [Dec. 1944–Aug. 1945; Oct. 1945–April 1946; 1949–Dec. 1950; Aug.–Oct. 1950; Dec. 1950–Dec. 1951; Sept. 1950–Jan. 1951]; PS/BOW/A/02: 001–006; 016–019; 032–047; 066–070; 091–093; 118–120; [Sept. 1944–July 1945; March 1955–May 1955]; PS/BOW/A/03: 001; 002–006; Clerkenwell: PS/CLE/A/01: 001–002; 016–020; 035–040; 052–055; 070–075; 088–091; 103–107; 119–123; 145–149; 170–175; 200–202; 237–241; Greenwich: PS/GRE/A/01: 005–009; 015–019; 027–030; 035–038; 045–046; 053–056; 065–067; 076–078; 087–089; 101–104; 236; Guildhall: CLA/005/02: 011; 018–019; 025–026; 032–034; 040–042; 048–050; 056–057; 063–065; 071–072; 078–079; 084–085; 092–094; 100–102; 108–116; 122–124; 131–132; 143–144; Lambeth: PS/LAM/A/01: 011–014; 027–031; 039–042; 054–058; 069–072; 087–090; 103–106; 127–129; 151–156; 182–187; PS/LAM/A/03: 001. Mansion House: CLA/004/04: 041–042; 046–047; 051–052; 056–057; 061–062; 066–067; 071–072; 076–078; 086–088; 096–098; 103–104; 109–110; 115–116; 131–139; 120–125; 140–141; 152–153; Marlborough Street: PS/MS/A/01: 001–005; 026–031; 045–050; 067–072; 097–102; 132–143; 166–172; 192–196; 220–227; 255–260; 288–294; 335–348; PS/MS/A/03: 001; 015–021; Marylebone: PS/MAR/A/01: 001–003; 019–024; 041–047; 060–065; 078–083; 100–105; 124–131; 149–154; 179–188; 221–228; 257–263; 308–318; 365–376; North London: PS/NLO/A/01: 001; 013–017; 025–028; 037–041; 049–052; 061–066; 075–080; 98–102; 122–127; 147–150; 172–177; 202–207; Old Street: PS/OLD/A/01: 001; 010–013; 029–035; 051–054; 067–071; 085–088; 099–103; 114–118; 133–137;

153–157; 173–177; 194–199; 226–229 [July 1960–Sept. 1960]; **South-West London:** PS/SWE/A/01: 001–003; 018–021; 032–037; 052–056; 068–072; 090–094; 112–115; 132–137; 157–162; 182–185; **Thames:** PS/TH/A/01: 005–006; 016–021; 040–045; 062–067; 084–089; 106–111; 130–135; 149–154; 167–171; 181–185; 196–201; 210–215; 233–237; 258–263; 285–291; 308; 318–327; 378–389; **Tower Bridge:** PS/TOW/A/01: 003–008; 030–034; 059–066; 085–090; 103–108; 125–130; 143–146; 157–160; 172–175; 186–190; 199–204; 217–220; 235–238; **West London:** PS/WLN/A/01: 006–007; 023–028; 048–055; 079–086; 120–123; 143–148; 167–173; 194–199; 210–214; 227–229; 242–246; 262–267; 278–283; 308–314; 338–345; 368–374; 400–409; 420; 433–441; **Westminster:** PS/WES/A/01: 014–020; 039–042; 060–063; 080–085; 101–104; 119–123; 139–143; 156–161; 172–177. **Woolwich:** PS/WOO/A/01: 001–002; 008–009; 020–021; 025–027; 036–044; 050–058; 067–072.

Data on female burglars' occupations, sentencing, and treatment post-conviction also gathered from London Metropolitan Archives, H.M.P. Holloway Calendars of Prisoners, 1914–39: CLA/003/PR/05/22; CLA/003/PR/05/24; CLA/003/PR/01/1; CLA/003/PR/05/23; CLA/003/PR/05/28; CLA/003/PR/05/27; CLA/003/PR/02/1; CLA/003/PR/05/29; CLA/OO3/PR/02/4; CLA/003/PR/02/5; CLA/003/PR/02/8; CLA/003/PR/02/10; CLA/003/PR/02/13; CLA/003/PR/02/12; CLA/003/PR/02/14; CLA/003/PR/02/15; CLA/003/PR/02/17; CLA/003/PR/02/18; CLA/003/PR/02/19; CLA/003/PR/02/20; CLA/003/PR/02/21; CLA/003/PR/02/22; CLA/003/PR/02/25.

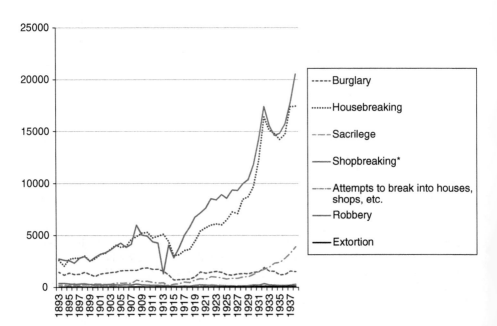

Chart 1. 'Class II Offences against property with violence' known to police in England and Wales, 1893–1938, recorded in the Home Office's annual report *Judicial Statistics for England and Wales.**

* The edition of *Judicial Statistics* for 1909 noted that offences recorded as 'Shopbreaking' also included breakings into warehouses and factories.

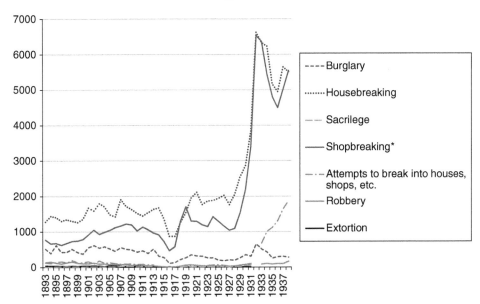

Chart 2. 'Class II Offences against property with violence' known to the Metropolitan and City of London police, 1893–1938, recorded in the Home Office's annual report *Judicial Statistics for England and Wales* and *Report of the Commissioner of Police for the Metropolis.**

* From 1914, figures for London are derived entirely from the *Report of the Commissioner of Police for the Metropolis*, in which the numbers collated by the City of London police did not feature (this is owing to the changed format of the *Judicial Statistics* series from 1914, which ceased to provide this information). As before, gaps in the statistics reflect years in which the format of reports delivered to Parliament changed and relevant information was omitted.

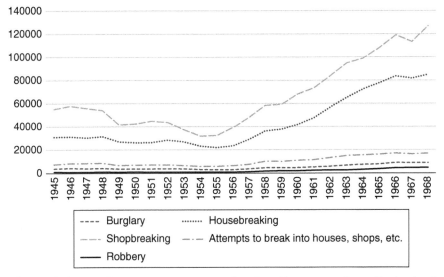

Chart 3. 'Class II Offences against property with violence' known to police in England and Wales, 1945–65, recorded in the Home Office's annual report *Criminal Statistics for England and Wales*.

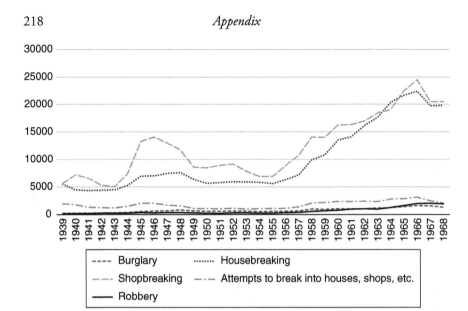

Chart 4. 'Class II Offences against property with violence' known to the Metropolitan Police, 1939–68, recorded in the annual *Report of the Commissioner of Police for the Metropolis*.

Table 1. Frequency and types of property stolen in London burglaries, 1860–1939.*

Type of property stolen:	'West End' (Westminster, West London, Marlborough St, Bow St, Marylebone, City Guildhall/Mansion House)	North (Clerkenwell, North London)	'East End' (Old Street, Thames)	South (Tower Bridge, Greenwich, Lambeth, South-West London, Woolwich)	TOTAL
Jewellery	56	15	27	36	136
Clothes	86	32	40	53	211
Food	20	7	10	8	45
Alcohol/tobacco	24	10	22	16	72
Furniture	11	0	2	3	16
Utensils (cutlery/plates/kitchen-ware)	43	18	10	30	101
Fabric	3	6	11	5	25
Works of art	2	0	1	1	4
Musical instruments	4	3	0	1	8
Ornaments (vases, urns, clocks)	20	4	13	15	52
Bicycles/motorcycles	3	0	0	3	6
Wireless radio sets, gramophones	4	1	2	3	10
Goods (inc. monies) total value under £10	140	26	94	67	327
Goods (inc. monies) total value between £10 and £100	73	17	17	44	151
Goods (inc. monies) total value between £100 and £1,000	10	1	2	3	16
Goods (inc. monies) total value over £1,000	0	1	1	0	2

* Numbers represent references to those types of goods stolen in burglaries either solely or as part of a larger haul of various kinds of belongings. As such, numbers featured here do not correspond to number of burglaries documented, but simply reflect their characteristics. Data taken from survey of burglaries at the Old Bailey (CCC), 1860–1913, and recorded in proceedings at the Metropolitan Magistrates Courts and City of London Justice Rooms, 1880–1939, sampled at five-yearly intervals.

Table 2. Occupations of those tried for burglary and possessing housebreaking implements by night, 1945–65, recorded in proceedings at the Metropolitan Magistrates Courts and City of London Justice Rooms, 1880–1939, sampled at five-yearly intervals.

Occupation:	All courts
Labourer (low skilled/casual, including painter/decorator)	442
Labourer (skilled): slater; carpenter; pipe fitter; builder; tiler; plasterer; welder/steel worker/metal cutter; plumber; locksmith	105
Service sector: hairdresser; florist; window cleaner; upholsterer; salesman; shop assistant; club assistant	59
Street trader	41
Soldier; seaman/Royal Marine; airman	125
Factory/mill work: machinist; warehouseman	73
No occupation declared*	275 (226)
Engineers mate; engineer	25
White collar work: clerk; accountant; commission agent; telephonist; printer; book keeper	35
Porter	33
Emergency services: fireman; rescue worker	6
Unemployed	165
Antique dealer	1
Baker; cook; butcher	32
Electrician; technician	16
TV/radio mechanic	4
Lorry driver; driver; bus conductor	52
Commercial artist	6
Wine butler; waiter; barman; café attendant	27
Greengrocer; fishmonger; costermonger; fruiterer	13
Apprentice; student	10
Bargee	1
General dealer	32
Domestic service: valet; butler; housekeeper; kitchen hand	10
Housewife	11
Motor mechanic	19
Handyman	1
Schoolboy	11
Van guard	12
French polisher	4
Laundryman	2
Messenger	7
Entertainment sector: acrobat; musician; theatre technician; fairground worker; cinema projectionist	10
Dressmaker; tailor; furrier; milliner; shoemaker	16
Rubber manufacturer	1
Coalman; miner	9
Optician; watchmaker	2
Traveller	1
Company director	3
Mortuary assistant	1
Photographer	1
Chemist	1
Pressman (journalist)	1

* The recording practices at Guildhall and Mansion House in this period meant that occupations of defendants were not listed, thus forty-nine of those in this number potentially may have had occupations they were unable to declare. The figure minus defendants at these two courts is given in brackets. Some of these may also, of course, have been unwilling to give their occupation in case word of their prosecution reached their employer.

Bibliography

I. MANUSCRIPTS AND ARCHIVES

BBC Written Archives Centre
TX 03/12/1975, Transcript of interview 'Kaleidoscope Special: Graham Greene in conversation with Ronald Harwood the day before the world premiere of his play THE RETURN OF A. J. RAFFLES', BBC Radio 4 (3 Dec. 1975).

British Telecom Archive
POST 33/1332, *Use of Telephone Circuit in Connection with Burglar and Fire Alarms: Adams Silent Burglar Alarm, 1921–1927.*
POST 33/1332, *Use of T.P. Circuits in Connection with Burglar & Fire Alarms: Radiovisor Parent Ltd.* (31 Oct.–19 Dec. 1930).
File *999 Emergency Calls.*

Cambridge University
St. John's College Library
Letter from Cecil Beaton to Greta Garbo (Sept. 1948).
Churchill College Archives
ARUP 2/108/6: Letter from Ruth Arup to Ove and Li Arup (2 Nov. 1965).
ARUP 2/108/6: Letter from Ruth Arup to Ove Arup (11 Nov. 1965).
GBR/0014/BEVN: Correspondence of Ernest Bevin.

Chartered Institute of Insurance Archives
9.94 Box 158, Law Accident Insurance Society, *Burglars and Burgling* (London, 1899).
9.701TEKN, file 'Early 1890s Prospectuses of Other Accident Offices'.
9.701 CN 8CHW9, file 'Correspondence and directory of clients: R. P. Walker & Son' (1904).
9.94 box 138 item 1, O. Buttifant, untitled article, in *How to Train a Young Agent, Written by 20 Successful Insurance Men* (London: 190?).

Geffrye Museum Archives
G. Harding & Sons Hardware Merchants and Manufacturers (Sept. 1905).

Harry Ransom Humanities Research Center, University of Texas at Austin
George Ives Papers.
British Sexological Society, Miscellaneous Series.

Library of the Reform Club, 104 Pall Mall, London
Unknown Author, *The Rules and Regulations with An Alphabetical List of the Members of the Reform Club* (London, 1896).

London Metropolitan Archives
CLA/003, *H.M.P. Holloway Calendars of Prisoners, 1914–1939.*
CLC/B 1999/007, *Chatwood Printed Items, The Chatwood Safe Co. Ltd* (1900–12).

CLC/B Box 72/1, 1999/007, *Descriptive and Illustrative Price List of 'Hobb's & Co.'s' Series of Locks and Lock Furniture* (1 May 1884); *Milner-Sales Catalogues* (1880–1915); *Descriptive and Illustrative Price List of 'Hobb's & Co.'s' Series of Locks and Lock Furniture* (1 May 1884).

CLC/B Box 72/2, file 1999/007, *Hobbs & Co.'s Wall Safes for Protection against Theft* (London: 1936).

CLC/B/002/10/01/008, *Exhibition booklet: Chubb's Patent Locks and Safes. International Exhibition, 1862. Class XXXI. No. 6017.* (1862).

CLC/B/002/10/01/009, *Chubb Collectanea Vol. 3 Part 3*: letter to Messrs Chubb and Son from Mr John Ellison (3 Mar. 1863).

CLC/B/002 Box 47, *Chubb's List of Patent Detector Locks* (Nov. 1907).

CLC/B/002 Box 244, *Chubb's Steel Strong Room and Party Wall Doors* (June 1905); *Chubb's Price List of Locks and Safes* (Oct. 1906).

CLC/B/002 Box 264, *Illustrated Price List of Chubb & Son's Patent Locks and Safes* (Oct. 1882); *Illustrated Price List of Chubb's New Patent Fire and Thief Resisting Safes, Vault Doors, Grilles, Strong Rooms, &c., Detector Locks, Japanned Boxes, &c.* (Oct. 1893); *Chubb's Locks, Door, and Window Fittings* (1 June 1894); *Illustrated Price List of Chubb & Son's Patent Lock's and Safes* (Oct. 1882); *Chubb's Locks, Door, and Window Fittings* (1 June 1894); *Illustrated Price List of Chubb's New Patent Fire and Thief Resisting Safes, Vault Doors, Grilles, Strong Rooms, &c., Detector Locks, Japanned Boxes, &c.* (Oct. 1906).

CLC/B/002, Box 309, *Safe as Houses* (London, 1939).

London Magistrates' Court registers

Bow Street (PS/BOW)
Clerkenwell (PS/CLE)
Greenwich (PS/GRE)
Guildhall (CLA/005)
Lambeth (PS/LAM)
Mansion House (CLA/004)
Marlborough Street (PS/MS)
Marylebone (PS/MAR)
North London (PS/NLO)
Old Street (PS/OLD)
South Western (PS/SWE)
Thames (PS/TH)
Tower Bridge (PS/TOW)
West London (PS/WLN)
Westminster (PS/WES)
Woolwich (PS/WOO)
MS15048, *Miscellaneous burglary insurance policy documents* (*c.*1900–10).

Mass Observation Archive
An Enquiry into People's Homes (London, 1943).

Museum of Domestic Design and Architecture
Egan, Michael, *The All-Electric Home* (London, 1931).
Harmsworth's Household Encyclopaedia (London, *c.*1900).
Humphry, Mrs. C. E. (ed.), *The Book of the Home* (London, 1909).
O'Brien, Thomas & Company, *Illustrated Catalogue of Builders Goods* (Jan. 1893).

National Archives of Scotland

CS253/2151, Summons at the instance of Mrs Mary Moscrop (with consent) against D. C. Thomson & Company Limited, 4 July 1919: Damages.

CS254/2161, Summons: The Right Honourable The Earl of Carnarvon against D. C. Thomson & Company Limited, 19 Dec. 1927: Damages.

CS257/3650, Second Division, Open Record in Causa Mrs. Olga Cook-Holmes against D. C. Thomson & Company Limited, 14 June 1932: Damages.

Old Bailey Sessions Papers Online <http://www.oldbaileyonline.org>

Trial transcripts, 1860–1912 (see Appendix for complete list).

Open University Police Archives

GB/2315/Police Manuals, *Instruction Book for the Guidance of the Metropolitan Police Force* (1912).

GB/2315/Police Manuals, *Home Office. Scientific Aids to Criminal Investigation. Forensic Science Circulars, No. 2* (Nov. 1936).

GB/2315/Police Manuals, *Home Office. Scientific Aids to Criminal Investigation. Forensic Science Circulars, No. 4* (London, May 1938).

Prudential Group Archives

Burn, Joseph, 'Newspaper Insurance', *Prudential Bulletin*, no. 3 (Dec. 1922), 379.

'The Kiosk at the British Empire Exhibition', *Prudential Bulletin*, no. 5 (July 1924), 641.

'Our Picture Gallery', *Prudential Bulletin*, no. 13 (Apr. 1932), 1992.

Royal Mail Archives

POST 33/148, *Security: Thefts from Post Offices, Insurance against Burglary Part 1* (1921).

POST 33/149A, *Security: Thefts from Post Offices, Insurance against Burglary Part 2* (1921).

Sheffield Local Archives

M.D. 5021, Letter from Charles Peace addressed to 'My poor Sue', 7 Feb. 1879, postmarked H.C.M.P. [Her Majesty's Convict Prison].

The National Archives

Board of Trade (BT)
Cabinet Papers (CAB)
Central Criminal Court (CRIM)
Foreign Office (FO)
Home Office (HO)
Metropolitan Police (MEPO)
Ministry of Information (INF)
Prison Commission (PCOM)
Supreme Court of Judicature: High Court of Justice (J)
War Office (WO)

University of Birmingham Archives

MS 127 box 5, E. W. Hornung Papers.

Victoria and Albert Museum

Photograph Album: *Daily Mail Ideal Home Exhibition* (March 1950).

II. OFFICIAL PUBLICATIONS

Acts of Parliament
Larceny Act 1861, 24 & 25 Vict. c. 96.
Larceny Act 1916, 6 & 7 Geo. V, c. 50.
Metropolitan Police Act 1933, 23 & 24 Geo. V, c. 33.
Offences Against the Person Act 1861, 44 & 45 Vict., c. 100.
Theft Act 1968, Elizabeth II. c. 60.

Hansard
House of Commons
5th ser., vol. 251 (15 Apr. 1931).
5th ser. vol. 279, cc. 1297 (26 June 1933).
5th ser., vol. 448, cc. 2591–2648 (20 Mar. 1948).

House of Lords
'Theft Bill', HL deb. vol. 290 cc. 78–86 (11 Mar. 1968).

House of Commons Parliamentary Papers
Cmd. 2605, *Report of the Committee on Housing in Greater London* (London, 1965).
Criminal Statistics, England and Wales (1938–68).
Judicial Statistics. England and Wales. Part 1—Police—Criminal Proceedings—Prisons
   (1860–1937).
Report of the Commissioner of Police for the Metropolis (1860–1968).
The Post Office London Directory for 1882 (London, 1882).

III. NEWSPAPERS AND PERIODICALS

Academy
Architects Magazine
Athenaeum
Bookman
Borough of Marylebone Mercury
Bromley District Times
Brisbane Courier
Bristol Mercury and Daily Post
British Citizen and Empire Worker
Cassell's Magazine
Chambers's Journal of Popular Literature, Science and Arts
City Jackdaw
Daily Chronicle
Daily Express
Daily Herald
Daily Mail
Daily Mirror
Daily News
Daily Telegraph
Dundee Courier
Era

Evening Gazette
Evening Standard
Evening Telegraph
Examiner
Financial Times
Freeman's Journal and Daily Commercial Advertiser
Gentlewoman and Modern Life
Glasgow Herald
Glasgow Weekly News
Gloucester Citizen
Graphic
Guardian
Het Nieuws Van Den Dag Voor Nederlandsch-Indië,
Hull Packet and East Riding Times
Ideal Home
Illustrated Police News
Ipswich Journal
Irish Times
John Bull
Judy, or the London Serio-Comic Journal
Kinematograph Weekly
Leeds Mercury
Le Figaro
Liverpool Mercury
Lloyd's Weekly Newspaper
London Journal
Los Angeles Times
Manchester Guardian
Monthly Film Bulletin
Morning Post
Nash's Pall Mall Magazine
News Chronicle
News of the World
New York Times
Nottingham Evening Post
Observer
Pall Mall Gazette
Picture Show
Picturegoer and Film Weekly
Play Pictorial
Police Gazette
Reynolds's Newspaper
South London Press
South Western Star
Star
Strand Magazine
Sunday Express
Sunday Times

The Economist
The People
The Scotsman
The Standard
The Times
Times Literary Supplement
Washington Post
Washington Times
Western Mail
Windsor Magazine

IV. FILM AND TELEVISION

Goodbye Mr Chips (United Kingdom: Metro Goldwyn Mayer, dir. Sam Wood, 1939).

Kate Purloins the Wedding Presents (United Kingdom: British and Colonial Kinematograph Co., dir. H. O. Martinek and Charles Raymond, 1912), *BFI*, http://www.screenonline. org.uk/film/id/727128/index.html (accessed 4 Sept. 2012).

Pett and Pott (United Kingdom: General Post Office Film Unit, 1934), http://www.btplc. com/Thegroup/BTsHistory/BTfilmarchive/1930s/ (accessed September 2015).

Raffles (United States of America: Vitagraph Company of America, director unknown, 1907).

Raffles, The Amateur Burglar (France: Gaumont Production Company, director unknown, 1910).

Raffles, The Gentleman Thief (United Kingdom: New Agency Film Company, producer and director unknown, 1911).

Raffles, The Amateur Cracksman (United States of America: L. Lawrence Weber Photodrama Corporation, Hyclass Producing Company, dir. George Irving, 1917).

Mr. Justice Raffles (United Kingdom: Hepworth Picture Plays, dirs. Gerald Ames and Gaston Quiribet, 1921).

Raffles (United States of America: Universal Jewel Production Company, dir. King Baggot, 1925).

Raffles (United States of America: Samuel Goldwyn Incorporated, dirs. Harry d'Abbadie D'Arrast and George Fitzmaurice, 1930).

The Return of Raffles (United Kingdom: W. P. Film Company, dir. Mansfield Markham, 1932).

Raffles (United States of America: Samuel Goldwyn Incorporation, dir. Sam Wood, 1939).

Raffles (United Kingdom: Yorkshire Television Ltd, dirs. Christopher Hodson, David Cunliffe, and Alan Gibson, aired 1975–7).

The Blue Lamp (United Kingdom: Ealing Studios, dir. Basil Dearden, 1950).

The Last of Mrs. Cheyney (United States of America: Metro Goldwyn Mayer, dir. Sydney Franklin, 1929).

The Last of Mrs. Cheyney (United States of America: Metro Goldwyn Mayer, dir. Richard Boleslawski, 1937).

The Life and Times of Charles Peace (United Kingdom: dir. William Haggar, 1905). Available to view at the British Film Institute.

V. BOOKS AND ARTICLES

Adickes, Sandra, 'Sisters, Not Demons: The Influence of British Suffragists on the American Suffrage Movement', *Women's History Review* 11:4 (2002), pp. 675–90.

Ahm, Povl, 'Arup, Sir Ove Nyquist (1895–1988)', *Oxford Dictionary of National Biography*, http://www.oxforddnb.com/view/article/40049 (accessed 12 Sept. 2017).

Aldrich, Richard D., *The Hidden Hand: Britain, America and Cold War Secret Intelligence* (London: John Murray, 2001).

Allport, Alan, *Demobbed: Coming Home after World War Two* (London and New Haven: Yale University Press, 2010).

Andersson, Peter K., *Streetlife in Late Victorian London: The Constable and the Crowd* (Basingstoke: Palgrave MacMillan, 2013).

Arnold, Dana, *Re-Presenting the Metropolis: Architecture, Urban Experience and Social Life in London 1800–1840* (Aldershot: Ashgate Publishing, 2000).

Arrow, Charles, *Rogues and Others* (London: Duckworth Press, 1926).

Atkinson, Rowland, and Sarah Blandy, John Flint, and Diane Lister, 'Gated Cities of Today? Barricaded Residential Development in England', *Town Planning Review* 76 (2005), pp. 401–22.

Auerbach, Jeffrey, *The Great Exhibition of 1851: A Nation on Display* (London and New Haven: Yale University Press, 1999).

Bailey, Peter, 'Conspiracies of Meaning: Music-Hall and the Knowingness of Popular Culture', *Past & Present* 144 (1994), pp. 138–70.

Bartrip, P. W. J., 'Troup, Sir Charles Edward (1857–1941)', *Oxford Dictionary of National Biography*, http://www.oxforddnb.com/view/article/60141 (accessed 21 Dec. 2016).

Baxendale, John, and Chris Pawling, *Narrating the Thirties: A Decade in the Making, 1930–present* (Basingstoke: Palgrave MacMillan, 1996).

Baybars, Taner, *A Trap for the Burglar* (London: Peter Owen, 1965).

Bearman, C. J., 'An Examination of Suffragette Violence', *English Historical Review* 120:486 (2005), pp. 365–97.

Beck, Ulrich, *Risk Society: Towards a New Modernity* (London: Sage, 1992).

Bell, Amy Helen, *Murder Capital: Suspicious Deaths in London, 1933–1953* (Manchester: Manchester University Press, 2015).

Bent, James, *Criminal Life: Reminiscences of Forty-Two Years as a Police Officer* (Manchester: J. Heywood, 1891).

Berg, Maxine, and Pat Hudson, 'Rehabilitating the Industrial Revolution', *Economic History Review* 45:1 (1992), pp. 24–50.

Berry, David, 'Haggar, William (1851–1925)', Reference Guide to British and Irish Film Directors, *BFI Screenonline*, http://www.screenonline.org.uk/people/id/449862/ (accessed 15 Jan. 2017).

Beveridge, Peter, *Inside the CID* (London: Evans Brothers, 1957).

Bill, Katina, 'Attitudes towards Women's Trousers: Britain in the 1930s', *Journal of Design History* 6 (1993), pp. 45–54.

Bingham, Adrian, *Gender, Modernity, and the Popular Press in Interwar Britain* (Oxford: Oxford University Press, 2004).

Bingham, Adrian, 'An Era of Domesticity? Histories of Women and Gender in Interwar Britain', *Cultural and Social History* 1:2 (2004), pp. 225–33.

Bingham, Adrian, *Family Newspapers? Sex, Private Life, and the British Popular Press 1918–1978* (Oxford: Oxford University Press, 2009).

Binny, John, 'Thieves and Swindlers', in Henry Mayhew and Others, *The London Underworld in the Victorian Period: Authentic First-Person Accounts by Beggars, Thieves and Prostitutes* (1861; reprinted New York: David & Charles, 2005), pp. 109–301.

Bishop, Cecil, *Women and Crime* (London: Chatto and Windus, 1931).

Biskupski, M. B. B., *War and Diplomacy in East and West: A Biography of Józef Retinger* (London: Routledge, 2017).

Black, Jeremy, *The Politics of James Bond: From Fleming's Novels to the Big Screen* (London: Praeger, 2005).

Blackstone, Sir William, *Commentaries on the Laws of England: Adapted to the Present State of the Law by Robert Malcolm Kerr, L.L.D* (3rd edn, London: John Murray, 1862).

Bland, Lucy, *Banishing the Beast: Feminism, Sex and Morality* (London: I.B. Taurus, 2001).

Bland, Lucy, 'The Trials and Tribulations of Edith Thompson: The Capital Crime of Sexual Incitement in 1920s England', *Journal of British Studies* 47:3 (2008), pp. 624–48.

Bland, Lucy, *Modern Women on Trial: Sexual Transgression in the Age of the Flapper* (Manchester: Manchester University Press, 2013).

Bold, Christine, '"Under the Very Skirts of Britannia": Re-Reading Women in the James Bond Novels', in Christoph Lindner (ed.), *The James Bond Phenomenon: A Critical Reader* (Manchester: Manchester University Press, 2003), pp. 168–83.

Booth, Charles, *Life and Labour of the People in London* (London: Williams and Norgate, 1887–1902).

Bourke, Joanna, 'Housewifery in Working-Class England, 1860–1914', *Past and Present* 143 (1994), pp. 167–97.

Bourke, Joanna, *Dismembering the Male: Men's Bodies, Britain, and the Great War* (Chicago: University of Chicago Press, 1996).

Bourke, Joanna, *Rape: A History from 1860 to the Present* (London: Virago, 2007).

Bowen-Rowlands, Ernest, *Seventy-Two Years at the Bar: A Memoir* (London: MacMillan and Co., 1924).

Boyle, Peter G., 'The British Foreign Office and American Foreign Policy, 1947–48', *Journal of American Studies* 16:3 (1982), pp. 373–89.

Brewitt-Taylor, Sam, 'Christianity and the Invention of the Sexual Revolution in Britain, 1963–1967', *Historical Journal* 60:2 (2017), pp. 519–46.

Broom, Herbert, *The Philosophy of Common Law* (3rd edn, London: W. Maxwell and Son, 1883).

Bruccoli, Matthew J., and Judith S. Baughman (eds), *Conversations with John Le Carré* (Jackson: University Press of Mississippi, 2004).

Bryden, Inga, and Janet Floyd, 'Introduction', in Inga Bryden and Janet Floyd (eds), *Domestic Space: Reading the Nineteenth-Century Interior* (Manchester: Manchester University Press, 1999), pp. 1–17.

Buettner, Elizabeth, '"Would You Let Your Daughter Marry a Negro?": Race and Sex in 1950s Britain', in Philippa Levine and Susan Grayzel (eds), *Gender, Labour, War and Empire* (Basingstoke: Palgrave MacMillan, 2009), pp. 219–37.

Bulloch, John, and Henry Miller, *Spy Ring: The Full Story of the Naval Secrets Case* (London: Secker and Warburg, 1961).

Burney, Ian, and Neil Pemberton, *Murder and the Making of the English CSI* (Baltimore: Johns Hopkins University Press, 2016).

Bush, Julia, '"Special Strengths for their Own Special Duties": Women, Higher Education and Gender Conservatism in Late Victorian Britain', *History of Education* 34:4 (2005), pp. 387–405.

Butler, C. McArthur, 'The Society of Architects, 1884–1913', *Journal of the Society of Architects* (Mar. 1914), pp. 184–95.

Butt, John, 'Life Assurance in War and Depression: The Standard Life Assurance Company and its Environment, 1914–39', in Oliver M. Westall (ed.), *The Historian and the Business of Insurance* (Manchester: Manchester University Press, 1984), pp. 155–72.

Caminada, Jerome, *Twenty-Five Years of Detective Life* (Manchester: John Heywood, 1895).

Cannadine, David, *Class in Britain* (London: Penguin, 1998).

Carrabine, Eamonn, *Crime, Culture and the Media* (Cambridge: Cambridge University Press, 2008).

Carter, Robert L., and Peter Falush, *The British Insurance Industry since 1900* (Basingstoke: Palgrave MacMillan, 2009).

de Certeau, Michel, *The Practice of Everyday Life* (Berkeley: University of California Press, 1984).

Champness, Arthur, *A Century of Progress: The General Life Assurance Company* (London: The Company, 1937).

Chapman, James, and Matthew Hilton, 'From Sherlock Holmes to James Bond: Masculinity and National Identity in British Popular Fiction', in Stephen Caunce, Ewa Mazierska, Susan Sidney-Smith, and John K. Walton (eds), *Relocating Britishness* (Manchester: Manchester University Press, 2004), pp. 126–47.

Churchill, David, 'The Spectacle of Security: Lock-Picking Competitions and the Security Industry in Mid-Victorian Britain', *History Workshop Journal* 80:1 (2015), pp. 52–74.

Churchill, David, 'Security and Visions of the Criminal: Technology, Professional Criminality and Social Change in Victorian and Edwardian Britain', *British Journal of Criminology* 56:5 (2015), pp. 857–76.

Clapson, Mark, 'The Suburban Aspiration in England since 1919', *Contemporary British History* 14:1 (2000), pp. 151–74.

Clark, Anna, *The Struggle for the Breeches: Gender and the Making of the British Working Class* (Berkeley: University of California Press, 1995).

Clark, Anna, *Scandal: The Sexual Politics of the British Constitution* (Princeton: Princeton University Press, 2004).

Clark, Anna, *Desire: A History of European Sexuality* (London: Routledge, 2008).

Clark, Geoffrey, and Gregory Anderson, 'Introduction', in Geoffrey Clark, Gregory Anderson, Christian Thomann, and J.-Matthias Graf von der Schulenburg (eds), *The Appeal of Insurance* (Toronto: University of Toronto Press, 2010), pp. 3–15.

Clarke, Comer, *The War Within* (London: World Distributors, 1961).

Cocks, Harry, 'Calamus in Bolton: Spirituality and Homosexual Desire in Late Victorian England', *Gender and History*, 13 (2001), pp. 191–223.

Cocks, Harry, 'Saucy Stories: Pornography, Sexology and the Marketing of Sexual Knowledge in Britain, c.1918–70', *Social History* 29:4 (2004), pp. 465–84.

Cohen, Deborah, 'Who Was Who? Race and Jews in Turn-of-the-Century Britain', *Journal of British Studies* 41:4 (2002), pp. 460–83.

Cohen, Deborah, *Household Gods: The British and their Possessions* (London and New Haven: Yale University Press, 2006).

Cohen, Deborah, *Family Secrets: Living with Shame from the Victorians to the Present Day* (London: Viking, 2013).

Cole, Simon, *Suspect Identities: A History of Fingerprinting and Criminal Identification* (Cambridge, Massachusetts: Harvard University Press, 2001).

Collins, Marcus, 'The Pornography of Permissiveness: Men's Sexuality and Women's Emancipation in Mid-Twentieth-Century Britain', *History Workshop Journal* 47 (1999), pp. 99–120.

Collins, Marcus, *Modern Love: An Intimate History of Men and Women in Twentieth-Century Britain* (London: Atlantic Books, 2003).

Collins, Wilkie, *The Moonstone* (1868: reprinted London: Penguin, 1994).

Conekin, Becky, *The Autobiography of a Nation: The 1951 Exhibition of Britain, Representing Britain in the Post-War World* (Manchester: Manchester University Press, 2003).

Conrad, Joseph, *The Secret Agent* (London: Methuen and Co., 1907).

Cook, Hera, 'The English Sexual Revolution: Technology and Change', *History Workshop Journal* 59 (2005), pp. 109–28.

Cook, Matt, *London and the Culture of Homosexuality, 1885–1914* (Cambridge: Cambridge University Press, 2003).

Cook, Matt, 'Law', in H. G. Cocks and Matt Houlbrook (eds), *The Palgrave Modern History of Sexuality* (Basingstoke: Palgrave MacMillan, 2006), pp. 64–86.

Cooter, Roger, *The Cultural Meaning of Popular Science: Phrenology and the Organisation of Consent in Nineteenth-Century Britain* (Cambridge: Cambridge University Press, 1984).

Corber, Robert, 'Resisting History: Rear Window and the Limits of the Postwar Settlement', *Boundary 2*, 19:1 (1992), pp. 121–48.

Cowman, Krista, *Women in British Politics, c.1689–1979* (Basingstoke: Palgrave MacMillan, 2010).

Cox, Pam, *Bad Girls in Britain: Gender, Justice and Welfare, 1900–1950* (Basingstoke: Palgrave MacMillan, 2002).

Crafts, Nicholas, 'Long-Run Growth', in Roderick Floud and Paul Johnson (eds), *The Cambridge Economic History of Modern Britain Vol. II: Economic Maturity, 1860–1939* (Cambridge: Cambridge University Press, 2004), pp. 1–24.

Cresswell, Tim, *The Tramp in America* (London: Reaktion, 2001).

Critchley, T. A., *A History of Police in England and Wales* (2nd edn, London: Constable, 1978).

Cromwell, William C., 'The Marshall Plan, Britain, and the Cold War', *Review of International Studies* 8:4 (1982), pp. 233–49.

Crone, Rosalind, *Violent Victorians: Popular Entertainment in Nineteenth-Century London* (Manchester: Manchester University Press, 2012).

Crook, Tom, 'Norms, Forms and Beds: Spatializing Sleep in Victorian Britain', *Body and Society* 14:4 (2008), pp. 15–35.

D'Cruze, Shani, *Crimes of Outrage: Sex, Violence, and Victorian Working Women* (London: UCL Press, 1998).

D'Cruze, Shani (ed.), *Everyday Violence in Britain, 1850–1950* (Harlow: Longman, 2000).

D'Cruze, Shani, '"Dad's Back": Mapping Masculinities, Moralities, and the Law in the Novels of Margery Allingham', *Cultural and Social History* 1 (2004), pp. 256–79.

D'Cruze, Shani, and Louise Jackson, *Women, Crime, and Justice in England since 1660* (Basingstoke: Palgrave MacMillan, 2009).

D'Cruze, Shani, and Sandra Walklate and Samantha Pegg, *Murder: Social and Historical Approaches to Understanding Murder and Murderers* (London: Routledge, 2006).

Davidoff, Leonore, and Catherine Hall, *Family Fortunes: Men and Women of the English Middle Class, 1780–1850* (London: Routledge, 2002).

Davie, Neil, 'Criminal Man Revisited? Continuity and Change in British Criminology, c.1865–1918', *Journal of Victorian Culture* 8 (2003), pp. 1–32.

Davis, Tracy C., *Actresses as Working Women: Their Social Identity in Victorian Culture* (London: Routledge, 1991).

Dawe, Carlton, *The Crackswoman* (London: Ward, Lock, and Co., 1914).

Deans, Richard Storry, *Notable Trials: Romances of the Law Courts* (London: Cassell and Co., 1906).

Deighton, Anne, 'Britain and the Cold War, 1945–1955', in Anne Deighton (ed.), *Britain and the Cold War* (Basingstoke: Palgrave MacMillan, 1990), 119–23.

Dennis, Richard, *Cities in Modernity: Representations and Productions of Metropolitan Space, 1840–1930* (Cambridge: Cambridge University Press, 2008).

Deriu, Davide, 'Capital Views: Interwar London in the Photographs of Aerofilms Ltd.', in *The London Journal* 35:3 (2010), pp. 266–73.

Devereaux, Simon, 'The Bloodiest Code: Counting Executions and Pardons at the Old Bailey, 1730–1837', *Law, Crime, and History* 6:1 (2016), pp. 1–36.

Dickens, Charles, *Oliver Twist* (1837–9; reprinted London: Penguin, 1994).

Dixon, Jay, *The Romance Fiction of Mills and Boon, 1909–1990s* (London: UCL Press, 1999).

Doan, Laura, 'Topsy-Turvydom: Gender Inversion, Sapphism, and the Great War', *GLQ: A Journal of Lesbian and Gay Studies* 12:4 (2006), pp. 517–42.

Doan, Laura, 'Primum Mobile: Women and Auto/mobility in the Era of the Great War', *Women: A Cultural Review* 17:1 (2006), pp. 26–41.

Doan, Laura, 'Queer History/Queer Memory: The Case of Alan Turing', *GLQ: A Journal of Lesbian and Gay Studies* 23:1 (2017), pp. 113–36.

Donnelly, Peter, 'Social Climbing: A Case Study of the Changing Class Structure of Rock Climbing and Mountaineering in Britain', in Aidan O. Dunleavy, Andrew W. Miracle, and C. Roger Rees (eds), *Studies in the Sociology of Sport* (Texas: Texas University Press, 1982), pp. 13–28.

Donovan, James B., *Strangers on a Bridge: The Case of Colonel Abel and Francis Gary Powers* (New York: Secker and Warburg, 1964).

Doyle, Arthur Conan, *Memories and Adventures* (London: Hodder and Stoughton, 1924).

Drake, David, 'Crime Fiction at the Time of the Exhibition: The Case of Sherlock Holmes and Arsène Lupin', *Synergies Royaume-Uni et Irlande* 2 (2009), pp. 105–17.

Eldridge, Benjamin P., *Our Rival, the Rascal: A Faithful Portrayal of the Conflict between the Criminals of this Age and the Defenders of our Society* (Boston: Pemberton Publishing Co., 1897).

Emsley, Clive, ' "The Thump of Wood on a Swede Turnip": Police Violence in Nineteenth-Century England', *Criminal Justice History* 6 (1985), pp. 125–49.

Emsley, Clive, *Crime and Society in England, 1750–1900* (London: Routledge, 1987).

Emsley, Clive, *Crime, Police and Penal Policy: European Experiences, 1750–1940* (Oxford: Oxford University Press, 2007).

Emsley, Clive, *Crime and Society in Twentieth-Century England* (Harlow: Longman, 2011).

Emsley, Clive, *Soldier, Sailor, Beggarman, Thief: Crime and the British Armed Services Since 1914* (Oxford: Oxford University Press, 2013).

Evergeti, Venetia, 'Notions of Home and Belonging among Greeks in the UK', in Louise Ryan and Wendy Webster (eds), *Gendering Migration: Masculinity, Femininity and Ethnicity in Post-War Britain* (Aldershot: Ashgate Publishing, 2008), pp. 105–20.

Faith, Nicholas, 'Obituary: Sir Denis Mountain Bt', *Independent* (6 January 2006), https://www.independent.co.uk/news/obituaries/sir-denis-mountain-bt-6112504.html (accessed 26 June 2018).

Felson, Marcus, and Rachel Boba, *Crime and Everyday Life* (4th edn, London: Sage, 2010).

Fishman, William J., 'Crime and Punishment', in Alexandra Warwick and Martin Willis (eds), *Jack the Ripper: Media, Culture, History* (Manchester: Manchester University Press, 2007), pp. 229–43.

Fleming, Ian, *Moonraker* (London: Jonathan Cape, 1955).

Fleming, Ian, *Casino Royale* (1953; reprinted London: Vintage Digital, 2012).

Floud, Roderick and Paul Johnson (eds), *The Cambridge Economic History of Great Britain Vol. III: Change and Growth* (Cambridge: Cambridge University Press, 2004).

Flower, Raymond, and Michael Wynn Jones, *Lloyd's of London: An Illustrated History* (Newton Abbott: David and Charles, 1974).

Foucault, Michel, *Discipline and Punish: The Birth of the Prison*, trans. Allen Lane (London: Allen Lane, 1977).

Francis, Martin, 'The Domestication of the Male? Recent Research on Nineteenth- and Twentieth-Century British Masculinity', *Historical Journal* 45 (2002), pp. 637–52.

Frank, Lawrence, *Victorian Detective Fiction and the Nature of Evidence: The Scientific Investigations of Poe, Dickens, and Doyle* (Basingstoke: Palgrave MacMillan, 2003).

Frazier, Robert, 'Did Britain Start the Cold War? Bevin and the Truman Doctrine', *Historical Journal* 27:3 (1984), pp. 715–27.

Froese, Paul, *The Plot to Kill God: Findings from the Soviet Experiment in Secularization* (Berkeley: University of California Press, 2008).

Frost, George 'Jack', *Flying Squad* (London: Youth Book Club, 1950).

Frost, Ginger, *Promises Broken: Courtship, Class, and Gender in Victorian England* (Virginia: University Press of Virginia, 1995).

Frost, Ginger, ' "She Is but a Woman": Kitty Byron and the English Edwardian Criminal Justice System', *Gender & History* 16:3 (2004), pp. 538–60.

Frost, Ginger, *Living in Sin: Cohabiting as Husband and Wife in Nineteenth-Century England* (Manchester: Manchester University Press, 2008).

Gardner, Viv, 'The Invisible Spectatrice: Gender, Geography and Theatrical Space', in Maggie B. Gale and Viv Gardner (eds), *Women, Theatre and Performance: New Histories, New Historiographies* (Manchester: Manchester University Press, 2000), pp. 25–45.

Gatrell, V. A. C., 'The Decline of Theft and Violence in Victorian and Edwardian England', in V. A. C. Gatrell, Bruce Lenman, and Geoffrey Parker (eds), *Crime and the Law: The Social History of Crime in Western Europe since 1500* (London: Europa Publications, 1980), pp. 238–337.

Gere, Charlotte, and Judy Rudoe, *Jewellery in the Age of Queen Victoria: A Mirror to the World* (London: British Museum, 2010).

Gervase, Charles, 'Maurice Durant', *London Reader of Literature, Science, Art, and General Information* (Jan. 1873), pp. 241–4.

Getzler, Joshua S., 'Jervis, Sir John (1802–1856), judge', *Oxford Dictionary of National Biography*, http://www.oxforddnb.com/view/10.1093/ref:odnb/9780198614128.001. 0001/odnb-9780198614128-e-14795 (accessed 26 June 2018).

Giddens, Anthony, *The Consequences of Modernity* (Cambridge: Polity Press, 1990).

Gissing, George, *The Collected Letters of George Gissing*, Vol. 7, ed. Paul F. Matthiesen, Arthur C. Young, and Pierre Coustillas (1897–9; reprinted Ohio: Ohio University Press, 1997).

Golding, C. E., *Burglary Insurance* (1921: 4th edn, London: Buckley Press, 1949).

Goodwin, John, *Sidelights on Criminal Matters* (London: Hutchinson and Co., 1923).

Gould, Jonathan, *Can't Buy Me Love: The Beatles, Britain and America* (London: Portrait, 2007).

Grandy, Christine, 'Paying for Love: Women's Work and Love in Popular Film in Interwar Britain', *Journal of the History of Sexuality* 19 (2010), pp. 483–507.

Grandy, Christine, ' "Avarice" and "Evil Doers": Profiteers, Politicians, and Popular Fiction in the 1920s', *Journal of British Studies* 50 (2011), pp. 667–89.

Grant, Matthew, ' "Civil Defence Gives Meaning to your Leisure": Citizenship, Participation, and Cultural Change in Cold War Recruitment Propaganda, 1949–54', *Twentieth Century British History* 22:1 (2011), pp. 52–78.

Grayzel, Susan, 'Liberating Women? Examining Gender, Morality and Sexuality in First World War Britain and France' in Gail Braybon (ed.), *Evidence, History and the Great War: Historians and the Impact of 1914–18* (London: Berghahn Books, 2003), pp. 113–34.

Griffiths, Arthur, *Mysteries of Police and Crime* (London: Cassell and Co., 1902).

Gullace, Nicoletta, *The Blood of our Sons: Men, Women, and the Renegotiation of British Citizenship during the Great War* (Basingstoke: Palgrave MacMillan, 2002).

Gurney, Peter, ' "Intersex" and "Dirty Girls": Mass Observation and Working-Class Sexuality in England in the 1930s', *Journal of the History of Sexuality* 8:2 (1997), pp. 256–90.

Hadlaw, Janin, 'The London Underground Map: Imagining Modern Time and Space', in *Design Issues* 19:1 (2003), pp. 25–35.

Haggard, Robert F., 'Jack the Ripper as the Threat of Outcast London', in Alexandra Warwick and Martin Willis (eds), *Jack the Ripper: Media, Culture, History* (Manchester: Manchester University Press, 2007), pp. 197–214.

Halén, Widar, *Christopher Dresser: A Pioneer of Modern Design* (London: Phaidon, 1990).

Hamlett, Jane, ' "The Dining Room Should Be the Man's Paradise, as the Drawing Room Is the Woman's": Gender and Middle-Class Domestic Space in England, 1850–1910', *Gender and History*, 21 (2009), pp. 576–91.

Hamlett, Jane, *Material Relations: Domestic Interiors and Middle-Class Families in England, 1850–1910* (Manchester: Manchester University Press, 2010).

Hammerton, A. James, 'Pooterism or Partnership? Marriage and Masculine Identity in the Lower Middle Class, 1870–1920', *Journal of British Studies* 38:3 (1999), pp. 291–321.

Hammerton, A. James, 'The Perils of Mrs Pooter: Satire, Modernity and Motherhood in the Lower Middle Class in England, 1870–1920', *Women's History Review* 8:2 (1999), pp. 261–76.

Hampshire, James, *Citizenship and Belonging: Immigration and the Politics of Demographic Governance in Post-War Britain* (Basingstoke: Palgrave MacMillan, 2005).

Harris, Alana, 'Love Divine and Love Sublime: The Catholic Marriage Advisory Council, the Marriage Guidance Movement and the State', in Alana Harris and Timothy Willem Jones (eds), *Love and Romance in Britain, 1918–1970* (Basingstoke: Palgrave MacMillan, 2015), pp. 188–224.

Harvey, David, *The Condition of Postmodernity: An Inquiry into the Origins of Cultural Change* (Oxford: Oxford University Press, 1989).

Hepburn, Allan, *Intrigue: Espionage and Culture* (London and New Haven: Yale University Press, 2005).

Hinchcliff, Tanis, and Davide Deriu, 'Eyes Over London: Re-Imagining the Metropolis in the Age of Aerial Vision', *The London Journal* 35:3 (2010), pp. 221–4.

Hitchcock, Tim, and Robert Shoemaker, *London Lives: Poverty, Crime, and the Making of a Modern City, 1690–1800* (Cambridge: Cambridge University Press, 2015).

Hodgson, Geoffrey, *Lloyd's of London: A Reputation at Risk* (London: Penguin, 1984).

Holden, Katherine, *In the Shadow of Marriage: Singleness in England, 1914–1960* (Manchester: Manchester University Press, 2007).

Hollows, Joanne, 'The Science of Spells: Cooking, Lifestyle, and Domestic Femininities in British Good Housekeeping in the Interwar Period', in David Bell and Joanne Hollows (eds), *Historicising Lifestyle: Mediating Taste, Consumption and Identity from the 1900s to 1970s* (Aldershot: Ashgate Publishing, 2006), pp. 21–39.

Holt, Richard, 'Cricket and Englishness: The Batsman as Hero', in Richard Holt, J. A. Mangan, and Pierre Lanfranchi (eds), *European Heroes: Myth, Identity, Sport* (London: Frank Cass, 1996), pp. 48–70.

Honeycombe, Gordon, *More Murders of the Black Museum 1835–1985* (London: Arrow, 1993).

Hopf, Ted, *Reconstructing the Cold War: The Early Years* (Oxford: Oxford University Press, 2012).

Hopkins, Michael, 'Continuing Debate and New Approaches in Cold War History', *Historical Journal* 50:4 (2007), pp. 913–34.

Hornsey, Richard, ' "Everything Is Made of Atoms": The Reprogramming of Space and Time in Post-War London', *Journal of Historical Geography* 34:1 (2008), pp. 94–117.

Hornsey, Richard, *The Spiv and the Architect: Unruly Life in Postwar London* (Minneapolis: University of Minnesota Press, 2010).

Hornsey, Richard, 'He Who Thinks, in Modern Traffic, Is Lost': Automation and the Pedestrian Rhythms of Interwar London', in Tim Edensor (ed.), *Geographies of Rhythm: Nature, Place, Mobilities, and Bodies* (Aldershot: Ashgate Publishing, 2010), pp. 99–112.

Hornung, Ernest William, 'In the Chains of Crime', *Cassell's Magazine* (June 1898), pp. 3–12.

Hornung, Ernest William, *Raffles* (New York: Charles Scribners Sons, 1901).

Hornung, Ernest William, *The Amateur Cracksman* (London: Grant Richards 1901).

Hornung, Ernest William, *Ein Einbrecher aus Passion* (Stuttgart : Verlag von. J. Engelhorn, 1903).

Hornung, Ernest William, *Le Masque Noir: Aventures de Raffles, Cambrioleur Amateur* (Paris: La renaissance du livre, 1907).

Hornung, Ernest William, *The Amateur Cracksman* (London: Eveleigh Nash, 1911).

Hornung, Ernest William, *A Thief in the Night* (London: Nelson Library, 1914).

Hornung, Ernest William, *The Amateur Cracksman* (London, John Murray, 1926).

Hornung, Ernest William, *A Thief in the Night* (London: George G. Harrap & Co. Ltd, 1926).

Hornung, Ernest William, *The Amateur Cracksman* (London: Readers Library Publishing Company Ltd., 1930).

Hornung, Ernest William, *The Amateur Cracksman* (London: Jonathan Cape Ltd., 1936).

Hornung, Ernest William, *The Complete Short Stories of Raffles* (1899–1905: Reprinted London: Penguin, 1987).

Hornung, Ernest William, *Mr. Justice Raffles* (1909: Reprinted Fairfield: Createspace Independent Publishing Platform, 2007).

Hornung, Ernest William, and Eugene Presbrey, 'Raffles, The Amateur Cracksman', in Ernest William Hornung, *The A. J. Raffles Omnibus* (1906; reprinted Ontario: Battered Silicon Dispatch Box, 2000), pp. 137–84.

Horsley, John William, *How Criminals are Made and Prevented: A Retrospect of Forty Years* (London: T. Fisher Unwin, 1913).

Houlbrook, Matt, *Queer London: Perils and Pleasures in the Sexual Metropolis, 1918–1957* (Chicago: University of Chicago Press, 2005).

Houlbrook, Matt, '"The Man with the Powder Puff" in Interwar London', *Historical Journal* 50:1 (2007), pp. 145–71.

Houlbrook, Matt, '"A Pin to See the Peepshow": Culture, Fiction and Selfhood in Edith Thompson's Letters, 1921–1922', *Past and Present* 207:1 (2010), pp. 215–49.

Houlbrook, Matt, *Prince of Tricksters: The Incredible True Story of Netley Lucas, Gentleman Crook* (Chicago: University of Chicago Press, 2016).

Houlbrook, Matt, and Chris Waters, 'The Heart in Exile: Detachment and Desire in 1950s London', *History Workshop Journal*, 62:1 (2006), pp. 142–65.

Howell, Philip, *Geographies of Regulation: Policing Prostitution in Nineteenth-Century Britain and the Empire* (Cambridge: Cambridge University Press, 2009).

Hubbard, Phil, 'Sex Zones: Intimacy, Citizenship, and Public Space', *Sexualities* 4:1 (2001), pp. 51–71.

Hutchinson, W. J., *A Policeman Puts You Wise* (London: The Police Journal, 1951).

Inglis, Fred, *A Short History of Celebrity* (Princeton: Princeton University Press, 2010).

Ireland, Richard, 'Criminology, Class, and Cricket: Raffles and Real Life', *Legal Studies* 33:1 (2013), pp. 66–84.

Jackson, Alan A., 'From Street to Train', *Journal of the Railway and Canal Historical Society* 34:1 (2002), pp. 34–7.

Jackson, Lesley, *Twentieth Century Pattern Design* (London: Mitchell Beazley, 2002).

Jackson, Louise, *Child Sexual Abuse in Victorian England* (London: Routledge, 2000).

Jackson, Louise, *Women Police: Gender, Welfare and Surveillance in the Twentieth Century* (Manchester: Manchester University Press, 2006).

Jackson, Louise, ' "The Coffee Club Menace": Policing Youth, Leisure and Sexuality in Post-War Manchester', *Cultural and Social History* 5:3 (2008), pp. 289–308.

Jackson, Louise, and Angela Bartie, *Policing Youth: Britain, 1945–70* (Manchester: Manchester University Press, 2014).

Jackson, Peter, and L. V. Scott, 'Introduction: Journeys in Shadows', in P. Jackson and L. V. Scott (eds) *Understanding Intelligence in the Twenty-First Century: Journeys in Shadows* (London: Routledge, 2004), pp. 1–28.

Jenkins, John, *British Propaganda and News Media in the Cold War* (Edinburgh: Edinburgh University Press, 2006).

Jeremiah, David, *Architecture and Design for the Family in Britain, 1900–70* (Manchester: Manchester University Press, 2000).

Jerram, Leif, *Streetlife: The Untold Story of Europe's Twentieth Century* (Oxford: Oxford University Press, 2011).

Jervis, Sir John, *Archibold's Pleading and Evidence in Criminal Cases* (20th edn, London: Sweet and Maxwell, Ltd., 1886).

John, Angela, ' "Behind the Locked Door": Evelyn Sharp, Suffragette and Rebel Journalist', *Women's History Review* 12:1 (2003), pp. 5–13.

Johnson, Paul, 'Conspicuous Consumption and Working-Class Culture in Late Victorian and Edwardian Britain', *Transactions of the Royal Historical Society* 38 (1988), pp. 35–7.

Johnston, Helen, *Crime in England 1815–1880: Experiencing the Criminal Justice System* (London: Routledge, 2015).

Jones, Ben, 'Slum Clearance, Privatization and Residualization: The Practices and Politics of Council Housing in Mid-Twentieth Century England', *Twentieth Century British History* 21:4 (2010), pp. 510–39.

Jones, Howard, *'A New Kind of War': America's Global Strategy and the Truman Doctrine in Greece* (Oxford: Oxford University Press, 1989).

Jones, Max, *The Last Great Quest: Captain Scott's Antarctic Sacrifice* (Oxford: Oxford University Press, 2003).

Joyce, Patrick, *The Rule of Freedom: Liberalism and the Modern City* (London: Verso, 2003).

Joyce, Simon, *Capital Offences: Geographies of Class and Crime in Victorian London* (London: University of Virginia Press, 2003).

Kemp, Sandra, and Charlotte Mitchell and David Trotter, *The Oxford Companion to Edwardian Fiction* (Oxford: Oxford University Press, 1997).

Kent, Susan Kingsley, *Sex and Suffrage in Britain, 1860–1914* (Princeton: Princeton University Press, 1987).

Kent, Susan Kingsley, *Gender and Power in Britain, 1640–1990* (London: Routledge, 1999).

Kent, Susan Kingsley, *Aftershocks: Politics and Trauma in Britain, 1918–1931* (Basingstoke: Palgrave MacMillan, 2009).

Kingston, Charles, *A Gallery of Rogues* (London: S. Paul and Co., 1924).

Klein, Joanne, 'Traffic, Telephones and Police Boxes: The Deterioration of Beat Policing in Birmingham, Liverpool and Manchester Between the World Wars', in Gerald Blaney (ed.), *Policing Interwar Europe: Continuity, Change, and Crisis, 1918–1940* (Basingstoke: Palgrave MacMillan, 2007), pp. 215–36.

Knight, Stephen, *Crime Fiction 1800–2000: Detection, Death, Diversity* (Basingstoke: Palgrave MacMillan, 2004).

Koven, Seth, *Slumming: Sexual and Social Politics in Victorian London* (Princeton: Princeton University Press, 2006).

Koven, Seth, *The Matchgirl and the Heiress* (Princeton: Princeton University Press, 2014).

Kozin, Alexander, 'Scrapbooking the Criminal Defence File', *Crime, Media, Culture* 4:31 (2008), pp. 31–52.

Kuhn, Annette, *An Everyday Magic: Cinema and Cultural Memory* (London: I.B. Taurus, 2002).

Laite, Julia, *Common Prostitutes and Ordinary Citizens: Commercial Sex in London, 1885–1960* (Basingstoke: Palgrave MacMillan, 2012).

Lamb, Frederick, *Forty Years in the Old Bailey: With a Summary of the Leading Cases and Points of Law and Practice* (London: Stevens and Sons, 1913).

Langhamer, Claire, 'The Meanings of Home in Postwar Britain', *Journal of Contemporary History* 40:2 (2005), pp. 341–62.

Latour, Bruno, *Reassembling the Social: An Introduction to Actor-Network Theory* (Oxford: Oxford University Press, 2005).

Laub, John H., and Robert J. Sampson, 'The Sutherland-Glueck Debate: On the Sociology of Criminal Knowledge', *American Journal of Sociology* 96 (1991), pp. 1402–40.

Law, Michael John, '"The Car Indispensable": The Hidden Influence of the Car in Inter-War Suburban London', *Journal of Historical Geography* 38 (2012), pp. 424–33.

Lawrence, Jon, 'Class, Affluence, and the Study of Everyday Life in Britain, *c.*1930–1964', *Cultural and Social History* 10:2 (2013), pp. 273–99.

Le Carré, John, *Call for the Dead* (London: Victor Gollancz, 1961).

Lefebvre, Henri, *The Production of Space*, trans. Donald Nicholson-Smith (Oxford: Oxford University Press, 1992).

Leffler, Melvyn P., *A Preponderance of Power: National Security, the Truman Administration, and the Cold War* (Stanford: Stanford University Press, 1992).

LeMahieu, Dan, *A Culture for Democracy: Mass Communication and the Cultivated Mind in Britain between the Wars* (Oxford: Oxford University Press, 1988).

Liddell, Guy, *The Guy Liddell Diaries: Vol. II: 1942–1945* (ed.) Nigel West (London: Routledge, 2005).

Light, Alison, *Forever England: Femininity, Literature and Conservatism between the Wars* (London: Routledge, 1991).

Loader, Ian, 'Policing and the Social: Questions of Symbolic Power', *British Journal of Sociology* 48:1 (1997), pp. 1–18.

Lobban, Michael, 'Broom, Herbert (1815–1882), legal writer', *Oxford Dictionary of National Biography*, http://www.oxforddnb.com/view/10.1093/ref:odnb/9780198614128.001.0001/odnb-9780198614128-e-3569 (accessed 26 June 2018).

Long, Vicky, 'Industrial Homes, Domestic Factories: The Convergence of Public and Private in Interwar Britain', *Journal of British Studies* 50 (2011), pp. 434–64.

Lonsdale, Frederick, *The Last of Mrs. Cheyney: A Comedy in Three Acts* (London: W. Collins Sons and Co., 1925).

Lucas, D. B., and C. E. Benson, *Psychology for Advertisers* (London: Harper and Brothers, 1930).

Lycett, Andrew, 'Fleming, Ian Lancaster (1908–1964)', *Oxford Dictionary of National Biography*, http://www.oxforddnb.com/view/article/33168 (accessed 2 Oct. 2017).

MacBrayne Lewis E., and James E. Ramsay, *One More Chance: An Experiment in Human Salvage* (Boston: Small, Maynard and Co., 1916).

Mackenzie, J. M., 'The Popular Culture of Empire in Britain', in Judith Brown and W. M. Roger Louis (eds), *The Oxford History of the British Empire: The Twentieth Century* (Oxford: Oxford University Press, 1999), pp. 212–31.

Madame Tussaud's Exhibition Catalogue (London: Madame Tussaud's, 1925).

Maguire, Mike, 'The Impact of Burglary Upon Victims', *British Journal of Criminology* 20 (1980), pp. 261–75.

Major, Patrick, and Rana Mitter, 'East Is East and West Is West? Towards a Comparative Socio-Cultural History of the Cold War', *Cold War History* 4:1 (2006), pp. 1–22.

Malchow, H. L., 'Public Gardens and Social Action in Late Victorian London', *Victorian Studies* 29:1 (1985), pp. 97–124.

Malyon, E. J., and Charles James, *The Lady Burglar, A Farcical Problem: French's Acting Edition* (London: Lacy's Acting Edition of Plays, 1897).

Manwaring-White, Sarah, *The Policing Revolution: Police Technology, Democracy and Liberty in Britain* (Brighton: Harvester, 1983).

Marcus, Sharon, *Apartment Stories: City and Home in Nineteenth-Century Paris and London* (Berkeley: University of California Press, 1999).

Marlow-Mann, Alex, 'Exploits of Three-Fingered Kate, The (1912)', *British Film Institute Online*, http://www.screenonline.org.uk/film/id/727128/index.html (accessed 16 Oct. 2012).

Marsh, Christopher, *Religion and the State in Russia and China: Suppression, Survival, and Revival* (London: Continuum, 2011).

Martin, Douglas, 'Anthony Cave Brown, 77, Historian of Espionage, is Dead', *New York Times* (2 Aug. 2006), http://www.nytimes.com/2006/08/02/arts/02brown.html (accessed 16 Aug. 2017).

Martland, Peter, 'Wright, Peter Maurice (1916–1995), Security Service Officer and Author', *Oxford Dictionary of National Biography*, http://www.oxforddnb.com/view/10.1093/ref:odnb/9780198614128.001.0001/odnb-9780198614128-e-57934 (accessed 29 June 2018).

du Maurier, Daphne, *Gerald: A Portrait* (1934: reprinted London: Virago, 2004).

Mauskopf, Seymour H., 'Pellets, Pebbles, and Prisms: British Munitions for Larger Guns, 1860–1885', in Brenda J. Buchanan (ed.), *Gunpowder, Explosives and the State: A Technological History* (Aldershot: Ashgate Publishing, 2006), pp. 303–40.

Mayhall, Laura E. Nym, *The Militant Suffrage Movement: Citizenship and Resistance in Britain, 1860–1930* (Oxford: Oxford University Press, 2003).

Mayhew, Henry, *London Labour and the London Poor, Vol. 4* (London: Charles Griffin, 1861).

McClintock, Anne, *Imperial Leather: Race, Gender, and Sexuality in the Colonial Contest* (London: Routledge, 1995).

McKenzie, Andrea, 'The Real Macheath: Social Satire, Appropriation, and Eighteenth-Century Criminal Biography', *Huntington Library Quarterly* 69:4 (2006), pp. 581–605.

McKernan, Luke, 'Haggar (Arthur) William (1851–1925)', *Oxford Dictionary of National Biography*, http://www.oxforddnb.com/view/article/42131 (accessed 14 Jan. 2017).

McKibbin, Ross, *Classes and Cultures: England, 1918–51* (Oxford: Oxford University Press, 1998).

McLaren, Angus, *Sexual Blackmail: A Modern History* (Cambridge, Massachusetts: Harvard University Press, 2002).

McLaren, Angus, *Playboys and Mayfair Men: Crime, Class, Masculinity, and Fascism in 1930s London* (Baltimore: Johns Hopkins University Press, 2017).

McLaughlin, Eugene, 'From Reel to Ideal: The Blue Lamp and Popular Cultural Constructions of the English "Bobby"', *Crime, Media, Culture* 1:1 (2005), pp. 11–30.

McMillan, F. D., 'Burglary Insurance', in Reginald C. Simmonds and Joseph H. Matthews (eds), *The Insurance Guide and Handbook Vol. II* (6th edn, London: C. and E. Layton, 1922), pp. 248–9.

McMillan, F. D., and F. J. Woodroof, *Outlines of Burglary Insurance* (2nd edn, London: C. and E. Layton, 1924).

Meier, William, *Property Crime in London, 1850–Present* (Basingstoke: Palgrave MacMillan, 2011).

Meier, William, 'Going on the Hoist: Women, Work, and Shoplifting in London, ca. 1890–1940', *Journal of British Studies* 50:2 (2011), pp. 410–33.

Meller, Helen, 'Urban Renewal and Citizenship: The Quality of Life in British Cities, 1890–1990', *Urban History* 22:1 (1995), pp. 63–84.

Menke, Richard, *Telegraphic Realism: Victorian Fiction and Other Information Systems* (Stanford: Stanford University Press, 2008).

Merchant, A (pseud.), *Six Years in the Prisons of England*, ed. Frank Henderson (London: Richard Bentley, 1869).

Mercier, Charles Arthur, *Crime and Criminals: Being the Jurisprudence of Crime, Medical, Biological, and Psychological* (London: University of London Press, 1918).

Miller, Elizabeth Carolyn, *Framed: The New Woman Criminal in British Culture at the Fin-de-Siècle* (Michigan: University of Michigan Press, 2008).

Miller, Wilbur R., *The Social History of Crime and Punishment in America* (London: Sage, 2012).

Moores, Chris, 'Thatcher's Troops? Neighbourhood Watch Schemes and the Search for "Ordinary" Thatcherism in 1980s Britain', *Contemporary British History* 31:2 (2017), pp. 230–55.

Moran, Joe, 'Imagining the Street in Post-War Britain', *Urban History* 39:1 (2012), pp. 166–86.

Morley, Sheridan, *David Niven: The Other Side of the Moon* (Sevenoaks: Hodder and Stoughton, 1986).

Mort, Frank, *Capital Affairs: London and the Making of the Permissive Society* (London and New Haven: Yale University Press, 2010).

Moss, Eloise, 'Cracking Cribs: Representations of Burglars and Burglary in London, 1860–1939', Unpublished D.Phil Thesis, University of Oxford, 2013.

Moss, Eloise, 'The Scrapbooking Detective: Frederick Porter Wensley and the Limits of "Celebrity" and "Authority" in Interwar Britain', *Social History* 40:1 (2015), pp. 58–81.

Moss, Eloise, '"Dial 999 for Help!" The Three-Digit Emergency Number and the Transnational Politics of Welfare Activism, 1937–1979', *Journal of Social History* 52:2 (2018), pp. 468–500.

Muthesius, Stefan, *The Poetic Home: Designing the 19th Century Domestic Interior* (London: Thames and Hudson, 2009).

Nead, Lynda, *Victorian Babylon: People, Streets, and Images in Nineteenth-Century London* (London and New Haven: Yale University Press, 2000).

Nead, Lynda, *The Haunted Gallery: Painting, Photography, Film c.1900* (New Haven and London: Yale University Press, 2007).

Neale, Alexa, 'Framing a Murder: Crime Scene Photographs in Mid-Twentieth-Century London', paper delivered to British Crime Historians Symposium, October 2016 (article forthcoming).

Neiswander, Judith A., *The Cosmopolitan Interior: Liberalism and the British Home, 1870–1914* (London and New Haven: Yale University Press, 2008).

Nelson, Deborah, *Pursuing Privacy in Cold War America* (New York: Columbia University Press, 2002).

Neocleous, Mark, 'Social Police and the Mechanisms of Prevention', *British Journal of Criminology* 40 (2000), pp. 710–26.

Newburn, Tim, *Criminology* (Cullompton: Willan, 2007).

Newman, Bernard, *Epics of Espionage* (London: Werner Laurie, 1950).

Newman, Bernard, *Spies in Britain* (London: Robert Hale, 1964).

Newman, Bernard, *Spy and Counter-Spy* (London: Hale, 1970).

Nijhar, Preeti, 'Imperial Violence: The "Ethnic" as a Component of the "Criminal" Class in Victorian England', *Liverpool Law Review* 27 (2006), pp. 337–60.

O'Connell, Sean, *Credit and Community: Working-Class Debt in the UK Since 1880* (Oxford: Oxford University Press, 2009).

Offer, Avner, 'British Manual Workers: From Producers to Consumers, *c.*1950–2000', *Contemporary British History* 22:4 (2008), pp. 537–71.

Ogborn, Miles, *Spaces of Modernity: London's Geographies 1680–1780* (London: Guilford Press, 1998).

Oram, Alison, 'Cross-Dressing and Transgender', in Matt Houlbrook and Harry Cocks (eds), *Palgrave Advances in the Modern History of Sexuality* (Basingstoke: Palgrave MacMillan, 2006), pp. 256–85.

Orange, Vincent, 'Trenchard, Hugh Montague, First Viscount Trenchard (1873–1956)', *Oxford Dictionary of National Biography*, http://www.oxforddnb.com/view/10.1093/ref:odnb/9780198614128.001.0001/odnb-9780198614128-e-36552 (accessed 16 Sept. 2011).

Otter, Chris, *The Victorian Eye: A Political History of Light and Vision in Britain, 1800–1910* (Chicago: University of Chicago Press, 2008).

Owen, Nicholas, 'The Soft Heart of the British Empire: Indian Radicals in Edwardian London', *Past & Present* 220:1 (2013), pp. 143–84.

Panerai, Philippe, Jean Castex, Jean Charles DePaule, and Ivor Samuels, *Urban Forms: The Life and Death of the Urban Block* (Oxford: Oxford University Press, 2004).

Parrinder, Patrick, 'Wells, Herbert George (1866–1946)', *Oxford Dictionary of National Biography*, http://www.oxforddnb.com/view/10.1093/ref:odnb/9780198614128.001.0001/odnb-9780198614128-e-36831 (accessed 29 Dec. 2012).

Parrott, Catriona, 'Little Means or Time: Working-Class Women and Leisure in Late-Victorian and Edwardian England', *International Journal of the History of Sport* 15 (1998), pp. 22–53.

Parry, Sir Edward Abbott, *The Drama of the Law* (London: T. Fisher Unwin, 1924).

Paslew, John, 'No Robbery', *Belgravia: A London Magazine* (June 1889), pp. 465–80.

Paul, Kathleen, *Whitewashing Britain: Race and Citizenship in the Postwar Era* (London: Cornell University Press, 1997).

Pederson, Joyce Senders, 'Victorian Liberal Feminism and the "Idea" of Work', in Krista Cowman and Louise Jackson (eds), *Women and Work Culture: Britain c.1850–1950* (Aldershot: Ashgate Publishing, 2005), pp. 27–47.

Petrow, Stefan, *Policing Morals: The Metropolitan Police and the Home Office, 1870–1914* (Oxford: Oxford University Press, 1994).

Pilbeam, Pamela, *Madame Tussaud and the History of Waxworks* (London: Hambledon and London, 2003).

Piper, Alana, 'Victimization Narratives and Courtroom Sexual Politics: Prosecuting Male Burglars and Female Pickpockets in Melbourne, 1860–1921', *Journal of Social History* 51:4 (2018), pp. 760–83.

Plain, Gill, *Twentieth-Century Crime Fiction: Gender, Sexuality and the Body* (Edinburgh: Edinburgh University Press, 2001).

Platt, Roger H., 'The Soviet Imprisonment of Gerald Brooke and Subsequent Exchange for the Krogers, 1965–1969', *Contemporary British History* 24:2 (2010), pp. 193–212.

Power-Berrey, Robert J., *Bye-ways of Crime with Some Stories from the Black Museum* (London: Greening and Co., 1899).

Prest, Wilfrid, 'Blackstone, Sir William (1723–1780), legal writer and judge', *Oxford Dictionary of National Biography*, http://www.oxforddnb.com/view/10.1093/ref:odnb/9780198614128.001.0001/odnb-9780198614128-e-2536 (accessed 26 June 2018).

Quinton, Richard Frith, *Crime and Criminals, 1876–1910* (London: Longmans and Co., 1910).

Rafter, Nicole Hahn, 'Criminal Anthropology: Its Reception in the United States and the Nature of its Appeal', in Peter Becker and Richard F. Wetzell (eds), *Criminals and their Scientists: The History of Criminology in International Perspective* (Cambridge: Cambridge University Press, 2006), pp. 150–81.

Readman, Paul, 'William Cecil Slingsby, Norway, and British Mountaineering, 1872–1914', *English Historical Review* 129:540 (2014), pp. 1098–1128.

Reddy, William, *The Navigation of Feeling: A Framework for the History of Emotions* (Cambridge: Cambridge University Press, 2001).

Rhodes, William M., and Catherine Conly, 'Crime and Mobility: An Empirical Study', in Paul J. Brantingham and Patricia L. Brantingham (eds), *Environmental Criminology* (London: Sage, 1981), pp. 167–88.

Richards, Jeffrey, 'The British Board of Film Censors and Content Control in the 1930s: Images of Britain', *Historical Journal of Film, Radio and Television* 1 (1981), pp. 95–116.

Richards, Jeffrey, and Anthony Aldgate, *Best of British: Cinema and Society from the 1930s to the Present* (London: I.B. Taurus, 1999).

Rickett, Denis, 'Salter (James) Arthur, Baron Salter (1881–1975)', *Oxford Dictionary of National Biography*, http://www.oxforddnb.com/view/article/31651 (accessed 31 July 2017).

Roberts, Lewis, 'The "Shivering Sands" of Reality: Narration and Knowledge in Wilkie Collins' *The Moonstone*', *Victorian Review* 23 (1997), pp. 168–83.

Robertson, James C., *The British Board of Film Censors: Film Censorship in Britain, 1896–1950* (London: Croom Helm, 1985).

Rodensky, Lisa, *The Crime in Mind: Criminal Responsibility and the Victorian Novel* (Oxford: Oxford University Press, 2003).

Roodhouse, Mark, *Black Market Britain, 1939–1955* (Oxford: Oxford University Press, 2013).

Roper, Michael, *The Secret Battle: Emotional Survival in the Great War* (Manchester: Manchester University Press, 2009).

Rose, Jonathan, *The Intellectual Life of the British Working Classes* (London and New Haven: Yale University Press, 2001).

Rose, Sonya, *Limited Livelihoods: Gender and Class in Nineteenth-Century England* (Berkeley: University of California Press, 1992).

Rose, Sonya, *Which People's War? National Identity and Citizenship in Wartime Britain* (Oxford: Oxford University Press, 2003).

Roth, Marty, *Foul and Fair Play: Reading Genre in Classic Detective Fiction* (London: University of Georgia Press, 1995).

Rowbotham, Judith, and Kim Stevenson and Samantha Pegg, *Crime News in Modern Britain: Press Reporting and Responsibility, 1820–2010* (Basingstoke: Palgrave MacMillan, 2013).

Rowland, Peter, 'Hornung, Ernest William (1866–1921)', *Oxford Dictionary of National Biography*, http://www.oxforddnb.com/view/10.1093/ref:odnb/9780198614128.001.0001/odnb-9780198614128-e-37572 (accessed 29 Dec. 2012).

Ryan, Deborah, 'All the World and her Husband': The Daily Mail Ideal Home Exhibition 1908–39', in Maggie Andrews and Mary M. Talbot (eds), *All the World and her Husband: Women in Twentieth-Century Consumer Culture* (London: Cassell, 2000), pp. 10–22.

Sala, George Augustus, *Madame Tussaud's Exhibition Guide* (London: Madame Tussaud's, 1900).

Saler, Michael, '"Clap if You Believe in Sherlock Holmes": Mass Culture and the Re-Enchantment of Modernity, *c.*1890–*c.*1940', *Historical Journal* 46:3 (2003), pp. 599–622.

Sanders, Lise Shapiro, *Consuming Fantasies: Labor, Leisure, and the London Shopgirl, 1880–1920* (Ohio: Ohio University Press, 2006).

Schlör, Joachim, *Nights in the Big City: Paris, Berlin, London, 1840–1930* (London: Reaktion, 1998).

Schwartz, Hillel, *Making Noise: From Babel to the Big Bang and Beyond* (New York: Zone Books, 2011).

Scott, Gillian, *Feminism, Femininity and the Politics of Working Women: The Women's Co-Operative Guild, 1880s to the Second World War* (London: Routledge, 2005).

Scott, Peter, *The Making of the Modern British Home: The Suburban Semi and Family Life between the Wars* (Oxford: Oxford University Press, 2013).

Seal, Lizzie, 'Discourses of Single Women Accused of Murder: Mid-Twentieth Century Constructions of "Lesbians" and "Spinsters"', *Women's Studies International Forum* 32:3 (2009), pp. 209–18.

Seal, Lizzie, *Women, Murder, and Femininity* (Basingstoke: Palgrave MacMillan, 2010).

Selverstone, Marc J., *Constructing the Monolith: The United States, Great Britain, and International Communism 1945–1950* (Cambridge, Massachusetts: Harvard University Press, 2009).

Shaw, Tony, 'Introduction: Britain and the Cultural Cold War', *Contemporary British History* 19:2 (2005), pp. 109–15.

Shaw, Tony, *British Cinema and the Cold War: The State, Propaganda and Consensus* (London: I.B. Taurus, 2006).

Shoemaker, Robert, 'The Street Robber and the Gentleman Highwayman: Changing Representations and Perceptions of Robbery in London, 1690–1800', *Cultural and Social History* 3:4 (2006), pp. 389–402.

Shore, Heather, *Artful Dodgers: Youth and Crime in Early Nineteenth-Century London* (Woodbridge: Royal Historical Society, 1999).

Shore, Heather, *London's Criminal Underworlds, c.1720–c.1930: A Social and Cultural History* (Basingstoke: Palgrave MacMillan, 2015).

Shpayer Makov, Haia, *The Ascent of the Detective: Police Sleuths in Victorian and Edwardian England* (Oxford: Oxford University Press, 2011).

Sibley, Norman Wise, *Criminal Appeal and Evidence* (London: T. Fisher Unwin, 1908).

Smith Wilson, Dolly, 'A New Look at the Affluent Worker: The Good Working Mother in Post-War Britain', *Twentieth Century British History* 17:2 (2005), pp. 206–29.

Smithson, George, *Raffles in Real Life* (London: Hutchinson and Co., 1930).

Smyth, Frank, *Cause of Death: The Story of Forensic Science* (London: Orbis Publishing, 1980).

Spraggs, Gillian, *Outlaws and Highwaymen: The Cult of the Robber in England from the Middle Ages to the Nineteenth Century* (London: Pimlico, 2001).

Springhall, John, '"Pernicious Reading"? The Penny Dreadful as Scapegoat for Late-Victorian Juvenile Crime', *Victorian Periodicals Review* 27 (1994), pp. 326–49.

Stafford, David, 'Spies and Gentlemen: The Birth of the British Spy Novel, 1893–1914', *Victorian Studies* 24:4 (1981), pp. 489–509.

Strange, Julie-Marie, *Fatherhood and the British Working Class, 1865–1914* (Cambridge: Cambridge University Press, 2015).

Stringer, Arthur, 'The Button Thief', *Pall Mall Magazine* (Oct. 1911), pp. 611–24.

Summerfield, Penny, 'Culture and Composure: Creating Narratives of the Gendered Self in Oral History Interviews', *Cultural and Social History* 1:1 (2004), pp. 65–93.

Sutter, Gavin, 'Penny Dreadfuls and Perverse Domains: Victorian and Modern Moral Panics', in Judith Rowbotham and Kim Stevenson (eds), *Behaving Badly: Social Panic and Moral Outrage—Victorian and Modern Parallels* (Aldershot: Ashgate Publishing, 2003), pp. 159–76.

Taylor, Becky, and Ben Rogaly, ' "Mrs. Fairly Is a Dirty, Lazy Type": Unsatisfactory Households and the Problem of Problem Families in Norwich 1942–1963', *Twentieth Century British History* 18:4 (2007), pp. 429–52.

Taylor, James, *Boardroom Scandal: The Criminalization of Company Fraud in Nineteenth-Century Britain* (Oxford: Oxford University Press, 2013).

Taylor, Vanessa, and Frank Trentmann, 'Liquid Politics: Water and the Politics of Everyday Life in the Modern City', *Past and Present* 211 (2011), pp. 199–241.

Thane, Pat, 'The Working Class and State "Welfare" in Britain, 1880–1914' *Historical Journal* 27:4 (1984), pp. 877–900.

The New Madame Tussaud's Exhibition: Official Guide and Catalogue (London: Madame Tussaud's, 1930).

Thomas, David, and David Carlton and Anne Etienne, *Theatre Censorship from Walpole to Wilson* (Oxford: Oxford University Press, 2007).

Thomas, Nick, 'Will the Real 1950s Please Stand Up? Views of a Contradictory Decade', *Cultural and Social History* 5:2 (2008), pp. 227–35.

Thomas, Ronald R., *Detective Fiction and the Rise of Forensic Science* (Cambridge: Cambridge University Press, 1999).

Thomas, Ronald R., 'The Moonstone, Detective Fiction, and Forensic Science', in Jenny Bourne Taylor (ed.), *The Cambridge Companion to Wilkie Collins* (Cambridge: Cambridge University Press, 2006), pp. 65–78.

Thompson, John B., *Political Scandal: Power and Visibility in the Media Age* (Cambridge: Cambridge University Press, 2000).

Thomson & Co., Ltd., D.C., *The D.C. Thomson Bumper Fun Book: An Account of the Activities of D.C. Thomson & Co.* (Edinburgh: P. Harris Publications, 1977).

Thomson, Basil, *The Criminal* (London: Hodder and Stoughton, 1925).

Thomson, Matthew, *Psychological Subjects: Identity, Culture and Health in Twentieth-Century Britain* (Oxford: Oxford University Press, 2007).

Thorsheim, Peter, 'Green Space and Class in Imperial London', in Andrew C. Isenberg (ed.), *The Nature of Cities: Culture, Landscape, and Urban Space* (New York: University of Rochester Press, 2006), pp. 24–37.

Tidy, Charles Meymott, *Legal Medicine* (London: Smith, Elder, and Co., 1882).

Todd, Selina, *Young Women, Work, and Family Life in England, 1918–1950* (Oxford: Oxford University Press, 2005).

Todd, Selina, 'Young Women, Work, and Leisure in Interwar England', *Historical Journal* 48 (2005), pp. 789–809.

Todd, Selina, 'Domestic Service and Class Relations in Britain, 1900–1950', *Past and Present* 203 (2009), pp. 181–204.

Todd, Selina, *The People: The Rise and Fall of the Working Class, 1910–2010* (London: John Murray, 2014).

Todd, Selina, 'Affluence, Class, and Crown Street: Reinvestigating the Post-War Working Class', *Contemporary British History* 22:4 (2008), pp. 501–18.

Tosh, John, *Manliness and Masculinities in Nineteenth-Century Britain* (London: Routledge, 2005).

Tozer, Malcolm, 'A Sacred Trinity—Cricket, School, Empire: E. W. Hornung and his Young Guard', in J. A. Mangan (ed.), *The Cultural Bond: Sport, Empire, Society* (London: Cass, 1992), pp. 14–39.

Troutman, Anne, 'The Modernist Boudoir and the Erotics of Space', in Hilde Heynan and Gülsüm Baydar (eds), *Negotiating Domesticity: Spatial Productions of Gender in Modern Architecture* (London: Routledge, 2005), pp. 296–314.

Turvey, Gerry, 'Three-fingered Kate: Celebrating Womanly Cunning and Successful Female Criminal Enterprise', *Journal of British Cinema and Television* 7 (2010), pp. 200–12.

Unknown Author, 'Lady Charmeigh's Diamonds', *London Society* 35 (Jan. 1879), pp. 1–16.

Unknown Author, *Charles Peace; or, The Adventures of a Notorious Burglar. Founded on Fact and Profusely Illustrated* (London: G. Purkess, 1880).

Unknown Author, 'Diana's Diamonds', *London Reader of Literature, Science, Art, and General Information* 48:1230 (Nov. 1886), pp. 97–101.

Unknown Author, 'Burglary Insurance', in J. B. Welson (ed.), *Pitman's Dictionary of Accident Insurance* (2nd edn, London: Sir I. Pitman's and Son, 1938), p. 44.

Van Der Vat, Dan, 'Obituary: Anthony Cave Brown', *Guardian* (17 Oct. 2006), online at https://www.theguardian.com/media/2006/oct/17/pressandpublishing.booksobituaries (accessed 16 Aug. 2017).

Vernon, James, ' "For Some Queer Reason": The Trials and Tribulations of Colonel Barker's Masquerade in Interwar Britain', *Signs* 26:1 (2000), pp. 37–62.

Vernon, James, *Distant Strangers: How Britain Became Modern* (Berkeley: University of California Press, 2014).

Vickers, Hugo, 'Beaton, Sir Cecil Walter Hardy (1904–1980)', *Oxford Dictionary of National Biography*, http://www.oxforddnb.com/view/article/30801 (accessed 12 Sept. 2017).

Vickery, Amanda, 'Golden Age to Separate Spheres: A Review of the Categories and Chronology of English Women's History', *Historical Journal* 36:2 (1993), pp. 383–414.

Vickery, Amanda, 'An Englishman's Home Is his Castle? Thresholds, Boundaries, and Privacies in the Eighteenth-Century London House', *Past and Present* 199 (2008), pp. 147–73.

Vickery, Amanda, *Behind Closed Doors: At Home in Georgian England* (London and New Haven: Yale University Press, 2009).

Waddell, Bill, *The Black Museum, New Scotland Yard* (London: Harrap, 1993).

Walkowitz, Judith, *Prostitution and Victorian Society: Women, Class, and the State* (Cambridge: Cambridge University Press, 1982).

Walkowitz, Judith, *City of Dreadful Delight: Narratives of Sexual Danger in Late-Victorian London* (Chicago: University of Chicago Press, 1992).

Walkowitz, Judith, *Nights Out: Life in Cosmopolitan London* (London and New Haven: Yale University Press, 2012).

Ward, Paul, *Britishness Since 1870* (London: Routledge, 2004).

Waters, Chris, ' "Dark Strangers" in our Midst: Discourses of Race and Nation in Britain, 1947–63', *Journal of British Studies* 36 (1997), pp. 207–38.

Waters, Chris, 'The Homosexual as a Social Being in Britain, 1945–1968', *Journal of British Studies* 51:3 (2012), pp. 685–710.

Watson, Katherine, *Poisoned Lives: English Poisoners and their Victims* (London: Hambledon and London, 2004).

Wavell, Brigadier A. P., 'The Training of the Army for War', *Royal United Service Institution Journal* 78 (February 1933), p. 258.

Wells, H. G., *The Invisible Man* (London: C. A. Pearson, 1897).

Wells, H. G., *Ann Veronica* (1909; reprinted London: Penguin, 2005).

Wensley, Frederick Porter, *Detective Days: The Record of Forty-Two Years' Service in the Criminal Investigation Department* (London: Cassell and Co., 1931).

Whitlock, Tammy C., *Crime, Gender, and Consumer Culture in Nineteenth-Century England* (Aldershot: Ashgate Publishing, 2005).

Wiener, Martin, *Reconstructing the Criminal: Culture, Law and Policy in England, 1830–1914* (Cambridge: Cambridge University Press, 1990).

Wiener, Martin, *Men of Blood: Violence, Manliness, and Criminal Justice in Victorian England* (Cambridge: Cambridge University Press, 2004).

Wildman, Charlotte, 'Miss Moriarty, the Adventuress and the Crime Queen: The Rise of the Modern Female Criminal in Britain, 1918–1939', *Contemporary British History* 30:1 (2016), pp. 73–98.

Williams, Chris A., 'Police Surveillance and the Emergence of CCTV in the 1960s', *Crime Prevention and Community Safety* 5 (2003), reprinted in Chris A. Williams (ed.), *Police and Policing in the Twentieth Century* (Aldershot: Ashgate Publishing, 2011), pp. 27–37.

Williams, Gordon, *British Theatre in the Great War: A Revaluation* (London: Bloomsbury, 2003).

Williams, Montagu Stephen, *Leaves of a Life: Being the Reminiscences of Montagu Williams Q.C.* (London: MacMillan and Co., 1890).

Wills, Abigail, 'Delinquency, Masculinity and Citizenship in England, 1950–1970', *Past and Present* 187 (2005), pp. 157–85.

Wolff, Larry, ' "The Boys Are Pickpockets, and the Girl Is a Prostitute": Gender and Juvenile Criminality in Early Victorian England from *Oliver Twist* to *London Labour*', *New Literary History* 27 (1996), pp. 227–49.

Wood, John Carter ' "The Third Degree": Press Reporting, Crime Fiction and Police Powers in 1920s Britain', *Twentieth Century British History* 21:4 (2010), pp. 464–85.

Woolf, Virginia, *The Voyage Out* (London: Hogarth Press, 1915).

Wright, Peter, *SPYCATCHER: The Candid Autobiography of a Senior Intelligence Officer* (New York: Viking, 1987).

Wrigley, Chris, 'Bevin, Ernest (1881–1951)', *Oxford Dictionary of National Biography*, http://www.oxforddnb.com/view/article/31872 (accessed 8 Aug. 2017).

Yorke, Peter, *William Haggar (1851–1925): Fairground Filmmaker* (Bedlinog: Accent Press, 2007).

Zedner, Lucia, *Women, Crime, and Custody in Victorian England* (Oxford: Oxford University Press, 1991).

VI. UNPUBLISHED THESES

Moss, Eloise, 'Cracking Cribs: Representations of Burglars and Burglary in London, 1860–1939,' Unpublished D.Phil Thesis, University of Oxford, 2013.

VII. REPORTS

Office of National Statistics, 'Two Hundred Years of the Census: London and Middlesex' (London, 2001), https://data.london.gov.uk/dataset/office-national-statistics-ons-population-estimates-borough (accessed 24 Dec. 2016).

VIII. WEBSITES

' "Cat burglar" der. of "Cat" n.', *Oxford English Dictionary*, http://www.oed.com (accessed 16 Sept. 2011).

'CGNU Life Assurance Ltd', https://heritage.aviva.com/our-history/companies/c/cgnu-life-assurance-ltd/ (accessed 26 June 2018).

'Das Praktina-System', http://www.dresdner-kameras.de/praktina-system/praktina-system.html (accessed 16 Aug. 2017).

'Fine Art and General Insurance Company', https://heritage.aviva.com/our-history/companies/f/fine-art-and-general-insurance-company-ltd/ (accessed 26 June 2018).

'General Accident and Employers Liability Assurance Association', https://heritage.aviva.com/our-history/companies/g/general-accident-and-employers-liability-assurance-association-ltd/ (accessed 26 June 2018).

'Ocean Accident and Guarantee Corporation', https://heritage.aviva.com/our-history/companies/o/ocean-accident-guarantee-corporation-ltd/ (accessed 26 June 2018).

'Monthly Weather Report of the Meteorological Office', 77:7 (July 1960), http://www.metoffice.gov.uk/binaries/content/assets/mohippo/pdf/e/n/jul1960.pdf (accessed 16 Aug. 2017).

'Monthly Weather Report of the Meteorological Office', 77:8 (Aug. 1960), http://www.metoffice.gov.uk/binaries/content/assets/mohippo/pdf/e/0/aug1960.pdf (accessed 16 Aug. 2017).

Index

Abel, Colonel Rudolph Ivanovich (Soviet spy) 189–90
Andersson, Peter 13–14
Anti-burglar technologies
    Alarms 9, 133, 135–7, 146–55, 160–1, 213
    CCTV cameras 15–16, 96, 135–6, 161–2
    Emergency number (999) 155–7, 160–2, 164, 213
    Locks and safes 11–12, 18–19, 101–2, 123, 132–5, 137–46, 153, 213
Anti-Soviet propaganda 186–9, 194–5
America
    Cultural exchange with 45–6, 53, 62–3
    Criminological influence 22–3, 128–9
Arnold, Dana 92–3
Arrow, Charles 63
Arts and Crafts Movement 141
Arup, Ove and Ruth 158–9

Barabanov, Second Secretary to the Soviet Embassy 196
Barnardo, Thomas 33
Barrington-Ward, Robin 194–5
Bateman, Jessie 54–5
Baybars, Taner 206
    A Trap for the Burglar (1965) 206–8, 212
Beaton, Cecil 158–9
Benney, Mark (burglar and journalist) 104
Bevin, Ernest 187–8, 192–7
Binny, John 24, 93–4
Bishop, Cecil 83–4
'Black' Museum 35–6, 110
Blackstone, Sir William 2–4
Blue Lamp, The (1950) 164–5
Bishenden, Dennis (burglar, rapist, and murderer) 174–7
Booth, Charles 13–14, 32–3
Bradford, Colonel Sir Edward 95
British Board of Film Censors (BBFC) 80
Buck, Mary (burglar) 74
Burgess, Guy 188–9, 204
Burglars
    'Cat' burglars 11, 19, 41–2, 84–5, 89–109, 208–9
    Cracksmen 16–17, 24–5, 63, 138–41
    Occupations of 9n.30, 25–6, 182–3, 220*t*
    'Professional' 4, 15, 18, 46–7, 113, 128–9, 208–9
    Racial stereotyping of 26–7, 96–7, 179–81
    Spy-burglars 20, 185–205
    Women 18–19, 44–5, 58, 66–88, 209–10

Burglary
    Armed 23, 32, 110, 164, 176–9, 212–13
    Commercial dimensions 11–12, 30, 48, 114–15, 136–7, 170–1, 174
    Fear of 11–12, 18–19, 91–2, 110–32, 210–11
    Legal definition of
        1861 Larceny Act 2–4
        1916 Larceny Act 2–4, 66
        1968 Theft Act 20, 184, 210–12
        Common Law 2–4
    Material residue of 19, 91
    Pleasurable narratives of 11–12, 16, 23–4, 44–62, 104–5, 209, 213–14
    Sentencing for 2–4, 68–9, 71
    Statistical indices of 12, 25, 59, 67, 97–8, 117–18, 160, 171, 217–18
Burglary Insurance 110–31, 159, 165–6, 174, 213
    Advertising 7, 113–26, 122*f*, 125*f*

Caminada, Jerome 36–7
Carr, E.H. 194–5
Cassell's Magazine 48–9
Cave Brown, Anthony 204
Chatwood's Safe Co. 132–3, 138–41
Christie, Agatha 208
Chubb and Sons Lock and Safe Co. 116–17, 132–3, 137–8, 141, 153, 170–1, 198, 200–1
Churchill, Sir Winston 196
Cinema 57–8
    Early film 37–8
    Second World War 4–5
Clarke, Comer 199–200
Cocks, Harry 50
Cold War 20, 185–205, 209
Collins, Wilkie 26–7
    The Moonstone 26–7, 143–4, 210–11
Colman, Ronald 58–9
Conan Doyle, Sir Arthur 10–11, 22, 43–4
    Sherlock Holmes 22, 47
Conrad, Joseph
    Secret Agent, The 96–7
Contagious Diseases Acts (1864, 1866, 1869) 68–9, 72–4
Crackswoman, The (1914) 79–80
Crawford, Joan 81–2
Crime Club 41–2

Criminal biography 16
Criminal celebrity 28–30
    Post-mortem 37–8
Criminology 33–5, 47, 63, 128–9, 133–5
Crone, Rosalind 30
Cross, Sir Richard 22–3

D'Cruze, Shani 46–7
de Havilland, Olivia 10–11, 61
Delaney, Robert (burglar) 103–4
Dennis, Richard 101–2
Detective fiction 46–7, 143–4
Dickens, Charles 16–17, 27–8
    Oliver Twist 16–17
Disguise 35–6, 40–1, 75, 83
    Cross-dressing 83
Domestic space 5, 18–19, 119–23, 132–57,
    171–4, 179–82, 200–1
de Certeau, Michel 8
du Maurier, Gerald 53–6
Dumphy, Thomas Patrick (burglar) 176

Economic depression 6, 11–12, 38–9,
    41–2, 97–8
Ede, Sir James Chuter 166, 194–5
Edgar, Nathaniel (Police Constable) 164–5
Emsley, Clive 6, 23
Eroticism 11–12, 44–5, 52, 103–4,
    143–4, 208

Fenians 22–3
First World War 1–2, 40, 56, 97, 120–1,
    124, 171–4
Fitt, Leslie (burglar and arsonist) 181–2
Fleming, Ian 185–8
    Bond, James 185–6, 201–2
    Moonraker (1955) 185–6
Foreign Office 186–90, 192–4
Forensic Science 19, 91, 105–6
France
    Sûreté 22–3
    Cultural exchange with 46–7, 62–3
Francis, Kay 59

Game, Sir Philip 97
Garbo, Greta 158
Gee, Ethel 204
Gender
    Masculinity 7, 51, 70–1, 120–3, 171,
        176–7, 209
    Women, perceived social roles 75, 153, 159,
        167–8, 176–7, 201–2
George, Lloyd 99–100
Gilmour, Sir John 104–5
Golding, C.E. 130
Goodwin, John 63
Grandy, Christine 80–1
Greene, Graham 64, 213–14
Griffiths, Arthur (Inspector of Prisons) 35–6
Gullace, Nicoletta 120–1

Hadlaw, Janin 99–100
Haggar, William 38
Hamlett, Jane 143
Hankey, Robert 190, 192
Harrington, Ellen (burglar) 71–2
Harvey, David 90
Hays Code (1930) 10–11
Henderson, Colonel Sir Edmund 97
Herd, Kathleen and John 1–2, 4–5
Hichens, Robert 11
Highway robbery 16–17, 47–8
Hobbs & Co., lock and safe manufacturers
    127–8, 132–3, 138–43, 153, 170–1
Home Office 4, 9, 23, 63, 80, 104–5, 150,
    160–3, 166–7, 169, 171–4, 183–4,
    194–6, 211
Homosexuality 177–8, 188–9
Hooper, Sarah (burglar) 68–9
Hopkins, Michael 187–8
Hornsey, Richard 98–9
Hornung, Ernest William 10–11, 48–50
    Raffles, A.J.
        Fictional characterisation 17–18, 43–5,
            171, 188–9, 203, 208–9
        Films 45n.12, 56–61
            Raffles (1925) 57–8
            Raffles (1930) 58–9
            Raffles (1940) 10–11, 59–61
        Homosexuality 50–1, 213–14
        Imitators 61–4, 66–7, 85–7
        Novels 10–11, 17–18, 45–6
        Theatre productions 45–6, 53–7
            Censorship of 56
        Television series 64–5
Horsley, John William (prison chaplain) 37
Houghton, Harry 204
Houlbrook, Matt 12
Housebreaking 2–4, 16–17, 25, 47–8,
    163–4, 171
Hutchinson, W.J.
    A Policeman Puts You Wise (1950) 166–8,
        209–10
Hutchinson, Edward (burglar) 179

Insurance companies
    Alliance Co. 198
    Eagle Star and British Dominions 121–4,
        171–4
    Fine Art Insurance Company 116, 126–9
    General Accident and Life Assurance
        Corporation 116–18, 126
    Goldsmith's and General Burglary Insurance
        Association 116, 118
    Guardian Assurance Co. 119
    Lancashire and General Assurance Co. 129
    Law Accident Insurance Society 110–13,
        116–17
    Lloyd's of London 115–16
    Mercantile Accident and General Guarantee
        Corporation 115–16

National Burglary Insurance
    Corporation 116–17
Ocean Accident and Guarantee
    Corporation 116–17
Prudential Assurance 7, 124–6
Security Company 116–17
Traders and General Insurance
    Association 129–30
Interior design 144–5
Ireland, Richard 46
Ives, George 50n.38

Jack the Ripper 4, 14–15, 27–8, 50
Jervis, Sir John 2–4
John Tann's Safe Co. 132–3
Joyce, Patrick 89–90
Juvenile crime 24, 68–9, 175–7

Karavaev, Boris 191–3, 195–6
Katasanov, Clerk to the Soviet Air
    Attaché 196
Khrushchev, Nikita 196
Kleptomania 69–70
Knight, Samuel Edward 126–9
Kroger, Peter and Helen 190, 197–8

Lady Burglar: A Farcical Problem, The
    (1897) 77–8
Langhamer, Clare 161
Last of Mrs. Cheyney, The 81–2
Life and Times of Charles Peace, The
    (1905) 37–8
Le Carré, John 187–8, 202–3
    Call for the Dead (1961) 202–3
    Spy Who Came in from the Cold, The
        (1963) 202–3
Lefebvre, Henri 90
Liddell, Guy 186–7
Light, Alison 208
Lloyd, Lydia (burglar) 74
London
    Administration 12–13
    Architecture 13–14, 19–20, 89–90, 94–5,
        97–103
    Popular imagination of 15, 92–3, 99–100
    Population of 13–14, 91–2, 97
    Post-war reconstruction 15–16, 183
    Underground railway 19, 98–100
Lonsdale, Gordon 200–1, 204
Lupin, Arsène 47, 63

MacMillan, Sir Harold 163
Madame Tussaud's 38–42
Maiden Tribute of Modern Babylon scandal
    (1885) 33, 49–50
Major, Patrick 187–8
Manningham-Buller, Sir Reginald 197–8, 202
Marshall Plan 187–8, 195–6
Mass Observation 161–2
Mayhew, Henry 24, 27–8, 93

MacLean, Donald 188–9, 204
McKenzie, Andrea 47–8
MI5 186–7
Mills ad Boon 54–5
Miller, Elizabeth Carolyn 70
Milner's Safe Co. 132–3, 138–41
Mitter, Rana 187–8
Mobility (criminal) 19, 89–112, 213–14
Molotov, V.M. (Soviet Foreign Minister) 195–6
Mort, Frank 12–13, 188–9
Muggeridge, Malcolm 194–5

National Crime Prevention Campaigns 162–3,
    166–7, 169–71, 182–3, 187–8, 211
Naval Intelligence Service 197
Newman, Bernard 187–8, 203–4
    Spies in Britain (1964) 203
Niven, David 10–11, 59–61
Nolan, Sally (burglar) 66–7

Parry, Sir Edward Abbott 22
Peace, Charles (burglar and murderer) 17,
    21–42, 50, 74, 110–12, 115–16,
    188–9, 208–9
Penny Dreadfuls 30–2, 35
Peterson, Sir Maurice (Ambassador) 193–4
Pheby, Minnie (burglar) 75–7
Phrenology 33–5
Piper, Alana 68–9
Police
    Autobiographies 36–7
    City of London 155
    Criminal Investigation Department 14–15,
        22–3, 106–7
    Metropolitan Police 14–15, 95–7, 104–8,
        155, 161, 163–6, 168, 170–1, 192–7
    Relationship with citizens 9, 135
    Reputation of 14–15
Portland spy ring 197–204
Poverty 14–15, 32–3, 182–3
Powell, Dilys 10–11
Powell, Enoch 179–81
Power-Berrey, Robert James 35–6
Privacy 135–6, 161
Prostitution 33, 49–50, 68–9, 72, 177–8

Radionova, Madame 193
Rape 16–17, 19, 133–5, 163, 174–6, 210–11
Representation of the People Act, 1918
    5–6, 69
Reform Act, 1832 5–6
Retinger, Dr Józef 186–7
Ring of Spies (1963) 200–1
'Risk society' 114
Robinson, Edward (Police Constable) 21–2
Rosenberg, Julius and Ethel 197–8

Saksin, Georgy Filipovich. (Soviet
    Ambassador) 190
Salter, Sir Arthur 189–90

Schlör, Joachim 11
Scott, Frederick (murder victim) 179–82
Scott, Sir Harold, Commissioner of
     Metropolitan Police 161n.14, 163–4,
     166, 192–3
Second World War 4–6, 59–61, 163–4, 166,
     175–6
Shandabylov, Captain 190
Shearer, Norma 81–2
Shoplifting 69–70
Smith, John William (burglar) 179–81
Smithson, George (burglar) 63–4
Soviet Embassy 187, 190, 196–7, 203–4
    School 192–3, 195–6
Spraggs, Gillian 16–17, 47–8
Stalin, Joseph 196
Storry Deans, Richard 36–7
Stolen goods, types of 113, 219*t*
    Cash 9–10
    Clothes 69–70, 145
    Jewellery 1–2, 19, 69–70, 98, 133–5, 143–5,
     159, 195–6
Surveillance 135–6, 161–2, 164, 190
Sweden, policing strategies 165–6

TASS (Russian News Agency) 193–4
Temporality 16–17, 19, 96–7, 188–9, 211
Thompson, Edith 14–15, 202n.82
Three-Fingered Kate (1909–1912) 80
Tosh, John 49–50

Truman, President Harry S. 191–2
Turvey, Gerry 80

Valentine, Anthony 64
Vickery, Amanda 2–4, 121–2, 132–3
Victimhood
    Celebrity 15–16, 158
    Female 11, 32, 210–11
    Idealised 4–5
    Middle-class 5–6, 119–20, 169
    Racism 169
    Upper-class 50, 119–20, 159
    Working-class 179–82
Vincent, Sir Charles Edward Howard 22–3,
    116–17

Walkowitz, Judith 13–14
Wensley, Frederick Porter (Detective) 83
Wells, Herbert George (H.G.) 49–50, 78–9
    Invisible Man, The 96–7
Wilde, Oscar 49–50
Williams, Gordon 56
Women's suffrage movement 68–71, 73–4,
    78–9
Woolf, Virginia
    Voyage Out, The (1915) 79–80
Wright, Peter 200–1

Zarubin, Georgiy Nikolaevich (Soviet
    Ambassador) 192